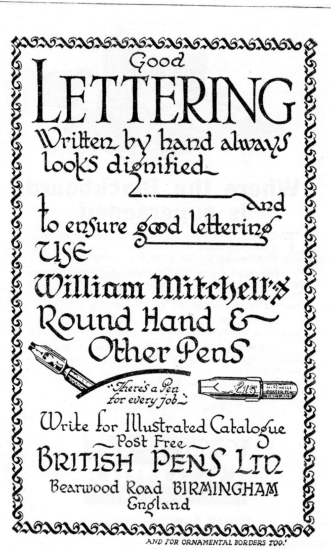

BOARD OF EDUCATION

HANDBOOK OF SUGGESTIONS

FOR THE CONSIDERATION OF TEACHERS AND OTHERS CONCERNED IN THE WORK OF PUBLIC ELEMENTARY SCHOOLS

Crown Copyright Reserved

LONDON
HIS MAJESTY'S STATIONERY OFFICE
Price 2s. 0d. net

CONTENTS

PREFATORY NOTE

The considerations which have led to the issue at the present time of a new edition of the Handbook of Suggestions for Teachers are explained in the General Introduction. While these considerations appear to the Board to call for a restatement of their views on the nature and scope of the work of the Public Elementary School, it seems desirable in this Note again to emphasise the character of the volume as a Handbook of Suggestions. The aim of the Board in issuing the present volume cannot be more aptly defined than in the following words from the original Prefatory Memorandum :—

> " Neither the present volume nor any developments or amendments of it are designed to impose any regulations supplementary to those contained in the Code. The only uniformity of practice that the Board of Education desire to see in the teaching of Public Elementary Schools is that each teacher shall think for himself, and work out for himself, such methods of teaching as may use his powers to the best advantage and be best suited to the particular needs and conditions of the school. Uniformity in details of practice (except in the mere routine of school management) is not desirable even if it were attainable. But freedom implies a corresponding responsibility in its use."

The need for a Handbook which attempts to present in a coherent form a statement of the principles under-lying the work of the schools and which brings together some of the results of practical experience will be apparent, not only to those actively engaged in the work of teaching, but also to teachers in training. The Board hope, therefore, that the present volume will be regarded as a necessary part of the equipment of every teacher in a Public Elementary School. It remains for the teachers themselves to apply and to adapt the standards and practice suggested in this volume to the particular circumstances of the schools in which they are at work.

E. H. PELHAM.

January, 1937.

FOREWORD

Unity and continuity are the leading ideas which have determined the arrangement adopted in this new edition of the *Handbook of Suggestions* in its treatment alike of the individual pupil, the school, and the subject matter of instruction.

The General Introduction deals with the school child, his natural and many-sided development, his reaction to his surroundings as a complete personality, and his preparation through his school life for full membership of a modern community : Part II deals with the three stages which form the units of the Public Elementary School system, each an organic whole and each having its specific function to perform ; Part III deals with the separate branches of the curriculum and shows how each is related to the main purposes of education and is developed continuously from the earliest stages to the end of school life.

In reading this book teachers will naturally give most attention to those sections of it which deal most directly with the particular type of school in which they are working, or the particular subject in which they are specially interested ; but they will, it is hoped, find in each section of the book something that will help them to view their own work as part of the general perspective.

PART I

CHAPTER I

GENERAL INTRODUCTION

SUMMARY OF CONTENTS

I. REASONS FOR THE PRESENT ISSUE

1. Recent changes in modern life.—It is not yet ten years since the last edition of the " Handbook of Suggestions for the Consideration of Teachers and Others concerned in the work of Public Elementary Schools " was published, but the development in educational thought and practice has in the meantime been so rapid as to make the issue of a substantial revision desirable.

Looking back we must all realise today how much the world in which the modern child is growing up has changed. The general standard of life has improved, and life itself is being lived at a faster rate. The universality of motor-transport, of broadcasting, and of the sound-film in the cinemas presents new features in the common life, while better housing, the increasing use of electrical and other mechanical devices, the probability of increased leisure and wider social contacts for all, with their opportunities for the enrichment of experience, make it necessary for those engaged in education to review their task afresh. It must be recognised that world distances have shrunk and that the peoples of today are nearer to each other and their lives more closely linked together than ever before.

2. Changing conceptions of education.—On all sides, moreover, there has been a steady growth of interest in educational problems, and the last three reports of the Consultative Committee of the Board of Education have reflected something of the concern of the public for the improvement of our educational system.* The reorganisation of the Public Elementary Schools has been accelerated by the appearance of these reports, and the experience of work in reorganised schools has

---

* *The Education of the Adolescent* (1926), *The Primary School* (1931) and *Infant and Nursery Schools* (1933), printed and published by H.M. Stationery Office, London.

resulted in a greater clarity in the definition of many of our problems. We realise more and more the importance of broadening the aims of education and of placing greater emphasis on the social development of children ; we appreciate more thoroughly the value of space and of activity in securing and maintaining their health and vitality, and we feel more deeply the need of relating what is taught in the schools to what is happening in the world outside. We have discovered in recent years a great deal, too, about how we should teach the various subjects of instruction, but at the same time we are also beginning to find that we shall have to know still more about how the child himself learns, and what things he should learn, if his subsequent development is to be as complete and as healthy as possible. In other words, in consequence of the changes that are occurring there has been a shift of emphasis in teaching from the subject to the child.

3. Increasing importance attached to individual differences among children.—In the schools themselves the changes we have mentioned have thrown into strong relief certain problems which were only mentioned in passing in the last edition of the Handbook, particularly those arising from individual differences among children. It is, moreover, imperative today that a handbook for the use of teachers should treat in some detail of the difficulties that arise from their having to adapt general principles to the requirements of changing conditions, especially conditions which militate against the success of the traditional forms of education. It will be found that an attempt has therefore been made in the present edition of this Handbook not only to deal with the needs of children of different types and at different stages, but also to take into account different lines of approach to the solution of the problems which confront us all. But a book of suggestions cannot do more than indicate the way to success, and its publication will not render less urgent or indispensable the need of personal resourcefulness and enterprise on the part of the teacher.

II. THE AIMS OF EDUCATION

A. HISTORICAL RETROSPECT

4. An early example of the best English tradition. —Enlightened aims in education are not peculiar to modern times. Since schools were first instituted some teachers in every age have taken as broad and liberal a view of education as the wisest men and women of today. Thus, we may quote a passage from the writings of Sir Henry Wotton (1568–1639) as an example in the best English tradition. It is a short account of what education embraces. " First, there must proceed a way how to discern the natural inclinations and capacities of children. Secondly, next must ensue the culture and furnishment of the mind. Thirdly, the moulding of behaviour and decent forms. Fourthly, the tempering of the affections. Fifthly, the quickening and exciting of observations and practical judgment. Sixthly, and the last in order, but the principal in value, being that which must knit and consolidate all the rest, is the timely instilling of conscientious principles and the seeds of religion."

5. The gradual widening of the Elementary School tradition.—The roll of honourable names in the history of education in this country is a long one, but not till recently has the best educational thought received official expression. In our own century the Code for use in Public Elementary Schools (1904–1926) contains a statement of aims from the pen of Sir Robert Morant which is as finely conceived and as nobly expressed as any that can be found. Nevertheless, education as represented in the common practice of the Elementary School in this country has not always adequately emphasised the most liberal and comprehensive views of what is required. Thus, we have seen the emphasis laid first on eradicating illiteracy, then on disseminating useful knowledge, in the hope that the mere possession of such knowledge would give culture, later, on training the separate " faculties," and later still on " developing intelligence," as though there were no differences between children in their natural endowment. None of these views would in itself now be regarded as a satisfactory account of the purpose of education. The emphasis in more recent years has been on the wider aim of an all-round training of character. The general approval which has been bestowed upon the Introduction to the 1904–1926 Code justifies our continued use of it as representing a great deal of what is best and most inspiring in our modern outlook.

6. The Introduction to the Code of 1904-1926.—

The Introduction runs as follows :—

" The purpose of the Public Elementary School is to form and strengthen the character and to develop the intelligence of the children entrusted to it, and to make the best use of the school years available, in assisting both girls and boys, according to their different needs, to fit themselves, practically as well as intellectually, for the work of life.

" With this purpose in view it will be the aim of the School to train the children carefully in habits of observation and clear reasoning so that they may gain an intelligent acquaintance with some of the facts and laws of nature ; to arouse in them a living interest in the ideals and achievements of mankind, and to bring them to some familiarity with the literature and history of their own country ; to give them some power over language as an instrument of thought and expression, and, while making them conscious of the limitations of their knowledge, to develop in them such a taste for good reading and thoughtful study as will enable them to increase that knowledge in after years by their own efforts.

"The School must at the same time encourage to the utmost the children's natural activities of hand and eye by suitable forms of practical work and manual instruction, and afford them every opportunity for the healthy development of their bodies, not only by training them in appropriate physical exercises and encouraging them in organised games, but also by instructing them in the working of some of the simpler laws of health.

"It will be an important though subsidiary object of the School to discover individual children who show promise of exceptional capacity, and to develop their special gifts (so far as this can be done without sacrificing the interests of the majority of the children), so that they may be qualified to pass at the proper age into Secondary Schools, and be able to derive the maximum of benefit from the education there offered them.

"And, though their opportunities are but brief, the teachers can yet do much to lay the foundations of conduct. They can endeavour, by example and influence, aided by the sense of discipline which should pervade the School to implant in the children habits of industry, self-control, and courageous perseverance in the face of difficulties; they can teach them to reverence what is noble, to be ready for self-sacrifice, and to strive their utmost after purity and truth; they can foster a strong sense of duty and instil in them that consideration and respect for others which must be the foundation of unselfishness and the true basis of all good manners ; while the corporate life of the School, especially in the playground, should develop that instinct for fair-play and for loyalty to one another which is the germ of a wider sense of honour in later life

" In all these endeavours the School should enlist, as far as possible, the interest and co-operation of the parents and the home in an united effort to enable the children not merely to reach their full development as individuals, but also to become upright and useful members of the community in which they live, and worthy sons and daughters of the country to which they belong."

B. THE PRESENT POSITION

7. Modern education must adapt itself to modern needs.—Since this was written certain aspects of life have assumed a greater importance than they had earlier in the century. In the modern world, education must take account of leisure no less than work. It will not be necessary to enlarge upon the fact that life is a less simple affair for all of us today. The citizens of tomorrow will be citizens of a more complex and more difficult world than that of yesterday. Social contacts are becoming more frequent and more varied, and children will need to learn to mix with a greater variety of types of individual than their parents probably knew and to understand the point of view of people in other lands besides their own. They will need, moreover, to accommodate themselves to sudden changes of process and method in the occupations they are likely to take up, and even to be prepared to transfer themselves from one occupation to another and from one part of the country to another. The individual, therefore, must not only become more adaptable as a worker, but must also be in a position to select for himself some worthy and useful way of occupying his free time. Believing, too, as in this country we do, in a system of democracy, we realise that the average citizen must be a man or woman of common sense and breadth of view and that the positions of high responsibility must be open to the ablest citizens irrespective of their origin. Obviously, therefore, the schools must offer every possible opportunity for serviceable talent to manifest itself, whatever direction it may take and however limited in range it may be, and must do all they can to ensure that their ablest pupils may pass on to suitable forms of higher education.

It follows, then, that the aim of education should be to develop to the full the potentialities of every child at school, in accord always with the general good of the community of which he is a member.

III. THE FUNCTION OF THE SCHOOL

8. Various factors in the educative process.—When we come to consider methods of arriving at the ends we have set before us a good deal of analysis is required. Failure to arrive does not necessarily lie in a lack of sympathy with the ends to be reached. It may also be due to our inability to plan our route or to not knowing which turning to take at a particular point of the journey. Education is not so simple a business as is often supposed. It is not enough for the teacher to collect together a mass of knowledge, and retail it to his class. Nor is it enough for his personality to be strong enough to make the children do what he wants them to do. No subject is such that the mere teaching of it will produce the results we require of the schools, and no method will work automatically. Education in fact depends both on the school environment and on the response of the children to the teaching as well as on the subject and the teacher.

9. Elementary education is a general education.— The wider ends before us cannot be reached, then, without the development in the children of certain general attributes ; habits that cannot be shaped without a good deal of drill ; skills that involve the integration of well-trained physical and mental elements ; knowledge which, if it is to be real knowledge, involves the power to see relations of increasing complexity and generality ; interests that issue from spontaneous self-direction ; and attitudes of mind that bespeak a growing sense of values. Any attempt to develop these attributes in isolation, however, must be unsatisfactory, sometimes dangerous. Unless under enlightened control, habit may obstruct the free play of intelligence ; skill in any direction may degenerate into unadaptable routine ; knowledge may be no more than mere lifeless information; interest may become so narrow and limited as to threaten the balance of personality ; while attitudes of mind may harden into intolerance of whatever is unfamiliar or new.

10. Attitudes of mind are as important as mastery of forms of skill.—We may thus say that there are two important aspects of every lesson taught, and the emphasis may rightly vary from one to the other as circumstances demand. In some subjects the emphasis may frequently be directed to securing proper attitudes of mind through the inspiration arising from worthy sentiment or the illumination that comes from fresh and exciting knowledge. In other lessons the emphasis may be upon habits as a preparation for the acquisition of skill, or on skills that are essential to creative work of any kind. The school, then, which seeks to give children the use of tools and tool-habits but does not interest them in the proper use to be made of them has hardly begun its task, while the school which seeks to inspire will have failed to fulfil its purpose unless it has also taught its children to achieve.

11. How the subjects of instruction may help to produce attitudes of mind and promote skill.—It would not be difficult to quote examples showing that the effectiveness of a given subject will depend on how far the teacher is alive to its general value as well as skilled in giving a training in its technique. Thus, one value of English is as a means of communication,—an important matter as civilisation becomes more complicated and increased command of the mother tongue necessary. Appreciation of this fact will serve to give reality to the teaching which it may otherwise lack. Or again, the realisation by the teacher that literature, in its higher sense, gives access to the deeper springs of life and conduct, should enable him to avoid undue concentration on the formal aspects of the subject matter and on verbal and grammatical niceties.

There are certain kinds of human experience that can be best summarised in mathematical terms, and there are certain ways of thinking that are most efficiently performed in mathematical symbols, so that the teacher should develop in his pupils an understanding of mathematical language and an aptitude for its use. But he must not overlook the necessity for accuracy in computation, or the wholesome discipline which comes from doing a piece of work with proper care and finish. Further, History and Geography will give the child a wider view of human life, and together with Science they should help him to understand better the world in which he lives.

Health Education, Physical Training, and Housecraft should help in developing in children both the desire and the ability to become healthier and happier citizens, while, finally, apart from a training in technique, the Arts and Crafts provide excellent opportunities for giving objective form and harmonious expression to many of the ideas and impulses of children.

12. A summary of what the School can do.—We may sum up the function of the school as being (1) to provide the kind of environment which is best suited to individual and social development ; (2) to stimulate and guide healthy growth in this environment ; (3) to enable children to acquire the habits, skills, knowledge, interests and attitudes of mind which they will need for living a full and useful life ; and (4) to set standards of behaviour, effort, and attainment, by which they can measure their own conduct.

13. The marks of a good education.—It is obvious that the school can fulfil these functions only if it insists on thorough and effective work in the various daily tasks it provides, but the ultimate test must be whether it assists in the development of citizens who desire the common good and are prepared to make sacrifices to secure and maintain it ; men and women, that is, who care for all that is lovely and of good report. For the fully educated person, we should do well to remember, is one who is enlightened in his interests, impersonal in his judgments, ready in his sympathy for whatever is just and right, effective in the work he sets himself to do, and willing to lend a hand to anyone who is in need of it.

14. The characteristics of a good school.—It will not be difficult to recognise a school which has such ends in view and has succeeded in a measure in realising them, for there the children will show the energy which comes from the natural flow of vitality, the knowledge which results from the free play of intelligence, the evident care and thoroughness which arise from a right sense of values, and the happiness which accompanies the feeling that they are doing things worth doing and doing them well.

IV. SOME IMPORTANT FACTORS IN EDUCATION

A. THE NATURE OF THE CHILD

15. How children differ from adults.—There is no need to labour the point that the teacher may put before himself the highest aims and be continually at pains to equip himself with the fullest knowledge of his subjects and the best technique for imparting it, and yet fail to teach successfully through ignorance of the essential things to be known about the nature of the children in his charge.

Children differ in many ways from adults : not only in constant bodily activity—which prompts them to run and skip where we are content to walk, to stand on their heads, to climb for the sake of fresh or novel views of their environment—but also in mental activity, as shown in their restlessness and love of excitement, and in their curiosity about thousands of things of little moment to adults.   They differ, too, in their need of talk and physical exploration as aids to comprehension when they meet with something new.   All these things are essential to proper growth and must be allowed for in their education.

16. The natural order of development.—The talents and abilities which we possess make their appearance in their own time and in their own order, often at no predictable instant.   The baby sits up when it is ready and not before.   It crawls when its power of locomotion is strong enough ; it does not speak until it realises that sounds imitated from others have meaning ; on arrival in the nursery class at school it shows that it can learn but can learn best through play, casually ; later the child is ready to learn through example, and later still through precept ; sooner or later the passion for individual play gives way before the superior attractiveness of team games ; and so on. " First the blade, and then the ear ; then the full corn in the ear." It is for the teacher to know the times and the seasons, and to make effective use of them.

17. The teacher must allow for individual differences among children.—Experience shows that human beings differ considerably from one another in their general make-up, and to the discriminating teacher those differences are quite obvious even in young children. Between the brightest and the liveliest on the one hand and the dullest and the most reserved on the other the range of intelligence and the degree of social adaptability are usually too great to justify any teacher in relying solely upon class instruction as a method of education.

The child learns in many ways, sometimes best as a member of a large group, sometimes best as a member of a small group, sometimes best individually. In short the teacher must study the various methods of learning as well as of teaching and know how to adapt his instruction to the several needs and capacities of his pupils.

18. Importance of the sentiments in the development of character.—The development of character is not wholly an affair of the intellect, since what are called the sentiments, each with its strong core of instinct and its body of feeling and ideas, play a predominant part in the shaping of the child's outlook on the world and in directing the trend of his energies and purposes. The teacher will, therefore, be constantly on the alert to discover how, under the influence of his teaching, the principal and most powerful of the human sentiments, such as the sense of justice and self-respect, are taking shape and forming themselves into a stable system in the personality of his pupils.

19. Mental growth is an organic process.—It is clear that a good deal more than is known at present has still to be learnt about the way in which children's minds grow and develop. The important thing to remember is that the teacher has to teach a child as well as a subject. In short, the school exists for education as well as for instruction.

Judged, then, on the widest grounds, no teacher will succeed in his task unless he appreciates what is meant by saying that human growth is organic : that progress in a child's development is rarely smooth and automatic, but is subject to spurts and halts and even reverses ; that children vary both in their general rate of development and in their potentialities ; that appetite for knowledge is as important as capacity for receiving it, and that very little real assimilation takes place without such appetite ; that we are determined largely by what we have lived through, and that in times of excitement, stress or fatigue we may display interests and indulge in activities which we perhaps thought we had entirely outgrown. This means that the teacher must be able to view the conduct of his pupils with the necessary detachment that comes with understanding.

From this point of view, development will be seen to consist essentially in the steady growth of the body in power and in capacity for finer and finer adjustment, in increasing control over impulse and in a fuller realisation of the probable consequences of one's actions, in the growing ability to entertain and act upon ideas that are not based upon merely immediate considerations, in the regulation of our emotional life through the formation of sentiments which ensure stability and strength of character, and in the sure if slow advance towards the enjoyment and practice of all that makes for a full and satisfactory life.

B. THE HOME

20. The influence of the home environment.— Naturally, too, since education is only partly a school process, the teacher will endeavour to keep in close touch with the life which the children themselves lead, so that his instruction may always be found to bear a proper relation to their experience as well as to their capacity and their degree of maturity in any particular direction.

The child is what he is partly by reason of his inborn nature and partly as a result of experiences in home and neighbourhood. From the home he will have derived his first habits, his first ideas of the world, and perhaps more important than these, his first standards of conduct. There, too, he will have acquired emotional attitudes towards other people which may influence him for good or ill throughout his life. Thus, for example, he may have become habitually rebellious towards, or over-dependent upon, his elders. In such cases the teacher should, at the beginning of the child's school career, content himself with trying to win him over gradually by sympathy and understanding to better relationships. It is particularly important to realise that any violent disturbance of a child's first attachments may have the most serious consequences, and teachers of young children, in particular, will make it their duty to become acquainted with the life of the home, and to enlist the parents' active sympathy for the work of the School.

21. The relation between school life and home life.— It happens only too often that children regard the things they do at school and the things they do at home as belonging to two different worlds having little or no connexion with each other. Yet many of a child's home activities, his hobbies, the books he reads, and the games he plays, have a not inconsiderable educational value, and much of what he learns at school might help to make his life at home fuller and more interesting. The teacher who takes an interest in his pupils' hobbies, who encourages them to bring to school things that they have made at home, and who can give them advice on how to surmount their difficulties and acquire good technique, will do much to promote their education indirectly. Conversely, the teacher who makes his instruction interesting and real to the children may well hope that in their leisure time they will of their own accord practise some of the skills they learn in school, accumulate further knowledge through reading or observation, or endeavour to express their own ideas through various media, and the effect of such activities will be all the more lasting because they are self-chosen.

C. THE NEIGHBOURHOOD

22. The influence upon the child of the life he leads outside school.—The neighbourhood, whether urban or rural, well-to-do or the reverse, must also exert a powerful influence on the child as he grows older. In most cases it will decide to a large extent the kind of speech he will use, the nature of a great deal of his activity, the interests he will pursue, the friendships he will make, and so on. We must also take into account the various social agencies that are at work in the district in which he lives, e.g. those provided by Churches, by clubs and by other organisations like the Scouts and Guides. Nor must we forget that a surprising number of children acquire a good deal of knowledge of current affairs, experience of unfamiliar ways of life and of art, literature and music, through the medium of cinema, wireless, newspaper and children's weeklies. It should be the business of the teacher to acquaint himself with what his pupils are acquiring through means such as these, so that he may make full educational use of them.

23. How the School can keep in touch with the home and the neighbourhood.—Some knowledge on the part of the teacher of the out-of-school circumstances and interests of his pupils is very desirable. He should know, if possible, how far these circumstances are affecting the physical development of his pupils, their personal habits and general outlook. It will follow that the possibilities of utilising the resources of the home and the neighbourhood for school purposes must be an ever-present concern with him.

Particularly must the teacher be careful, if he disapproves of the local influences which are at work in the child mind, not to express his disapproval in terms likely to arouse opposition or resentment. He must beware lest his attitude be mistaken for one of superiority on his part and so make children ashamed of their parentage or their neighbourhood.

Viewing their work as a whole teachers will naturally avail themselves of every opportunity for bringing about an intimate relationship between school, home and neighbourhood. They and all others connected with education should do their best to dispel the harmful error—which the old formal system of examination tended to foster—that the work of the schools is a mystery not to be penetrated except by the initiated. The great interest which has been aroused by Educational Weeks, by exhibitions of school work, and by displays of school activities of various kinds, shows that the public is eager to know what is going on in the school. But of all the outside public, the parents clearly have the best right to be informed as to what the school is doing for their children. Many head teachers make it known that they will be ready to see any parent at certain hours. " Open days " for parents' visits are also a useful institution. On these occasions parents find themselves able to discuss matters of common interest with teachers and managers. Medical inspection has provided another valuable opportunity for consultation with parents. A day on which the school's achievements during the year may be reviewed is yet another means of linking the school with the outside world.

24. The study of environment as a basis of wider studies.—As far as possible the educational resources of the neighbourhood—its historical, geographical and scientific possibilities—will naturally be made use of by schools. Visits should be paid to neighbouring centres of interest, and constant reference might well be made to the environment for illustrations of what is being dealt with in class. Instances have been noted of children gaining a useful knowledge of the various industries and railway connexions of the country by following the fortunes and journeys of their favourite cricket and football teams, while other children have been found to learn a good deal about geographical position and distances from following in the shipping columns of the newspapers the progress of teachers on their way to take up exchange posts overseas. Many other instances will at once suggest themselves. An interest in remoter things must necessarily be grounded in this kind of activity.

V. THE SCHOOL AS A MEANS OF EDUCATION

A. ITS LIFE

25. Schools necessary in a modern community.— The Public Elementary School owes its existence to the fact that the vast majority of parents have neither the leisure nor the means to prepare their children for a full life in a modern community. It began with the task of providing, on the secular side, instruction in the Three Rs., leaving the home to provide training in other directions. But mere competence in the Three Rs. is no longer considered enough as the end of schooling. There is more and more which the nation must have that the parents cannot give, if it is to survive and maintain its standards of life and civilisation. In the national system of education there must be scope for the free growth of intelligence and adaptability, and the school must see that such scope exists.

26. The School provides a consciously modified environment.—The limits within which the school works should, however, be clearly understood. It is a consciously modified form of the child's environment but it is only a part of his total environment. It cannot provide him with a full life, since it cannot take the place of the home, or the neighbourhood, nor can it furnish proper substitutes for all the experiences which healthy and fortunately placed children will usually find for themselves ; moreover it cannot provide the situations in which children learn to adapt themselves, as they must, to the rough and tumble of life. People are apt to suppose that habits which are inculcated in one kind of environment will function automatically in another. Perhaps the greatest unsolved problem of education is to find a way of ensuring that the qualities of mind and character that are made to blossom freely enough under the protective care of the school will continue to flourish afterwards under the less sheltered conditions which the children will experience later on.

27. The value to the child of the school environment.—Nevertheless, the school may have a life of its own, the missing of which may be a serious loss to any child. Its various concerted activities, its protective sympathy, its care for health, its power of evoking—through the prestige of its traditions and loyalties—a sense of security and a regard for an ordered and worthy mode of living, are of inestimable value. The School is concerned with child life, not with adult life, but it can encourage and provide experience of a pattern similar to that met with in adult life. Thus, it may cultivate an alertness of outlook and a sense of values about conduct which will stand in good stead not only the child himself but also the community in which he lives.

Where a school is fortunate enough to have a canteen on the premises, for children whose homes are too far off to allow of their returning to them in the midday interval, an excellent opportunity is afforded for training children to be of service to one another and to take their meals in seemly fashion. A freer discipline than is possible in the classroom, and social intercourse with others who differ in age as well as in attainments, may be turned to excellent account where teachers are alive to the wider possibilities of education.

B.　ITS DISCIPLINE

28. The basis of discipline.—Discipline is the means whereby children are trained in orderliness, good conduct and the habit of getting the best out of themselves, all of which are essential to the well-being of the school. Discipline may take various forms, but the crucial test of its soundness is whether it represents a real sense, on the part of the children, of the rightness of the behaviour that is expected of them. It cannot be considered good unless it is founded upon worthy ideas of conduct that are becoming, or have become, embedded in the children's characters. An outward show of order can, of course, be maintained by force or fear, but mere repression is effective only while the children are immediately under the authority that exercises it. When they are released from this authority, they tend to revert to other modes of behaviour and, if discipline has not become self-discipline, they may be left at the mercy of any dominant unruly personalities or of the caprice of the moment.

The basis of good discipline then, is a willing acceptance by the children of the school's standards of behaviour. This can only be achieved if the school provides a way of life that they can understand, and this implies that the school must take account of their present interests and propensities and must lead them on to the things to which they may rightly aspire. It must be a way of life that the children recognise as something better and fuller than they could devise for themselves, for only thus will it be able to absorb their energies and command their loyalty. If the work of the school is congenial and its purposes are understood there need be no fear that the children will be unwilling to face spells of intensive work which in other circumstances might be mere drudgery to them. At every stage of school life, and among children of all grades of ability, it has been the experience of competent teachers that children willingly concentrate for considerable periods of time upon tasks that are suited to their capacity. Continual change, excitement and novelty, to which teachers sometimes have recourse through misunderstanding the educational doctrine underlying the use of the " interest," are no less prejudicial to the true purposes of education than unrelieved monotony of work.

29. The maintenance of discipline.—Once the children have become interested in their work, in the sense that they are eager to do their best and ready to take pains, they will recognise the value of such rules as they are expected to observe, when they know that those rules exist solely for the well-being of the school as a whole and of each member of it. Rules will, of course, be necessary for the maintenance of good discipline, but their successful working will largely depend upon the way in which they are administered.

The teacher should, therefore, aim at exercising a steady but sympathetic form of control in the interests of order and sound development, and in doing so he will take for granted the existence in his pupils of a desire to behave and work sensibly. Such rules as he makes will depend for their nature and number on the age and maturity of the children for whom they are made. They will not appear unreasonable and they will not make impossible demands. Whether the rules themselves are intended to represent a standard of behaviour which is desirable or one which is compulsory will also depend on the same factors.

The importance of good sense and stability in the control of a school or a class requires no emphasis. It needs good sense to know what to treat as calling for interference and when to interfere, while stability in those responsible for the training of children is equally important. Experience has shown that unfortunate results follow from both undue severity and excessive indulgence, and also from incalculable alternations of these two forms of unwise treatment.

30. Discipline at the Infant School stage.—It would be absurd, for example, to insist upon infants conforming to rules which have a remote or infrequent application. With children of this age the teacher will work largely by suggestion and example. She will set patterns of the conduct which she wishes to see imitated and will praise those who conform. She will be careful, too, not to create in any child a sense of its own general unworthiness by stigmatising him as " naughty " on the basis of some specific act of which she disapproves. The desire to please the teacher and to be on good terms with her is a strong motive in the behaviour of young children at the infant stage.

31. Discipline at the Junior School stage.—With both Infants and Juniors some allowance must be made for their general liveliness and active curiosity. Any form of discipline which requires them to remain seated and physically inactive for long periods will be out of place in a modern school. Another characteristic, important in the Junior School child, is his tendency to appeal to the authority of his teacher against those of his companions with whom he has some dispute. As a result of his experiences in this direction he begins to acquire a strong sense of what is fair and what is unfair, so that it is essential that the authority of the teacher should be such as to command respect as being fair and impersonal. The teacher who allows his authority to manifest itself as the expression of impulse and personal irritation will not have the best influence on his pupils.

32. Discipline at the Senior School stage.—In the Senior School the possibilities of a certain amount of self-government among the pupils will have to be considered. A growing sense of the need for order and security in the common life will bring with it an interest in seeing that these conditions are established on an acceptable basis. With the growth of such an interest the teacher will become less and less a person who imposes arbitrary rules and more and more the guardian of the common interests of all who are under him. It will be his aim, accordingly, to create an environment in which each pupil may find it worth while to express what is best in his nature. When the teacher fails, he should ask himself, therefore, whether his control is too repressive, too slack, or too capricious, whether his rules make for security or anxiety, and whether he has allowed proper scope for the expression of the energies and intelligence of his pupils.

33. Changed conception of discipline in recent years.—In conclusion, it may not be out of place to say that one of the greatest changes in elementary education in the last half century lies in the gradual recognition on the part of teachers that the superiority of the adult over the child is a matter of length and width of experience and not of moral quality, and that few children are so unreasonable or unmanageable by nature as not to respond to the calmly exercised control of an intelligent teacher who has their best interest at heart.

34. Punishment.—As a result of this change there has been a great decrease in the amount of punishment inflicted, whether corporal or of other kinds. In the best schools, in fact, there is now very little punishment at all, and corporal punishment may be altogether absent. Tradition and public opinion in a school may in themselves be sufficient deterrents with most children, though undoubtedly individual cases may occur where the active intervention of the Head Teacher is called for and stern measures may be justified.

C. ITS PREMISES AND EQUIPMENT

35. School premises and the amenities of civilised life.—The school cannot perform its function adequately unless the premises themselves are an example of what we naturally associate with a civilised life. Thus, the building should be dignified and pleasing as well as conducive to health. The internal decorations should be bright and attractive, with specimens of good craft-work and suitably chosen pictures placed to the best advantage. The school, moreover, should give an impression of order and cleanliness, reflected, for instance, in the care of books and apparatus, in the proper storing of clothes in well-kept cloakrooms, and in the tidy appearance of the playground and offices. Wherever possible, too, the dreary appearance of the typical school playground should be relieved by trees, shrubs, lawns and flower gardens.

The school should, in short, be a source of comfort and inspiration to the children while they are young, as a place where, for an important part of their day, they can pursue their studies in a friendly, healthy and civilising atmosphere. It will thus do something to help to give good standards which will be of real service to the children when they grow up.

D. ITS ORGANISATION

36. The need of organisation whenever people work together in groups.—Where numbers of people have to live or work together there must be organisation ; the larger the group the more necessary it will be. But such organisation should be as little restrictive as possible. Over-direction may render the activities of a school unreal and its life largely artificial. It will be universally agreed that there are some things too important to be subordinated to the smooth running of the school machinery.

37. Various kinds of grouping desirable in a school.—Faced with the task of arranging for a school to work under the most satisfactory conditions, we should ask ourselves what things are best done by the school taken as a whole, by groups of classes working together, by classes of the traditional type, by sections within such classes, and by children working in voluntary association or individually.

Thus, there are needs which may be met by assemblies of the whole school, e.g. for prayers, prize-givings, celebrations of all kinds and broadcasts of great events. Groups of classes may well be brought together to enjoy the experience of mass music-making, or to be entertained by dramatic performances and other kinds of display which are given by individual classes or groups. In many schools children are encouraged to join circles and clubs which meet outside school hours, and these are obviously of the greatest value in cultivating co-operation and group-life on the one hand, and self-confidence and intellectual independence on the other. Again, there are few schools nowadays where children do not at some time or other work together in sections within their classes ; the practice is common where classes are not homogeneous, where groups have to be formed for co-operative work in particular tasks, and where certain children need separate attention.

38. The value of individual work to children at every stage of school life.—Individual work, too, is a common feature of school work in an increasing number of schools. It must play an important part in Infants' education—since little children do not learn all at once to act as members of a group,—in Junior Schools, where practice in acquiring skill needs varying amounts of time from child to child, and in Senior Schools, where the cultivation of individual talents and interests is of vital importance.

39. The function of the traditional " class ".—The traditional class, organised mainly for instruction in the " Three Rs " is the most familiar of all school groups. Classes in schools are still necessary and always will be, but we must be quite sure why we have them. It is their existence as water-tight compartments in the school organisation which is no longer justified. Classes are homogeneous when they contain children at the same stage of maturity and with common intellectual needs. Too great a range of age or intelligence has an adverse effect on the work in any class. Where, however, there is a satisfactory degree of homogeneity, a community of interest is soon aroused which makes for a class spirit, for healthy rivalry among the children and for economy of effort on the part of the teacher. The situation is thus favourable for such activities as are the common staple of class work along traditional lines. The younger or more retarded the child the more must he have the continual support and sympathy both of a group with which he is thoroughly familiar and of a teacher whom he has learnt to understand. He will be lost if the group with which he associates is too large or if he comes to it too infrequently. But as he grows older he must learn to mix freely with, and hold his own in, groups of less permanent character. Only in this way will he acquire self-confidence and the power to adapt himself to changing social circumstances.

VI. CLASSIFICATION

A. BY ATTAINMENT OR BY ABILITY

40. Promotion by attainment and promotion by ability.—Where a school is large enough to have a staff of several teachers it is a natural thing for them to share the responsibility of the work by each taking charge of a roughly equal number of children. The question then arises how the children should be allocated to their teachers, whether, e.g. the classes thus formed should be arranged on a basis of age, or of ability, or of attainments.

When less was known about mental development in children classification by formal attainments, irrespective of age or ability, was the rule. But classification of this kind began to disappear with the rigid system of promotion, which was the result of the old annual external examination.

The system of annual examinations was dropped more than forty years ago, but the sort of curriculum formerly imposed on schools is by no means a thing of the past. With the disappearance of the annual examination, however, teachers found it possible to take individual ability more and more into account in the promotion of children from any one class to another. In consequence, the custom spread throughout the country of pushing the brighter children ahead as they mastered their lessons, so that they might work with the highest classes while they were still eligible by age to enter for competitive examinations, e.g. those of the " Junior Scholarship " type.

The argument for promotion by ability has been reinforced by the doctrine of " mental age " which has become familiar during recent years. We know now that in a Junior School, for example, the teachers may have to deal with children whose mental ages range from $5\frac{1}{2}$ (which is about that of a dull entrant of $7\frac{1}{2}$ years) to $16\frac{1}{4}$ (the " mental age " of an extremely bright child of $11\frac{1}{4}$ years). It would be folly, therefore, to ignore the ability factor in organisation when it is of such great significance as these figures indicate.

B. BY AGE

41. The child's physical and social development a matter of age rather than ability.—It may, of course, be claimed that the intellectual training which bright young children have received through rapid promotion in accordance with their capacities is in many ways good for them. But physical growth and social development do not necessarily keep step with intellectual progress. Indeed, it is now questioned whether the practice of promoting bright young children to classes where, on the average, the pupils are considerably older, has been an unmixed blessing. For this reason, many teachers have felt that it would always be better to arrange for bright children to proceed individually in their school studies as far as they are intellectually capable but to remain still in the company of their equals as regards age, physique and character. Moreover, we must not forget that in the traditional type of school the promotion of the bright child may have meant the retardation of his slower fellow, if the inclusion of a young child in a high class has entailed the exclusion of an older one. In fact, too much attention to securing the rapid promotion of bright children has been a potent cause of general backwardness in many schools. Indeed, in schools where classification follows the old lines, with rapid promotion of the brighter children, the pupils of any one age are to be found as a rule spread more widely throughout the school than can be justified in the light of modern knowledge. We may say, then, that there is an increasing disposition to take age more fully into account in classification, and as far as possible to deal with individual differences among children of the same age by means of sectional treatment.

C. BY " STREAMS "

42. Promotion in reorganised schools.—It was the recognition of the difficulties of classification in schools organised on traditional lines that led to the formulation of the Hadow principle of reorganisation, the adoption of which would make it possible to have in Junior and Senior Schools both promotion by age and classification by ability at the same time.

The extent to which the Hadow principle can be applied must depend on the number of children available for classification. Where circumstances permit, it is desirable that a Junior School should be at least large enough to have an A and a B stream, and a Senior School to have an A, a B, and a C stream. This means Junior Schools of six to eight classes, and Senior Schools of nine or ten classes, where annual admissions from the contributory schools are the rule and the leaving age is 14+. Where, however, six-monthly promotions are the rule, then twice the number of classes will be needed if the same advantages in classification are to accrue. Single-stream Junior and Senior Schools usually present special problems of their own, but in scattered areas there is often no alternative.

The gain here, as in every reorganisation, is the opportunity of concentrating upon the problems of the separate stages of school life.

43. Classification in large schools.—Among the larger reorganised schools it will generally be found that, as between the two-stream and the three-stream school, there is an important difference in the actual composition of the classes. In the former type of school the classes in both the A and the B streams will commonly include a larger proportion of children of more or less average ability than will either the A or the C classes in the latter type. Unless this difference is fully appreciated, there is a real danger that in the two-stream school the teaching may demand too much from the less able children in the A stream and too little from the more able children in the B stream.

It is also worthy of note that where A, B and C classes are in existence, the B class may very well be made a little larger than the A or the C class, since the distribution of ability among children is such that more cluster around the average than fall towards the extremes. This means that a well selected B group will usually be more homogeneous than an A or a C group of the same size. In fact, some Authorities have thought it worth while, where the numbers have allowed of it, to organise Senior Schools in four streams : A, B^1, B^2, and C.

In any case, to get the full benefit of a Hadow reorganisation, relatively large numbers and annual promotions are essential. These conditions alone make it possible to meet the needs of different types of child by providing continuous and complete courses of work of a differentiated kind which can be followed uninterruptedly by each type of child for the whole period of his attendance at school.

D. THE BACKWARD CHILD

44. Treatment of backward children in reorganised schools.—The arrival of the Hadow school has made it less necessary to organise special classes for " dull and backward " children of the type that were once fairly common in large schools. Experience showed that children put into such classes seldom continued over a period of years to make such progress as would justify their segregation from the rest of the school. No doubt this was partly because undue emphasis was laid on subjects and skills in which these children were deficient, and partly because there were, as a rule, few facilities for development along more favourable lines. There was often too little difference in the treatment of children whose backwardness was due to innate dullness and of those whose retardation could be attributed to some extraneous or removable cause.

In the lowest stream of the Hadow school the dull or backward child may follow a continuous course that has been purposely planned with a view to enabling him to make full use of his particular powers and interests. The curriculum can be more closely adapted to his needs and the methods of teaching employed can be clearly directed towards securing a more lively response on his part. Such a curriculum will be simpler than the curriculum for the average child without necessarily being one which would appeal to children much younger in age ; that is to say, it will deal with things that interest children of the same age as those who are being taught in " C " classes rather than stop short at a point usually reached by much younger children in the same school. The methods employed will demand a greater amount of physical activity. They will involve more frequent movement, a good deal more practical work in all subjects, and a much fuller use of pictures, models and objects, since a first-hand acquaintance with what is being dealt with in lessons will usually be essential to understanding. It may be added that in many schools a very small proportion of children will be found who cannot be taught effectively by ordinary methods. For such special cases the teacher may find it useful to avail himself of the advice of the School Medical Officer or the aid of the psychological clinic, where one exists.

VII. THE CURRICULUM

A. SUBJECTS AND ACTIVITIES

45. Origin and growth of the present school curriculum.—In every Public Elementary School a definite course of work is mapped out for the children to follow. The time-table usually shows it as divided up into a number of subjects and activities. The curriculum thus represented has arisen in a somewhat haphazard way. It has, in most cases, no philosophical basis and cannot be said to have evolved organically. It began as a simple combination of Religion, Needlework and the "Three Rs," and new subjects were added from time to time under pressure from public opinion. The introduction of each new "subject" caused a certain amount of dislocation in the existing curriculum and a great deal of argument and heart-burning about the time to be given to old and to new subjects. It was natural, too, that a new subject should at first be treated more or less in isolation and be imperfectly related to the rest of the work. It may also be noted in passing that when the curriculum was less crowded than it is now there was a tendency to divide "subjects" into numerous branches, which in their turn came to be regarded as "subjects" themselves. Thus, English has been known to figure on the time-table under as many as a dozen different sub-headings.

46. Principles underlying the curriculum.—The changes which have been made from time to time in the curriculum have no doubt been inspired by a feeling that the school should contribute more effectively than before towards fitting boys and girls to play their part worthily in home, workshop and neighbourhood, as happy and useful men and women. In short, our attitude towards the curriculum has been influenced, even if only obscurely, by a desire to assist children to acquire or develop the habits, skills, interests and sentiments which they will need both for their own well-being and for that of the people among whom they will live.

It is, in fact, being increasingly recognised that the various subjects of the curriculum represent certain forms of skill and certain branches of knowledge which have proved to be of importance in the experience of the race, and which have to be taught to each succeeding generation. From this point of view it is the function of the school to preserve and transmit the traditions, knowledge and standards of conduct on which our civilisation depends; and, if the child at school is to assimilate the various highly systematised bodies of subject-matter presented to him, due regard must be had to his natural interests and to the way in which he acquires his everyday experience.

The organisation of the work of a school in terms of subjects has its advantages, particularly for the brighter and more mature pupils, but the teacher must constantly be on the alert to counteract the disadvantages of such a plan. For example, a subject deals largely, as it must, with generalised experience which may have no appeal for the young child who prefers to learn by first-hand experience; and for him any division of experience into separate time-table subjects is at best an artificial business, and in any case results in a great deal of his school work becoming unreal and lacking in any purpose he can comprehend. To give it factitious purpose by encouraging the children to compete for marks is to defeat one of the ends of education, which is to make boys and girls alive to the intrinsic interest of the subjects they are studying.

Again, undue concentration on subjects as such too frequently means that a great deal is taught which is of no clear value to anyone who is not a professional scholar. Not that the teacher must confine himself to teaching those things which have obvious bread and butter value. The question " What is the use of teaching *this* or *that* ? " must not be interpreted too narrowly. Often the things that have little utilitarian value may nevertheless be justified because of their power to illuminate and refresh the mind. The thorough study of a subject, moreover, by children able to grapple with it, should result in creating in them a habit of mind, and an appreciation of the value of method and a spirit, all peculiar to the subject, which they can carry to the solution of problems which might otherwise baffle them completely.

48. The relation of " subjects " to activities and first-hand experience.—At the same time, studies which have a disciplinary value must have vitality and meaning in their presentation if they are to contribute to a child's development. In childhood, vigour and zest for learning are the best basis for the production of a well-trained mind. This means that the younger the child the more must he be provided with suitably selected first-hand experience if he is to grow up satisfactorily. The experience of other people can have little meaning for him if he has had no corresponding experience of his own to give it point and significance.

It follows, therefore, that a division of the curriculum into separate subjects is more easily justified at the Senior School level of development than at the Infant stage. In the Infant School it will be natural and right to arrange activities of various kinds which cannot be classified in terms of any single subject, and even at later stages it will often be advisable to encourage work of a kind that calls for the application of what has been learned in a number of different subjects. It is not to be supposed that the need of a large number of different " subjects " will be felt as soon as the child enters school at the age of five. In fact, the emergence of " subjects," in the stricter sense of the term, is determined by the pupils' experience and degree of maturity. It will, therefore, be for the head teachers of each school to decide at what stage any particular body of experience should be treated as a specific " subject," and this will depend on the circumstances of the school and the stage of development reached by its pupils. Even after it begins to be treated separately, a subject will have appropriate activities associated with it, while, in addition, there will always be many useful and educative activities that cannot be linked up satisfactorily with single subjects of study, and may be dealt with as " projects ".

49. The main branches of the curriculum.—The Public Elementary School of the present day, apart from the incidental, but none the less important, moral and social training that it provides, includes in its normal curriculum, in addition to religious instruction, a number of activities and subjects which may conveniently be grouped under the following heads : Health and Physical Training ; Music ; Art and Craft and the various other forms of practical instruction ; English, History and Geography ; Nature Study and Science ; and Mathematics.

It is not possible to lay down any rule as to the exact number of the subjects which should be taken in an individual school. The choice, indeed, cannot be in practice absolutely free. Every normal child must acquire the power of speaking his own language, of reading and writing it, and also some knowledge of arithmetic and measurement. Similarly the importance of Health and Physical Training, on the one hand, and of Practical Instruction, on the other, is so great that no one would propose their omission from the curriculum of an Elementary School. But in selecting other subjects the decision is not always so easy : the curriculum must vary to some extent with the qualifications of the teaching staff. This principle is specially applicable to small schools, taught by only one or two teachers. In such schools there may be no teacher on the staff capable of dealing adequately with some particular subject or subjects. When this is the case, it may be wise to omit the subject altogether rather than to teach it badly or half-heartedly. In such schools, however, excellent work is sometimes found being done by teachers who, without having marked gifts in a subject themselves, have learnt nevertheless to release and guide the interest of their pupils in that subject.

50. The advantages and disadvantages of specialisation by the school staff.—In a large school staffed by several teachers it should not be necessary to omit any of the usual subjects. The problem in such a school is to make full use of the diversity in tastes and abilities which is almost sure to exist among the staff. Specialisation on the part of the teachers is the result of the attempt to utilise this diversity for the benefit of the school as a whole. The adoption of specialisation, particularly in senior classes, is often greatly to the advantage of both teacher and taught, and if used with judgment it is quite compatible with the exercise of the strong influence which the class teacher should have upon the characters of his pupils.

But although specialisation may raise the standard of work in a school the system has its dangers. For example, it may lead to unhealthy competition for pre-eminence among the various subjects in which the teachers specialise; it may mean that subjects are taught in isolation from one another; and it may result in the interests of the children being over-looked, owing to their class-teacher seeing too little of them. Thus he may see so little of his class-teacher as to be without the guidance and sympathy which are his due. Further, the balance of the curriculum may be upset, and important matters may escape attention because they are no one's business in particular. Handwriting, for example, may degenerate; and indeed, a carelessness may develop in more than one direction. Moreover, owing to the conflicting demands made by different teachers, the school as a whole may lack unity of aim and purpose. It will obviously be the duty of the head teacher to watch carefully the operation of specialised teaching in order to avoid these dangers, and to take steps to see that someone is responsible for the well-being and progress of each individual child, either the class teacher or a person whose functions are akin to those of a tutor or housemaster.

51. Certain general activities related to the curriculum.

—Though it will often be found that emphasis is laid in these pages on the recognition of childhood as a stage in itself, and on the importance of taking the interests and the capacity of children into account in planning the syllabus and devising the methods of teaching, the ultimate purpose behind all the work of the school is to fit the pupils to take their part worthily in the life of the community which they themselves later on will help to form.

This purpose guides the selection of the subjects of instruction: it also suggests the inclusion of certain more general activities which, though allied to one subject or another, may conveniently be referred to separately here, as instances of the part that the school can play in contributing to the life of the community. Among such activities may be mentioned the lessons on the training in temperance,[1] road safety,[2] the development, whether through the History or the Geography or the Nature Study lessons, of an interest in, and a feeling for, the beauty of the English country-side,[3] and the teaching of thrift, or the wise use of money, which is valuable alike for the individual and the State.[4] Matters such as these afford scope for practice as well as precept—but the methods used to deal with them will naturally vary according to the circumstances of the school.

B. INDIVIDUAL NEEDS

52. Variations in the curriculum according to local conditions.—Variations in the curriculum will often correspond to the special needs and circumstances of the scholars. They will show themselves rather by differences of emphasis on some subjects or parts of a subject than by the omission of a subject altogether. In a rural school under a competent teacher, for example, nature study

---

[1] Reference should be made to Chapter III of the Board's *Handbook of Suggestions on Health Education*, published in 1933 by H.M. Stationery Office, London, price 6d.

[2] See the Report of the Inter-Departmental Committee (England and Wales) on *Road Safety among School Children*, published by H.M. Stationery Office, London, in 1936, price 6d. net, the *Highway Code* issued by the Ministry of Transport and various pamphlets issued by the Safety First Council.

[3] The publications of the Council for the Preservation of Rural England (4 Hobart Place, London, S.W.1.) provide much valuable information on this subject.

[4] Practical training in thrift can be given through a School Savings Association or a Penny Bank. Membership of an affiliated National Savings Group gives the children immediate access to the facilities for shorter or longer period saving which are provided by the three State-controlled thrift organisations,—the Post Office Savings Bank, the Trustee Savings Banks, and the National Savings Committee. Habits of thrift acquired by this means

may properly occupy an amount of time which would, as a rule, be excessive in a school situated in the heart of a town. The course of Arithmetic for a school where the majority of pupils take up industrial pursuits will differ from that of a school where the majority of pupils pass on to commercial life. It is frequently found that there are traditional crafts or callings around which the life of a locality is centred and it may be desirable to take these into account in planning a curriculum. Again, it is particularly the duty of the head teacher of a Senior School to discover where the special aptitudes and interests of his pupils lie so that he may arrange for their proper development.

53. The differing requirements of boys and girls.— The most obvious and general reason for variation in curriculum is difference of the pupils in sex. Young boys and girls can be taught together with mutual advantage, but as the years pass on the gulf between the boys' and the girls' courses rapidly widens. It is not merely

---

during school days can be continued without interruption of method when the children leave school.

The National Savings Movement provides simple schemes for group saving through a School Penny Bank or Savings Association which enables members to invest in the Post Office Savings Bank, a Trustee Savings Bank, and National Savings Certificates. On 30th September, 1936, the number of School Savings Associations and Penny Savings Banks affiliated to the National Savings Committee in England and Wales was as follows :—

Elementary	21,022
Secondary with Grant	880
,, without Grant	39
Technical	127
Special	77
Private Schools	230
Public Schools	74
Advanced Education. (Training Colleges, etc.)	11
Total	22,460

that older girls are instructed in various subjects, e.g. needlework, domestic subjects, and infant care, which are only rarely taken by boys, and that boys receive various kinds of manual training which are not usually taught to girls. Difference of sex must also affect to some extent the treatment of many ordinary subjects in the curriculum. This is obvious in the case of lessons in Health and Physical Training ; but the experience of teachers seems to show that in subjects such as Arithmetic and Geography a course suitable for boys often requires considerable modification if it is to serve the needs and interests of girls. This matter is clearly one of some difficulty in Mixed Schools. Where private study methods have been adopted it is possible to introduce some difference in the courses of work arranged for the older boys and girls. Classes may be broken up into groups, and to each group different types of exercise in Arithmetic may be set ; the English courses, while containing much in common, may be based on a library including books specially suitable for reading by girls and by boys respectively. Obviously in every large mixed school under a headmaster there should be a mistress who has special responsibility where the girls are concerned. The converse would hold good in a mixed school under a headmistress.

C. THE SMALL RURAL SCHOOL

54. The curriculum of the small rural school.— There are many small "decapitated" schools up and down the country in which the head teacher and an assistant teach 40 or 50 children ranging in age from 5 to 11 years, and others still of the older type with children of from 5 to 14 years of age. The older children aged eleven and upwards, however, are being increasingly taught in separate Senior Schools. Both types of smaller schools are found in districts where farming is the principal industry and where the children are familiar with the outdoor life of the farm, its livestock and the wild life of the neighbourhood. One of the first aims of the teacher here will be to teach the children how to express their ideas clearly about all these things in speech and in writing, so that what they learn in school may lead them to think with a fresh interest about what they see out of school. But the curriculum should not be narrowly confined to rural affairs, although the teacher will not neglect to draw freely upon such material ready to hand as can be used to vitalise almost every subject of instruction. Teachers will rightly lay special emphasis upon those subjects which they are best qualified to teach, but it is specially desirable that they should be interested in plant and animal life and have some training in drawing and simple handwork. The more interesting features and the traditions of the neighbourhood should not be overlooked.

55. The treatment of Infants in these schools.— In many country schools all the children up to the age of seven or eight are taught by one assistant teacher. The difficulties of this arrangement are obvious, and they are best surmounted where the application of modern Infant School methods succeeds in teaching the younger children how to occupy themselves usefully and happily. To foster this habit of mind in children, to give them suitable opportunities for social and practical experience, to train them to talk clearly, to teach them the beginnings of reading, writing and arithmetic are, next to care for the children's physical welfare, the most important matters at this stage.

56. The treatment of older children.—With the children whose ages range approximately from 8 to 11 or 8 to 14 the problem is to provide systematic and progressive instruction within a single class. The difficulty has been met in certain subjects by the use of graded series of text-books of which there is now a large supply available. Since these books are intended for all types of schools, careful selection from their contents may be advisable in any particular school, and certainly additional exercises should be devised by the teacher. In any case actual instruction will still be necessary.

Some rural teachers have succeeded in developing a technique by means of which they take an oral lesson with one half of the class while the other half are engaged in working alone. There are of course other variants of this technique possible, but in any case the child in the small rural school has through force of circumstances to spend a considerable portion of his time in independent study.

It need hardly be said that in these small schools the children should have an adequate supply of varied and interesting books. It will naturally be difficult to draw up a syllabus, especially in History and Geography, which will meet the needs of children who will spend three or four years in the same class. The usual method is to plan one course for the younger children and one for the older children and to vary these from year to year. This is the best perhaps that can be done in the circumstances.

In schools under a mistress, the question how best to occupy the boys' time when she herself is teaching the girls needlework, calls for her serious consideration. The principle should be that the boys are occupied with something which is as useful to the boys as needlework to the girls, for example, scale drawing, surveying, or certain forms of handwork.

Gardening forms part of the course in most rural schools. Scientific gardening is only possible where the facilities are adequate and the teacher has the necessary knowledge. In schools for children under eleven some amount of plant cultivation may well form part of a scheme of nature study and add greatly to the amenities of the school.

57. The one-teacher school.—In the still smaller schools in which one teacher is in sole charge of some 20 children, there is even greater need for resourcefulness on her part. It is inevitable that a simpler form of curriculum should be adopted, in view of the fact that the requirements of the younger children make great inroads on her time. On the other hand such small schools may, in their intimacy and informality, have something akin to the life of a family.

D. SCHOOL BOOKS

58. The various types of books available for school use.—At the present day a better and more varied choice of books is open to the Public Elementary School than at any previous time. Books for use in school may be divided roughly into three main classes : Literature proper, books of information and books of pupils' exercises.

(i) *Literature, prose and verse.*—In the first place come books which children read because they find there a reflection of human experience which has an intrinsic appeal to them. If these books are worth anything as books, the children will derive something of value from reading them, though they may not read with this end consciously in view. Such books in most school libraries are limited to stories in prose, though books of poetry and plays, which undoubtedly appeal to many children, deserve to find a place more often than they do. Nor is it necessary that all stories read for enjoyment should take the form of fiction. True stories of historical incidents, of travel and exploration, of invention and discovery, are equally worthy of inclusion in the school or class library for the children's private reading. Each story or poem in these books is an artistic unit and must be read as a whole, if it is to be fully appreciated.

(ii) *Books of information.*—A second class of book essential to the life of the School is that which is read, or referred to, for the information which it contains. Of the standard text-books intended for the use of adults the majority are too difficult in language and in ideas for use by children of Elementary School age, though there are some fields of knowledge in which this may not apply, such for instance as Natural History. Many school text-books have now been published which have been specially written to provide children with knowledge of facts that fall outside their own range of experience, and these are often characterised by freshness of treatment and novelty of appeal. Sometimes in their effort to make themselves attractive they contain little information of value, or resort to devices which are more appropriate to story-books than to books which are primarily designed to provide children with information for their study of some branch of knowledge. There are others, however, which are merely dull compendia. They may be useful in preparing for examinations, but contain a great deal of information of doubtful interest for the immature mind : e.g. dates of minor events in history, or lists of unimportant geographical details.

In recent years it has become the practice to introduce, especially into craft-room libraries, books which are written in order to explain how certain practical operations and processes can be carried out by the learner. Thus there are books relating to weaving, knitting, needlework, woodwork and metalwork, and various hobbies. The present and future value to a child of being able to make use in a practical way of books of this kind is clearly very great.

These last two types of books of information obviously need not be read from beginning to end, though it will often be necessary to make a full study of some particular topic dealt with in them.

Among books of information may also be included certain kinds of reference-book. These contain a large amount of information other than that immediately required for class or school use, and are consulted mainly for such details as are required from time to time. Examples of such books are dictionaries, encyclopædias, gazetteers, almanacs and certain books of statistical information.

(iii) *Books of pupils' exercises.*—The third main class of school book is the manual, or class-book, of exercises designed to provide the teacher with material on which the children can be set to work by themselves. These, it is clear, are an adjunct to, and not a substitute for, teaching. They may be very useful to the teacher who wishes to give practice to a class or to individuals, but the teacher must not allow such a book to become his master rather than his servant.

59. The uses of books.—It often happens that a book primarily intended for one of the three purposes indicated above is used for some other purpose as well. For instance, a story-book, especially if it has been previously read and enjoyed, may well provide passages for practice in reading aloud or for language study. Such a use of the book is both sound and reasonable, but it must not be supposed that it is usually wise to divert a book from its original purpose, and, in particular, to use a book of information for a lesson in reading aloud is mere waste of time.

(i) *Literature, prose and verse.*—Methods of using books of prose and verse literature are dealt with in Chapter XI of this Handbook and need not be discussed here.

(ii) *Books of information.*—The private study of books of information is a common feature of the work of the Public Elementary Schools, particularly in schools for older children. Such study is not likely to be successful unless the children have been trained from the earliest stage to attend to the meaning of what they read, and unless the language and the ideas in their books are well within the range of their comprehension.

To train a child to make use of text-books, so that it naturally occurs to him to go to them instead of relying for all his information on teachers, is a task which calls for a high measure of skill and patience. Every specialist teacher in a Senior School, for example, should aim at getting, in addition to the ordinary class-books, a supply of interesting and informative books on his own subject, of which his pupils will make use as a matter of course. Unless this habit of consulting books for information becomes part and parcel of the Senior School pupil's make-up it is doubtful whether we can claim that we have taught him to read in any real sense of the word.

In consulting dictionaries and other works of reference, such as those mentioned in Section 58 above, children should learn how to obtain a desired piece of information as easily and as rapidly as possible. For this they need some training in the use of an index or table of contents and some knowledge of what is meant by certain signs and abbreviations in common use.

(iii) *Books of pupils' exercises.*—It is not to be doubted that books of pupils' exercises serve a useful purpose in giving the children opportunity for practising various kinds of technique. At the same time these books, unless they are employed with discretion, suffer from two disadvantages. In the first place, a teacher who relies too largely on them surrenders thereby his responsibility for the choice, order, and treatment, of his subject-matter. The books, having been compiled for the use of schools in general, do not necessarily fit the needs of the individual school, class, or pupil. In the second place, the exercises contained in them are to this extent artificial that they are not derived from the circumstances of the school and the children's own experiences.

It is obvious that a teacher from his own knowledge of his school and his pupils can evolve more stimulating and more appropriate exercises than are to be found in any book. Thus, for instance, the text-book example in Arithmetic which asks school girls to calculate the weight of 217 locomotives has less real significance to them, and perhaps to the teacher, than many problems with which they will naturally find themselves confronted in the course of a week in the classroom, the Housecraft room or their own homes. Similarly with many of the school or classroom activities it is possible to devise for boys and for girls exercises not only in Arithmetic but in other subjects as well, to which interest and value will be given by the fact that their practical purpose is immediately apparent to the children themselves.

E. MECHANICAL AIDS (VISUAL AND AUDITORY)

60. Some mechanical aids to teaching.—Teachers today are not limited to the printed word and to the illustrative material found in books or even to the things that may be immediately observed by the children as means of supplementing their instruction. The films and the wireless are two examples that occur at once as alternative forms of assistance. Other mechanical aids are the gramophone, the epidiascope, the projection-lantern and the micro-projector.

61. The use of films and wireless broadcasts.— The films and wireless have already begun to play an important part in education and there is every prospect of their becoming even more important. It must be remembered that they do not so much introduce us to a new kind of education as provide additional opportunities for making existing forms of teaching more concrete and interesting and for linking up the work of the school with what is going on in the outside world. Certainly, the teacher who is able to employ films or wireless as an aid to instruction may find in one or the other of them an instrument for infusing fresh life and purpose into his syllabuses. But the attention of children usually needs guiding and directing, as otherwise what has been introduced as an aid may become a danger. Many teachers have worked out a proper technique for getting the best out of mechanical aids. This technique will emphasise, as a rule, the importance of adequate preparation and skilful following-up. It may be added that schools which do not possess either a film projector or a wireless set may still in many districts do a great deal for their pupils through the sympathetic discussion of what the children see at the local cinemas or hear by wireless at home.

F. THE TIME-TABLE

62. Principles for drawing up time-tables.—Every school is required to have a time-table showing how the time at the disposal of the teachers is allotted for the various subjects and activities over a given period, usually a week. A certain amount of discretion will generally be allowed to the class-teacher in the subdivision of the main times set apart for a subject so that a teacher may employ any period as he finds it desirable. The time-table will also show a summary of the hours and minutes devoted, on the average, to the various school activities and will account fully for the whole of the school time. Thus, periods for assembly, registration, recreation, change of rooms, and dismissal will each find their place in the weekly total.

The younger the children in attendance, the more broadly will the division of the time available be treated, but always the nature of the balance between the main activities will be indicated. Some Head Teachers of Infant Schools, for example, show, in separate colours, the periods set apart for different types of activity so that at a glance the gradually increasing amount of time devoted, e.g. to formal work in the " Three Rs," can be seen. In this connexion it may be useful to observe that the younger the child the shorter will be the periods of formal work required of him. In schools where the older children are taught by specialist teachers in special subject-rooms, the necessity for making full and proper use of the accommodation brings with it its own time-table problems. For example, since the periods spent in the various subject-rooms will need in many cases to be roughly equalised, these subjects may have to be given more time than formerly. This will, however, mean that a broader treatment will be possible and a greater variety of occupation within each of the periods allotted for use. In every school the time-table will be an embodiment of the principles on which the curriculum is based, and the summary of times and the allocation of the subjects and activities to different parts of the day will show where the emphasis of the work lies.

It will usually be desirable to plan the periods of the time-table so that each lesson brings a real change of occupation or interest. A sedentary period or part-period, for example, should be followed, wherever possible, by one of greater physical activity, and a period or part-period of formal work by one in which other than the purely intellectual functions of the mind are employed.

G. SCHEMES AND SYLLABUSES

63. Some general principles.—The curriculum followed in any school will be found set out in the Head Teacher's scheme and the class teachers' syllabuses of work. It is considered essential nowadays that each teacher should possess a copy of the complete scheme of work for the school, so that he may be able to understand the part which he is called upon to play in the education of the pupils. There is no need for the school scheme to be set out in great detail : it will be the duty of the class teachers to interpret, in accordance with the peculiar needs of their pupils, what the Head Teacher is aiming at in drawing up the school scheme. To particularise, for example, exactly what the English composition exercises should be for a term or so in advance is to introduce undesirable rigidity into the teaching. After all, the syllabus must be made to fit the child rather than the child made to fit the syllabus. Some elasticity must be allowed or the possibility of adaptation to changing circumstances will disappear.

A good syllabus does not consist merely of a list of headings taken from some text-book. It should indicate aims as well as content, and give particulars of methods of approach to be followed and types of activity to be employed. In reorganised schools it is becoming increasingly common for the schemes and syllabuses for A, B, and C streams to be differentiated not only as regards their difficulty and amount but as regards their method of approach. This is but a natural application of the principle that forms of education should be suited to the needs of those who receive them. The further application of the principle will no doubt be a feature of the work of the schools in the next decade. Where the system of specialised teaching is in force it will be a paramount duty of the Head Teacher to see that the separate schemes are properly related to one another and that those important matters which are not necessarily connected with any single subject in their entirety nevertheless do not escape attention.

VIII. THE HEAD TEACHER AND HIS DUTIES

A. ORGANISATION AND DIRECTION

64. The Head Teacher as a leader.—It will be obvious that the tone and well-being of a school must largely depend upon the quality of the Head Teacher's leadership. While his duties will vary considerably in accordance with the type of school he finds himself in, a certain breadth of outlook and energy in direction will characterise all that he does. Unless he himself is a person with some live intellectual interest of his own, he can hardly expect to exert any lasting influence on the intellectual growth of his pupils.

It will be an important part of the Head Teacher's duty to direct the work of his assistants, particularly of those who happen to be in their probationary year. He will himself set them an example of professional craftsmanship worthy of their emulation. He will endeavour always to keep himself in touch with the latest developments in the practice of teaching and show generally a flexibility of mind combined with an unyielding loyalty to principle which will win the respect of his staff. It will also be his privilege to prove to them by his own activities that the best teacher is not one who is merely a purveyor of lifeless information or a drill sergeant in the field of the " Three Rs " but one who has a real concern for intellectual, ethical and aesthetic advancement. Moreover, he will be a person with some powerful interest of his own of educational value which will give purpose and individuality to all that he does.

65. The value of staff conferences.—To make the most of his staff and keep them in touch with the work of the school as a whole is so obvious and important an object for the Head Teacher that he should try every practicable device to secure it. Periodical conferences are one necessary part of the school routine which are invaluable in promoting unity of aim. They should be held regularly to discuss progress made, changes in the scheme of work, or modifications of method, and to put teachers in possession of what is being done in other parts of the school. Such conferences are particularly necessary in reorganised schools where one of the marks of a good Head Teacher is the successful delegation of duties.

B.　TEACHING AND SUPERVISION

66. The Head Teacher as a teacher.—It should be a first principle with every Head Teacher himself to do a regular amount of actual time-table teaching. In small schools he has no choice in the matter. He has perforce to do the main part, or even the whole of the teaching himself ; sometimes the success of a small school is due to this very fact. In large schools the head teacher who is anxious to make his influence felt to the best advantage will arrange a programme of work to be taken by himself, which must, of course, vary greatly according to his special tastes and circumstances. It should have the invariable qualities of being actual teaching and not mere supervision of others, of being regular, and of being so planned that every child in going through the school comes at some time or other under the influence of the one teacher who should have the most to teach him. In schools of intermediate size many different forms of organisation may be employed, but all should provide an opportunity for the head teacher to fulfil his duty as teacher.

67. The value of conferences in groups of re-organised schools.—It is now an important duty of head teachers to represent their schools at conferences called to co-ordinate the work of several reorganised schools working together in a group. Such a system is not likely to work smoothly and harmoniously unless the teachers are fully alive to the fact that they are engaged in a common task and realise that education is a continuous process. For this reason, regular conferences at which all the schools in a group are represented are essential.

C. THE TRAINING OF YOUNG TEACHERS

68. The treatment of the teacher on probation.—
The head teacher will frequently have to assist young
teachers fresh from the Training Colleges to derive full
advantage from their "probationary year." Such
teachers have rarely had the experience in managing large
classes which fell to pupil teachers in the past ; and they
cannot reasonably be expected at the outset to exhibit the
same ease in maintaining the externals of discipline. But
in most cases this difficulty is merely temporary, and is
overcome with the help of sympathetic advice from the
head teacher as to the technique of class management.
He should, however, beware of carrying direction of their
work so far as to check initiative or discourage them from
attempting to carry out any fresh methods which they
may have learnt in their course at the Training College.
Lack of practical skill in the theorist is no proof of the
worthlessness of his theories, and the wise head teacher
will get from his young assistants all the new ideas he
can for trial, and, if necessary, for amendment in the
light of further experience. He should make a point
of ascertaining what special qualifications and interests
they possess and should take these into account, as far
as possible, in arranging their work.

D. THE INTERNAL EXAMINATION

69. Why the teacher tests his pupils.—Every
teacher who is interested in his work will wish to form
from time to time a sound and reliable estimate of the
value and effectiveness of what he has done for his pupils.
He will naturally make use at fairly frequent intervals
of informal tests, in order to find out whether a particular
process has been mastered or a particular piece of knowledge acquired, or whether a particular method is likely
to prove successful ; yet there will be times when the
need is felt for a more comprehensive review of the work
done in a school or in part of a school.

70. Limitations of examinations.—The traditional method of making such a review is through the children's performance in examinations, whether external or internal. But, with the enlargement of the scope of his work in recent years and with the increasing emphasis which is being laid upon those aspects of education which do not lend themselves readily to formal examination, the teacher's survey needs to be correspondingly broader and not limited to what is precisely measurable for the purposes of an examination mark-list.

The teacher will realise that examinations, though they may, if properly conducted, be effective measures of skill, knowledge and intellectual ability, can tell us little, and that only by implication, about other things which are equally important, such as feelings and sentiments, or strength and persistence of endeavour.

71. An examination should be no mere ceremony.—Nevertheless the internal examination will still have its place in every well organised school, even if it is recognised that a Head Teacher who does not avail himself of the traditional methods of examination may nevertheless have a more intimate knowledge of his school and his pupils than one whose examinations are ill-conceived in purpose and restricted in range. So much time and energy have been wasted by teachers in the past in discovering with great ceremony, and by the elaborate machinery of formal examination, either what was already patent to them or, if not, what often was hardly worth discovering, that the question of the proper function of the internal examination may profitably be considered afresh.

72. The aim of the internal examination.—The purpose of the internal examination is to reveal important facts about the school and the progress of its pupils which are not otherwise discoverable or are only discoverable with difficulty. A detailed knowledge of the work of the classes and of the progress of individual children is essential to the proper organisation and successful management of any school. If the Head Teacher does not know with some degree of certainty whether his pupils are making the progress which they are capable of making, whether his classification of them is satisfactory, whether their attainments compare favourably or not with those of previous years, whether his schemes of work are as suitable as they might be, and so on, he and his staff will be working with less efficiency than they might and under a self-imposed handicap which need not exist.

What a good internal examination should do for a school, then, is to show the Head Teacher and his staff how far this or that pupil has caught the purpose of his lessons, whether he is getting what he needs from them, what he is capable of when fully extended, how far he can adapt himself to unusual conditions, what he has actually gained in the way of permanent knowledge, skill and interest, and, consequently, what modifications of objectives and methods are desirable.

73. Some dangers of examinations.—It is important, however, to bear in mind that examinations may unwittingly determine what is actually done in a class as well as measure its effectiveness. A Head Teacher may be fully justified, in certain circumstances, in limiting his examination of a class to what has been done in the " Three Rs," but unless he takes other aspects of the work of the class into account in forming his judgment of the value of its teacher's effort, it may follow that little else but the " Three Rs," as he examines them, will receive adequate attention.

Again, the importance of the internal examination may, on account of the high place it occupies in an unwisely managed school, become unduly exaggerated in the eyes of the pupils. The fear of an approaching examination has been known to rob school life of a good deal of its spontaneity and freshness. If an examination, for example, is employed to demonstrate the backwardness of a dull section of children, term after term, and year after year, it must be of doubtful value, but where it is arranged to give children an opportunity of displaying the full range of their powers, and provide them with proof of the increase in their mental stature, it will clearly have a stimulating and not a depressing effect.

74. How observation is related to examination.—

It will be obvious, then, that the expert Head Teacher will not make the mistake either of supposing that he can know his school and his pupils completely by means of his examinations and mark-lists, or that he can entirely dispense with them and rely upon day-to-day observation and impression for his knowledge of how the work of his school and of his pupils stands. But if his examination work is enlightened and searching, it will naturally show itself in the occasional modification of his schemes of work and the re-classification of his pupils. If his day-to-day observation is well directed and the impression he forms well grounded, they will be seen reflected in the increasing success of his examinations in giving him the knowledge he seeks and in his power of varying his methods of getting at it. It will thus be through alert observation and intelligent purpose in examination that the Head Teacher will ensure the greater vigour and the surer progress of his pupils.

75. The Head Teacher's part. Conditions of success.—

In small schools the Head Teacher may well have to do most, if not all, of the examining himself. In larger schools, especially in Senior Schools, he will naturally delegate much of the routine work to panels of teachers in the different subjects, though he himself will retain the responsibility for the conduct of the examination as a whole and will no doubt wish to do his share in the work of marking.

Success in the conduct of an examination involves three things : a clear conception of what it is desired to find out ; knowledge of the particular technique required for a particular purpose ; and knowledge of how to evaluate the work done by individual children.

76. Various purposes of examination.—Thus the Head Teacher may wish to know how the work of his school compares with that of others and may on occasion make use of some of the standardised tests now available in a certain number of subjects. He may wish to know how the work of his school or part of his school compares with that done in previous years. Obviously he cannot do this unless the nature and difficulty of the tests he sets and the standard of marking are sufficiently like those of previous years to make comparison possible.

He may wish in the reports he sends to parents to indicate in an objective and easily understandable form how a child's progress compares with that of his fellows and in what branches of his work he is relatively strong or relatively weak, using for that purpose perhaps actual marks, or estimates based on a five-point scale (A, B, C, D, E), or the child's position in class in the various subjects. If he wishes to give a fair impression of the child's achievements in various directions, he will find it necessary to go beyond the restricted range of the traditional examination and to assess in some way attainments that have not come within its scope.

77. Variety of attack needed.—Thus the nature of the tests the Head Teacher sets will vary in a good many ways. Tests for younger children will naturally involve little written work. They may be largely oral and be concerned with promise rather than actual achievement ; or they may take the form of picture tests or performance tests. A test of a term's work, based on the class teacher's syllabus and records, will be more detailed than one which seeks to discover whether back work has been kept in mind. So a test in reading aloud will be very different from one in the comprehension of matter read ; a test in speed and accuracy in arithmetic will differ from one in problems ; and a test to see whether things worth remembering have been remembered will differ from one to see whether knowledge can be intelligently applied.

78. The importance of preserving an even standard.—It will be the Head Teacher's business to see that an even standard of assessment is kept from term to term and year to year by all who are engaged in the work. Where the object of an examination has been to ascertain whether principles have been understood, or reading matter comprehended, or whether knowledge can be applied by the pupils in a variety of ways, it will be found that the majority of children reach a standard which is not far removed from the average. Many of the marks, therefore, will be in the neighbourhood of the average mark, (which should be about 50 per cent. if the fullest scope for an effective spread of the marks is desired), and there will be relatively few children obtaining very high or very low marks. Where, however, the test deals in a straightforward way with things that should be generally known— " mechanical " arithmetic, for instance, or spelling, or salient facts in History or Geography—it may well happen that the majority, or even all, of the children obtain high marks.

79. The use to be made of the results of the internal examination.—Having the necessary information before him the Head Teacher is in a position to consider how far things are proceeding satisfactorily, what children need special attention, what steps should be taken to secure improvement, or in what directions the syllabus and methods of approach need modification.

These matters he will discuss fully and freely with his class-teachers and specialist teachers, and if they have the tabulated results together with his suggestions, which on occasion he will be well advised to commit to writing, they will be in a position to proceed in the next stage of their teaching in a businesslike manner.

It is usual to go through the marked papers with the children and to acquaint them with the table of results. A child who has worked a test will naturally wish to know where he has done well and where he has gone wrong. It is inadvisable that he should be too much concerned with whether he has done better or worse than his neighbours, but it is right to provide some objective standard against which he can measure his strength and weakness and gauge his progress.

80. School Records.—It is usual for teachers to keep some record of work from day to day. In the preliminary stages of school life, where the emphasis is largely on spontaneous activity and individual development, the keeping of class records of work has but a limited value because of the difficulty of making them objective and comparable. Nevertheless, records of some kind must be kept and, indeed, in most schools which include young children it is customary to keep some account of individual progress. This may take the form of records made by the children themselves, of observations written down by the class teacher, of marks awarded as a result of some significant test which admits of objective comparison, or of a special record card.

.All these are useful, but the record-card, properly related to the other forms of record, has a special value inasmuch as it will serve to show a child's progress as he moves through one class or school stage to another, will do something to bring about continuity of treatment, and will save the time which is so often wasted in the effort to discover what has already been discovered.

The wholly satisfactory form of record has yet to be devised. If it is to be of real help to the teacher in his work, as it should be, it will not be over-elaborate, nor entail excessive clerical labour ; it will be more concerned with the points in which a child differs from his fellows than with those in which he belongs to the common average ; it will give information, on the one hand, about the more permanent factors in his make-up, his health, his physical defects if any, and the nature of his home, his temperament, his native ability, and on the other, it will deal with the changes represented by his successive stages of achievement ; it will wherever possible be based upon objective standards of assessment rather than depend upon personal impressions ; and it will be wide enough in scope to enable the reader to form some picture of the development of the child as a whole.

PART II

PREFACE

THE THREE STAGES IN OUR SCHOOL SYSTEM

1. Children's development is continuous and different children develop at different rates.—The three chapters which follow deal with the education of children in infancy, in early childhood, and in later childhood ; and their titles correspond to the main divisions of our present school system. In such a system it is necessary, for reasons of administrative convenience, that children should enter or be transferred from a school or department at a particular age, but it must not be supposed that at this age there occurs in all children simultaneously any radical alteration. The normal development of the individual child is subject to no sudden breaks and falls into no clear-cut stages. Growth, though it may not be regular, is a continuous process, and no one can say of any child that at a particular moment he ceases to be an infant or begins to be an adolescent. Moreover, children develop at different rates, so that there is inevitably between one stage and another of our school system a wide overlap, for which each type of school must make due provision.

2. Classification by " streams " : some of its dangers.—In view of the different rates at which children develop, it is only right that, where numbers permit, they should be classified in " streams," commonly referred to as " A," " B," and " C " streams, according to their scholastic powers ; and indeed our school organisation would be ineffective if it made no attempt to meet the wide variation in ability that is known to exist. But a word of warning is needed on the tendency to label individual children or individual classes in a manner which suggests some fundamental and lasting difference. The methods of grading on which the organisation of a school is based cannot be exhaustive and should not be regarded as giving final assessments of human value : their true purpose is to give the children better chances to master their school-work and to develop gifts of different kinds. The qualities and interests that children have in common by reason of their racial inheritance and their share in the life of the community are fundamentally of far greater importance than any differences of ability ; and the exigencies of organisation should not obscure the fact that all children have an equal claim to oppor-tunities of cultivating whatever talents they may possess and equal rights in the corporate life of their school.

3. A full life at each stage the best preparation for later life.—The differences of educational treatment that are suggested as suitable for the successive stages of school life are based on the principle, stated in the General Introduction to the present Handbook, that children's talents and abilities appear in an orderly sequence and not simultaneously. The order in which they appear is sufficiently regular to make systematic education possible, though differences in the rates of growth are in themselves such as to make uniform methods of treatment for all children inappropriate. Each new power of body or mind as it emerges must be nurtured by the right kind of experience, and, if that experience is to fit the child for independent life in a modern community, it must be drawn largely from the world of present realities rather than from the world of books. The school must be open to all the beneficial ideas and influences that are at work in the world of today, while still preserving its function as a shelter within which children can exercise in safety their immature powers of feeling, thought, and action. These are the considerations on which is based the appeal made in the following chapters for a wide range of social and realistic activities in the schools.

4. Children need experience of both freedom and discipline.—The kind of experience needed by children at any particular stage of growth is that which enables them to discover their newly developing powers and to exercise, measure, and prove them. If children are to find themselves they must be allowed a sufficient degree of freedom ; if they are to develop their powers to the fullest they must be prepared to accept the appropriate discipline and training.

5. The main differences between the three types of school.—While children should have experience of both freedom and discipline at each stage of school life, the relative emphasis placed upon either will vary from stage to stage. Thus the Infant School is primarily a place in which children learn to find themselves, and a greater measure of freedom is appropriate there, while formal exercises and testing occupy a minor place. In the Junior School the systematic practice of bodily and scholastic exercises will assume a greater importance, for at this period, as will be seen from what is said later on, children take a conscious pleasure in acquiring skill and in measuring themselves against their companions. At the end of the Junior School stage comes the time when the general capacities of the children are assessed in accordance with the promise they have so far shown in school and their specific performance in suitable tests, in order that they may proceed to that form of post-primary education for which they are best suited. The Senior School stage is in no sense a time of final proving, but it should at least be a time in which the children have begun to settle down to courses of study that suit their special gifts, and in which they will have a chance to show their worth in some enterprises of their own choice and conception.

CHAPTER II

THE NURSERY AND INFANT SCHOOL STAGES

SUMMARY OF CONTENTS

I. THE PLACE OF THE INFANT SCHOOL IN OUR EDUCATIONAL SYSTEM

1. The Infant School peculiar to this country.—This country may well be regarded as the home of the Infant School. In making school attendance compulsory at the age of 5, a lower age than that adopted in any other country, the Education Acts of 1870 to 1876 both recognised and perpetuated a type of school which, established as much for social as for educational reasons, was already in existence and had already developed its own technique and its own tradition.

2. Its usual age-range is from 5 to 7+.—In England an Infant School is administratively a school that is designed for children between 5 and 7 years old. It is true that in many areas children are admitted to school before the age of 5, but these children should be in the Nursery School or Nursery Class rather than in the Infant School proper. It is true, again, that many Infant Schools retain children to the age of 8, and some to the age of 9, and that there are also Infants in many schools with an age range of 5 to 11 or 5 to 14; but in such schools it is usual to regard the children under 8 as forming a separate group and as requiring different treatment from the children above that age. Experience, in fact, has shown that there are distinct advantages in an educational system which includes, where possible, separate departments for children between the ages of 5 and 7+, and that a school which concerns itself specially with this stage, short as it is, has a certain unity of its own and a definite function to perform. It is therefore advisable as a rule that where their numbers are sufficient the Infants should constitute a separate department. Such a department need not be large; in fact, very large departments are not altogether suitable for young children, for the demands of organisation are apt to interfere with the freedom and spontaneity which are so necessary at this stage. Moreover the larger numbers mean that the children have on the average a longer journey to school and may run greater risks on the way, while the teachers find it more difficult to maintain contact with the parents. On the whole, 250 to 300 seems to be a very good size for an Infant School.

3. Promotion from the Infant School to the Junior School.—The present tendency is to make promotions from one department to another once a year only, and for many reasons this is a sound practice.

It is undesirable that a child, whatever his ability, should be moved from the atmosphere of the Infant

School before the age of 7+, and this means that where transfers are made annually the groups transferred should consist of children over 7 and under 8, with an average age of $7\frac{1}{2}$. It is hardly necessary to say that wherever this represents a higher age of transfer than that formerly adopted it should be accompanied by a correspondingly higher level of development on the part of the children. Even then, however, there will be some children who at the time of transfer have made little progress, for a child who is naturally dull may, through the accident of his date of birth, be transferred when he is not much over the age of 7. To retain such children in the Infant School or Infant Section for a longer period than their fellows is an expedient which can be justified in very exceptional cases only. The Junior School, therefore, will have to face the task of dealing with a small proportion of children whose attainments so far are rudimentary, and to be content if they have at any rate developed as far as their abilities warrant.

II. THE CHILD OF FIVE

4. The Infant School aims at the development of the child along natural lines.—The Infant School differs from other schools in that it starts with the untaught child. For this reason, no doubt, teachers in Infant Schools have been especially interested in studying the nature of the child and have made it their aim to encourage the development of his native potentialities rather than to force him into a uniform mould. That this is a sound aim may well be judged from the success with which it works in practice. It has always, however, to be borne in mind that education is a continuous process which does not stop at the age of 7, and the teacher of even the youngest children should not be unaware of the aims of the Junior and the Senior Schools.

A school which admits term by term, or even at more frequent intervals, a succession of young children must make it its first business to provide for these children a suitable environment, in which, under the stimulus and guidance of their teachers, they may enlarge their experience, acquire useful habits, widen and deepen their mental powers, and begin to develop certain skills.

5. Some characteristics of the child of five.—Even at the age of 5, children vary considerably in ability, in temperament, and in their attitude towards others, but their common characteristics are sufficiently numerous and pronounced to make possible a form of school life in which all can participate.

The child of five is physically active and restless. He is still the creature of relatively uncontrolled instincts which prompt him to spontaneous and vigorous if somewhat fitful action and which show themselves especially in his love of play. His natural curiosity leads him to ask many questions and he is constantly seeking to enlarge his experience and acquire control over his environment. His emotions are still often violent, but short-lived, though they may have their lasting effects ; and he is very dependent on the affection of grown-ups, in whom he places implicit trust. Socially he is undeveloped, being still in his own eyes the centre of all things, but at this stage he shows a disposition to associate with small groups of other children.

6. Treatment of children on entry to school.—Such a child, accustomed as a rule to somewhat informal conditions at home, does not at first adapt himself very easily to school life, which even in the freest schools must and should contain a certain element of regularity. It is therefore a wise plan to treat the newcomers as a " Reception Class," giving them conditions and equipment that will make it possible for them to occupy themselves in a natural manner and enjoy a life which in many ways resembles that of a good home. In the free atmosphere of such a class valuable opportunities occur of studying the needs and characteristics of individual children, and, if necessary, taking early steps to prevent the development of undesirable traits.

7. Some things the child learns before he comes to school.—It would be a mistake to imagine that the child, though untaught, has learnt nothing before he comes to school. For the very young child the home offers the best training ground, provided of course that it is a reasonably good home. By the age of five a child has amassed a considerable though unsystematic knowledge of his own small world. His sense perceptions are as acute as those of an adult and perhaps more vivid, though as yet they lack the full significance that results from longer and wider experience. He has probably acquired a number of useful habits and some power of doing things for himself, like dressing and feeding himself, though his performance in these matters is apt to be slow and laborious. He has already an individuality of his own and may before this time have been subjected to some of those early and strong impressions which often have a lasting effect on personality. He has, as a rule, a working knowledge of small numbers, and, above all, he can talk fairly fluently and has a vocabulary far more extensive than is commonly supposed.

8. Not all homes are satisfactory.—When the effect of home life has been to develop the child on the lines indicated above the school has a good foundation on which to build. Unfortunately there are homes in which the children are not under good influence, and indeed whole areas where, owing to bad housing conditions, a low standard of living, the fact that the mothers are employed, or other causes, they do not develop as they should. The task of the school then becomes a difficult one, and it may well find itself unable to repair the damage already done. Prevention is better than the attempt to cure, and the Nursery School or Nursery Class can do valuable work in providing, so far as is possible, the conditions and the training associated with a good home, where these do not exist.

III. THE NURSERY SCHOOL

9. The Nursery School as a substitute for a good home.—The Nursery School, admitting children as early as the age of two and retaining them till they are five, is concerned with an important, even a critical, stage of development. Under bad conditions in very early childhood the seeds may be sown of much trouble in later life, mental as well as physical, just as good conditions may well produce habits and attitudes of mind which will form the foundation of good conduct.

It is these good conditions that the Nursery School seeks to create, so that, as in the good home, a healthy growth may be fostered of body, mind, and character. It cannot be expected that the school will provide all that the home does. On the other hand, it may provide some things in a higher degree than the home : a more ordered experience, perhaps, a more stimulating life, and especially a wider range of companionship.

10. Its care for the health of the child.—It is, however, in the field of preventive medical activity that the Nursery School offers particular advantages ; for one of its principal aims is the nurture of debilitated children by providing for their physical welfare and wholesome development. This it achieves by undertaking frequent medical examinations, by supplying nutritious and well-balanced meals, and by creating an environment favourable to growth in an atmosphere relieved of much of the strain which is inevitable in the ordinary home.

Important results are obtained by the early detection and treatment of defective eyesight, defective hearing, dental decay, weakness of mental capacity and behaviour difficulties ; while the cure of some of the sequelae of infectious diseases before the age of five may save attendance at a Special School in later life. The value to the nation of such preventive work is obviously very great.

11. Some characteristics of a good Nursery School.—The small child will find in the Nursery School an atmosphere of natural affection, a feeling of space and security, an ordered and regular way of life. He will be on friendly terms with teachers and others who minister to the needs of children, and he will have at hand the material through which he may develop his powers and enlarge his experience, not only within the school precincts but also outside ; for he will be made acquainted with the neighbourhood, which, even in the poorest districts, has abundance of life and interest.

Where the school has the right aims and uses the right means the children will show the gaiety, the curiosity, the friendliness, and the spirit of adventure which are as desirable as they are characteristic of this period of life, and the natural poise which shows that they are acquiring powers of self restraint as well as of self expression.

12. The daily programme.—There will be no timetable in the ordinary sense of the term, but the daily programme will have a definite framework. This arrangement will give the child the feeling that he lives in a stable world and will foster in him regularity of habits, yet the programme will be elastic enough for him to exercise initiative and learn to adapt himself to changing experiences. There will be set times for meals—in many Nursery Schools the children have breakfast, lunch, dinner, and tea, at school—for attention to personal hygiene, and for rest. The intervals between these

fixed periods will be devoted to those activities which
are appropriate to children who have not long learned
to walk and to talk, and who manifest the independence
of spirit that comes with these accomplishments.

Such activities may be said to fall roughly into two
groups.   On the one hand are those which arise
spontaneously from the children's overflow of natural
energy or from their interest, permanent or passing, in
the things around them.   On the other hand are those
over which the teacher exercises a directive influence,
with a view to encouraging the children to join in co-
operative effort, awakening them to new ideas, or leading
them to realise possibilities in themselves of which they
are as yet unaware.

13. Free activities.—The first group will include
the playing with large realistic toys—carts, wheels,
perambulators, dolls and their accessories, Teddy bears,
large boxes, and planks, large blocks and other building
material—through which the children will indulge their
love of make-believe and find an outlet for their
exuberance of spirit ; the use of the Jungle Gym, slides,
balancing bars, jumping steps and other kinds of
specially designed apparatus by which control of the
larger muscles is developed ; such exercise in manipulation as is involved in opening and shutting doors,
setting tables, sweeping and dusting, arranging flowers,
filling and carrying vessels of water, digging in the sand
pit or garden, or using toy hammers and other simple
tools ; the first steps in responsibility and foresight
through the care of living things in the school or the
garden ; and quiet sedentary occupations with materials
or apparatus chosen to give specific training—all the
better when they are self-corrective in operation—
such as puzzles, beads for threading, Montessori
apparatus, building and constructive material, scissors,
paste, and picture-books.

In this programme there will be, both for the individual child and for the school, an ordered succession of periods of noisy activity and periods of quiet occupation, but there will be throughout a running accompaniment of talk. While the children are thus engaged the teacher will be no mere spectator. She will watch over their safety, observe their choice and use of material for play, give timely suggestions for new occupations or for fresh possibilities in familiar occupations, and her conversation will continually provide for them the vocabulary and phraseology with which they can put their experience into words.

14. Directed activities.—To the second group—the directed activities—belong the various forms of music and rhythmic movement, listening to or relating stories, discussing pictures, chanting rhymes; observing or talking about matters of interest, such as things seen in the street or new toys; walks and visits to the park, the shops, the railway bridge, a blacksmith's forge, a house in course of erection, or even, it may be, a country holiday, undertaken in order that the children may become familiar with a wider and more varied life than that within the school or their own homes.

15. What the child learns in the Nursery School.— Thus in the Nursery School the children will spend a busy and active time with alternations of regularity and freedom, of vigorous movement and restfulness, of spontaneous activity and directed activity. They will have passed quite naturally, yet encouraged by the teacher and aided by opportunity, from the stage when their play consists mainly of random activity that may be discontinued at any moment to the stage when their play is directed to a conscious end and is not discontinued until that end is accomplished. They will constantly be meeting new experiences and increasing their powers of taking in fresh impressions by eye, by ear, or by muscular sense ; they will be winning a progressive mastery over voice and limbs, and cultivating those simple skills of hand that are essential to the arts of creative expression ; and they will be on the way to becoming responsive to what is good not only in simple music, literature, and art, but also in human conduct.

Such a school will have achieved its aim, if the children who have been through it are found to be healthy and vigorous, active and even graceful in movement, deft with their hands, ready of speech, eager to learn, able to look after themselves, companionable and willing to respect the rights of others, and altogether well suited to begin the next stage of school life.

IV. THE NURSERY CLASS AND OTHER CLASSES FOR CHILDREN UNDER FIVE

16. How the Nursery Class differs from the Nursery School.—A Nursery Class usually differs from a Nursery School in that it is always attached to an Infant School and its minimum age of admission is three instead of two. Its hours of attendance are those of the Elementary School, it does not aim at providing medical supervision and care to the same extent, nor does it usually provide meals other than the mid-morning lunch. Conditions will naturally vary according to local circumstances. A Nursery Class, however, is not fulfilling its proper function unless its numbers are reasonably small, and unless the children have space for free movement, facilities for the practice of personal hygiene, for the mid-morning lunch and for the afternoon rest, a supply of toys and apparatus, and a place where they can play in safety out of doors.

17. The similarity of aim.—In spite of these differences in the facilities offered, the aims of the Nursery Class are identical with those of the Nursery School and it is, therefore, unnecessary to add to what has already been said. The more closely the former approximates to the latter, within the limits of its circumstances, the more successful is it likely to be, and, as it is an actual part of the Infant School, it makes possible continuity of method throughout the Nursery and Infant School stages.

18. Children under five in Infant Schools or Classes.—In some districts it is still the custom to admit into the Infant Schools children of four or even of three without making special arrangements for them. The wisdom of admitting them at all in such circumstances is questionable, especially when, as happens in rural areas, they form so small a group, taught in the same class as children of five, six, or seven. To offer detailed suggestions as to the best way of dealing with these children once they have been admitted is hardly practicable, so widely do conditions vary from school to school. The wise teacher will do what she can to provide some at least of the elements of the Nursery School régime described above, even if, to take an extreme instance, she can give them no more than a corner of the room and some toys to play with during part of the day.

19. The connexion between School and Home.— The home is always a potent factor in the making of character, but its influence on the child is perhaps strongest before the age of five. The teacher who is concerned with children who are still in so many ways dependent on their parents will make it part of her duty to get into touch with the homes, in order not only to get a better understanding of her pupils but also to enlist the co-operation of the mothers and fathers. The Nursery School has been particularly successful in securing this co-operation, by making contact with the homes, welcoming the visits of parents, encouraging their practical help, and forming active Parents' Associations.

Such contact is evidently easier to establish when the children are young, but once established it may be expected to persist, with mutual advantage, through later periods of school life.

V. THE PREMISES AND EQUIPMENT OF THE INFANT SCHOOL

20. The type of building most suitable for Infants. —The Infant School which admits children at the age of five has on the one hand to provide an environment and a training appropriate to a particular stage of their development and on the other hand to ensure, so far as is possible, that each child begins his progress at the point he has already reached and continues it at the pace which corresponds to his abilities.

The building which provides the best environment for Infants has much the same qualities as the Nursery School, that is to say it is sunny, well lighted, airy, and well warmed in winter. Spaciousness in the premises as a whole and the class rooms in particular is of especial importance, because at this stage activity of mind is closely associated with activity of body, and the child needs room not only for his games and other forms of physical training but also for those purposeful activities in the classroom which should occupy a considerable portion of his day. For the same reason the furniture, preferably small tables and chairs, should be light and easily handled. Every school needs either a hall or playroom, with a piano, and the larger schools can make good use of both. Some schools may be fortunate enough to have in addition a room not occupied by a class which can be put by the school to many useful purposes.

21. Its amenities and equipment.—If the social training is to have reality, the premises must offer adequate facilities and seemly conditions for the exercise of personal hygiene. The appearance of the school and the way in which it is decorated will undoubtedly have considerable influence on the children, and the provision of suitable pictures, not hung too high, and of a few objects possessing some beauty of colour or form may do something to foster discrimination and a sensitiveness to beauty. Equally important are the appearance and arrangement of the class rooms. Here the individual teacher will have opportunity to exercise her good taste and to provide an example of order and beauty to the children. A completely equipped school would contain not only picture-books for the younger and reading books for the older children and small apparatus and simple toys such as bricks, balls and hoops, but a certain number of things more commonly found in the Nursery School than the Infant School, such as cups, plates and tablecloths for the mid-morning lunch, small brooms and dust pans, toy wheelbarrows and perambulators, instruments for a percussion band, jigsaw and other puzzles, a dolls' house, or apparatus on which the children can learn to climb and balance.

22. The surroundings and playground.—A playground is of course a necessity. Yet a mere playground, however good its surface, affords but limited facilities. Schools which possess a sandpit, a garden where the children can cultivate their own plots and observe flowers, shrubs, and birds, or a grass plot on which they can romp freely, are fortunate in what they can do for their pupils.

Few schools possess all the amenities that constitute the best environment for Infants and many fall lamentably short of the minimum desirable. Yet even where the external conditions appear to be most unpromising remarkably good work is often done in making the most of limited opportunities and in providing the essentials of a sound education.

VI. METHODS OF CATERING FOR THE NEEDS OF INDIVIDUALS

23. Individual differences among children of five.
—It has already been said that the training given
should as far as possible be adapted to the needs of the
individual child. Among the children who enter the Infant
School at the age of five there may be some who are
vigorous and intelligent and others who are retarded,
delicate, or badly brought up. It may be found that
among the children who have been in a Nursery School or
Nursery Class there is a somewhat greater degree of
general development of a kind that is valuable both in
itself and to the school. To endeavour to teach all these
children as if they were on exactly the same level would
be to make a serious mistake. Even at this early age the
creation of opportunities for individual progress presents
no insurmountable difficulties. Probably most schools
nowadays arrange for children to work at times either
individually or in small groups, and this has been found
to have a special appeal for young children, who are still
animated by a spontaneous urge to explore things and
still tend to immerse themselves in their own occupations
without much regard to what others are doing.

24. Group activities.—Much use will, doubtless, be
made of those corporate activities of a realistic kind
which make it possible for each child, working as one
of a group, to engage himself in the particular operation
which appeals to him most. The better the equipment
of the school, the more it will provide suitable opportunities for this. Such activities as setting a table,
tidying up a room, arranging flowers, arranging the
contents of a dolls' house, building a castle of bricks,
looking after living creatures, making simple toys,
playing at shops and other forms of dramatic play, are
enjoyed by children without any consciousness that by
practising them they acquire something of value. Their

enjoyment is in itself worth while, for childhood—a stage in itself—is more than a preparation for maturity, and there is no doubt that children learn a great deal naturally through spontaneous and undirected play.

But so far as the school itself is concerned, these activities will, in addition, provide the best foundation for future development if the teacher herself understands their value and their possibilities and takes steps to ensure that they do not degenerate into mere barren repetition, or take the form of that apparently aimless kind of play which marks an earlier stage of childhood. She will need to realise that the Infant School, especially in the first year, is concerned largely with the development of forms of behaviour, native powers, and personal qualities, bodily control and balance, for instance, carefulness in manipulation, capacity for purposeful effort, ability to co-operate with others and readiness to do so, in which are contained the potentialities of subsequent growth in one direction or another. Such qualities should manifest themselves, as is explained later on in this chapter, not in this or that activity only or in this or that period of the time-table, but in a variety of activities and at many times during the school day. Later on, as knowledge grows with experience and ideas become systematised, these qualities will tend to become associated in school with particular subjects of the curriculum and with particular forms of skill.

Although the aim is the development of qualities which are thus general in character, the teacher is after all concerned not with abstractions but with living children, and what matters most of all is the way in which these children feel, act, and think. She will endeavour, as far as lies in her power, to provide for them activities in which they can express themselves whole-heartedly and without self-consciousness, because in them they find genuine purpose, satisfaction for their native impulses and scope for more than one side of their nature.

25. Individual occupations.—Many schools, either from lack of facilities for such activities as those referred to above or as a supplement to them, provide what are known as individual occupations. These need not be restricted to the more formal exercises in reading and number, but may well include jigsaw and other kinds of puzzles, matching pictures and patterns, sorting out different small objects, making designs with various material, and some manipulative toys. Apart from the fact that they require little space, these occupations have advantages in that they call for no great expenditure, give the children an opportunity of busying themselves profitably in a quiet way, and are concerned with material which allows of the occupations being so graded that progress may easily be noted not only by the teacher but also by the child.

Here, as with the group work already mentioned, it is important that the teacher should realise the precise value and purpose of the occupations. On the one hand, they serve as a useful preparation for reading, writing, and number, while, on the other hand, they may well be continued side by side with the more formal instruction ; for they contribute in a measure to the formation of certain ideas and conceptions and to the recognition of spatial and other relations, e.g. of resemblance and difference, which become increasingly important at a later stage.

VII.   CLASS ACTIVITIES AND LESSONS

26. Class activities.—However much attention is given to group work or individual work every school will need to set aside a good deal of time for activities in which a whole class can participate—singing, dancing, physical training, games of various kinds, story telling, and a good deal of the training in speech.

27. Class lessons.—Some of these class activities will develop into " class lessons " in the upper part of the school. The older Infants will have reached the stage when they respond to the stimulus of numbers. They will have begun to take an interest in one another's ideas and experiences and to feel the need of guidance in thought and in performance.

Such lessons take various forms and serve various purposes. The teacher may relate to her class stories and experiences that enlarge their range of ideas or aid the growth of good sentiments, encourage them to discuss things seen or things done, help them to think clearly and to express their thoughts adequately, show them the best way of doing certain things, or give them exercises which will promote the development of skill. Her success will depend on the extent to which she meets what the children feel to be their needs at the time and on her power of enlisting their active co-operation.

VIII.   ORGANISATION

28. The Infant School commonly organised on an age basis, with provision for new admissions.—The special feature of the organisation of the Infant School is that, as children may be admitted all through the year, the numbers in the lowest class and the length of time any child stays in it may be uncertain. In a school which has the good fortune to retain the same staff throughout the year it is usual to start with a skeleton class at the bottom and allow it gradually to fill. Where, as happens in some places, it is only in the latter part of the year that the school has its maximum number of pupils, a classroom is at first left empty, to be occupied by a new class when the additional teacher is appointed. In the great majority of the schools, though

some prefer a different kind of organisation, the classification is mainly by age, and this seems to accord well
with their circumstances and the kind of training they
give.   In a school of over 200 children there will be at
least two classes which will be due for transfer at the
end of the year ; and the average age of the one will be
about six months higher than that of the other and the
children in it proportionately more advanced.

IX. THE CURRICULUM

**29. The curriculum a matter not of subjects but of
experience and activities.**—In any school however
much the immediate concern may be with the teaching
of subjects the underlying aim is always a general
training, and the younger the child the more that general
training is in evidence.   This is particularly true of the
first year of the Infant School, where so much of the
time is spent in joyous activities, which, though largely
instinctive in origin and apparently without ulterior
purpose, provide the best preparation for the more
serious occupations of a later day.   As the children grow
older they acquire more capacity for sustained effort and
for relating means to ends, but play is still an important
element in their school life.   The older Infants are still
interested in the relations between things themselves
rather than in the relations between ideas : their desire
is to experience, to experiment, to develop skill, rather
than to acquire systematic knowledge, and for them
thinking is closely associated with doing.   For this
reason it is best to envisage the curriculum of the Infant
School not in terms of subjects at all, but in terms of
experiences and activities.

**30. Not all the training given is represented in
the syllabus or the time-table.**—Much of the training,
and that not the least valuable part of it, is such that
it cannot always find a definite place in the curriculum

or time-table. It will often be going on incidentally and unobtrusively ; yet, if it is to be a real training, the teacher must never lose sight of it.

It is necessary, for instance, that the children should acquire certain good habits, of personal hygiene, of cleanliness and tidiness, of consideration for others, of courteous speech and good manners. Many children on first entering school will be found to be deficient in varying degrees in some of these habits and will need to be initiated in them as the first step in school life. It is not, however, enough to establish good habits. They must be maintained and actively practised throughout at least the Infant stage if they are to become a lasting part of character.

Certain useful and habitual actions, the washing of hands, the putting on or doing up of garments, the distribution or removal of material used in the classroom, are performed by young children slowly and not always efficiently. At first the performance of these actions will need a good deal of time and supervision, but if they are kept up as part of the ordinary routine of the school they will eventually become so speedy and precise as to be practically automatic. There will no doubt be times set apart for the younger children to engage in some of them ; with the older Infants they will, apart perhaps from the mid-morning lunch, occur incidentally during the ordinary occupations of the day. In either case the teacher will see to it that the practice of good habits is not confined to certain times and seasons, but becomes an integral part of school life. She will aim in fact at making these habits so much a part of the school tradition that the children will practise them without question and as a matter of course.

31. The development of character.—In some important elements of character the child who is approaching the end of his course in the Infant School has changed considerably since the time when he began it. His emotions are less intense and less liable to rapid changes from one extreme to the other, and are beginning to assume a certain stability which favours the development of sentiments, such as the sentiment of fair play; his actions arise less from the immediate promptings of instinct and more from settled purpose which is not far removed from a sense of duty; and he is not so self-centred, for he is beginning to take an interest in the world around him and the people in it as having an independent existence of their own. The development, through habit and reason, of a proper control of the emotions is of first importance; on the other hand, any attempt to create emotional states in the minds of the children should carefully avoid methods which may result in insincerity, sensationalism, or weak sentimentality.

In general, the teacher will seek at this stage to form character not only through direct training in good habits, but by making use also of experiences and conditions in which development can take place in a natural way. The school itself with its corporate life will provide the conditions in which growth may best take place. The teacher will have done her part, if due insistence is laid on good habits, if occupations are provided which call for purpose, care, and effort, if activities are encouraged which offer scope for the expression of feeling, and if ideals of conduct are presented through the religious teaching and sometimes also in the story lesson.

32. Training in self-help and social training.— Given the right conditions this more general side of the school training will result in development along two lines. On the one hand, the child will have become far more capable of looking after himself. He will be able to attend to his personal wants, keep himself clean and tidy, look after his own possessions, and carry out a number of tasks without an undue amount of supervision or help. On the other hand, he will be able to play his part as a member of a small society. He will know what is fair to others as well as to himself, and be ready to assume some responsibility for what affects the welfare of his school or his class ; he will perform his part in group activities, and render help to his fellows when they need it ; and he will have acquired some of that grace of manner, sympathy with others, and readiness to exchange ideas, which contribute so much to the happiness of a community.

33. Principles underlying the curriculum.—The experiences and activities which occupy the greater part of the day in the Infant School may be grouped in various ways, according to the purpose they serve, the materials or apparatus they require, or the place in which they are carried on. The teacher who is drawing up a syllabus or arranging a time-table will probably have regard to the way in which they serve as a preparation for the various subjects in the Junior and the Senior Schools. Such a view is entirely reasonable, provided that two things are kept steadily in mind. In the first place, there should be no attempt to introduce prematurely into the Infant School forms of activity which are more appropriate to the Junior School. The first year of the Infant School should be a period of general preparation, and the activities of the second year should arise naturally from this preparation and should be developed in difficulty and complexity at a rate which corresponds to the general development of the child. In the second place, it is particularly true of the Infant School that no one activity or group of activities can be said to function separately. The activities have so much in common that to divide them into watertight compartments has been found to result in waste of time and power and in poverty of training.

34. Training in rhythm.—As an example may be mentioned what is often called rhythmical training, a side of education which has a strong appeal to young children and which without doubt is valuable to them in a great many ways. Such training commonly takes the form of bodily movement to music, and this is the natural way of introducing it. Given in this way it forms a good preparation for the various kinds of dancing that now figure on the time-tables of most schools, but if it goes no further than this its full value will not have been attained. Through singing or chanting, with or without the accompaniment of music, or playing in percussion bands, the sense of rhythm will be strengthened, and it may be expected to display itself in the children's speech, in their art, and in many other activities.

35. Training in bodily control.—An important group of activities is that relating to physical movement. From his play the younger Infant will learn in the first place control of the larger muscles and will gradually acquire balance, speed of movement, quickness of response, ability to move gracefully and rhythmically to music, and skill in the management of balls, hoops, or ropes. At the same time through building with bricks, setting a table, and many other of his occupations, he will acquire that nicety of touch and delicacy of adjustment that will enable him to undertake various forms of handwork, drawing, and writing. But even in his second year at school his handwork will be varied in character and such as to call for constructive powers and the expression of ideas rather than a high degree of skill. The learning of crafts belongs to a later stage of school life.

36. Opportunities for first-hand experience.—It is probable that not enough attention has been paid in schools to the importance of first-hand experience. Many weaknesses in later education may be traced to the fact that in the early stages children have had too limited a range of impressions, or their impressions have lacked clearness and vividness. The wise teacher will arrange that the children have opportunity for a variety of experience during school hours, and will encourage them to take advantage of the opportunities within their reach out of school.

By observing flowers or living creatures in the school grounds, in the nearest park, or in any open country near the school, by cultivating small gardens, by growing plants in pots or window boxes, by keeping aquaria or breeding cages, the children will be laying a foundation for Nature Study and Biology ; by observing their surroundings, the things in the shops, the changes in the weather, the movement of the sun, they will be preparing for the later study of Geography. Their interest in people who serve the community—for instance, the Policeman, the Postman, the School Nurse, or the Dustman—will introduce them to the idea of social interdependence and later on make History more alive to them ; while an interest in Physical Science may well have its beginning in experiments with mechanical toys, examination of the ways in which the school is heated, lighted and ventilated, or observation of the machines that may be seen at work in most places.

37. Enlargement of experience through stories, talks and other means.—Valuable as such experience is in itself it is neither possible nor desirable that a child's experience should be all first-hand. The teacher can add greatly to his stock of ideas by reading or relating to him stories, by talking to him about interesting events, and by showing him pictures and objects. Stories, of course, have a strong appeal to children, who obtain through them their first ideas of History and Literature and learn something of how human beings feel and behave.

38. Translating experience into language.—It need hardly be said that it is only when they receive expression in some form or other that these impressions are likely to be clear, lasting, and part of a genuine body of knowledge. Of all forms of expression language is by far the most important, especially at the Infant School stage ; for to translate experience into words is the basis of intellectual development. There should therefore be ample opportunity for talk and discussion. The younger Infants talk most readily about things which they are doing at the moment ; the older Infants retain impressions longer and are quite capable of discussing in class experiences that are over. The teacher will encourage them to relate freely things they have done or seen, to compare and contrast, to express their likes and dislikes, and to exchange ideas. In these discussions and descriptions she will, of course, encourage the children to put into language experiences which involve the ideas of number or measurement, and will help them to express those experiences definitely and in such a way as to make their reasoning clear. She will often find it necessary to supply the word or phrase which will fit a child's need, and if she does this at the right time and in the right way she will be helping him to make a step forward. She will not be content, however, to help merely in increasing the extent of his vocabulary, but will do what she can to ensure that the language he uses has full and vivid meaning.

39. Other forms of expression.—Important as expression through language undoubtedly is, it is far from being the only form of expression. In the Infant School in particular other forms should have their due place. The children should have full opportunity to express their ideas and experiences through drawing and painting, through handwork, and through miming and other dramatic action. In these ways they can often express themselves more completely and find an outlet for the natural impulse to create something.

Through music, dancing, the saying of poetry, or through practising various kinds of decoration and design, they can find vent for feelings of which they are hardly conscious themselves, but which are none the less real.

From a child's expression of his ideas and feelings, provided that it is genuine and spontaneous expression, the understanding teacher can indirectly learn much about his inner life that might otherwise be quite unknown to her.

40. Speech as a kind of skill.—From another point of view it is possible to regard the use of language as a sort of skill. Certainly in their second year the children should learn to pronounce their words and phrases clearly and correctly, to produce the voice pleasantly, and to speak connectedly and intelligibly. This may mean that a good deal of time will be devoted to speech exercises, even including speech drill, but these should never degenerate into the lifeless routine which deprives the children's speech of its most attractive qualities, expressiveness and animation.

The introduction to what is generally regarded as correct speech should be gradual. No attempt should be made to impose suddenly on young children a form of speech which is so far removed from their natural mode of expression that it is largely dissociated from their home life and inhibits their natural flow of ideas.

41. Learning to listen.—It should not be forgotten that to cultivate in children the power of listening attentively and with understanding is to endow them with a gift which is hardly less valuable than the power to speak well.

42. The beginnings of the " Three Rs".—Reading, writing, and number, are three important skills in which children are commonly expected to have made considerable progress before they leave the Infant School.

Opinions differ as to the best age for introducing the children to them, and it is clear that this must depend a good deal on the development of the individual child. Rapidity of progress and thoroughness of mastery depend so much on previous preparation of a general nature that it is wisest with the majority of children to postpone formal instruction in all three until about the age of six.

43. Skill in reading.—Thus during their first year the children would be acquiring the power of speech that is a necessary preliminary to reading, but they would also constantly be seeing printed words and realising the use of books. Doubtless they would pick up a great deal incidentally from seeing the titles of books or pictures, printed directions, or the written names of members of the class. Of methods of teaching children to read it may be said that no method is satisfactory which results in attention to the symbol at the expense of the meaning. Since the end is to train people to read rapidly the children should have some practice in reading as grown-ups do, by taking in the meaning of a whole group of words at a single glance. If children are to learn to read books by themselves in the early stages, as they usually wish to do, they must know something of the sounds of the letters in order to read new words, and they will understand these sounds all the better if they learn them in connexion with their speech training. Finally, they should have frequent opportunity of reading aloud passages with which they already have some familiarity, so that they may be able to give a fluent and expressive rendering.

44. Skill in writing.—Of the teaching of writing it need only be said that the exercises at this stage should always have meaning. Most Infant Schools find it advantageous to teach the children—who are at the same time learning to read—to use the symbols which resemble those they see in print. Before they leave the Infant School, the children should be expected to write at a reasonable speed, and to spell correctly words that they have often seen. Through their work in drawing and making patterns they should acquire the manual control in making curves that will help them later, when the time comes for cursive writing. Written " Composition " as such does not belong to the Infant School, but some children enjoy putting down their ideas on paper and should be allowed to do so.

45. Skill in arithmetical calculation.—Number teaching is too often a matter of training children in the manipulation of written symbols. Infants are quite capable of making simple calculations, even without the use of objects, and of making them rapidly and accurately. There is, however, a real danger that skill of this kind may be cultivated at the expense of the very thing that makes it worth while. Arithmetical skill is not an end in itself ; and its acquirement should be preceded and accompanied by exercises in which there is a strong element of reality. This is advisable because in the situations occurring in everyday life which demand the use of number it is necessary to select the relevant data and decide on the processes to be employed, before the calculations can be performed.

46. For arithmetical calculation experience is a necessary prelude to the use of symbols.—To begin with, then, the child will need plenty of varied experience which involves the idea of number, not only in actual counting, but also in different kinds of measurement. Next, as has already been said, he will have practice in putting that experience into words and into some sort of logical arrangement. Finally, as his ideas become more exact, he will learn to express his experience through the use of the symbols that represent numbers or numerical operations. In this way he will be enabled not only to be skilful in the use of figures, but also to know what he is doing and why he is doing it.

X. THE TIME-TABLE

47. The time-table should reflect the ideas under-lying the curriculum.—The time-table of the Infant School will reflect the ideas underlying the curriculum. The more free and varied the life of the school the less rigid will the time-table be, while the greater the stress that is laid on activity the less will the time be cut up into short periods. In the first year of the Infant School the time-table should be somewhat similar to that suggested for the Nursery School. In the second year it will naturally be more detailed and will vary according to the circumstances of the school. In drawing it up, however, certain principles will always have to be kept in mind.

There are, for instance, certain fixed times, for registration, for religious instruction, and for recreation, which are regulated by Code requirements, and certain periods which must be earmarked for a particular form of activity because the hall or playroom is at that time allocated for this purpose to a given class or classes.

A time-table with minute subdivisions or very short periods defeats its own ends. Children should have time in which to finish whatever they are busied with, and, though they tire more quickly of some things than of others, they are capable, if interested, of applying themselves for surprisingly long periods to some occupations, for example handwork. Moreover they will not all finish their tasks at the same moment and, where group or individual methods are adopted, several different occupations may be going on simultaneously. For these reasons it is now usual to arrange for the inclusion in the time-table of a number of long periods perhaps an hour in length, assigning them to two or more activities, without stating when one will end and another begin, or how they will be distributed among the sections of the class at a particular time. This is far from implying a haphazard allocation of time. It is easily seen that if children are to maintain their freshness and interest throughout the day their occupation must follow a certain alternating sequence. Thus, after listening to a story they will be ready for some form of bodily activity, or after a reading lesson they may enjoy handwork or drawing.

48. Preserving the balance in the various forms of activity.—The summary of the time-table will show whether regard has been paid to this last requirement, to the extent that it makes clear what proportion of the time is allocated to physical activity, to observation and inquiry, to expression, or to formal instruction. Where the arrangement is as elastic as has been suggested above, the time analysis cannot show the exact amount of time assigned in a week to any particular activity or group of activities, but it can at least indicate how much a child is intended to spend on the average in this way.

Such freedom as this, however, imposes on the teacher the further duty of seeing that a proper balance between the various activities is preserved in actual practice. This can best be done by keeping from day to day a brief record of how the children have occupied their time and consulting it at frequent intervals to see what adjustments are needed to redress the balance.

XI. THE TEACHER AND HER TASK

49. The qualities of a teacher of Infants.—The
teacher of Infants has no easy task. She needs above all
things an interest in and a liking for young children,
and the capacity to win their good will and trust.
She must have knowledge, but that in itself is not
enough, for freshness and vitality are even more
important ; and as her function is to guide as much
as to instruct she should have a sympathetic understanding of human nature.

50. Her methods of teaching.—The methods she
uses, provided that they are based on sound principles,
should be her own, for with these she is most likely to
be successful. But she will have to beware of two
dangers to which the Infant School is particularly liable.
In the first place, she must avoid aiming at results
which, though superficially attractive, do not represent
genuine progress. In the second place, while encouraging
the free and spontaneous development of the children
in ways such as have already been suggested, she will
not interpret this freedom as implying that she can be
content with anything less than the best effort and
accomplishment of which the children each in his
degree are capable.

XII. TESTS AND RECORDS

**51. How to ascertain and record individual
progress.**—The value of a teacher's personality and of
her methods of teaching can be estimated only in terms
of the all-round development of her pupils. She must
therefore always be on the alert to observe signs of
progress or retardation, and she must have standards
by which to judge.

The Infant School is no place for examinations.
But this does not mean that steps should not be taken

to ascertain periodically what progress has actually been made. However general the training that is aimed at, its effects can only manifest themselves in what the children do and how they behave, and the only proof that a skill has been acquired lies in the fact that a child does a thing skilfully. Hence informal tests will be given from time to time in accordance with the principles explained in the General Introduction, and the results recorded in some simple and intelligible form. There are, it is true, many important aspects of a child's growth which it is hard to test or to record in this way, and it is particularly difficult to devise any kind of record which gives a complete picture of the development of the child as a whole. Yet some at least of the individual work done in the Infant School, and that not only in reading, writing and number, lends itself to organisation in the form of a series of graded steps, and, where this is so, it is easy and useful to keep records of the progress made by each child individually.

XIII. THE RESULTS OF INFANT SCHOOL TRAINING

52. The characteristics of a good Infant School.— An Infant School that is animated by the principles indicated in this chapter will be a place where life has all the freshness and vividness of early childhood, and where activities are pursued in a spirit of lively adventure. It will have provided the children with many new interests ; and it will have given them in a measure suited to their age and maturity both the freedom and the discipline, through which their awakening sense of group membership may best be developed. Its product should be a child who, in comparison with the child of five, is self-possessed, responsible, independent, and capable of devoting himself to a straightforward task with a remarkable intensity of purpose and a high regard for the proper way of performing it.

53. Similarities and differences between children in their development.—So far as the simple physical and social habits are concerned development is largely a matter of age and training and should not differ greatly as between one child and another at the end of the school course ; but, where activities are concerned which are not matters of routine, there will be marked variation in achievement. Hence it is undesirable in this field to lay down any fixed standard which all Infants may be expected to reach. Where conditions are normal, however, it is probable that the great majority of the children will have acquired considerable facility in speech, and in reading, writing, and number, the sort of proficiency that has been summarised in sections 43–46 above.

Differences in attainment, and indeed in most other respects, are natural and inevitable among children at the end of their course in the Infant School, but what has been said in this chapter will show that behind these differences lies a common training with a common purpose. Expressed briefly, this purpose is to give the children experiences that will help them both now and later to adjust themselves to life in a civilised community.

CHAPTER III

THE JUNIOR SCHOOL STAGE

SUMMARY OF CONTENTS

I. THE JUNIOR SCHOOL. ITS ORIGIN AND DEVELOPMENT

1. The Junior School as a new form of organisation.—The Junior School, which is the final stage of primary education, is intended for children between the ages of 7 and 11, though in practice both the lower and the upper age-levels are found to vary considerably. It did not come into being because children of this particular age-range were known to have special needs and to present special problems. It arose through the successive splitting off of the Infant and the Senior School from the original type of Public Elementary school for children of all ages. As yet the Junior School is young, its traditions are still in the making, and its full potentialities unrealised, but already it has shown a surprising vitality and has opened up new vistas of educational progress that promise well for its future. Separation from the other types of school has given an impetus to the study of the characteristics of children between the ages of seven and eleven, but it has also brought difficulties inseparable from introducing yet another division into what after all is a single process of continuous organic growth. The transfer from stage to stage almost inevitably entails a temporary check in progress and only by the closest co-operation between Infant, Junior, and Senior Schools can the loss be reduced to a minimum.

2. The Junior stage no longer regarded as one of mere passive preparation.

—For a long time the work of Standards I to IV, the counterpart of the modern Junior School, was based upon the idea that the period of childhood which they covered was pre-eminently a time for a narrow and rigorous treatment of the "Three Rs". It was a common belief that the rote-memory of the child was then at its best, and his nature so plastic as to retain almost indelibly the impressions of any lesson learnt. Particularly did the notion prevail that the mind of the child at this age was a tool to be fashioned and sharpened for the more serious work of the later stages of education.

The danger in this view is, of course, that the minds of children may be regarded merely as passive instruments in the hands of the teacher. But as Professor Whitehead has said, "The mind is never passive . . . You cannot postpone its life until you have sharpened it. Whatever interest attaches to your subject-matter must be evoked here and now ; whatever powers you are strengthening in the pupil, must be exercised here and now."

3. The modern view : a systematic course based on children's natural interests.

—One of the main concerns of the Junior School will be to discover those activities of child life which promise the best combination of immediate interest and permanent value. The work of exploration demands close observation of the spontaneous behaviour of children and systematic study of their development. We must take note of the things which seem to them to be most significant in the life of the world about them, and find out in what sort of terms they explain to themselves the events that make up their life. We must study the growth of their language and familiarise ourselves with the words, phrases, and modes of expression, that pass into currency at this stage, and with the forms of literature that have the strongest attraction. We must discover their compelling motives and modes of activity and be able to say what things make the deepest appeal to their feelings. In all these things the Junior School child differs in greater or lesser degree from younger and older children, and only upon an understanding of his particular qualities and immediate needs can his education be rightly conducted.

But to take advantage of dominant interests as they arise does not mean that the course which the school provides should be wholly opportunist or unorganised. Inherent in each stage of growth are the resources of the earlier stages and the potentialities of the later ones, and it would be folly to ignore at any moment either the experiences which the child has hitherto had or the qualities which the school aims at developing. The school cannot evade the duty of planning a systematic course of activity for its pupils ; nor can it escape its responsibility to the public for maintaining proper standards of achievement in the fundamental subjects.

II. THE AIM OF THE JUNIOR SCHOOL

4. A full and active life not dominated by external standards.—There is every reason why the aim of the Junior School should be set out in terms of the nature of its pupils rather than exclusively in terms of subjects and standards of achievement. It would, indeed, be anomalous if on the one hand Infant School teachers were to be encouraged to plan a life of free activity for little children, and on the other hand the teachers of Senior School children were to be asked to arrange courses of work suited to the varying capacities and interests of their pupils, while at the same time the Junior School child had still to do nothing but follow the traditional track with an imposed curriculum and an external standard of achievement. If it is wrong in the Infant and Senior Schools to ignore the capacities and interests of children it must be equally wrong in the Junior School. But it by no means follows that children should decide entirely for themselves exactly what and how much they should do or learn, irrespective of the requirements of the society in which they find themselves. The course of instruction for children which will appear reasonable to most teachers will be one which can be followed with due regard both for the welfare of the child and for that of the community of which he is a member.

It is not to be expected that Junior School teachers will be able to free themselves at short notice from the external standards to which they have so long been accustomed. Indeed, it may be some time before they can win the same measure of freedom as is commonly conceded to their colleagues in other departments. Already, however, many Junior Schools have profited by adopting the more generous ideas set out in the Hadow report on *The Primary School*, and the movement thus started will no doubt gather momentum as the years go by.

It will be the aim, then, of the Junior School to provide an education which is suited to the nature of children between the ages of seven and eleven as well as to give a satisfactory form of preparation for the years beyond.

III. CHARACTERISTICS OF CHILDREN AT THE JUNIOR SCHOOL STAGE

5. Physical and mental stability.—To say that those responsible for Junior Schools should arrange a life which is suited to the nature of children between the ages of seven and eleven is not helpful unless we can say in some detail how Junior School children differ from children of other ages, and, consequently, what healthy progress between the ages of seven and eleven consists in.

At the outset it is well to remember that the Junior School period is one in which the child enjoys a life of relative physical and mental stability. School attendance is usually good and comparatively fewer cases are brought to the notice of those in charge of Child Guidance Clinics. This fact, however, does not lessen the need for teachers to keep a watch upon individual children and to maintain close touch with parents, School Medical Officers, and others concerned with the health of the child, for children of this age may pass through phases of ill-defined disturbances of body and mind, which only those who know them intimately can detect and remedy.

At all ages, the physical well-being and mental balance and general progress of children depend upon their vigour of body and vitality of interest, so that it is as important during the Junior School period as at any other time to see that no child suffers from preventable weakness of body or unsettlement of mind.

6. Juniors delight in exercising bodily skill.— Physical development during the Junior School period is characterised by progress from the pleasure of displaying energy for its own sake to the enjoyment of actions calling for the exercise of some specific form of bodily skill. During the recreation intervals children of seven may indulge in activities such as " playing at horses " which call for little conscious effort at improvement, but older pupils will concentrate assiduously on the practice of skilled movements involving co-ordinations of mind and body that are increasingly difficult to perfect. Top-spinning, walking on stilts, turning " cart-wheels," and doing hand-stands, are examples of skills of hand or body that each generation of young children seems impelled by some inner necessity to try to master. This growing ability to control bodily movement in the service of ends not to be reached without some difficulty will be reflected in their Physical Training syllabuses.

7. Their propensity to self-assertion and competition.—The pleasure which the growing child finds in the display of physical power shows itself in his social life. He enjoys asserting himself in various ways against his companions. He is frequently given to boasting of what he can do better than they can, whether he is justified or not. His individualism finds expression in work as well as in play, so that getting more sums right than his neighbours will be as pleasurable as beating them on the playing field. The problem of the Junior School teacher is to guide the individualistic expression of this energy into healthy channels ; to check the spirit of competition when it is likely to hinder the emergence of more important qualities, as, for example, when a struggle for " marks " may destroy the possibility of an interest in a subject of study for its own sake. In this connexion it will be well to instil in the mind of the child the idea that, while he may find it possible to excel in one direction, this is no evidence of an all-round superiority. An appreciation, moreover, of the abilities of others is essential to a right sense of his own.

8. Their reactions to the opinions of others.— As the junior child passes up through his school he shows signs of a growing recognition of the fact that he is a member of a group which he must consider as of equal importance with himself. He appeals less and less frequently to the authority of the teacher against his class-mates, and he is less and less inclined to give quick expression to every feeling of resentment which a check to his aggressiveness may arouse. The opinions of his fellows begin to carry weight. At the same time he shows less confidence in his valuation of his own efforts. Faults in technique—as in art work, which is an excellent example—begin to affect his outlook, and a great deal of the spontaneity and freshness which gave such charm to all he did at an earlier age may disappear. It is important, therefore, that nothing should be done to deepen his occasional sense of failure. We have not yet learnt how to steer children past this difficult age with entire success, but a discerning teacher who is able to keep alive in his pupils a sensible belief in their powers and a desire to excel will do much to make the problems of this age easier of solution.

9. Their love of collecting.—A characteristic of children during this period which may be utilised by teachers in promoting social as well as intellectual development is the tendency to collect things. Most children find pleasure in collecting shells, picture-cards, stamps, etc., and as they grow older the pleasure derived from the mere act of collecting is supplemented by that of exchanging, completing sets of things, and arranging and re-arranging them. Teachers should see that there are suitable opportunities for the expression of this tendency. Already it is common to find children making collections of nature specimens and of pictures that illustrate lessons in Geography and History. But the tendency must not be allowed to get out of hand. Some positive knowledge should follow from the activity; for example, a child who collects postage stamps should be expected to talk with some accuracy about countries and their location on the globe.

10. Their attitude towards the external world.— During the Junior School period the child's view of the world undergoes considerable change. He loses the habit so common in infancy of attributing the things that happen in the world of nature to the action of personified forces and begins to recognise the operation of the laws of cause and effect. The child of 11, for example, may understand the analogy between the formation of clouds and steaming breath on a frosty morning, but would not explain the clouds—as a boy of six is known to have done—by saying they were made by someone breathing in the sky. Mental development of this kind is a matter of natural growth which should not be unduly forced ; so that, while it ought to be normal for the child of eleven to expect effects to follow upon natural causes in unvarying sequence, it would be folly to expect children of seven to acquire the same out-look merely as a result of a few lessons. The best form of education in this connexion is one which allows children to become actively acquainted with the rich treasure-house of nature and to feel something of its reality and its romance.

11. Their interest in persons.—It is a commonplace of educational theory that little children learn best through the active exploration of their environment. Experimentation is as necessary in the sphere of personal relations as in the physical world. One method of discovering what other people are like and how they think and feel, which is not always treated sympathetically, is that of imitating their behaviour. History and Literature lessons give children glimpses of what human life can be outside the limits of their own relatively narrow experience, but the lessons will be incomplete unless opportunities are provided which will allow children to feel for themselves what the people they hear and read about were like.

Young children are naturally inclined to put their conceptions of other modes of life into dramatic play, and so it is important that children in the Junior School shall have ample space, as, for example, in a commodious school hall, in which they can give free rein to their dramatic propensities. Through a free expression of these, children find their way to maturer forms of speech, feeling, and behaviour, and when their conceptions of life are thus openly expressed in dramatic action faulty ideas are exposed and can more easily be set right.

12. General ability and special talents.—Finally, some reference to modern doctrines as to the nature of intelligence may be made here. It is agreed widely today that Junior School children have not arrived as a rule at the age when specific talents have begun to take permanent shape. With a few exceptions, particularly, perhaps, musical talent, the appearance of a special gift during early childhood is not necessarily a sign that a permanent talent is there. A good performance in any direction is more likely to be a sign of good general powers. Thus, an ability in art or handwork is more likely at the junior school age to be an expression of the child's general intelligence than of anything more specific. What is very important for teachers to remember is that the intelligence of children best develops, and the chances of powerful special gifts of permanent value appearing are best secured, when the educational environment is as rich and varied as it is possible for it to be.

IV. THE ORGANISATION AND DISCIPLINE OF THE JUNIOR SCHOOL

13. Ways of securing differentiation of curriculum and methods in large and small schools.—The reorganisation of schools has made it possible to provide courses of education which take into account some of the broad differences in the physical and mental characteristics of children. Much naturally must depend upon the size of the school. In very large concentrations there may be as many as three parallel classes for each age group, and it will be relatively easy in such cases to classify the children approximately to suit their varying needs. But even in these schools it is not always realised that careful and intelligent differentiation in the curriculum, syllabuses of work, and methods of training and teaching, is also needed to secure the full benefits of better classification. The relatively homogeneous class of a large three-stream school may itself be subdivided for group-work, and opportunities can thus be provided for independent thought, effort, and activity. For many purposes, too, the children can profitably be allowed to work individually ; for example, in some Reading and Arithmetic periods, in various kinds of expression work, and, in general, wherever a child has special needs or displays exceptional talents. Individual methods of teaching which have proved so valuable in the Infant School in helping children to master the earlier stages of learning to read, write and calculate arithmetically should by no means be abandoned in the Junior School.

In smaller schools, children of widely different types, and in very small schools, of ages also, must inevitably be grouped under one teacher. The difficult problems inherent in such an organisation may be at least partially solved by a well-planned routine involving a judicious mixture of individual, sectional, and class instruction and activity.

14. Varieties of classification in mixed Junior Schools.—The mixed school is of course a necessity where the numbers are small, but the main arguments for and against co-education seem to apply less to the Junior School stage than to later stages of education. Where the numbers are large enough to permit the effective classification of boys and girls in separate departments Local Authorities sometimes prefer this arrangement, for administrative reasons. Classification by sex is not unknown, however, in Mixed Junior Schools, which are sometimes organised with parallel classes for boys and girls separately, instead of with classes containing both boys and girls graded according to ability or attainment. In schools so organised some of the chief advantages of large concentrations of children are unnecessarily sacrificed. It is no doubt desirable to separate the boys and the girls for physical training, but this should be a simple matter to arrange.

Cross-classification, not necessarily on a sex basis, has been tried in some schools for other purposes (e.g. instruction in Arithmetic) and with proper safeguards such a plan may prove to be a valuable incentive to individuals. Chapter V of the Hadow Report on *The Primary School* describes interesting experiments on these and other lines.

15. Desirability of limiting specialist teaching.— A child of Junior School age seems to thrive better in the care of a good all-round " general practitioner," whilst a succession of different teachers during the day tends to debar him from the continuous care and oversight he seems at this stage to need. Nevertheless, any appropriate special qualifications possessed by the staff, should—especially, perhaps, in Art, Music and Physical Training—be freely utilised, both for the preparation of schemes in particular subjects, and, if thought expedient, for specialist teaching throughout the school.

16. Discipline in the Junior School.—The changes that are taking place in the work of the Junior School cannot but bring a new conception of discipline. Discipline in the Junior School must lead gradually from the freedom of the Infant School to the self-direction of the closing stages of Senior School life. There must be, as at all stages, sufficient control by the teacher to permit the systematic carrying out of the school programme. If the activities of the school are to be profitable to all its members, they must be orderly ; if they are to be continuous and purposeful, they must be guided into suitable channels. But the maintenance of order and the guidance, for which children look naturally to their elders at this age, can be provided without harmful repression by teachers who understand the needs of their pupils and can share their interests and their moods.

There must be, in the daily programme, times when the children can discharge their high spirits in various kinds of vigorous activity ; there must also be periods, which should increase in length as the children grow older, when they are called upon for spells of quiet effort and attention. The chief factor in creating the atmosphere in which young children can grow in self-control and consideration for others is the personal example of the teacher, for children respond gladly to one who is genuinely concerned for them and can lead them on to new adventures of mind and body. They are, however, no less quick to discern in their teachers any weakness of purpose or lack of sympathy, though the disorderliness, with which they sometimes react to such conditions, brings them no real satisfaction.

V. THE JUNIOR SCHOOL CURRICULUM

17. The importance of activity and experience.— In their Report on *The Primary School* the Consultative Committee sum up their views on the curriculum in the words : " The curriculum is to be thought of in terms of activity and experience rather than of knowledge to be acquired and facts to be stored ". These words have been perhaps more frequently quoted than any others in the Report, and their general acceptance by the educational public is a warrant of the soundness of the principles they embody. The rest of the paragraph in which the quotation occurs makes it clear that the choice of activities and experience shall be such as to lead the child to a realisation of the fundamental interests of life in so far as they lie within the compass of childhood, to set him on the way towards self-control and to awaken his imagination and sympathies so that he may be ready to follow in later years the highest examples of excellence in life and conduct.

18. The relation between experience and knowledge.—In this view, life, as it presents itself day by day to the child, is the main subject of study and the unifying principle of the curriculum. The task of curriculum-making is that of selecting experiences which will enable the child to enter directly as by his own activities, or vicariously as by reading or hearing of the experiences of others, into the full heritage of childhood ; not childhood as an isolated thing, but as linked with home and an ever-widening environment, with family and ancestry, with friends and the people of his own country, and with mankind at large.

A word of caution, however, is needed here. To emphasise activity and experience is not to belittle the value of the knowledge that they bring. Indeed, unless they bring knowledge that will serve present and future needs, experience and activity lose a great deal of their value. Moreover, there is some knowledge so important for immediate use and future progress that regular drill or constant practice is needed to make it permanent ; knowledge of the addition, subtraction, and multiplication tables is an obvious example of this.

19. The development of language.—It is not possible here to enter into details of how to apply the general principle to all branches of the curriculum. A few illustrations only can be given from the various types of activity which gradually differentiate themselves into separate subjects of study during the period of Junior School life. Speech and the arts of communication and expression by means of language will still have a pre-eminent place. As new experiences and new ideas come into the child's life, new words and new forms of expression will have to be acquired ; as he realises more clearly how things and events are related to one another in time or space, or as cause and effect, he will naturally use new forms of sentence structure in speaking of them. For example, clauses introduced by *when, where, but, because, although,* will become more frequent and their significance and right use will have to be understood. To the general growth of language each subject will contribute a new store of potential imagery and a new stock of ideas, facts and words. Each subject will bring its particular way of arranging its facts and describing them. From all sides ideas will flow in such profusion into the child's mind that it will be beyond the power of any teacher to regulate, exercise and discipline them all, but in trying to foster the growth of language he should at least recognise the main sources which supply the ideas that give it life and colour, and should draw as freely as possible upon them to strengthen and enrich the child's command of the written and spoken word.

20. Music and rhythmic movement.—Music and the arts of expression through rhythmic movement have no less important a place in the Junior School than in schools for older and for younger children. At the Junior School stage children's pleasure in them is perhaps greater and more spontaneous than at other stages, because they have gained more assurance than when Infants in using their voices or their band-instruments, and they are not yet subject to the embarrassing influence of self-consciousness which so often assails them in adolescence. In the Junior School it will be

more important to preserve the children's freshness by
means of a wide range of simple songs and rhythmic
exercises than to hurry them on to grapple with more
complicated musical patterns. Increased skill in
reading music and better control of voice and limbs
will come with practice under good guidance, but harm
may be done by concentrating exclusively upon a highly
polished performance of just a few songs or exercises.
Music has at all stages a justification in itself because
it allows children to give disciplined expression to
feelings that are common to the group of which they
are members ; the sense of unity which they experience
deepens the feelings and increases the delight in expressing them. In the recitation of poetry and in collective
verse-speaking, too, the same spirit may be awakened and
fostered.

21. The beginnings of Art and Crafts.—At this
stage a powerful motive in Art and Craft work will be
the impulse to reproduce on a realistic scale the simple
dwellings and appliances of which he learns in the world
about him, or from his fellows through the lore that each
generation of children conserves for the next. When
left to their own devices children pursue these crafts
at home, in the garden, or on some neighbouring waste
ground or common. The task of the school is to preserve
the child's spontaneity and allow opportunities for its
expression which are suited to the more confined space
and the small-scale materials available in school.
Pictures and models will naturally abound in schools
which recognise the child's compelling interest to make
things. In the beginning, zest and inventiveness are
more important than exactness or finish, but no course
should satisfy either teacher or child that does not
eventually lead to livelier realism, better design and
more precision in the finished product. Such marks
of progress should appear even in the freer type of

Art which is proving in many schools to be an invaluable means of developing the child's innate sense of colour and his love of rhythm and design.

22. The romantic element in the Humanities.— In Literature, History and Geography the human and romantic features have at this stage the greatest appeal ; stories of child life and animal life, biographies, and stories of travel and adventure are popular. If at times we should be inclined to deplore that the child mind yields too readily to the lure of things that are highly coloured, exaggerated, or exceptional, it should at least be remembered that through meeting the unusual the child first begins to look carefully at what is familiar. By acquaintance, through reading history and fiction, with people of other times and places, the children come to a better knowledge of themselves.

23. The romance of the external world.—In Science teaching, too, the wonder and romance of Nature—which practical work in the garden should emphasise—will be the dominant notes. In this field it is specially important that phenomena that are striking or extreme should be brought into relation with the commonplace—the lightning with the sparks on the frosted electric tramway, the cloud with the steaming kettle—so that the children may as they grow older get glimpses of the order that underlies variety, of regular sequences of change, and of laws that run through a wide range of diverse events. The daily happenings of the street, the changes of the sky, the seasonal progression of field, park, and garden, which an active experience in work there will yield in the greatest measure, supply an unending succession of topics, but the teacher's own work will be well done only if he selects for special attention those facts that illustrate a few simple principles and provide a groundwork of knowledge in which later on the child will discern the working of scientific law.

24. The child's own experience as the basis of mathematics.—The mathematical syllabus calls for serious investigation and experiment. It has grown up in obedience to the dictates of a logical scheme of development along lines that have left the natural propensities of children of this stage unheeded. We should consider what quantitative aspects of the child's experience are important to him and use these interests to develop the fundamental skills that belong to them. Some features of the growth of his interests are plain to see. His possessions are more numerous and more valuable, so that questions of price, barter, and saving, arise. His physical powers are greater ; he can walk further, lift greater weights, jump higher and further, and run faster, and he becomes interested accordingly in the questions, How much ? How far ? How high ? How fast ? He has lived longer and is beginning to have a surer sense of time, though his time-sense, especially as regards historical chronology, is notoriously slow in attaining even a moderate degree of exactness. Such considerations as these must be taken into account in drawing up the Arithmetic syllabus. If the subject matter is sufficiently real and interesting as it may be, e.g. through simple practical exercises in weighing, measuring, etc., and oral shopping calculations—then the drill which is needed for the mastery of mechanical processes will be undertaken with the zest which the young child brings to all those activities that have a natural appeal for him. To restrict the Arithmetic lessons exclusively to the working of the text-book examples may deprive the work of much of its real value.

VI. STANDARDS OF ATTAINMENT

25. The danger of expecting a common standard of attainment.—The Junior School contains the full range of abilities found among children attending Public Elementary Schools. The spread of attainments therefore will be proportionately greater than in the Senior School, from which the cleverer children will have been drafted away to centres of higher education. Any attempt, therefore, to prescribe a common standard of attainment may be misleading, since it is agreed that the educational treatment of children should be suited to their individual abilities and attainments. What can be said clearly, however, is that whatever his grade of ability the child must be expected to do whatever he is called upon to do as well as in him lies. No excuse ought to be offered for any slipshod work, as shown, for example, in careless handwriting, grossly inaccurate Arithmetic, slovenly speech or reading. If the best work that a child can produce under a particular syllabus or method of treatment is not good, then this indicates that the syllabus or the treatment is unsuitable for him. It will be found that no lowering of the standard of the Three Rs need follow the adoption of a broader conception of the curriculum. It has been already amply demonstrated that the new conception can lead to better and more lasting results than those which have been attained in the past.

But attainments within the Three Rs are not the only things to consider. Improved health and physique and better performances in Art, Handwork and Music must also be accredited as merits. The mark of the best modern Junior Schools is that in the Three Rs they are as good as if not better than the middle " standards " of the traditional all-age school and very much more alive and interesting in an increasing variety of ways.

26. Comparing standards of achievement.—One advantage which the modern Junior School teacher has over teachers of the past is that he can make use of standardised tests for the purpose of measuring the achievements of his pupils and of noting how they compare with those of other children. In addition, the increase in the number of short courses organised by the Board and by Local Authorities, the freer encouragement of teachers to visit other schools, and frequent exhibitions of school work, are helping to disseminate new ideas and to establish better standards of work, and are breaking down to some extent the isolation often felt by teachers who work in areas of scattered population.

27. The common stock of knowledge.—In every syllabus there will be parts dealing with knowledge which should become a permanent possession of the pupils. The teachers should recognise these clearly and take the necessary steps to establish such knowledge on a sound basis. The familiar Bible stories, the commoner myths and legends of the past, the episodes most frequently alluded to in the works of great writers, incidents in the lives of some outstanding characters in History, key-knowledge in Geography, acquaintance with the flora and fauna of the countryside, and so on, can only be established by frequently recurring to them from term to term, or year to year. Stories told in one class may be read in the next, passages from them used for closer study at yet a later stage, and by purposeful recurrence to any important theme or set of facts knowledge gained may be deepened and made lasting. Any passing reference to well-known characters in history or fiction or to parts of the globe covered in the school course should have a clear and definite meaning to the child. Good team-work on the part of the staff of every school is needed to get a satisfactory standard of knowledge of essentials, whether in the multiplication tables or in less easily summarised forms of knowledge.

28. Dangers of special preparation for external examination.—At the end of the Junior School stage comes the time of selection for Special Places in Secondary Schools, and it is natural for teachers in

Junior Schools to be concerned that every child who is fit for a Special Place shall have his chance to gain it. But it is not the chief business of the Junior School to prepare children for the Special Place Examination ; and to warp or impoverish the curriculum of the school, as is sometimes done, by giving undue prominence to examination subjects, not only sets up manifestly unfair conditions of competition, but is also contrary to the best educational interests of all the children involved, many of whom may not even sit for the examination at all.

As our knowledge of the means of diagnosing children's abilities increases and it becomes possible to discern with greater certainty the true marks of fitness for specialised education at the higher stages, it may be expected that the task of preparing children for Special Places in Secondary Schools will be accomplished without involving the temptation to interfere with the normal course of the work of the Junior School. Till then, the way of safety lies in providing, as a natural part of the school course, sufficient scope for even the brightest, so that they may take the examination in their stride.

29. The needs of the specially bright child.— Teachers do not always realise that the bright child as well as the dull child needs some special provision ; otherwise, not only his mental but his moral development also may be hindered, for he may have few chances within the limits of the Junior School of learning to attack and to persevere with a task worthy of his capacity or of experiencing the stimulus and joy of achievement arising from real thought and effort. Resourceful and intelligent teachers have shown that it is possible to provide appropriate training and work for such children without sacrificing those of average ability.

30. The treatment of dull and backward children.

—Children who are inherently dull, or who are backward from other causes, are to be found in every Junior School, and many different methods of dealing with them have been tried. It is beyond the scope of this chapter to describe any of these experiments, but it may be worth while to emphasise the point that, in the larger reorganised Junior Schools, attention can be more definitely focussed upon what is admittedly a very difficult and hitherto unsolved problem. Whatever method of dealing with such children may be adopted, it is of the highest importance that the teacher should not merely refrain from depressing and discouraging them by, unconsciously perhaps, suggesting that they are inferior beings, but should do all in his or her power to make them hopeful and to strengthen their self-respect and determination to succeed.

31. The importance of the Junior School in our educational system.

—In conclusion, the Junior School represents a stage of school life which is clearly equal in importance to the stages above and below it, demanding no less careful and precise definition and deserving of the fullest opportunities of developing its own life, identity, and technique. What it will become we cannot yet foresee, for further studies of early childhood may justify bold departures from the types of curriculum and educational treatment that have hitherto been regarded as suitable. But in the words of the Hadow Report on *The Primary School*, it should not be regarded " as a mere interlude between the Infant School and later stages of education . . . It is continuous with both, because life is continuous, and it must be careful, accordingly, to preserve close contact with both. But, just as each phase of life has its special characteristics, so the Primary School has its special opportunities, problems and difficulties. The essential point upon which all else depends is that the work of teaching children between the ages of 7 and 11 should be recognised as not less fascinating, less exacting, less fraught with human interest and social significance, or less worthy of teachers of the highest attainments, than any other part of the educational system."

CHAPTER IV

THE SENIOR SCHOOL STAGE

SUMMARY OF CONTENTS

I. HISTORICAL SETTING

**I. The development of " advanced instruction "
in Elementary Schools.**—The first two chapters of
the Hadow Report on *The Education of the Adolescent*
sketch the development of post-primary education up
to 1925. They give an account of a long series of
experiments which goes far back into the history of
Elementary Education. A point that emerges clearly
is that until recently nearly all attempts at separate
provision for post-primary education were planned to
meet the needs of selected children. Such, for example,
was the purpose of the Higher Grade Schools developed
at the end of last century and of the Higher Elementary
Schools that grew up after 1900. Their descendant in
the Elementary School system of today is the selective

Central School. The Education Act of 1918 did much indeed to encourage Local Education Authorities to provide specially for the needs of the older children in their schools; but the main purpose of these so-called " advanced courses " was to ensure that the older and cleverer children did not mark time in their last years. Nevertheless, it was being realised with increasing clearness that some form of post-primary education might be possible for all children; a number of Authorities attempted to put this into practice and the Hadow Report expressed a policy which already had very considerable support.

2. The freedom from external examinations allows the Senior School to cater for all grades of ability.—The non-selective Senior School is, therefore, the typical product of the Hadow scheme of reorganisation, the purpose of which is to ensure that all the older children shall receive the same consideration and equal opportunity. When reorganisation is complete, every child, whatever his ability, will begin at $11+$ a new phase of his education. In a fairly large Senior School it is possible to classify the children both by age and ability and to arrange courses that differ not only in degree of difficulty but in methods of approach. The Senior School is free from the compulsion of external examinations and is at liberty to frame a curriculum in which more importance is attached to the need for a full and active life and less to academic instruction.

3. Its need for space and special facilities.— These wider opportunities demand more space and special equipment, and Local Authorities have recognised this in their provision of new premises and in the remodelling of old ones. The plan of a modern Senior School building embodies a new conception of the activities of the school. Much of the work must still be done in class-rooms of the traditional type, but of these some will be reserved for such subjects as Geography, which need an appropriate background and equipment of their own ; and one room may be set aside for the purposes of a Library. There is, too, a well-furnished Science Room. Each of the practical activities—drawing and painting, light craft-work, woodwork and metalwork, needlework and housecraft— is carried on in a room specially planned for its purpose, and a part of the site may be set aside for gardening and poultry-keeping. Facilities for physical training are given prominent place ; where there is no gymnasium there is at least a hall with simple gymnastic apparatus ; there may perhaps be a changing room and shower-baths. Sometimes there are ample playing fields. The hall is the scene of the school ceremonies and assemblies, through which the child can realise the unity and importance of the community to which he belongs ; it serves, too, for dramatic, musical or rhythmic activities which need more space than the ordinary class-room affords, and for the various purposes for which two or more classes can be grouped. The grounds are attractively laid out ; the internal decoration of the building is pleasing ; lastly its very design has a simplicity and fitness for purpose which make it at once a distinguished public building and a worthy background for the life of the school.

A number of Senior Schools will no doubt have to carry on in old and out-of-date premises for a long time to come. A solution of the difficulties of the small Senior School has yet to be found and many Authorities are forming large Senior Schools even at the cost of providing transport for some of the children.

4. Its staffing is important.—But helpful as good premises can be they do not make the school. Good work can be and has been done under unfavourable conditions ; but the success of a school depends in the long run on the personal influence of its teachers. Authorities have given much thought to the staffing of Senior Schools, and the Training Colleges have adapted themselves to the new needs. Many of the teachers of the Senior School are chosen for their special qualifications or for their experience in teaching various branches of the work.

5. The need for bold experiment.—It is clear that the superiority in staffing, premises and equipment which the selective Central School used to possess is fast disappearing. The chief advantage that remains to it is the extra year of school life which it usually provides. But it must be recognised that the Senior School has not yet taken its place in public estimation as a true form of " Secondary " education. It is true that many schools have already made great advances and that many new modes of educational treatment are here and there being tried, but, in the main, experiment in the Senior Schools has so far been cautious. This is probably natural and wise ; for there was much of value in the old system that might have been lost by a rash break with tradition. But the full value of the Senior School will not be generally recognised until the curriculum, outlook and methods of teaching have been boldly reshaped. This is not to imply that the Senior School should imitate the Secondary School. The Senior School must provide a form of education that will convince the public that all children are receiving the sort of instruction from which they best can profit.

II. CHARACTERISTICS OF THE CHILD AT THE SENIOR SCHOOL STAGE

6. The Senior School child compared with the Junior School child.—The most obvious difference between the Senior School child and his younger companions lies of course in his greater fund of experience and his larger store of memories, by virtue of which he has a firmer and more confident grasp of the present, a better understanding of the past and more power to anticipate the future. But it is not alone in an increase of experience and memories that his growth consists; there is a great difference in the way in which their elements are inter-related in his body and mind. His feelings, thoughts and actions are becoming organised in larger groups and more stable patterns which may dominate through the whole of his life.

7. His greater power of self-control.—Many of his characteristics may be summed up as increased power of self-control. Consider, for example, the way of a group of seven-year old boys with a football and the behaviour of a team of boys of 13 years who are playing a game of football. The kicking of the younger boys is random and impulsive, their movements are individualistic and unorganised, and they may give way to tears or temper when accidentally hurt. By contrast the footwork of the older boys is deliberate and controlled; they have learnt to play as a team; they understand and abide by a complicated set of rules, and they have learnt in a large measure to restrain their feelings and tempers.

Better co-ordination of bodily movements is not a matter of muscles alone; it means also awareness of several things simultaneously. The older child can see out of the tail of his eye as well as directly in front of him. This is shown by his quicker responses in dangerous situations—the frequency of street accidents to pedestrians, for example, diminishes greatly after the age of 10 years—and by his ability to deal with fire and with edged tools in his practical work.

8. His greater power of abstract thought.—The mental life of the older child shows similar features.

Ie is able to hold together in his mind a set of diverse icts and to discern a meaning in them as a whole, as, or example, when he interprets a picture or a fable. 'o some extent he is able to suspend his judgment until e knows all the facts of a situation. He is learning o carry in his mind a number of outwardly dissimilar leas, to abstract from each such elements as they have 1 common and to make simple generalisations about hem. He is passing from the stage in which he learnt ⊃ recognise isolated cases of cause and effect to the tage in which he becomes conscious of general laws.

9. His greater emotional stability.—With the hange in the child's manner of thinking comes a change n his emotional life. As his understanding widens his eelings become attached to larger things ; sympathies, ɔyalties, ideals begin to take shape and to cover more omprehensive fields of experience. Instead of being ubject to the short-lived impulses of early childhood, is emotional life begins to settle down under the steady nfluence of the stable sentiments which are the main lriving force of conduct in adult life. This is seen in he emergence of the group-loyalties of gangs, clubs, teams .nd school, and in the altruistic dreams of adolescence. ;roup-sentiments cannot be formed without group- ·nterprises, nor can worthy ideals grow in the absence ɔf fitting examples of conduct. Unless the school does ts share in directing the child's natural feelings and mpulses into proper channels there is a danger that hey will find an outlet in unruly or perverse individual ɔonduct and in undesirable forms of social behaviour.

10. His special interests and abilities.—At the ʒenior School stage, too, the permanent special interests .nd abilities are beginning to emerge and to link them- selves with the child's aspirations for a future career ⸱nd with his desires for particular leisure occupations in he future. Unless he feels that the school-work takes account of his special capacities and personal needs and will help him in later life, his interest in it is likely to wane.

11. His greater independence.—With the growing sense of power and self-control springs up a greater desire for independence. This fact must be recognised, though not to the extent of granting the child unfettered freedom which he has not the knowledge or the confidence to use wisely. In his newly discovered world of wider relationships and social contacts he is still unsure of himself and often only too conscious of his liability to stumble; he tends to oscillate in an unpredictable fashion between childish and adult forms of behaviour. The mixture of self-assertion and self-distrust in early adolescents makes them inclined to hide their thoughts and to resist suggestions from grown-ups, to be impatient and critical under authority. For children's well-being at this stage it is therefore all the more necessary that they should not only be allowed to do certain things of their own free will but that they should also understand the reason for the things that they are called upon to do.

12. The differing needs of boys and girls.—A description of the general characteristics of the child of 11–15 years would be seriously incomplete without reference to sex differences. The Senior School stage is a critical one in the growth and development of boys and girls and the differences between them become increasingly apparent, as regards both appearance and behaviour. In mental capacity and intellectual interests they have much in common, the range of difference in either sex being greater than the difference between the two sexes. But in early adolescence the thoughts of boys and girls are turning so strongly towards their future roles as men or women that it would be entirely inappropriate to base their education solely on their intellectual similarity. In some ways their education must be alike and in others it should be different, but as yet no settled conclusion has been reached as to the manner and extent of the resemblances and differences ; in this field there is still ample room for intelligent experiment.

It is undeniably important that boys and girls should learn to know each other and to share the interests they have in common, but it is no less important that they should exercise the powers and develop the interests that are peculiarly their own. Where boys and girls are taught in separate departments some means should be devised for securing the first condition ; where they are taught in the same school it is equally necessary to see that the second is ensured, and this is perhaps the more difficult of the two. The boys' natural vigour and love of activity make it difficult in a Mixed Senior School to provide equal opportunity for girls either in the classroom or in social leadership.

II. GENERAL CONCEPTION OF THE LIFE OF THE SENIOR SCHOOL

A. *ITS SOCIAL LIFE*

13. The importance of social training.—By its social life, its curriculum and its methods of teaching the Senior School must do all it can to safeguard the privileges and foster the characteristic powers of later childhood. For unless the children's early growth is vigorous and healthy they will not easily reach the higher mental development or become capable of the wider forms of co-operative effort and the larger loyalties that adult life should bring.

As they approach adolescence children become more interested in different forms of behaviour and more critical of their teachers' mode of government, and it is particularly important in the Senior School that those in authority should not only be firm and just but also moderate and discriminating. Since school is the first public society of which the child forms a unit, his social behaviour is greatly influenced by his experiences there and his future attitude to authority elsewhere can hardly fail to be in some degree affected by these. Modern dictators have given practical proof of their interest in school training, but the healthy existence of a great democracy calls for habits of self-discipline, patience, tolerance, even interest in differences of opinion, which are far more difficult to cultivate than mere subservience to an imposed pattern of behaviour, and which therefore demand correspondingly more intelligent and careful preparation at school.

14. The need for some measure of freedom for the pupil.

—The first essential for social training is an environment which itself exemplifies the qualities it is desired to foster. Training for responsible citizenship cannot be given under a régime of either extreme severity or over-indulgence. There are occasions when a teacher must be able to exact prompt and implicit obedience, as, for example, in the practice of fire-drill but there are also times when both classes and individual respond better to a wise tolerance than to peremptory correction.

Children cannot help being sensitive to the social standards which they find in force around them, even though they may rebel against them, and in this sphere at least example is immeasurably more effective than precept. So while the teachers must retain sufficient control to ensure that the work of the school is efficiently done, they must also give the children scope to develop a corporate life of their own. It has been said in the preceding chapter on the Junior School that children must be allowed to make experiments in the sphere of personal relationships ; in the social, as in the intellectual sphere the " heuristic " method has a place, though in neither should it be the only one to be used.

There are dangers in giving adults absolute control over young people, for even well-meaning adults are apt to use children as a means of satisfying their own conscious or unconscious desires. There are some adults, for instance, who find in unquestioned authority over children a compensation for a feeling of inferiority towards people of their own age, and others who strive unwisely to impress their own unfulfilled desires or ambitions upon children who are unable to share them. Only people who are reasonably contented in their own life, who are independent in thought yet tolerant and friendly towards others, can enter into children's lives in such a way as to allow them to grow naturally without becoming too dependent in thought and feeling upon their elders.

15. The question of self-government.—The delegation of some measure of authority to senior children is often advocated as a means of training them in social responsibility, and many schools have instituted prefect systems. There can be little doubt as to the wisdom of assigning definite duties to children in respect of the orderly upkeep and daily routine of the school. Some of these should be distributed as widely as possible; the performance of others may be considered as a special privilege and assigned to those worthy of the responsibility. The selection, however, of a few individuals to exercise disciplinary powers over the behaviour of others is a different matter. As has been said, such authority demands a certain maturity and stability of mind which can hardly be expected in children of Elementary School age. The fourteen year old rarely feels at ease in face of the great changes that are taking place within him. At the same time the various social activities of the school should provide plenty of opportunities for the exercise of natural gifts of leadership in the pursuit of common interests. The maintenance of order should be the natural outcome of a corporate sense of good manners; where this exists, few external sanctions are found necessary, and there is little need to delegate the right to exercise them.

16. School societies and other social groups.—

Upon the social ideals that animate the school as a whole will depend the character of the smaller social groups within the school; for social interests there will be whether within or without the law. Where the government is autocratic, societies and clubs, if officially approved, will be imposed upon the pupils as an essential part of school life, and compulsory hobbies and clubs may fall into line with compulsory games. But where there is a spirit of comradeship between teachers and pupils the children will willingly follow the leadership and accept the guidance of teachers in clubs and societies of a more or less permanent kind; and where reasonable freedom has been attained other groupings will arise spontaneously which only demand from teachers occasional suggestion or criticism. Some of these latter will prove short-lived and limited in appeal; when they come to an end there is no need for artificial respiration. Some will wax and wane according to the special talents of the school community. Others will be more general and lasting. It is for the staff to discover and encourage the beginnings of likely interests.

Where optional courses are organised, the particular preferences there discovered are a good starting-point for the formation of societies to pursue these interests further; a census of children's leisure occupations will sometimes give useful clues. Even an interest in the local " pictures " can be turned to good purpose by the school by means of reports, discussions, and special visits. It is important here to point out that, as the Consultative

Committee's report on *The Education of the Adolescent* very clearly explains, a Senior School is most seriously hampered in its social development if the school building is monopolised by other organisations during the evening.*

17. Enlisting the interest of the parents.—Any school that knows its business will embrace the opportunity of strengthening the bonds between school and home by approaching the parents before making any definite arrangements for the children to pursue voluntarily after school hours the interests that they have developed in school. It has not seldom been the case that parents have shared in their children's hobbies, and the joint work has been presented at school, to the greater interest of all concerned.

18. The social value of mid-day meal.—Where Senior Schools draw their pupils from a wide area and are consequently obliged to make arrangements for their mid-day meal on school premises, an opportunity arises for social training of a more intimate kind. To share a common meal has been regarded from the most primitive times as a ritual of unity or friendship, and the school dinner may well be given a dignity befitting this tradition. Good manners have at least as much to do with social well-being as good scholarship, and they have the great advantage of lying within the reach of all who receive appropriate training. Boys and girls may learn to show courtesy at the dinner-table to children who are strangers to them in lesson-time. Under one large rural Authority, which makes special provision for school canteens, the boys wait at table in turns, and everything is done to make meal-time of social value to the children as well as pleasant in itself. The best of food can only nourish the body if it is served in peace,

---

* Chapter XI, pp. 246–7, *The Education of the Adolescent*, H.M. Stationery Office, London.

and the experience of dining at school in unhurried comfort will bring this fact home to children more effectively than eloquent exhortation. Life in School Camps or on School Journeys offers even more obvious opportunities for friendly training.

19. " Houses " and " teams " valuable not only for purposes of competition.—The formation of " Houses " cutting across class organisation has done much to bring children of differing age and outlook together, and the introduction of " Teams " or groups within each class has brought something of sportsmanship into the work. The value of group experience, however, depends in the last resort upon the ends which it serves. There is, of course, some value in group-experience as such, since it gives to each individual the feeling that he does not live to himself alone but that his actions are of moment to the group of which he forms a part. But, if the group can accomplish something that is of permanent or passing value to the school as a whole, or, better still, if it can perform some service for a cause not directly related to the school, it will have taught its members more of the real value of co-operative endeavour than if it is solely concerned with competition with other groups for marks or places awarded for routine school activities. It is also important to remember that if everyone is to give of his best to the group, the whole organisation must be so guided that it does not trespass too far upon the liberty of any one individual. The very keenness with which some children pursue the interests of their team or house may lead them to ignore those larger interests which concern the whole school and every one of its members.

20. The transition from school to employment : the need for experiment.—Towards the close of their school life children's thoughts are naturally occupied with their future careers. Reference is frequently made to " the bridge between education and industry ", but so far as the bulk of children are concerned the gulf between the two territories of work remains as yet unspanned. There seems to be in fact no relationship between a child's life in his last period of school life and his early experiences as a wage-earner, whether in respect of his activities, hours of labour, material conditions, or type of supervisor. His life changes overnight, and this at a time when his own development of body and mind is at a crucial stage. Clearly some bridge should be provided for him, but if it is ever to be built the work must be the concern of both authorities, and they must frame a common plan.

There are few parts of the educational field in which wise experiments are more urgently needed than in this. Many schools have flourishing Old Scholars' Clubs, which might do good service in exploring these problems.

B. CURRICULUM

(i) GENERAL CONSIDERATIONS

21. The curriculum should cater for differing abilities and interests.—In making a curriculum for the Senior School two major difficulties have to be faced. The first is the growing divergence of individual interests and abilities, which renders a single curriculum for all types of children unsuitable ; the second arises from the specialised equipment, classroom space and teaching power, which may be called for by the sharper differentiation of the subjects of instruction at this stage.

As yet we are more skilled in discerning differences of ability and interest than in setting up educational objectives for children of different orders of intelligence, or in devising suitable methods of treatment for different types of children. It is generally recognised that there must be differences of objective and treatment, but it is still not unusual to find common syllabuses for two or even three different " streams ", the practice being palliated by the explanation that the duller children are not expected to go so fast or so far as the brighter ones.   Such explanations as this are merely confessions of failure to grasp the realities of the situation.   Not only is there among the children the wide diversity in mental capacity to which reference is made in Chapter I ; but there are also great differences in physical and social development, in temperament, interests and experience. And while it is impossible to take full account of all these things, the only hope of dealing with the most weighty of them lies in making a series of syllabuses that differ radically in content and treatment.

22. It should not make excessive demands on the children.—As the teaching of the various subjects comes to need special techniques and falls into the hands of different teachers, the problem arises of adjusting the claims of the subjects so as to get a curriculum that is both properly balanced and within the children's powers of assimilation.   There are so many branches of knowledge and there is so much in each worth knowing, that one is tempted to make excessive demands on the children. A child who could assimilate a minimum curriculum drawn up independently by subject specialists even in their most yielding mood would be a paragon far removed from the ordinary child, and the traditional type of school syllabus contains far more information than any normal child can master.

For that portion of the school population that we call the " B " stream the contents of the curriculum should be simpler and more realistic, the treatment more varied and practical, and the results more lasting than they have been hitherto. For the " C " stream children we may be well content if we can train them to behave sensibly in the commonplace situations of life, to mix freely and confidently with their fellows, and to maintain the sturdy self-respect that comes from a knowledge that they can do the simple, essential things of life. In the " A " stream there are some, but not all, who can face successfully a wider and more advanced curriculum than that of the old all-age schools ; the proportion of these more intelligent pupils varies, of course, from place to place according to the extent to which facilities are available for transfer to other places of further education.

23. It should be related to the immediate needs and interests of the children.—In the Senior School it is even more difficult than in the earlier stages of education to co-ordinate the various subjects of instruction, but here, too, the first consideration should be to focus the curriculum as sharply as possible upon the immediate interests and needs of the child. The school must help to explain and illuminate to the child the world as it impresses itself upon his senses day by day, and as he tries to impress himself upon it by his creative activities ; and the explanations must be suited to the state of maturity that he has reached. The more clearly the child realises that the work of the school relates to matters which directly concern him, the more readily will he identify himself with all that the school stands for. To ensure this is more important even than to devise a curriculum which is well-balanced from the academic point of view. For however well-rounded and logically arranged a course of lessons may be, it will leave upon each child a different impression. While lessons must be systematic and progressive and the course as representative as possible of the chief human interests and activities, it is well to remember that though a balanced diet will help it cannot compel digestion.

24. It should be varied and flexible. Some experiments.—A good curriculum will be varied and flexible, and will provide for opportune use of unforeseen happenings in daily life. It will be extremely rare for any of the major subjects to be entirely omitted, but it may happen that some are allotted, either temporarily or throughout the course, a relatively small place. It should not be considered an absolute necessity that all children should spend a measured amount of time during each week on every subject; there are other ways of maintaining the balance of the curriculum. Sometimes indeed there are advantages in taking a longer period than a week as the unit of time within which all the subjects of the curriculum are covered. As interest and skill develop the repeated interruptions of work entailed by the short periods of the ordinary time-tables become more irritating and the waste of time involved in getting clear of one activity and under way in the next more evident. Neither in the work nor the leisure occupations of later life are the children likely to be subject to such conditions, and it should be the duty of the Senior School to prepare them in some measure for long periods of work and for persevering in the chosen occupations of their leisure time.

Many interesting experiments with this end in view have already been made. For example, some schools have taken pairs of subjects such as History and Geography, which receive about the same amount of time per week, and have dropped one of the pair for a term, giving double time to the other, compensating the next term by taking the second of each pair and dropping the first. For incidental reasons, too, it may be desirable to hold up, say, part of the History course until the children have mastered the geographical setting of a particular series of events, or to lessen the amount of Geography in order to establish certain mathematical principles that are essential for full understanding. With even the best of team-work between teachers it is impossible for each to foresee all the needs of the others and for all to keep precisely in step. Good planning and an understanding by each of what the others are doing will help to keep a fairly even front, but every teacher must assume some responsibility for the incidental teaching of subjects ancillary to those in which he specialises.

(ii) SUBJECTS AND ACTIVITIES

25. Common elements in school curricula.— However much the curricula of individual schools may differ in points of detail, there are several broad groups of subjects that should always be represented. Health and Physical Training, Music, Art and Craft and the various other forms of practical instruction, English, History, and Geography, Natural Science, and Mathematics, must all find a place, not in isolation but as far as possible interwoven with each other. In the children's minds are pooled all the resources derived from their different studies ; teachers can do a great deal to help them to mobilise all these resources in the pursuit of a particular study. All subjects have their historical and geographical setting, their quantitative and scientific aspects ; all are expressed in the common medium of language and all afford some opportunities for using the constructive or decorative arts. There are some studies—for example, that of the simple features of civic life—which are peculiarly fitted to serve as a meeting-ground for knowledge gathered from many different fields ; and there are, besides, many co-operative enterprises, such as school concerts and dramatic performances, and many projects, such as village surveys or studies in local history, in which children with widely different talents can all contribute something to a common end that calls for and justifies their best efforts.

(a) Health Education and Physical Training

26. The special contribution of the Senior School.—Health Education and Physical Training are among the most important activities included in the curriculum of the Senior School. They have a direct and obvious bearing on the life and well-being of the individual and the community ; for the school must teach children to live healthily if they are to get the best out of life both at school and afterwards. It is for the teachers in the Senior School to continue and develop further the training in habits of healthy living, begun at the earlier stages of schooling, in such a way as to secure that it is carried over into adolescent and adult life. But the Senior School teacher has also a special contribution of his own to make. It is his privilege " to lay the foundations of a health-conscience in the minds of the English people of the next generation, and to teach the children to realise more fully the fundamental motives and means of healthy living, to understand the debt which one generation owes to another, and to cultivate a wider vision of what contributes towards ' the betterment of man's estate '."*

(b) The Arts and Practical Activities

27. Expression through various forms of Art.— As their intellectual life becomes more complex and greater demands are made upon the children's power of self-control, the need for some outlet in art grows more urgent. Physical energy can be released in games and other exercises, but children who are bewildered and disturbed by the emotional tangles of early adolescence do not always find the way to peace on the playing-field. The rhythms and patterns of art, whether musical, literary, decorative or constructive, may bring them satisfaction and help to give a balance to their lives. Moreover art can foster the power to perceive the patterns and ryhthms of the life which goes on around

---

* From the introduction, p. 12, of the Board's *Handbook of Suggestions on Health Education*, 1933. Published by H.M. Stationery Office, London, price 6d.

them, a power which may give them fuller understanding of the life they read about in books.

If, as we are told, the essential quality of art is " felt life," the art of schools must be directed to this end rather than to the mastery of any special technique. Where art is a vital experience the pupils themselves will want to be taught a helpful technique ; where it is not, no amount of technical accomplishment will be valued by them except as a means of earning money. It follows therefore that the teacher's " right " or " wrong " can give no lasting standard to the pupils ; his duty lies rather in rousing and directing their attention to forms which they may find enlivening to see or hear or touch. Different abilities are to be found in sense-perception as well as in intelligence, and since some children will prefer sounds to sights, there seems to be no good reason for making all seniors follow a course in all the arts. Certainly in their last year of school life there should be some opportunity for those who dislike any one of the arts to drop this and give extra time to the others.

28. Practical occupations and craftsmanship.— Senior school children demand realism in their practical occupations, and so it is right to shed from their practical instruction the element of make-believe which is one of the chief attractions for younger children. It is indeed the obvious practical interest of the crafts which makes them the most appropriate mode of expression for many boys and girls. The typical forms that their work takes are Housecraft, Woodwork, Metalwork, Gardening and the allied rural subjects, as well as lighter crafts such as Weaving, Bookbinding and Pottery. Not all of these appeal equally to every child, but there are very few children for whom one or other of them does not fulfil an elemental need of their nature, the need to do, or to make, or to grow things. Educationally, too, all alike are valuable in that they provide a means by which the children's thinking and planning can be put to the hard test of practicability. When the child tries to put his ideas into material form he discovers that tools and materials will only serve the purposes he has in mind if he knows at first hand their possibilities and submits to their limitations. He learns, too, more surely than in any other way, that to be effective he must be exact. The results of his work deal impersonally but faithfully with any imperfection of planning, any misunderstanding of the nature of the materials, and any carelessness or lack of skill in execution. From the bright child who should learn that the true test of thinking lies in action to the dull child who learns only to take pleasure in homely crafts, practical instruction is for all children a fundamental part of education. It should foster a delight in honest craftsmanship and a delight in good design and finish, and for many it will lay the foundation of lifelong interests and leisure occupations.

(c) The Humanities

29. The function of the Humanities.—The content of these subjects is human life in place and time, and in the sphere of thought and feeling. Their purpose is to interpret this life. They can indeed claim to be taught for their own sake ; each has its intrinsic interest from which a skilful teacher can stimulate in his pupils tastes that will last a life-time. But individual interests will languish unless they are rooted in the life of today ; the teaching will be directed to exploring the child's daily experience and its background of past and present. However realistic the treatment, much of the material will necessarily be derived from second-hand sources, from books above all ; so that History and Geography as well as Literature will serve the purposes of English, in training the pupils' powers of

oral and written expression and of intelligent reading
and listening, and in making them free of the world of
books. The knowledge gained on the way will not be
mere memorising of facts ; it must be charged with
" accurate imagination " and should be the data from
which the child can form general notions of the behaviour
of man in relation to his environment. These subjects
are in fact social studies, not only feeding private
interests but helping the pupils to realise themselves as
members of a community.

(d) The Sciences

30. The scope of the Science teaching.—The
child of today lives in an environment that has been
profoundly modified by Science. The task of the Senior
School is to give him some idea of the methods by which
man has discovered so many of the laws of nature, of
the immense power that these discoveries have put at
his disposal, and of the uses to which he is putting his
knowledge. So far as is possible under school conditions,
the pupil should learn how scientists carry out their
work ; he should be given an opportunity to look at a
series of facts carefully and to seek an explanation of
their interrelationships ; he should submit tentative
conclusions to the test of experiment ; he should learn
to decide on evidence and to discount prejudice ; in
other words he should begin to acquire a scientific habit
of mind. He should gain some conception of how
science is transforming life in the home and in the
world outside, and of the wealth, variety and inter-
relations of living forms, plant and animal, which
surround him. He should make some study of the
human body and of the conditions for its healthy
functioning. An attempt should be made to create
lasting interests by developing hobbies that will help to
fill leisure time when school is left behind.

(e) Mathematics

31. The character of the course.—Mathematics is concerned with a different way of thinking. At the Senior School stage children bring to the study of the subject a fuller experience of quantities, both numerical and spatial, and greater powers of abstract thought such as Mathematics demands. Most of them are beginning to understand abstract ideas such as ratio and proportion on which so many arithmetical processes are based, and such generalisations as are embodied in the use of easy formulae or in the properties of the geometrical figures ; some of the older ones, too, may be ready to begin Algebra, the study of the general properties of numbers. The vocabulary of the more advanced parts of the Arithmetic syllabus, as illustrated by such words as average, profit and loss, percentage, discount, interest and the like, will become familiar to them through the talk of adults and through their reading, and they will be able to apply it to their own transactions and experiences.

The course will fix and extend the knowledge and the skill in arithmetical operations gained in the Junior School, and teach the children to apply their new powers to the affairs of daily life and school ; it will also have to prepare them to deal with situations requiring numerical knowledge that lie ahead of them. Their experience of accounts, gained in school affairs such as meals, concerts, saving banks and societies, school journeys, excursions, gardening or poultry-keeping, will introduce ideas that are current in the larger world of finance, and will be used to lead up to such questions as buying by instalments, investments, pensions and insurance. The use of graphical methods will provide them with a new means of representing and interpreting arithmetical data. Their work in practical subjects, mechanical drawing, surveying and design will provide material that will serve as a basis for the study of Geometry.

(f) Extra Subjects

32. Commercial subjects, if included, for some pupils only.—A question that frequently arises in the Senior School is whether or not to include subjects that have a vocational bias. The commonest subjects of this kind are shorthand, book-keeping and the office arts. In some schools there is a good deal of external pressure brought to bear upon the teachers to take these subjects in order that the children's chances of obtaining employment may be bettered, and it is not unusual for schools to hold out the opportunity of learning them as an inducement to children to stay on after the normal school leaving age. They are only valuable when built upon a solid groundwork of general education and especially upon a sound knowledge of English. Proficiency in them can best be acquired by a relatively short course of intensive practice, and except under skilled teaching there is a serious danger of children acquiring bad habits which have to be eradicated later. In general, teachers will do well to resist the intrusion of vocational subjects upon the curriculum up to the school-leaving age, and only teach them after that time to selected children if they can do so thoroughly well and without detriment to the interests of the other pupils.

33. Foreign languages : conditions determining their inclusion.—There are good reasons for desiring in our Senior Schools some extension of the practice of teaching a foreign language, a matter in which we are far behind other countries, but the conditions under which a foreign language can profitably be taught are by no means universally found. The first essential is that the children who take it shall be reasonably proficient in the use of their own language. Other conditions are that the course shall be sufficiently long and the lessons frequent enough to guarantee at the end a satisfactory degree of facility in speaking and reading the foreign tongue ; a daily lesson for about three years under competent teaching seems necessary to ensure this standard being reached. French, German and Spanish are the languages mostly commonly taught at present in Senior Schools. The choice has depended partly on the qualifications of the teacher, partly on the foreign trade relations of the locality. An important factor is the quantity of literature suitable for children of Senior School age which is available in the language chosen.

C. SELF-EDUCATION AND THE USE OF BOOKS

34. Training in the use of books.—The statement in the last issue of the *Handbook of Suggestions* that self-education should be the keynote of the older children's education is one that still holds good. The phrase has, however, many meanings. Perhaps the commonest interpretation that we find in practice is that the children must have opportunities for independent study, and particularly that they must learn how to use books. The practice of silent study has increased of late years, but it has been mainly directed to routine study of chapters from a text-book rather than to the purposeful reading that arises naturally out of the pursuit of an interesting topic. The results have not been as satisfactory as had been hoped for partly because of insufficient training in the art of reading for information, an art that is by no means easily acquired, and partly because unsuitable books have been used. To take a text-book written for class-purposes, which assumes continual help and exposition by the teacher, and to hand it over to the child for his unaided use is to court failure. The wording and content of books must be radically simplified if the full benefits of private study are to be gained.

35. The school library.—The aim of private study is to ensure that the pupil by the time he leaves school can use a work of reference sensibly and shall have come to treat books as natural sources of knowledge and interest. What is important is not the sum of information gained but the habit and the attitude of mind that have been formed. If this habit and this attitude are to last after the child has left school he must be shown how to use not only books but a library. Few schools as yet are fortunate enough to be able to house their books in a special room, a " library " in the best sense, whose atmosphere as much as its equipment will foster both serious study and recreative reading and where in wise hands and for the right children " browsing " may be encouraged. But it is now recognised as desirable that the Senior School should possess a library, and the number of schools that have one will no doubt increase as years go by. Meanwhile much can be done by means of well-stocked bookshelves for home and class-room use, and by close co-operation with the local Public Library.

36. The use of the Public Library to be encouraged.—A habit of reading formed while the child is still at school may easily die away after he has left if he is not brought into touch with the local Public Library. The wise teacher will persuade as many of his pupils as he can to join and will show them how to do it. Where the Public Library is close to the school chosen pupils may well make use of it in school time. The teachers not only of Literature but of such special subjects as Crafts, Science, History and Geography, should know what books suitable for their pupils are in the Public Library, and these are not always found in the so-called " children's section ". Time and trouble can be saved if a committee of teachers in a district can work together and pool their information. The local librarian will no doubt give every help and will supply from time to time titles of books recently added. Selected lists of suitable books, especially of those bearing on immediate interests and studies, can be posted in the class-room and the children can keep their own library suggestion book. In these and other ways the teacher can do much to direct his pupils' choice of books and develop a lasting fondness for reading.

Reading may be an enrichment of life or an escape from it ; if the escape is always into a world of trivial make-believe, the effect may be to weaken the individual's powers of facing the difficulties of everyday life. Nevertheless the teacher will do all he can to encourage the reading-habit. It is in his pupils' hands to make what use they can of it in after-life.

37. Self-education and self-direction.—But self-education means more than the acquisition of skills that will enable the child to pursue his studies when school-life is over. It means also the cultivation of the desire for further education and the habit of using the resources developed in school to the pursuit of personal ends. To achieve these objects the school must encourage in every way the growth of the children's powers of self-direction. Already many schools have made a great advance along this line. The means used are numerous : in some schools part of the school time is set apart for occupations chosen by the children themselves : in others there is a great development of hobby activities in out-of-school time ; in many schools children with special interests are encouraged to prepare lectures and demonstrations to be given to the rest of their classes and are given guidance in " reading round " subjects that are specially attractive to them ; sometimes also it is possible to give children with exceptional gifts special opportunities to cultivate them. The more the children can be made to feel that the school recognises their qualities as individuals the more likely they are to

value the contribution that it makes to their own development and to continue to use in later life the endowment it
provides.

IV. ORGANISATION

38. The importance of flexibility in organisation.
—It is now generally agreed that the organisation of the
Senior School should be determined primarily by the
need for differentiation of curriculum, and that this
involves classification by streams. Such a classification,
however, will provide no more than a simple framework.
The problem for the Head Teacher is how to modify
this to suit his own school and how to make it flexible
to meet its varying needs. The various groupings that
may occur within a given school, and the general purposes
for which they may be used are summarised on page 29
of the General Introduction. For certain purposes
reclassification on some basis other than general ability
may be necessary. There may be classification according
to aptitude for special subjects, e.g. needlework, or to
provide for individual choice of occupation, as already
described. In a Mixed School, apart from activities
like Physical Training where boys and girls are taught
separately as a matter of course, there may be other
subjects, e.g. Geography and Science, where the advantage of catering for their respective interests may out-
weigh the disadvantage of grouping classes from two
streams. Teachers are often found who can teach a
subject, e.g. Science, much better to one sex than to the
other.

**39. Organisation in small groups for certain
purposes.**—For Handicraft and Domestic Subjects a
half-class unit is now generally accepted, and where the
Senior School is self-contained it is possible to arrange for
this teaching without drawing children from several
classes. The half-class unit makes for simplicity of
organisation. Small classes may be necessary for other

subjects, e.g. for certain forms of Craft work or for practical Science. The Head Teacher, with a fixed staff at his disposal, has to consider whether or not the gain is neutralised by large classes elsewhere. For example, to send a small party of children on a School Journey in charge of several teachers may be excellent in itself. Care should, however, be taken that the sacrifice of the other work is not too great. If "remainders" have to be grouped in consequence the value of the journey from the point of view of the school as a whole may be diminished. Staffing in other words should not be unduly concentrated on a few children in order to introduce special subjects. If, for example, only a few children are ready for a foreign language, it may be unwise to introduce it, especially if the group has to be drawn from several classes.

40. Organisation by " streams " and the problem of the dull child.—Organisation by " streams " has one serious danger. Many children of less intelligence before they enter the Senior School, will have been taught in classes with children brighter than themselves, and their relative failure, especially with the academic subjects, may already have impressed upon them a sense of their inferiority. It will be one of the main tasks of the senior school to counteract this. Something may be done to avoid the suggestion of inferiority by giving the " C " classes an attractive name, or by numbering all classes in order. Every effort should be made to find some pursuits in which the less intelligent children can excel, and to assign them responsible duties that they are able to carry out. What is far more important, however, is that the staff should regard the training of these children as at least as important as that of their more gifted schoolmates. To turn such children into contented and useful citizens is not only a more difficult task but it is at least as important. In the past when schools were so organised that these children could not receive the special attention that they need, they too often left school lacking in self-respect and with a sense of inferiority fixed upon them. It is a sufficient comment on this fact that the great majority of those who have come in conflict with the law after leaving school were originally what we now call " C " children. Further the " C " class besides being difficult to teach commonly has a wider range of ability than the " B ", and usually a wider range than the " A ", class. This is a strong argument for making it smaller.

41. The problem of the " leavers."—Groups of children in their last year at school present special difficulties. There are a few schools where the majority of an " A " stream, often encouraged by a course which is made specially attractive in the last term, will complete a three or four years' course. More often children leave term by term, so that the leavers' groups fall in numbers. The importance in these cases of providing self-contained terminal syllabuses, so that each child's course may be complete in itself, is dealt with elsewhere. The fact that there are smaller groups at the end of the educational year makes it possible to conduct the work on individual lines, to make special provision for the choice of occupations for future leisure, and to make a special effort to form a habit of self-direction in work and recreation before leaving school. Though the leavers' groups will be small it is obviously difficult to reduce their number without sacrificing the main principle on which the senior school is organised—differentiation of curriculum.

42. Staffing should be stable.—The most suitable staff for a Senior School cannot be determined solely on the basis of numbers on roll. It should as far as possible be stable throughout the educational year. The Head Teacher should be in a position to plan his organisation at the beginning of the year. If normal fluctuations in numbers are allowed to influence the staffing it is very difficult for him to maintain a steady policy, and the advantages of " stream " classification are apt to be lost. Considerations that should be borne in mind in fixing the size of a staff are the need for leaving some margin over the bare minimum necessary to teach the ordinary classes so that organisation may be flexible, the desirability of occasionally forming small groups for special purposes, and the need for keeping within bounds the amount of out of school preparation and correction expected of each assistant.

Something can be done to economise staff and make organisation more flexible if the Head Teacher, where he has no class of his own, arranges his teaching so that someone else will be set free as a matter of course. Occasional relief will be given by the grouping of classes for special purposes, e.g. a wireless lesson, as described in the General Introduction.

43. Teachers with special qualifications.—The staff must include a number of teachers with special qualifications and interests and should be so well balanced that the more important educational requirements can be fully met. This is only possible, especially in small schools, if the requirements are carefully thought out and borne in mind whenever a new appointment is made. It is most important that the staff should not be merely thought of in terms of number and that the Head Teacher should be consulted before vacancies are filled.

44. The work of the specialist teacher.—The arguments for and against specialisation are set out in the General Introduction. The Head Teacher of a Senior School will naturally have to consider this problem in the light of the special abilities and tastes of his staff. He will bear in mind that while specialist knowledge and skill may be particularly valuable in the " A " classes knowledge of and sympathy with children are even more important in the " C " classes ; that while the specialist need not and often cannot cope with most of the teaching in his subject he may be especially valuable in laying down a policy, drawing up a syllabus, deciding on equipment, etc. ; that if the staff includes an experienced teacher with special qualifications, some use should if possible be made for them, though it may be unwise to make him a specialist in the ordinary sense ; that it is in the long run just as bad or worse to confine a teacher for a long period to a single subject as to a single class ; that change of work and the assigning of special responsibility often have surprisingly good results. Many valuable specialist teachers owe their success to the fact that they set out to improve their qualifications for a task which in the first instance was arbitrarily assigned to them.

45. Devolution of authority.—The problem of specialisation is really part of the much wider problem of devolution of responsibility. While the head of any large organisation must ultimately be responsible for the whole of it, his success will largely depend on the wisdom with which he assigns responsibility to others. The school in which the Head Teacher does little else but organise and the staff little else but teach is probably not managed in the best way. In large Mixed Schools it is customary to appoint a Senior Mistress who is responsible for the discipline and general welfare of the girls.

V. THE ASSESSMENT OF RESULTS IN THE SENIOR SCHOOL

46. The Head Teacher's need of a clear criterion in internal examinations and tests.—Teachers and taught alike welcome the chance of testing their work from time to time, so as to find out how they stand. The problems of the internal examination have already been discussed in Chapter I, to which the reader is referred for more detailed suggestions. It is only necessary to emphasise here that much of the work of the Senior School is difficult to assess. If tests are confined to what is measurable, what is not measurable tends to be neglected. In Art and Craft, in wide reading of Literature, in the working-out of practical topics in Mathematics the tangible results are not the only ones that matter ; what is important in such work is the quality of the experience that lies behind it and this can hardly be summed up in quantitative terms. One cannot give marks for an attitude of mind. None the less the Head Teacher will wish to assure himself that such activities have been worth while ; he should have definite ideas of the results that may be expected, and when these cannot be measured he must have some clear criterion by which to judge if they have been well done. Where he has to rely in the last resort on personal impression, he will make clear the evidence—often only unconsciously recognised—on which the impression has been formed.

47. The advantages of freedom from external examinations.

—The Senior School is still in the experimental stage and will remain so for some time to come. It is therefore unwise to introduce outside influences in the shape of external examinations that would almost certainly tend to stereotype methods and curriculum and to cramp the initiative of the teachers and the independent development of the school. Success in an outside examination does indeed give children a sense of achievement, in itself desirable ; but it is a confession of failure to suggest that they cannot get full satisfaction from the normal work of the school. In any case the number of children who can be presented for such examinations is small. The proper aim is to make sure that every child, whatever his ability, shall leave school with the sense that he has completed something that has been worth the doing. If the work is organised so that children can see the beginning and end of each unit of the course and comprehend it as a whole, then the completion of each such unit can provide them with the consciousness of a job well done. It is within the discretion of the Head Teacher to frame his own leaving examination on the results of which a leaving certificate may be awarded ; the value of this will depend largely on the local prestige of the particular school.

48. The importance of teaching things that will endure after school life is finished.—To a great majority of its pupils the Senior School is the last stage of school life. Those who are in charge of it cannot evade the insistent question whether the school is fostering the knowledge, habits, interests and attitudes of mind which the child needs in order to pursue an almost independent course through the years that separate him from the full status of citizenship and to serve him in good stead when he attains that status. If the children have lived a full life in the earlier stages of education and have come up to the Senior School fresh and unsated, they may find it a pleasant and satisfying place and yet be unprepared for the final wrench from its shelter and its associations. No small part of the training of the school must be directed towards emancipating its pupils, and ensuring that they shall carry forward into adolescence as many as possible of the interests and activities that they have pursued at school. When school life is over, only those activities will endure which have acquired a sufficient momentum through a long period of self-direction and independence and have been drawn, as it were, into the main stream of the children's own lasting interests. This survival is worth securing even at the cost of curtailing the traditional school activities or of modifying them to suit the genius of the locality or of the teachers.

The real value of a school, then, must be judged by it
lasting effects upon the children rather than by thei
attainments at the time of leaving school, importan
though these attainments are as evidence of abilitie
put to good use.   Knowledge gained in school studies i
bound to fade from the memory if it is not kept fresh by
constant use, and skills inevitably diminish when
opportunities for practice are withdrawn.   But if
within the fields of learning and activity to which the
school has introduced them, the children have come to
know and to care for things of real worth, if they have
formed habits of honest endeavour and have known the
joy of worthy achievement in the exercise of such talents
as they possess, then one may hope that they will
continue to use well and wisely the gifts with which the
school has endowed them.   The children who leave
our Elementary Schools at the age of 14 or 15 will have
their part to play in shaping the society of the future
All the natural propensities of mankind that make for the
ordered development of society will have germinated
and made some progress towards maturity before school
life is over.   It is for the School to see that free conditions
of growth and exercise are provided for those qualities
of mind and heart which make for individual excellence and the common good.

PART III

PREFACE

THE VARIOUS SUBJECTS OF INSTRUCTION

1. Unity of the curriculum.—In this part of the present Handbook the main divisions of the curriculum, —commonly known as " subjects," though some might more appropriately be called " activities,"—are dealt with separately. It is true enough that education should be thought of as a unity and not in terms of individual subjects, and certainly it is not possible to divide the curriculum into self-contained compartments any more than it is to divide the mind of a child into separate faculties. " Subjects " are no more than aspects of a many-sided training ; but, so long as this is borne in mind, it is convenient to deal with them in detail one by one and to show how the ever-widening curriculum of the Senior School contains nothing that is not begun at the Nursery and Infant School stage and continued in the Junior School. The curriculum, in fact, may be likened to a fan, each leaf of which has its origin in the activities of the youngest children.

2. Valuable forms of school training that do not appear in a list of " subjects ".—It must not be supposed that the chapters which follow can deal with the whole of what is learnt in school. They cannot deal, for instance, with the valuable training that is given through the social life and daily routine of the school, and the personal influence of the teachers, or with the religious teaching which most people will agree has a powerful effect on life and character. Again, there are a number of activities which do not belong specifically to particular subjects, but involve the application of several subjects to one piece of work, and are all the more valuable on that account. Examples

of such activities—to which it would be not inappropri.
ate to apply the term " project,"—are the productio.
of a play, the making and use of model theatres an.
puppets, school entertainments of various kinds, or
school magazine.

3. The " Three Rs ".—Finally what are sti.
called the " Three Rs " are not dealt with specifically
That is not to say that they are less important tha.
they were or that any school should be content wit.
a low standard in them.   It is rather that they ar.
best regarded as forms of skill, as means to furthe.
ends, and are best acquired in close connexion wit.
the other subjects or activities.

4. How " subjects " may be classified in groups.—
The subjects which constitute the normal curriculum
of the Elementary School are so intimately related on.
to another, both in actual content and in the sort o.
training they provide, that no hard and fast classification
is possible.   Indeed, it will be found in several parts
of this Handbook that they are grouped differently
for different purposes.

In the following brief summary the grouping—which
is in no way intended to indicate any order of relative
importance,—is based partly on the natural interests
to which the different subjects appeal and partly on
the extent to which they involve abstract thought.

(a) *The physical side of school training.*—Bodily health
and bodily control depend to no small extent on home
environment, but the school can do much to further
them through the knowledge and practice of hygiene,
through attention to good posture, and through physical
training, organised games and the various forms of
dancing.

(b) *Expression through various forms of art.*—The
natural tendency to express through outward form

and satisfying arrangement ideas that are especially interesting or moving finds its outlet in the arts, whether creative or interpretative. The arts most commonly practised in school—and none should be without its effect in awakening the sense of beauty—are rhythmic movement, music, painting, drawing and modelling, decorative work of various kinds, dramatisation, recitation, verse speaking, reading aloud, and the writing of verse and some kinds of prose composition.

(c) *The crafts.*—The crafts, which appear to originate from an instinct to construct, are closely associated with some of the arts, in that good craftsmanship involves as well as manual skill the use of satisfying form, colour, and design. This is particularly true of such of the traditional crafts as it is possible to teach in the practical work rooms of the Elementary School.

(d) *Housecraft and gardening.*—The domestic arts, which aim at the making of healthy and satisfying home life, and gardening, especially now that more attention is given to other than its purely utilitarian aspects, partake of the nature of crafts. It is easy to see how both of these can profit by association with the arts.

(e) *English.*—Practice in the understanding and use of English occurs, for good or ill, almost continuously throughout the school day. It is almost exclusively through language that teaching is carried on, and the teacher's success depends in no small degree on the clearness and precision with which he expresses himself and the extent to which his words are understood. Thus English, whether it is regarded as the art of receiving and conveying ideas through the spoken or the written word, or as the means of forming ideas, that is to say, as the instrument of thought, is something much wider than a subject that can be confined to set periods of the school time-table.

(*f*) *Foreign languages*.—Where a foreign language is taken, its study in the Elementary School may be regarded partly as an indirect way of providing the children with increased skill in the use of their own language and partly as one of the humanities.

(*g*) *The study of humanity*.—The three subjects through which, in particular, children learn something which they cannot learn by direct experience about human beings, how they feel, think and act under various conditions, their hard struggle along the road of progress, their relations to their environment, and the relations of one community to another, are Literature, History and Geography.

(*h*) *The sciences*.—The last named of these three has much in common with the Sciences, which arise out of the study of nature, whether animate or inanimate, and of some of the works of man, and are concerned with a number of general principles and with methods of reasoning and discovery.

(*i*) *Mathematics*.—Arithmetic in its elementary form is no doubt a skill, of value in so far as it serves certain very practical everyday needs ; but it is also part of the wider field of Mathematics, the study of ideas of number, time and space, that are of great importance in the world of science.

CHAPTER V

HEALTH AND PHYSICAL TRAINING

SUMMARY OF CONTENTS

I.   HEALTH EDUCATION

I. The importance of forming healthy habits.—In view of the publication by the Board in 1933 of the *Handbook of Suggestions on Health Education** it is not necessary here to do more than mention a few simple principles upon which its recommendations are based. Primarily, of course, health is healthy living and not a subject to be taught.   Children are far more likely to acquire habits of healthy living through being trained to perform the actions upon which health depends than through merely receiving instruction which is mainly theoretical in character.   Left to themselves, young children will not perform these acts by the light of nature.   They require to be initiated into a life of health.   They should accordingly be required to perform certain actions as a matter of regular routine : for example, the use of the handkerchief, the necessary attention to clothing before and after physical exercise, the care of the feet, hygiene relating to the use of swimming baths and the ventilation of classrooms, etc. Older children will be interested to know the reason

---

* Issued by the Board of Education, printed and published by H.M. Stationery Office, London, price 6d.

F

for such practices and the teacher should satisfy their reasonable curiosity. Anything in the way of ambitious instruction in anatomy and physiology should however be avoided.

2. Some mistakes to be avoided.—It is fatal to the formation of healthy habits and the creation in the pupil's mind of the right attitude towards health to attempt to separate theory from practice. Against two mistakes, in particular, it is necessary for the teacher to be on his guard. One mistake is to regard the treatment of health as a separate subject of the curriculum. The fact is that health education is naturally and intimately connected with physical training, housecraft, and natural science, particularly in its biological aspect. It can no less profitably be linked up with other subjects, such as geography and history. There are, for instance, few more interesting themes than the effect on the settlement and development of the Empire of the great discoveries in tropical medicine or the influence of great epidemics on the social, the industrial and the political progress of the nation.

The other mistake is to fail to relate instruction in health to the habits of the individual and the needs of the community. The practice and study of health must form, from the first, part of the everyday life of the school. Only so will health education come to be connected in the mind of the child not only with duties to his comrades, his school and his home, but also with the welfare and happiness of the nation at large.

II. PHYSICAL TRAINING

A. SOME GENERAL CONSIDERATIONS

3. The place of Physical Training in the school curriculum.—During the period of growth it is essential that children should have frequent opportunity for bodily activity. For them, as for any other young animals, free and active movement is as necessary for health and development as are fresh air, sunshine, pure water, suitable food and ample sleep. Games and other physical activities provide a necessary outlet for the natural impulses of children and the real but easy discipline associated with them is one of the best means of training in self-management. Physical training helps children to build up strong, beautiful and graceful bodies and to keep them fit. It is probable, too, that the development of the brain itself is to a considerable extent connected with bodily activity. This, certainly, seems to be true of young children and there is reason to believe that it is true also of backward children at a later age.

Qualities, also, that are desirable in the future citizen —self control, self respect, courage, decision, good temper and a sense of well being—are promoted when the body as well as the mind is rightly educated. Moreover, in so far as many forms of physical activity call for combined effort and prompt co-operation on the part of a number of individuals, they are of value to the community in promoting and fostering a healthy public spirit.

Opportunity for such training must be given by the school, for it must be remembered that all children, even those brought up under healthy conditions with opportunities for play and bodily exercise, spend in sedentary work at school the best hours of the day,—hours when light and sun are strongest and when their potential energy is at its greatest. Circumstances in the home life of many children diminish their chances of making their bodies strong and healthy, and the school must therefore afford them every opportunity it can for full development. The child of sub-normal health is sent to the open-air school and enjoys there the special advantages of sunshine, fresh air and space for free exercise unhampered by superfluous clothing. It is just as important to provide adequate facilities for the healthy development of the normal child who is the more able to take advantage of them.

4. Facilities needed for a satisfactory course.—The first essential for carrying out a comprehensive scheme of physical training is a suitable place in which to exercise and play games. Practically all schools have playgrounds though unfortunately many are ill-adapted for this purpose. The question of indoor accommodation is important and a gymnasium or physical training room is a necessity, if the modern type of training is to be properly carried out. There are many days in the year when outdoor lessons are impossible, and when, in many schools, classroom lessons, though obviously a makeshift, are the only alternative. Preparatory training in games can be given in a playground but full enjoyment and the acquisition of real skill in games and athletics are only fully obtainable, by senior boys and girls in particular, when regular use is made of a playing field. Children in schools which have only hard-surfaced playgrounds are debarred from some of the best and most advanced games.

To carry out the scheme of physical exercises and games given in the 1933 Syllabus a certain amount of inexpensive apparatus is required. The training in schools has suffered considerably in the past from lack of apparatus and until sufficient is provided and is used regularly in every lesson, progress will be slow.

The provision of a daily period of organised activity is most important and should be the aim of all schools dealing with children from 7 to 14 years or over. Schools which make such provision find that the loss of working time is amply compensated for by the more effective use the children make of the remaining time devoted to ordinary school work. The principle of " the daily period " should be observed even in schools where as in many Senior Schools, the older children are able to follow a more advanced scheme of gymnastic training, which demands a longer lesson period. When the longer period can be arranged on some days only in the week, on each of the other days there should be a shorter and vigorous lesson of not less than 20 minutes. Such an arrangement will do much to ensure that the general vigour, alertness and vitality of the children, which the training is intended to produce, lasts throughout the day and that good posture is maintained.

5. Clothing and Footwear.—In view of the emphasis which the modern practice of physical training places on agility and freedom of movement, it is important that children should be suitably clad and shod when taking part in physical exercise and games. As few clothes as possible should be worn, for reasons of hygiene as well as to allow of unhampered movement. The dress worn should be light and loose, and it is important, too, that it should not hide the outline of the body, or else bad faults of posture may be disguised.

Fortunately, more rational views have been taken in recent years of clothing in general and successful efforts have been made by teachers and others to secure that a more suitable type of dress is worn by children. In some areas singlets and shorts or even shorts alone for boys, and for girls knickers and blouse, or a simple one-piece dress allowing of free movement, have been adopted as the normal dress for physical exercise lessons and games. Changes of dress necessary for such purposes should be made before the children go out into the playground or playing field. The way in which children dress for their physical training—and this does not necessarily depend on cost, except perhaps for footwear,—is an indication of the value attached to it by a school and not infrequently of what may be expected in actual performance.

In an increasing number of schools the teachers responsible for Physical Training change into suitable attire for the lessons. This not only enables them to teach or coach more competently and in greater comfort, but it also sets an excellent example to the children.

6. Detection of children unfit for Physical Training.—Every teacher responsible for Physical Training should be able to decide which children are temporarily unfit to undertake the full course of gymnastic training. Children who while they are at rest give no indication of physical unfitness, sometimes show symptoms of breathlessness or excessive fatigue after exercises ; they should be excluded from Physical Training until a medical opinion has been obtained. The Physical Training of girls should be in the hands of women teachers, and that of boys in the hands of men teachers.

7. The habit of good posture.—The habit of maintaining good posture is one of the most important contributions to personal hygiene that physical training has to offer. It is a habit which can only be said to be established when the framework of the body and its supporting muscles are so formed and trained by suitable exercise that the child adopts at all times a good posture as the most natural and least fatiguing for him. Good posture of the body is necessary if the maximum of effect is to be achieved with minimum expenditure of effort. Bad posture breeds fatigue, and fatigue bad posture, and so on in a vicious circle. Correct posture not only ensures a more skilful use of the body, but also results in the self respect and confidence, which come from good poise and graceful carriage.

The appreciation of good poise and bearing, whether in movement, in standing or in sitting, should be cultivated not only during the gymnastic exercises but at all times. The bad effect on posture of maintaining one position for any length of time is now generally recognised, and in most schools frequent opportunities for movement are now given. More attention is also being devoted to the most suitable means of support for the body, when sitting in seats and at desks. Children who are uncomfortable and wrongly supported when sitting cannot be expected to maintain good posture for any length of time.

B. THE MAIN FORMS OF PHYSICAL ACTIVITY IN THE SCHOOL COURSE

8. What Physical Training includes.—The term " Physical Training " as used here includes gymnastic exercises, games and athletic sports, swimming, dancing, boxing, etc. No one of these is sufficient in itself to constitute an all round training in general fitness and physical development ; each is valuable for its own particular effects and all should be included if possible in the Physical Training programme.

The purpose of gymnastics is to secure certain definite effects on the structure and functions of the body, such as the controlled and balanced use of all joints and muscles. Such training gives poise and control of the limbs and is, therefore, an excellent preliminary to the more individual and skilled physical activities involved in work or recreation after school days are over.

Games, athletic sports, swimming, dancing, and boxing are of great value in contributing towards a general condition of health and well-being. The direct appeal they make to the natural interests of the child and the discipline and training inherent in them are sufficient reasons for the claim that they constitute an indispensable part of physical training. Swimming has of course an additional value and usefulness entirely its own. Dancing, especially if based on early training in rhythmic movement, helps to give poise and grace. Because of its contribution to bodily and mental health it deserves to be included in the education of all children.

9. Gymnastics.—Systematic gymnastic exercises are necessary to aid growth and harmonious development of the body and to ensure the full range of movement in the joints. They help to give increased bodily control and enable the individual to use his strength to the best advantage. They constitute, therefore, a most useful foundation for many forms of bodily skill and activity as well as a valuable preliminary to, and accompaniment of, games and sports, especially those which require prolonged exertion. Through these exercises the body is enabled to withstand considerable exertion without injurious results ; the risk of overstrain, especially of the heart, is minimised, and weak and under-developed children often acquire strength and stamina, so that they can take their place on the playing fields with their naturally more vigorous companions.

Suitable courses of gymnastic exercises are described in the Board's publications on Physical Training but, in order to obtain full value from them, the teacher must possess the necessary vigour and inspiration and must thoroughly understand the purpose and the correct way of performing the exercises.

10. Games and Sports.—The educational value of games lies in cultivating a spirit of true and chivalrous sportsmanship. Success in this direction has, of course, little to do with direct teaching ; it depends largely upon the general tone and atmosphere of the school. The teacher's own example is a most potent factor, and the more closely he is able to identify himself with the children's play-time interests, the more influence he is likely to have.

Children are not likely to derive the fullest advantage from their participation in games, unless sufficient equipment is available to keep each member of a class fully employed. The simple apparatus needed for games in the playground is not expensive : it is often possible to make some of it in the school. Unless the teacher aims at developing in his pupils a satisfactory degree of skill and proficiency in the playing of games, the games themselves have little educational value, whether for the purpose of immediate training, or as a means of implanting a love of games for rational and healthy recreation in after life. The games played, just as much as the physical exercises, should be appropriate to the children's age and capabilities. To obtain the best results, it is necessary to follow a graded scheme beginning with the simple individual play of the youngest children and progressing, in the degree of skill and co-operation required, to the highly organised games, suitable for the older pupils, such as net-ball, shinty, hockey, rounders, cricket and football. Where the requisite grounds and prepared pitches for these latter games are not available the children need not be denied the benefit and interest of organised team play : for there are several good games such as touch-and-pass, rounders, stoolball, field handball, skittle ball, and long ball, which do not require much space or any specially prepared ground.

The games should have for their object the benefit of all the children in the school, and this is best achieved through some such organisation as a house system, which includes all and encourages each to take a part and to do his best according to his capacity. The formation of a school team for playing inter-school matches is useful and legitimate, when it is based on an organisation for games which includes all the children and its achievements are regarded as a test of the general training given in the school. Competition of this kind is neither legitimate nor desirable, when the attention is given to a school team at the expense of those children who are not likely to find a place in it.

The 1933 issue of the Board's Syllabus contains a large section devoted to games. Teachers responsible for the games of a school will be interested not only in the description of suitable games, but also in the suggestions on organisation, on individual practice and team play, on coaching and on the part played by the children themselves in the management of their games as well as in the directions for the care of apparatus and grounds and many other allied subjects.

11. Swimming.—Swimming should be regarded as an integral part of health and physical training. Unless the school has its own bath, which rarely happens, swimming must necessarily take place away from the school ; it is, therefore, desirable that close co-operation should exist between those in charge of the arrangements for swimming and the head teachers. Whenever possible, swimming instruction should be in the hands of members of the school staff. Generally it is inadvisable for a teacher to enter the water while engaged in teaching a class of beginners. It is, however, essential that he should be skilful in obtaining the confidence of his pupils and have the ability to encourage in them self confidence and a fearless attitude of mind. He must also have a thorough knowledge of the various strokes and of the best methods of organising class instruction when the children are in the water.

12. Dancing.—The type of dancing taken varies with the conditions and with the knowledge and ability of the teacher. Many schools will probably confine themselves to the national and folk dances of this and other countries. A certain number may be able to go further and include a more specialised type of dancing, but the rhythm and character of the dance should always be emphasised and the dances built up gradually from natural movements to simple steps.

In all dancing the music should be in the inspiring and guiding force and the accompaniment to dancing should receive special attention. For a large number of folk dances gramophone records are obtainable ; alternatively, the teacher, or even the children themselves, may be able to play the violin, pipe or mouth organ.

The dancing lesson should be a period of stimulating and enjoyable rhythmic activity giving definite training in easy, light and harmonious movement of the whole body. Every child should take part and have an equal share of the teaching given.

C. ADVANCED TRAINING AT THE SENIOR SCHOOL STAGE

13. Development of the training at the Senior School stage.—The Board's Syllabus of Physical Training gives a full scheme of training up to the age of 12. At the moment its new features and the fact that it envisages a higher standard and a wider scope of Physical Training than are common in the schools today make its use practically universal in all Schools. But Senior Schools will soon be ready to provide their pupils with a more advanced training than that described in this book. Already the introduction into Senior Schools of gymnastic apparatus, fixed and portable, the right use of which has been learnt by teachers at approved courses, has revolutionised the work in those schools.

14. Specialisation by Teachers.—The practice is increasing in Senior Schools of confining the teaching of gymnastic exercises to two or three teachers who are interested in and have special aptitude for this work. Any teacher " specialising " in this way should make it his business to attend courses from time to time in order to keep in touch with the modern practice and methods of teaching the subject.

The importance of teachers acquiring practical knowledge of both the right execution and the right method of teaching advanced exercises cannot be over emphasised. In particular, exercises on apparatus— a new development in the elementary school curriculum —must be adequately safeguarded. The training given in approved courses has already been mentioned. This may be supplemented by courses for teachers conducted by Organisers of Physical Training in their own areas. Advanced work cannot safely be undertaken by teachers who have not been trained to teach the use of apparatus, but steps have been taken in co-operation with certain Training Colleges to secure a supply of teachers qualified in this way, by the provision of advanced courses in Physical Training for teachers intending to take up work in Senior Schools.

15. Accommodation : Indoor and outdoor.—To ensure continuity of training and to allow for a more advanced course it is most desirable that Senior Schools should possess a gymnasium or large room which can be used for physical exercises. Special measures must be taken to secure adequate ventilation and to avoid dust. Since space is an important consideration in modern physical training all unnecessary furniture should be excluded. Where new gymnasia are erected changing rooms and shower baths are desirable.[1] Indoor accommodation is required particularly for apparatus work and when weather conditions make outdoor work impossible, but the good habit of exercising in the open air should on no account be abandoned. When it is

[1] Board of Education Educational Pamphlet Physical Training Series No. 14, *Memorandum on the Training, Construction and Equipment of Gymnasia in all types of Schools and Educational Institutions, 1936*, printed and published by H.M. Stationery Office, London, price 1s. 0d. net.

not convenient to carry the apparatus outside, the lesson can be conducted partly indoors, partly out of doors. The provision of playing fields for Senior Schools is a widely recognised necessity, and little need be said in its support here. Girls should have equal facilities with boys. More detailed suggestions relating to the use of playing fields are contained in the Board's Pamphlet *School Playing Fields*. Reference should be made more particularly to Sections 4, 7, 8, 11 and 12 of the Pamphlet.[2]

---

[2] Board of Education Educational Pamphlet, No. 80, *School Playing Fields*, printed and published by H.M. Stationery Office, London, price 4d.

CHAPTER VI

MUSIC

SUMMARY OF CONTENTS

I. SOME GENERAL CONSIDERATIONS

A. MUSIC IN THE SCHOOL

I. The place of music in education.—The value of Music in school life is now so well recognised that it is unnecessary to discuss it at length. Like the other Arts, Music is an expression of deep-seated instincts in human nature. Its appeal is no doubt fundamentally to the feelings and emotions; but it has its intellectual side also, and this is of no small importance. For children Music has a special value, in that, particularly in its rhythmic aspects, it involves bodily activity, controlled and harmonious effort in accordance with appropriate patterns and designs, and the sharing in a common emotional and intellectual experience with a common purpose in view. A training which includes rhythmic expression, the correct and pleasing use of the voice in singing, the use of such instruments as are possible in schools, the concerted rendering of Music that is in itself worth while, and the appreciation of some of the works of great musicians can do much alike for the individual and for society in general.

2. Formation of a taste for music the main aim of the teaching.—Since the last edition of this Handbook there has been a noteworthy enlargement of scope and range in the treatment of the subject in Public Elementary Schools, to such an extent, indeed, that teachers generally find it impossible to include in the Music syllabus all the new branches of the subject that may rightly be recommended as educationally sound. Their appearance in the syllabus, however, is undoubtedly due to the growing realisation that singing is a means and not an end. The end is now regarded as the training of the musical instincts towards the formation of a taste for, and an understanding of, music. But though there has been this shifting of emphasis, singing must still be regarded as the best and most convenient means to use towards the fulfilment of this end. The encroachment of any of the new aspects of musical training upon the proper proportion of time allotted to song singing and sight singing must be strongly condemned. If the increased recognition of the value of such wider musical education is to have its due effect, adequate time will, of course, be required for the subject.

3. Listening to good music.—Listening to good music is an important part of a child's education. A school fortunate enough to be situated in a district where there are well managed children's concerts should take every opportunity of attending and profiting by these concerts; and in addition concerts given by the school itself are strongly to be recommended as a stimulus to the musical life of the school. In this connexion, individual talent should be sought out and encouraged. The attendance of classes or choirs at Children's Festivals is also a splendid stimulus, especially because of the opportunity afforded of hearing other school choirs and of joining in the singing by the massed choirs. The teacher also can benefit greatly by the advice and suggestions offered by the adjudicator or director.

Interest in music may be further encouraged by the formation of Music Clubs or Societies which meet out of school hours. The most obvious form of these voluntary activities is the School Choir or Choral Society; but there is room for organisations of a more general type, such as listening and discussion groups and dinner-hour concerts; other activities will no doubt suggest themselves.

4. Equipment and provision for music teaching.— Every effort should be made to secure an adequate equipment for the teaching of Music. First in order of importance is the need for a good piano in every school or department. Next, care should be taken that a fair proportion of the general requisition is allotted to the purchase of song books, sheet music, and a manuscript book for each pupil. Plenty of blackboards should be available in the room used for Music teaching; the staff lines on the boards should not be too close together, and should be plainly visible from the furthest corner of the room. A good gramophone is desirable, as also are pictures showing orchestral instruments, charts illustrating musical history, and a well chosen selection of readable books, while, for use in Infant and Junior Schools, an adequate supply of good percussion-band instruments, charts, scores and parts is necessary where Percussion Band work is part of the curriculum.

As it is now generally recognised that nothing but suitable good music should ever be used for school purposes, little more need be said on this subject here. A basis of folk and national songs is essential. The great output of beautiful unison and part songs written by many of our distinguished composers make it possible for a school to have a large repertoire of first-rate British songs, as well as a fairly wide acquaintance with the songs of the great masters. It should be noted that the practice of copying the voice parts of copyright songs on the blackboard, or of reproducing voice parts by some other method, is illegal, inasmuch as it is an infringement of copyright. Every endeavour should be made to procure an adequate supply of printed copies.

For children at the Senior School stage, even in the smallest school, a collection of readable books on Music is desirable. Some of these books will appeal principally to the keener spirits ; a few will be in general demand. The provision of one of the periodicals for young musicians will be a stimulus to the children to read and enquire for themselves.

B. PLANNING THE COURSE OF INSTRUCTION

5. Need for a unified scheme.—There should be no difficulty in planning a syllabus which includes song singing, sight singing (including ear-training) and several of the appropriate new activities. But it is important that a unified scheme of Music teaching should be followed by the same children at different stages of their school life in a particular group of schools. Those responsible for the teaching of Music at the Infant, Junior and Senior School stages respectively, should keep in touch with one another, in order to ensure that a pupil is not subject to a disconcerting variety of method, or an irksome repetition of subjects to be studied, in the course of his school career. Continuity of method and progressive grading of the work are essential.

It will be seen from the foregoing outline of the possibilities of Music in elementary education that the more modern ideal makes greater demands on the musical abilities of the teacher than did the more limited ideals of the past. He should, therefore, do all in his power to fit himself for the task. Freshness of outlook and a knowledge of better methods can be gained by attending teachers' courses from time to time. He should never allow himself to get into a rut of teaching, and he should miss no opportunity of broadening his musical knowledge and of improving his practical ability.

6. The scope of the course.—The work at each of the three stages of the Elementary School course should be so planned as to give due weight to singing, on the one hand, and, on the other, to " musicianship." By this term should be understood that training of the musical instincts towards the formation of a taste for and an understanding of music, which is the end to be achieved alike by this instruction in singing and by the other musical activities in which the children will have an opportunity of engaging.

In the following summary the musical exercises and activities which are recommended for inclusion in the course, where practicable, at the Infant, Junior and Senior School stages respectively, are arranged for convenience of reference under the two headings " singing " and " musicianship."

(i) *THE INFANT SCHOOL STAGE*

(a) *Singing* :—

Nursery rhymes and singing games.—Simple unison songs.—Very easy rounds.—Breathing.—Simple voice-training.

(b) *Musicianship* :—

Imitation of phrases.—Time names.—Recognition of note values.—Simple rhythmic movement on the lines of the B.B.C. course.—Percussion band.— Simple modulator exercises.

In the upper part of the school : very simple sight-singing, from suitably graded books.—Preliminary preparation for country dancing.—Attendance at festivals.

(ii) *THE JUNIOR SCHOOL STAGE*
(a) *Singing* :—

National and folk songs.—Singing games.— Rounds, canons and descants.—Suitable classical and modern unison songs.—Breathing.—Voice Training.

(b) *Musicianship* :—

Rhythmic movement and (possibly) percussion band work.—Easy musical dictation in (1) rhythm, (2) pitch, (3) rhythm and pitch combined.—More advanced sight-singing and further work in staff notation.—Recognition of cadences.

More advanced modulator exercises. Such theory of music as is suggested by the songs and other forms of music used for school purposes.—Pipe making and playing.—Country dancing.—Attendance at children's concerts and festivals.—The B.B.C. Junior Course.

(iii) *THE SENIOR SCHOOL STAGE*
(a) *Singing* :—

Traditional, classical and modern unison and part songs.—Rounds, canons and descants.—The singing of bass parts by older boys.—Breathing. —Voice training.

(b) *Musicianship* :—

More advanced sight-singing and dictation in staff notation.—Melody writing.—The aural recognition of chords.—Study of musical form.—The B.B.C. Senior Course.

More advanced work in rhythmic movement where suitable.—Country dancing, Morris dancing and sword dancing.—Attendance at concerts and festivals.—School orchestra.—Preparation for school concerts, carol services, operas, etc.

In the remaining sections of this chapter the various aspects of school music are dealt with in detail. The sections on Ear Training and Sight Reading, Rhythmic Movement and Folk Dancing contain suggestions as to the way in which the instruction may be developed progressively through the successive stages of the school course in Music.

II. SINGING

7. Interpretation the chief factor in enjoyable song-singing.—A singer should have but one aim when he is singing a song : to reflect the character of the song. To this one aim all the details of training in the technique of singing must be made contributory and subservient, or the singer will have failed to give his message to an audience. A sound technique is of primary importance to the singer in the physical sense, inasmuch as it supplies him with the means to his end ; but it must ever be remembered that it is not an end in itself. It is therefore advisable for teachers, while steadily training the voices of their pupils, and cultivating an impeccable intonation and ensemble, to insist on interpretation as the first and foremost requisite for enjoyable song singing ; otherwise the spirit of the song will have no message for its hearers. Moreover, it will be found that if the character and mood of a song be reflected by the singers, they will the more easily be able to produce the right quality of tone, the appropriate phrasing, and the significant enunciation proper to the style of the song. It may be justly said that interpretation will often induce an improved technique, but that technique will not of itself induce a good interpretation.

It is unfortunate that it is beyond the power of any teacher to instil the feeling of a song into children by recognised pedagogic methods; they can only be encouraged to feel, and appealed to for the vocal reflection of the feeling. The response is more often than not generous.

But there are pedagogic methods for the teaching of technique, and the wise teacher will make full use of these.

8. Breathing.—Correct breathing is essential to good phrasing. Breath control ensures continuity and length of phrase. Breath should always be taken in through the nostrils if time and opportunity permit : e.g. before the beginning of a song, or towards the end of an intervening instrumental passage. The lungs should be quietly and steadily filled, without the raising of the shoulders, or the protrusion of the abdomen. Short, quick breathing, so often necessary in the course of a song, should also be practised.

9. Voice Training.—The training of the head voice downwards is a fundamental principle. But this need not preclude the giving of exercises with other objects. The whole dynamic range of tone from *pp* to *ff* should be covered, and all the various vowels and consonants should be practised. The exercises should also vary in *tempo* from very quick to very slow. They should sometimes be made expressive of various emotions.

This can be done by setting suitable sentences to the exercise, which may perfectly well be unaccompanied, e.g.

This exercise may be sung to such words as

" Singing is a joy " (whole-hearted enthusiasm) or " Peace at eventide " (serene contentment) or " Furious howls the storm " (titanic energy), or " Toll for the brave " (the dignity of sorrow)—the word " Toll " to be sung to the first two crochets.

A serious attempt to reflect the character of any of these sentences will be an excellent training for song singing, which, after all, is the purpose of voice training. The exercises should always be in pattern formation. A few suggestions are given below.

It will not be beyond the powers of a teacher to invent new exercises of this kind ; and he may also encourage the children to invent melodic phrases. The vocalising of songs, phrase by phrase, will be found a useful exercise. The exercises should, and can easily, be made really enjoyable and interesting. High notes should be practised constantly ; a young child's voice normally can easily take high A or B flat, but it should be remembered that as boys, and indeed girls, approach adolescence, they are less likely to feel comfortable when singing high notes.

The tone must never be allowed to become non-resonant, even in the very quiet exercises ; it should

be unaffected, and all strain must be checked instantly.
Resonant humming will prove a valuable corrective to
harsh, unmusical tone.

10. Enunciation.—As a rule, far too little attention is
given to enunciation. Good enunciation is essential
to the expressiveness of a song. It goes without saying
that the enunciation must have clarity; the outline
of the words must be clear, and the vowels must
be pure.

But beyond this there is a more subtle and difficult essential to be acquired : significance. This is often mistakenly termed " Expression," which is generally a matter of merely singing more loudly or softly. True significance can only come from a just appreciation of verbal values. The words of any sentence must be stressed rightly, and grouped correctly, if the sentence is to mean what the singer wishes it to mean. The stresses in song should approximate as closely as possible to those in speech,—irrespective of bar-line accent or varying note values.

Thus, in the sentence " He shall lead me forth beside the waters of comfort," the word " lead " and the first syllable of " waters " and of " comfort " should have *strong* stresses, the word " forth " and the second syllable of " beside " should have *medium* stresses, the remaining words and syllables having *weak* stresses.

It is a good plan to get the singers to practise speaking the words of a song naturally, at the same time noting where the stresses in the words occur ; then for the singers to sing the words, preserving the same stresses, and taking care to lighten the tone on less important words and syllables. At the same time the shape of the musical phrase must not be sacrificed.

It is important that full value should be given to consonants. Such words as " strength," for example, loses significance if the consonants are slurred over. It should be remembered that in English speech consonants not only give clarity of outline, but also a rich significance. In this connexion opportunities should be found for collaboration with teachers responsible for speech training.

11. Phrasing.—The grace of song depends largely upon the singer's conception of its phrasing.

Continuity is of the utmost importance. There must be no gaps in the outline, no shortening of note values, and no breaking of the phrase on account of faulty breath control. For example, " Drink to me only with thine eyes, and I will pledge with mine," is, musically, one continuous phrase, and it demands steady breath control to fill the whole phrase with tone, and to achieve a perfect *sostenuto*.

On the other hand, a perfect *sostenuto* in a song like " The British Grenadiers " would not be appropriate. In this song most of the notes require a separate and pointed attack. Without this treatment the song would lack vigour.

The contour and the rise and fall of a phrase should be carefully studied. Generally a slight increase of tone is desirable in an upward tendency, and a decrease of tone in a downward tendency. For example, in the passage

> " O, don't deceive me ;
> O, never leave me ;
> How could you use a poor maiden so ? "

If the same amount of tone is used throughout, the effect is dull and uninteresting : but if each of the phrases received a slight *crescendo* and corresponding *diminuendo* the music becomes more interesting. It may be noted that the climax of a phrase is not always at the top of the curve. In the above example the climax of the first phrase happens to come at the top ; but in the last phrase it comes at the word " use," which is one degree below the highest note of the phrase.

12. Rhythm.—Rhythm is the life of song. It means more than time. A choir may be fastidiously correct in its note values, and yet sing unmusically. If the " lilt " or " sway " of the song is not caught by the singers, the song cannot be said to have come to life. Appropriate *tempo* is an important factor. Unsatis-factory rhythm is often the result of taking a song

either too quickly or too slowly. Experiment wil
decide what is the appropriate *tempo* of a song.

The rhythm of a song should never be interrupted
merely for the purpose of making a picturesque effect.

13. Tone.—A good " normal " tone is a necessary
foundation, yet it is seldom required in song singing
since it has constantly to be adapted to the character
of the song, and must be coloured by its mood. To
use the same tone for such a variety of songs as " Who is
Sylvia ? ", " Rule, Britannia ", " Early one Morning ",
" Boney was a Warrior ", and " Golden Slumbers "
would have the effect of reducing them all to a dead
level of insignificance.

A good blend is sometimes difficult to secure in a
choir. One or two voices may stand out from the others
by reason of the different quality. Two " reedy " voices
in a choir of " fluty " voices can easily cause an unsatis-
factory blend. " Sing with your ears " and " Listen to
your neighbours " are two effective directions to give in
this contingency.

Vitality of tone must never be lost.

14. Intonation.—Many reasons are given for faulty
intonation or, in other words, singing out of tune.
Fatigue and atmospheric conditions are sometimes
said to be contributory causes, but ultimately there are
but two reasons : singing without listening and faulty
production. Listening is of vital importance to good
intonation. A choir of well-trained " listening " singers
never sings out of tune, however tired it may be or
whatever the atmospheric conditions may be. Humming
is an excellent corrective ; for it is easier to listen when
humming than when singing. Another corrective is to
transpose the song up for flatness, down for sharpness.

15. Ensemble.—This is generally taken to mean
" being together in point of time," and this is

undoubtedly an essential. But the word should also connote unanimity of spirit. All the singers should feel in the same way, express in the same way, vary their tone in the same way, phrase in the same way ; they should, in fact, sing as one.

16. Marks of expression.—Marks of expression are never absolute in value ; they are relative to the character of the song in which they occur. There are many kinds and degrees of *f* or *p*. A *crescendo* in the " Halle-lujah chorus " is quite different in kind and degree from a *crescendo* in " Farewell, Manchester." Such directions as *poco accel* or *poco rit* require careful consideration. The tendency in general is to exaggerate them.

The signs $<$ $>$ are often only half obeyed ; the singers generally find it easier to make the *crescendo* than the corresponding *diminuendo*. " Get back to where you started from " is a golden rule in this respect. A *crescendo* or a *diminuendo* should be graded carefully. Directions as to *tempo* also require careful consideration, e.g. *Andante*, which is often mistakenly interpreted as " slow."

17. Part singing.—This should only be attempted when, beyond all question, the unison singing is satis-factory. Even then, great care must be taken that the tone does not deteriorate. It is far too common an experience to hear a choir at a festival sing a unison song with attractive tone and, immediately after, sing a part song with unpleasant tone. Any tendency to force the tone, or to strain, in the under part, must be checked immediately. A sufficient number of singers must be allocated for the second part, so that they will not have to shout to make their part effective. A good balance is essential in part singing. Part songs for equal voices have an obvious advantage over songs in which the second part is confined to the lower register.

It need hardly be said that the practice, once not infrequent, of singing only the treble and alto parts of a four part chorus has nothing to commend it.

Canons, Rounds and Descants should be practised as preparation for part singing, though it must be remembered that the balance required in descant singing is by no means the same as that in the ordinary two-part song.

The same singers should not always sing the second part.

In mixed choirs it is advisable that each part should consist of both boys and girls, since in this way a better blend of tone may be expected.

III. EAR TRAINING AND SIGHT READING

18. Graded instruction necessary at every stage of the course.—The teaching of Music should include at every stage suitably graded instruction in ear training and sight reading.

The training of the ear to listen carefully and intelligently is of great importance and should form a definite part of every music lesson throughout the school. Experience shows that if it is methodically taught from the early school stages upwards, children can be trained to read simple music at an early age and that only about one per cent. turn out to be really tone-deaf.

(i) *THE INFANT SCHOOL STAGE*

19. Free expression and rhythmic training.—When they first come to school many young children may have something to unlearn about Music as a whole, so that at first it may be advisable to let them have plenty of free expression in, and movement to, music in order to prepare the right kind of environment in which the desire to know more about music will spontaneously grow. The resourceful teacher will, no doubt, devise many ways in which this feeling for music may be fostered and developed.

As it is now generally agreed that education in music should begin with some form of rhythmic training it is suggested that the French system of teaching rhythm can be used to great advantage in the early stages of this work. It is based on the sense impression given by the sounds of certain monosyllables, the combination of which imitates the rhythm of the musical phrases. These time names are as valuable in the teaching of rhythm as are the solfa names in the teaching of pitch.

20. Progressive development of the instruction.— When the children are ready for an advance from the elementary stages of free expression work in music these names should be introduced gradually and may be practised from the blackboard in much the same way as the solfa names will be learnt at a slightly later stage.

Recently it has been found that the rhythm names can be put to excellent use in Percussion Band work : indeed, it would be hard to find an easier or more interesting way of introducing them. (See section **34** below.)

A useful exercise at this stage is for the teacher to tap or clap a series of simple rhythmic patterns and require the children to imitate them. At a later stage, however, they may be encouraged to give their own individual ' answers ' to the various patterns set by the teacher. This is valuable, too, as breaking the ground in preparation for such melody making as they may be called upon to do when they have made further progress in ear training.

The next step will be the recognition of pitch, i.e. which of two sounds is the higher or lower, wide intervals, e.g. **dm', s'd,** being used at first. The hands may here be brought into play, the teacher and children moving them up and down according to the variation of pitch. In general, the visual training involved in tracing the rise and fall of a tune by movements of the hands has much to commend it.

The children should have adequate practice in imitating short phrases, especially sequences, sung to a definite rhythm by the teacher to the solfa names : e.g.

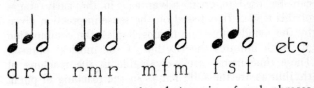

d r d   r m r   m f m   f s f   etc

but it is essential that the whole series of such phrases should be sung rhythmically and without a break from start to finish.

The next step will be to introduce the solfa names on the blackboard in scalewise order, the class singing the appropriate names as the teacher points up or down the scale, including upper **r** and **m** as well as lower **t** and **l**. Then simple stepwise phrases such as those suggested above may be patterned by the teacher and imitated by the children as she points them on the board. If this work is done by small groups in turn, as it undoubtedly should be, it will probably extend over many weeks.

21. From modulator to stave.—To bridge the gulf between the modulator and the stave, which to some seems so formidable a venture at this stage, the old-fashioned method of using the thumb and fingers of one hand as a stave and pointing on it with the other as if it were a modulator is recommended as a practical means of transition.   In this the children can participate by using not only their voices but their hands in imitation of the teacher. After working on these lines the class is ready to sing as before short phrases from the solfa names, which are now written on the stave, but are later superseded by notes, of equal value, e.g. all crochets or all minims. With a large stave drawn on the blackboard, its lines being at least three inches apart, useful exercises in reading can be given by the teacher using a movable note, i.e. of cardboard attached to a pointer, and practising from left to right with it, while the class sings the appropriate solfa names. Many successful teachers find the " mental effects " and their corollary, the hand-signs, useful, but these are not essential.

It is immaterial in which key a start is made, but key C enables young children to reach upper **r** and **m** without strain and key G brings lower **t** and **l** within easy range. There are those who advocate the principle of changing the key for each successive exercise even at this early stage, but progress is likely to be steadier and more uniform if the children are able to find their way about one key first. Other keys should then be taken according to the sight reading requirements of the class, for it is important that the reading should not be confined to any one key for too long a period.

22. Reading from the stave.—In some Infant Schools good use is made of class books for sight reading from the stave. It is important that they should be so well graded that a number of exercises may be sung at every lesson without repetition. As a spirit of confidence on the part of the class is an essential asset, since fluency in reading is the main purpose of this work, the first steps should be real steps and not hurdles. Moreover, the reading should invariably be done by groups within the class rather than by the whole class reading together, and both rhythm and solfa tune practice should be given from the blackboard for a few minutes at the beginning of every reading lesson. Before each exercise, the teacher should clearly set the *tempo*, or rate, and the children should be encouraged to look ahead as they read. Side by side with the reading, practice in the converse process of giving the rhythm and solfa names of the notes of short phrases should be taken.

By the time they pass from the Infant School stage children may be expected to be able to give the solfa names of any stepwise progression sung or played by the teacher and to read a scalewise tune in simple rhythm; for while there are many experienced teachers who regard the tonic chord, **d m s**, as the most satisfactory starting point in ear training and sight reading, it has been found that the use of stepwise exercises during the first stages of the work is more conducive to confidence and progress.

(ii) *THE JUNIOR SCHOOL STAGE*

23. Exercises in rhythm and pitch.—At the beginning of the Junior School stage, careful revision of the work done in the Infant School is advisable, but when the class as a whole is ready to move forward, more difficult exercises in rhythm and pitch will be attempted. As each new rhythm name is introduced, its corresponding symbol will be drawn on the blackboard and used in conjunction with those which the class already knows, for further rhythmic practice. Indeed, it should be possible for children by this means to overcome the ordinary difficulties of rhythm during their Junior School course.

24. The use of the modulator.—The great value of the modulator when rightly used lies in the help it should give the children in anticipating any difficulties which may occur in sight reading from the staff. In pointing on the modulator, however, care should be taken that the passage does not become a series of ungainly and disjointed skips with no definite rhythm or melodic design. The exercises should consist only of such intervals as the children are likely to meet with in the music they sing, and some simple phrases should be chosen which will allow for regular breathing spaces

Fully in keeping with this suggestion is the practice of using for this purpose tunes which the class already knows, the teacher pointing them on the modulator and the children singing the solfa names.

Later, they will be expected to sing the tunes to the correct solfa names without the help of the pointer. It need hardly be said that the tunes chosen should be free from rhythmic difficulties, as the main object of such exercises is the accurate pitching of intervals. Then the same tune should be pointed on the staff immediately after it has been pointed on the modulator, the teacher using, perhaps, the movable note referred to in a previous section, and the children singing the solfa names as before. It must be remembered, however, that when the teacher points to a note on the modulator he has told the children what note to sing, but when he points it on the staff they have to think for themselves what its solfa name is before they sing it. Ability to read the solfa names of a tune pointed on the staff is, therefore, a real step towards reading. In such ways the class will have learnt a large number of tunes with the solfa names attached.

25. Sight-reading and singing songs by ear.—The introduction of class books for sight reading from the stave should be effected as early as practicable, if indeed this has not already been done during the Infant School stage. When they are introduced, however, it is essential that they should be really well graded : for example no consecutive exercises should involve fresh difficulties in rhythm and pitch at the same time, for fluency is at first the most important aim. In the early stages the class should read through each exercise to the rhythm names and then sing it to the solfa names : when, after a lapse of time, the exercises are used again, they may be sung to any vowel sound or quietly hummed. Whatever mistakes are made, the children should be encouraged to continue to the end, maintaining the time.

Later, the reading of songs may be attempted in this way, though as many songs as possible should of course be taught by ear until the children can read them without difficulty. Moreover, the practice of learning carefully chosen songs by ear at this stage provides many excellent opportunities for quickening their powers of musical apprehension.

It is highly desirable, where possible, to have daily practice in sight-reading from books and some form of ear training. Where this is impossible, such practice should form part of every Music lesson.

It should be borne in mind that a mistake in rhythm or in time is more serious than a mistake in pitch. In general, no exercise should be sung through more than once in the same lesson, and a number of exercises should be taken without unnecessary comments. If this is done, it will be found that the class will sing the last two or three exercises with much more fluency and accuracy than they sang the first. It should be the exception rather than the rule for the whole class to sing through any exercise together. The necessity for sectional and even individual work throughout the whole school course cannot be too strongly emphasised. If the children in each class are divided into a convenient number of groups, the phrases, which in the best reading books are marked, can be shared out among them, preferably by indications made by the teacher during the singing of the exercise.

The little theory of music that is required at this stage, e.g. time signatures, keys, and clefs, should be introduced quite informally as it is required, whole lessons devoted to the teaching of theory being out of place.

26. Musical dictation.—At some period in the Junior School course—the earlier the better—musical dictation should be associated with the ear training.

and the children should be encouraged to set down on paper what they hear, singing it through once or twice beforehand. It is better to start with the dictation of rhythm, the teacher patterning a short phrase in rhythm names only and the children writing down the corresponding symbols. Thus, if the teacher patterns such a phrase as " Taa, Taa-tai, Taa-aa," the class would be expected to write down ♩ ♫ ♩, or simply | ⊓ ♩, (which, for the purpose of rhythmic dictation, is quite sufficient). In many schools, however, the use of an ingenious form of musical shorthand enables the children to write down any simple rhythm they hear more fluently.

The next step would be for the teacher to sing or play—at first without accompaniment—a tune with which the children are already familiar and then to ask them to write down its rhythm either in staff notation or in the shorthand. For this purpose hymn tunes are often suitable, as they seldom involve any serious rhythmic difficulties.

Side by side with this, much practice should be given in the solfaing of short melodic phrases, taken at first from tunes the children know, hummed by the teacher ; but when it comes to writing them down, it is essential that at first they should be very short and simple. It is evidently more satisfactory that the majority of the class should be able to write down with facility **d r m**, or **s f m**, than that a very small proportion only should be able to reproduce with difficulty **d l s d' f r m**.

Later, short phrases will be written by the class on the stave. Children should be able to take down a musical phrase with fair rapidity, if they are to profit by the work in its later stages. At first stems need not be added : e.g.

etc.

For black notes, as above, round heads are not required, and are simply a waste of time. When stems are added the strokes should be thin and they need not actually join the heads : e.g. :

Dictation of rhythm and pitch combined should be attempted as the ability of the class to write each down separately develops. This may be done by first singing or playing a familiar musical phrase and requiring the children to reproduce its rhythm on paper. As an example, let the first two bars of " The Vicar of Bray " be taken, the rhythm of which should appear on paper as :—

The tune will then be heard again, and the class will be asked to insert the bar lines and at the next hearing to write down the solfa names over the symbols, thus :—

from which the transcription to the staff notation is easy. After much practice the children should be able to write down in staff notation any simple phrase without the help of these intermediate steps.

The ability to recognise cadences in their more familiar forms, especially in relation to phrase endings, might be expected of children about this time.

It cannot be urged too strongly that, if real progress in ear-training, sight-reading and dictation is to be made, the use of the solfa names should become instinctive.

(iii) *THE SENIOR SCHOOL STAGE*

27. Revision of the earlier work.—At the beginning of the Senior School Stage careful revision of the work done in the Junior School is advisable. When this has been done, the minor mode may be taken on the modulator and then pointed on the staff. The teacher may follow this up by pointing tunes which are written in a minor key and well known to the class. A number of suitable exercises should then be read from the books at each lesson until the peculiar difficulties are mastered, whether the " lah minor " or " doh minor " system is used.

If the children have had sufficient previous experience in the correct pitching of " *fe* " and " *ta*," modulation to adjacent keys should present no serious obstacles : further, it is essential that they should be able not only to recognise that the " doh " of the original key has changed, but also to give the new " doh " its correct letter name. The order of the keys may be seen most clearly, perhaps, from a glance at the following table :—

$$C^\flat \mid G^\flat D^\flat A^\flat E^\flat B^\flat F \mid C \mid G D A E B F^\sharp \mid C^\sharp$$

If theory is rightly described as the grouping and classification of musical facts that have been already learnt through practice, it is clear that many of these will have been introduced from time to time in the course of the sight reading lessons. These will include the note values of semibreves, minims, etc., the letter names of the notes of the scale with special relation to the piano keyboard, the numerical description of intervals, the clefs, the cycle of key signatures, time signatures, the construction of the scale, and a knowledge of some of the more common musical terms. Up to this stage, no doubt, most of the reading will have been done from graded exercises, but it is important that these should give place to songs and instrumental tunes as soon as the teacher is satisfied that his class read fluently enough for this purpose. At the same time, themes from the works of the great composers can be cyclostyled or written on the blackboard for the class to read and, if necessary, to memorise. This greatly enhances the value of the lessons in which works of this kind are studied. The older boys should be introduced to the bass clef and sing chiefly from it, the passages sounding an octave higher than written. Where there are boys, however, who are able to sing at the actual pitch they should, of course, do so.

For practice in ear-training and dictation, short phrases containing more difficult intervals will now be attempted, and then longer phrases will be taken.

28. Chord analysis.—Some teachers will rightly want to do work in simple chord analysis. Much can be done with the help of the piano and of dummy keyboards, made of wood or cardboard, in encouraging older children to fit simple chords to suitably chosen songs during their class lessons. Ability to harmonise a melody at the keyboard is, after all, only a development from the recognition of cadence to that of other chords. If a chord can be recognised by the class when played by the teacher, any child should be able to find it on the keyboard.

Work of this kind is usually approached by setting exercises for distinguishing the notes of a chord. If, for example, a chord of two notes be played, the solfa name of the upper one being given, the class will be asked to sing, and then to name, the lower. Then as progress in recognition is made, a chord of three notes will be taken and treated in much the same way. This would be followed by dictation of two-part, and later of three-part, chords.

The triads may be quickly learnt by some such exercise as the following, which should be sung slowly at first and then quickened as it becomes more familiar :—

In like manner, the first inversion may be introduced and quickly memorised :—

Other methods of introducing the triads will no doubt be attempted and tested, but it is essential that the necessity for careful listening should be insisted upon throughout and that nothing should be committed to paper which cannot first be heard correctly through the ear. Listening to music gains in interest when there is some background of harmonic appreciation.

29. Melody making.—With expert help and guidance, children may be taught to compose simple tunes; but to ensure that they do not write down what they do not hear, it is advisable to confine their earliest efforts to vocal extemporisation. If the idea of question and answer, which is the basis of melody making, has already been presented by tapping or clapping in rhythmic form during the Infant stage, the next step is for the question and answer to be sung. First the children may be told to sing a fixed question, to which the teacher improvises various suitable answers: then the rôles may be reversed, the teacher improvising various questions to which the children reply with a fixed answer. When this principle of phrase balance has been established in their minds, pairs of children may be encouraged to do the same, the teacher suggesting the rhythm if necessary. The writing down of these tunes will afford additional practice in musical dictation. Excellent use may be made of the words of nursery rhymes and, indeed, of suitable verse in their poetry books, as soon as individual children are able to improvise the whole tune with reasonable fluency. When they are competent to write down correctly what they hear or sing, they may be expected to write down tunes that they hear mentally, without the necessity of vocalising them first.

IV. RHYTHMIC MOVEMENT

30. Conditions and facilities for rhythmic training.—One of the valuable developments of recent years in the teaching of music has been the use of rhythmic movement as a means of helping children to experience music, to understand the structure of the tunes they hear, and to express their knowledge in a way that is fundamentally satisfying and natural to them. Such training may take many different forms, some of them

highly systematised ; but valuable rhythmic work can
be undertaken profitably by any teacher with sufficient
musical ability to take the class singing.

The ideal conditions for such work are : good floor
space, a class of children so dressed that their garments
do not hamper free movement, a good piano, a sensitive
and competent pianist who is also able to demonstrate
the necessary movements and to inspire the class, and
a stock of first-rate tunes, however simple. Much
valuable work can, however, be done in very different
circumstances. If floor space is limited small groups
can take turns to move to music while the rest of the
class is singing, playing pipes or percussion instruments,
or even making simple hand or foot movements whilst
seated in their desks. The piano can be supplemented
by the pipe or percussion band or singing. It is sometimes found possible to combine two classes when the
numbers are small so that one teacher plays while a
second teaches and demonstrates. The pianist who has
the necessary ability and knowledge will find it possible
to illustrate particular points by improvising simple
tunes containing, for example, the regular repetition
of a rhythmic pattern ; this should not be overdone
or a valuable opportunity of widening the children's
musical repertoire will be lost.

National and folk songs, folk dance tunes, nursery
rhymes and good hymn tunes will provide a storehouse
of fine material from which a choice can be made to
suit the varying capacities of the pianists ; some of the
simpler compositions of the great masters are easily
accessible, within the power of most players, and
attractive and easy to interpret. Beyond this there
is a wide range of compositions, both modern and
classical, which can be drawn upon by the pianist of
greater skill, and it is most desirable to build up a school
library of suitable works of this kind. Care must be
taken to avoid poor material in the form of inferior

compositions specially written down to what is supposed to be the children's level.

Fuller descriptions of the kind of work done, and detailed suggestions for the type of work suitable for each stage will follow, but there are certain features which should characterise the work at all stages. It is essential that from the very beginning the children's movements should be unaffected, that the pupils should grow in the power both to relax and to control and that there should be liberation from the stiff, awkward or unnecessary movements that are too often caused by the wrong kind of environment.

Children who have had teaching of the right kind show by the beauty and grace of their movements what the work has done for their bodies. Response to the stimulus of a fine tune, controlled expression through bodily movements, and a satisfaction of the rhythmic instinct, should make for health of mind as well as of body.

31. Some practical considerations.—Certain specific teaching must be given, and some definite forms of movement adopted to represent such things as note values and pulse. Unanimity of movement has a special beauty and value of its own, and the children can use these definite forms when the structure of the tune they are interpreting is suitable. At other times the movements may illustrate the form of the composition more freely and be in less detailed accordance with note values. A skilful teacher may find it possible to allow the children to express their own ideas of the character of the music.

The teacher should not read into the music an idea that the composer has not intended, nor force upon the class expressions of emotion that are not natural to the children at the stage of development which they have reached, nor should the movements become stereotyped like those associated with the " action song."

The music should not suffer any mutilation, and the pianist should avoid any such unmusical treatment as, for example, the undue stressing of the first beat of a bar.

It has been found from experience that boys react to this work differently from girls. They often require more robust and vigorous movement, but, given the right teaching from a man or woman whose opinion they respect and who believes in the work, they will take naturally to it, and show none of the self-consciousness or ungainly movement which is sometimes attributed to them.

Rhythmic movement, when the children listen intelligently, and assimilate and express fine tunes so that they become a part of themselves, is a very practical and valuable form of musical appreciation, which, moreoever, results in the awakening and development of the children's own creative faculties.

32. Development of the work through the successive stages of the school course.—(i) *The Infant School stage.*—There might well be a short daily lesson at this stage. The course may begin with relaxation exercises, and others, not necessarily in response to music, in which the children perform simple movements rhythmically, for example those illustrating pulling, sweeping, hammering. Response to tunes that invite walking, running, skipping, rocking and so on may follow.

The children can listen and show the change in movement when the pianist plays loudly, softly, quickly or slowly, and should be taught to listen for the end of a tune. The half-way point of a simple tune can be shown by a change of direction or position. Phrasing is most important, first of all in regular phrases, then in irregular. Phrasing and also simple form—(for example, "ternary" form, A B A) can be shown either by the movements of different groups in turn, or by individual movements of body or arms.

At some point in the course it is useful to teach note values in connection with the rhythm names and definite foot movements, for example a walking step for " taa," a running step for " taatai," a skipping step for " taafe," a step-bend for " taa-aa."

Simple one bar rhythmic patterns regularly repeated may be taught at first, or a familiar tune with a very obvious pattern.

Arm movements may be used for 2, 3 and 4 pulse measures. It is wise here not to teach any movement that will conflict later with the recognised method of conducting.

The climax of a tune may be recognised and illustrated in some form of group or individual movement. The children can invent simple dances and games to illustrate the form of some of the tunes they hear.

(ii) *The Junior School stage.*—If the Juniors have had no previous experience of rhythmic work all the preparatory work indicated in the Infant School section must be taken. The Juniors will have more control but in all probability a larger proportion of relaxation exercises will be needed. The lessons now may be a little longer and possibly less frequent but the method may be used at any time as an illustration or corrective in the music lesson.

Any of the suggestions in the Infant School section may be used, but the work must develop. More definite teaching in form may be given and the children may be introduced to such terms as " binary," " ternary." The class may be taught to step more difficult rhythms, and to listen to and step bass and treble. Canons and rounds may be stepped, movements may be made for the different forms of cadences, and changes of key may all be shown by movement in groups.

(iii) *The Senior School stage.*—If the Infant and Junior School course has been followed, the work may be developed as a regular lesson for the class, or as an optional subject for those children who find it of especial value, or as an occasional method to be used at any time in the Music lesson. If there has been no previous training, it is not too late to begin.

Presuming a previous course there may be some revision of the Junior work and the development of the study and illustration of form, such as, for example, fugue and rondo. An understanding of counterpoint may be acquired by stepping all the independent parts. Recognition of more difficult subjects and the invention of dances, and so on, may be included in the course.

V. FOLK DANCING

33. The instruction at successive stages of the school course.—Dancing, and especially folk dancing, has come to be recognised as a most important form of the apprehension and expression of music. Its rhythmical qualities, and the fact that a good dancer must be able to study and appreciate a tune and then use his full mental and physical powers to express it in concerted motion, make it a proper part of a musical training. English folk dancing has such a wealth of beautiful tunes and such a variety of dances that it will easily supply the full wants of any school in this direction.

(i) *The Infant School stage.*—As with other forms of music, so with dancing, the Infant stage is one of preparation. The danger to avoid is to try to obtain at this age elaborate results for purpose of display. The first aim should be to teach the child to listen to a tune, to feel, though not necessarily to describe, its pulse and rhythm and to recognise and learn by heart and sing tunes and parts of tunes. With this should go the power to move in accordance with a tune, not in a set pattern at first, but simply in time with it, using the ordinary steps of English Country dancing, walking, running and skipping; and learning to start with the music and, by knowing the tune as a whole, to feel when the tune, and therefore the movement, are about to end. Detailed technical instruction is out of place at this stage, but great attention should be given to freedom of movement and to the avoidance of stiffness in the arms, shoulders and carriage of the head; and children should be taught to run and skip with a free and natural spring, without the pointing of the toes or holding out of skirts which are proper to some other kinds of dancing. Once these fundamentals have been grasped, the children can easily learn some of the simplest Country Dances, though this involves a considerable advance in difficulty, since to remember the pattern and order of a dance is much harder, for a child, than to move, almost instinctively, to a tune. The dances chosen must therefore be very simple in construction.

It should not be necessary to say that the quality of the musical accompaniment is vital to good dancing and, if there is no good pianist, it is better to use a gramophone, for which a sufficient number of folk dances have now been recorded. Little children, because of their shorter stride, need to have the tunes played faster than would suit an adult.

(ii) *The Junior School stage.*—Careful training in listening is still imperative, and the children must learn that the tune comes before the dance and that they cannot do the latter properly till they thoroughly know the former. It will now be possible to spend more time on the technique of the dances, and the children can learn to watch for their own place in the set and to adjust their movements and positions to those of others.

As soon as possible they must learn to dance in any position in a set and with any partner.

The quality of the step must be watched : it should be a clear, but not high, spring, from one foot to the other, with the knee firm but not stiff, the waist muscles firm and the upper part of the body quite free. In the skipping step the weight of the body should be in front of the feet. For all movements the weight of the body should be put forward beforehand, not allowed to fall back on the heels. As a singer takes breath before singing, so a dancer poises himself before he moves.

For Country dances the habit of boys and girls dancing together should be ingrained at this stage. The boys however may also well be taught the Sword dances of Northern England, which are men's dances and appeal more strongly to boys than to girls.

(iii) *The Senior School stage.*—Given enough time and intelligent teaching, Country dancing can now be carried to a high pitch of excellence. But too difficult dances must not be attempted, and stress should be laid on the dance as a continuous whole, with a character of its own, and not as a succession of separate movements. Failure to observe this leads to dancing that is correct but lifeless. Boys and girls should dance together whenever possible, and both sexes may be taught how valuable dancing is for their games and physical training.

Besides Sword dances, boys may now begin Morris dances. These involve strong muscular effort and are therefore best reserved for boys of 11 and upwards, while the physically weak should not attempt them. Only the easier dances should be attempted, and the teacher himself must be properly trained and be prepared to get results slowly. Girls can dance the Morris, but it is essentially a man's dance. The temptation to give displays of dancing in public before the children are fit for it should be resisted. On the other hand, folk dance festivals, where the dancing has to stand the test of criticism and other children's dancing can be watched, are most valuable. But care must be taken that the festival team do not monopolise too much of the time at the expense of the rest of the school.

The Hall is the best place for dancing : if a playground or grass be used the music must be slower. Light shoes make dancing much easier and should always be worn.

A school band, with pipes or mouth organs and a drum, can do much to help the dancing and is a delightful and profitable form of musical activity. To teach folk dancing well is difficult, and it is not enough merely to be able to get safely through the dances which it is proposed to teach. A much wider and deeper background of theory and practice is required. The tunes must be carefully studied, both in themselves and in relation to other tunes. The character of each dance must be appreciated, as well as the fact that the steps and figures of a dance are no more than the bare words of an actor's part, which are dead until he gives them life.

Finally, English folk dancing has its roots in English folk lore. Teachers will find much in its history that will interest children, will give atmosphere to their dancing and will acquaint them with one of the characteristic aspects of the social history of the English people.

VI. PERCUSSION BANDS

34. Purpose and scope of this activity.—In recent years the principles underlying the formation of percussion bands have undergone considerable change. Formerly the instruments in use were of poor quality, being regarded as mere toys, and the teacher was content to regard the ' playing ' as a form of harmless relaxation which the children appeared, for a season at any rate, to enjoy. The music used on these occasions was often trivial or banal, and in an unequal contest to gain a hearing the ' players ' were usually more successful than the pianist. In fact, the whole idea seemed purposeless.

More enlightened teachers, however, have seen in the percussion band a means of introducing young children to the first steps of rhythmic reading in staff notation. This is achieved by the use of charts and, later, of individual parts which are written out in the same way as those from which the percussion player in an orchestra would play. It has been found by experience, too, that the class as a whole will progress with greater speed and uniformity if this part of the work is carefully graded.

It is immaterial whether the teacher or a succession of children conduct the band, but it is important that the beat should be clearly seen by all the players, and that only recognised methods of conducting should be employed. If, however, a child does conduct, his directions, whether right or wrong, should be followed by the teacher as well as by the band.

That the music chosen should be worth hearing goes without saying, but it is sometimes forgotten that the instruments should be accompanying the piano or gramophone, and not vice versa, so that the children should be encouraged to listen for the music all the time. This is not a counsel of perfection incapable of realisation, but a matter of considerable practical importance in view of the fact that progress in music must depend primarily upon the development of the listening ear, so that the sooner the habit is formed the better.

With this object in view several National Songs, classical pieces, and other suitable works have been edited with Percussion band parts, thus giving young children the opportunity of actually taking part in the performance of such pieces in the only way possible for them at this early age. A number of gramophone records of those pieces, also, have been made in order to facilitate the introduction of band work in schools where there is no one on the staff who is competent to play the piano sufficiently well.

Band work may be introduced at any stage, of course, in the Infant or Junior School, but it is certainly not beyond the average capacity of the 5-year old and, therefore, might well be introduced early where conditions allow and circumstances permit. Experience has now proved that the Percussion band, in the hands of an alert and musicianly teacher, fosters and develops children's inborn sense of rhythm and gives them the thrill which is invariably associated with all concerted work of the best type.

There is no reason why this work should not be continued in the Junior School, provided that it is genuinely continuous and not carried on by a teacher who takes no account of the stage which the children have reached in the Infant School. In the later stages of the work, the band parts should not merely reflect the melodic tone of the music, but should approximate more closely to the percussion parts of an orchestral score.

In some Senior Schools, too, the experiment has been tried with the most backward pupils—and has been found to have succeeded in quickening their powers of concentration and in arousing their interest and has given them something both useful and interesting to do, which other classes in the school do not do, and perhaps, for lack of practice, could not do.

VII. PIPE BANDS

35. Value of pipe-making and pipe-playing.—In a growing number of schools the art of pipe making and playing is being taught. Those most commonly made and used are the treble (Key D), alto (A) and tenor (D), which are proportioned according to Eastern peasant tradition, that is to say, with the simplest possible fipple heads on a wide bamboo bore thus giving a mellow, musical tone. The range is ten notes of the diatonic scale, with all the intervening accidentals, which are obtained by cross-fingering. These pipes can be made, given the few requisite tools, for a few pence, and suitably embellished, if desired.

Work of this kind is valuable in many ways. The ear training involved in the making of a pipe, which is built up note by note by ear, is useful. The importance of careful tuning cannot be insisted upon too strongly. If there is failure in this respect, it is due far more to lack of care and standard than of ability. Moreover, through frequent use of such an instrument when completed, the ear becomes accustomed to the fixed sounds of the scale and the player begins to acquire a sense of absolute pitch. Further, mastery of the pipe gives children ample opportunity for sight reading and transposition, as well as for improvisation and the making of melodies.

The importance of phrasing correctly, which involves good breath control, is rightly insisted upon by the best teachers, for no musical activity is of any aesthetic value unless it tends to develop in the pupils a keener sense of musicianship.

From time to time every music teacher in the Senior School is faced with the problem of the boy whose voice is changing and of the proper course to pursue. The first inclination no doubt would be to encourage him to take up the study of some orchestral instrument, if suitable tuition were available ; but this would frequently be a difficulty, and the musical pipe provides one solution, at any rate, for the teacher who feels diffident about his ability to deal with the boy's voice at this stage.

In company with others such a boy will learn to play in two, three and four parts and thus gain first hand experience of music with which he would otherwise never have come into contact. Moreover, if he develops an interest in pipe playing is it unreasonable to hope that he will desire, at a later stage, to test his ability at playing a genuine instrument of the orchestra ? For where interest in ensemble playing has been aroused in early childhood through the Percussion band, and sustained later on by means of the Pipe band, the formation of a school orchestra would appear to be the normal corollary.

These pipes are useful, too, for accompanying Country dances, and can sound effective in combination with or in contrast to the singing class, the string class, or the Percussion band.

VIII. APPRECIATION OF MUSIC

36. Appreciation should permeate all the teaching.—It is now generally understood that the function of the teacher who takes a class in " Appreciation of Music " is to inculcate an understanding of music. This understanding will add greatly to the enjoyment of music. Appreciation should not be regarded as a separate subject, but rather as permeating the whole of the music teaching. Opportunities will be found in Song singing, Sight singing, Aural Training, and other branches of the subject.

The first step is to cultivate the children's power of listening. This should be begun in the Infant School, by means of Rhythmic Movement and the Percussion Band. From very simple beginnings, such as the recognition of high and low pitch, final cadence, and rhythmic pattern, can be developed a genuine musical sense. From this comes the ability to imitate phrases, and to add satisfactorily balanced cadential phrases to short phrases supplied by the teacher. From this to Melody writing is but a step, leading to the understanding of simple forms through the stringing of melodic phrases together, as exemplified in National songs. This is an excellent preparation for the understanding of more extended forms, such as the Rondo and the Minuet and Trio. The clear cut form of a Fugue, simply considered, makes it an excellent listening study for a class of children.

The teacher should talk as little as possible. His explanations should be carefully prepared, so enabling him to be concise and brief.

For wider study a gramophone with a stock of good records is essential. Gramophone records have the additional advantage of enabling the teacher to introduce the instruments of the orchestra to the children though of course attendance at children's concerts where the instruments of the orchestra may be seen as well as heard will make this classroom knowledge come alive.

The children should sometimes be allowed to hear a piece of music without any explanation from the teacher, giving their own ideas of its form and characteristics to the teacher afterwards.

The importance of the training of the ear in connexion with this subject cannot be too strongly emphasised. No one can properly appreciate music if he cannot listen properly.

Some general idea of musical history can be given incidentally in the course of the teaching, without attempting a series of lessons on the subject.

IX. SCHOOL BROADCASTS

37. Broadcast lessons and the schools.—Good reception is a primary requisite for the effective use of the music lesson as of all wireless lessons. Further, the course selected should be one suited to the powers and understanding of the children. Most of the courses assume a certain preliminary knowledge and a certain amount of preparation and following up on the part of the teacher, who should be prepared with the help of the pamphlets published terminally by the B.B.C. to anticipate difficulties and resolve misunderstandings as they occur. An elementary course, however, designed for small schools where it may happen that there is no teacher with musical gifts on the staff has much to recommend it, and it may well enable children to acquire some musical knowledge who would otherwise be deprived of the opportunity. But for schools where there are members of the staff well qualified to take music the broadcast lesson will doubtless make its chief contribution through features not ordinarily available in schools—in particular, through the concert lessons.

Children taking wireless lessons should be supplied with manuscript books and pencils, and with copies of the relevant B.B.C. pamphlet.

X. FESTIVALS

38. Competitive and non-competitive festivals.— Festivals are of two kinds, competitive and non-competitive, the latter being a new and flourishing development.

(i) *Competitive festivals*.

The competitive Festival ought to be, and now generally is, conducted with the competitive principle kept in strict subordination to the educative value derived from hearing a number of other schools and receiving a reasoned judgment from an experienced adjudicator. Performance by the massed choirs is most valuable and ought not to be omitted, where the nature of the song and other conditions allow.

Undue concentration on the one or two pieces set for a Festival is contrary to the spirit of music ; occasionally however it happens that for some time before a Festival no other music is practised but the ' test-pieces.' The wise teacher will know that the danger of staleness in such conditions is very real, and he will give the children plenty of change. If the right spirit is caught from the beginning a test-piece may often be at its best at about the sixth lesson or so after it has been begun.

(ii) *Non-competitive festivals.*

The non-competitive Festivals usually aim at bringing together a large number of schools from a comparatively small area. They are often found to succeed where the competitive type of Festival has not been established or has lapsed for want of support. They afford an incentive to schools that do not feel themselves sufficiently good to enter into a somewhat specialised competition but desire the training and inspiration which a great co-operative effort can give them. There is no reason why the two movements, competitive and non-competitive, should not flourish side by side; the aim of both is educational.

Massed rehearsals and concerts, frank and informal criticism delivered in private to the conductors, and a wide selection of songs are among the many advantages secured by the non-competitive Festival, which may be found more fully described in the Board's Educational Pamphlet No. 95 (*Recent Developments in School Music*).

XI. CONCERTS FOR SCHOOLS

39. Some points suggested by past experience.— The practice is growing of organising Concerts for school children at which children from a number of schools attend by arrangement. A few points arising out of past experience may be helpful :—

(1) The concert should not greatly exceed $1\frac{1}{4}$ hours.

(2) The most interesting type is found to be the orchestral concert. A full orchestra is a sure attraction, but children will listen to a string orchestra if it is competent.

(3) Much chamber music is apt to be somewhat intimate for large audiences, and nearly all such music is in extended form, which taxes the powers of concentration of inexperienced listeners. But if the programme is carefully chosen, and the programme is varied by solo instrumental work, or songs sung by a soloist, or singing by the audience, such concerts can be successful. From the point of view of expense, they are in some localities the most convenient type.

(4) There are obvious possibilities in concerts comprising such items as solos and duets, preferably instrumental, and performances by various types of choir.

(5) The selection of the programme is of the greatest importance. Descriptive pieces, suites, tone-poems, ballet music and the like seem to be the most easily appreciated. It goes without saying that modern composers and British composers should be represented as well as the ' classics.'

(6) If notices can be sent round early to schools, a brief description of the pieces will probably assist teachers to acquaint their pupils to some extent with what they are to hear. Any symphonic movement, in particular, requires some previous preparation if it is to be heard intelligently. Themes can be quoted, perhaps memorised, and the general idea of the form grasped. In addition to illustration on the piano, gramophone records are sometimes useful. But preliminary preparation should not be overdone.

(7) At the concert, it is beneficial for an expert to give a brief talk. It must not be academic in character, and it is not always easy to find the right speaker—one who will combine with a lightness of touch some solidity of matter, and who will be content to be brief. The talk need not be given

all at once ; for example, the instruments of the orchestra will be better understood, if they are not taken in rapid succession from the first Violins to the Glockenspiel, but are dealt with in two talks or perhaps three, incidentally as it were, during the remarks on a piece which is about to follow.

(8) At some point in the concert it is a good thing for the children assembled to sing, to orchestral accompaniment, a song or two which they have prepared. This need not take more than a few minutes.

XII. THE SCHOOL ORCHESTRA

40. Composition and training of the orchestra.— Among the out-of-school musical activities that are to be met with in many Senior Schools few are more interesting than the formation of a school orchestra. Many children now learn to play the violin and other instruments after school hours and the schools have put this fact to good use.

Early training in Percussion Band work is an excellent preliminary for orchestral work later. Children who have had the advantage of playing in a properly con- ducted Percussion Band will have had experience of taking part in ensemble work, of reading a part, of following a conductor's beat, and of counting rests accurately. If the school possesses or can command the loan of some of the bigger stringed instruments, an enterprising boy or girl may be attracted towards the viola or the 'cello, while a musical child will find little except physical difficulty in mastering a " tonic and dominant " part on the double bass. In schools that have experimented with a pipe band, a potential supply of wind-players is at hand : in any case the possibilities of wind instruments should not be lost sight of ; their great advantage, apart from portability, is the com- paratively short time required to obtain reasonable proficiency for simple orchestral work. Of the woodwind the flute and clarinet, and of the brass the cornet, have perhaps most to recommend them. It may be found possible to attract members of the staff to deal with some of the more intractable instruments. Unless the orchestra is unusually complete it is probable that the piano part will be needed : this should not be a mere transcription of the full orchestral score—it should rather be a specially written part calculated to supply the place of missing instruments or possibly to support, without elaborate figuration, instruments which, though not missing, are for any reason unreliable.

The music chosen should combine the merits of being good in itself and being playable. There are nowadays plenty of suitable publications, both original pieces and arrangements by reputable and experienced composers. If an orchestra has for some reason to undertake some piece that requires a more advanced technique than the players possess, it is usually practicable to simplify passages or transfer them from one instrument to another. A viola part, for example, can almost always be " faked " for a third violin. The conductor should at all times be prepared to re-score to this end, and the labour involved is amply compensated for by the increased effectiveness of the performance. There is a great deal of truth in the saying : " The best music for school orchestras is that scored by the conductor who knows the habits and peculiarities, the merits and defects, of the ephemeral personnel of his own band."

It cannot be too strongly urged that a substantial proportion of every practice should be devoted to sight-reading, which among other advantages encourages fluency and agility, fosters a spirit of self-reliance, and widens the repertoire. The music read should, of course, be carefully graded according to the capacity of the players.

CHAPTER VII

ART AND CRAFT

I. THE COMMON AIMS IN THE TEACHING OF ART AND CRAFT

1. Design—the common ground of the arts and crafts.—The chief purpose in combining the hitherto separate chapters on " Drawing " and " Handwork " and substituting for them a single chapter with the title " Art and Craft " is to stress the importance of design, which forms the common ground shared by Handicraft with Drawing and every other form of graphic art.

Design, which among other qualities, includes proportion, harmony, rhythm and pattern, is an essential element not only in all forms of expressive art, whether Music or Literature or such " fine arts " as Painting or Sculpture, but also in all forms of Craft work, whether executed in wood, metal or other material. The various arts, which are primarily concerned with the expression in outward form of ideas and experiences which make some special appeal to the artist, have each its own technique. Whatever he creates or interprets, the artist seeks to achieve something that will cause both in himself and in others a feeling of satisfaction,—similar perhaps to what we experience in our response to the works of nature—through the use of design appropriate to the medium he has chosen. So, too, the crafts, which are primarily concerned with the making of serviceable things in various materials, have each its own technique. The good craftsman, whilst suiting his treatment of his material to the particular end he has in view, seeks, like the artist, to arouse similar feelings of satisfaction by the use of appropriate design. Thus, design,—the character of which is determined, in each art, by the experiences it expresses and the medium employed, and, in each craft, by its practical purpose and the material used,—provides a link between the arts and the crafts.

2. Only certain kinds of " art " and " craft " dealt with in this chapter.—The present chapter deals with only those forms of art, which are known as the " graphic " or " plastic " arts, and the appeal of which is primarily to the eye, and those forms of craft which are frequently spoken of as the traditional crafts. Between these crafts and drawing, painting, modelling and kindred activities the underlying connexion is particularly close and it is important that teachers both of art and of craft should lay greater emphasis than they have done in the past on good design, which here includes the right use of materials, sound workmanship, good proportion and appropriate decoration.

Though the use of the term " art " in this chapter is restricted to graphic and plastic art, this limitation, necessary for the sake of convenience, should not be taken as implying either that what is said of them does not hold good, *mutatis mutandis*, of the other forms of artistic expression which have their part to play in a general education, or that the domestic crafts and gardening will not depend for life and interest on the extent to which they, too, exhibit the touch of the artist.

3. The need for co-operation between the art teacher and the craft teacher.—" Art " and " handicraft " then, are not two separate sections of the curriculum which imply different outlooks ; they should properly be regarded as part and parcel of one important branch of teaching. Bookbinding, for instance, provides a useful example of a craft in which artistic considerations and qualities of good workmanship must be associated if it is to be successfully practised ; it is immaterial whether it be put into a pigeon-hole labelled " art " or into one labelled " handicraft." This does not mean that drawing and design done on paper should not play an important part in the work of the school, but it is essential that the same spirit should govern both art and craft work throughout the school and that there should be no unreal distinction or artificial barrier between them.

But if we are to make the best possible use of the available teaching power, it follows that all concerned with art and craft must be very willing and ready to work together with a common aim and that anything in the nature of watertight compartments must be avoided. Moreover, co-operation should not be assumed to be complete when the art and the craft teachers have entered into a successful partnership. The spirit which is made manifest in their teaching should permeate the whole school, and the choice of fittings and decorations should result in the provision of a cheerful and inspiring environment for all school activities.

4. The appreciation of design.—The school should do its utmost to provide each new generation as it passes through it with the power to appreciate and to demand well designed homes and well designed articles of all kinds. To achieve this the children themselves should be placed in a bright and cheerful environment, and surrounded with pleasant and soundly made articles of daily use. Secondly, the things they make in the handicraft or art room should be fully considered from the point of view of good design. There is, of course, a place for bringing to the attention of school children, specifically, what is good in design in everyday use outside the school ; but the first thing to do is to attend to their immediate surroundings and to see that no ugly, overdecorated or unsuitable things of any kind are permitted to be made in the school.

5. The importance of art and craft in daily life.—There has been a tendency in the past to look upon some subjects of the curriculum as means of acquiring such knowledge or skill as would have a practical bearing on life, but to look upon art as an ornamental frilling, more or less desirable, applied to the fabric of education, admirable, possibly, as a preparation for leisure, but having little contact with everyday affairs. If, however, a wider view is taken, and art and craft are regarded as including design, as suggested above, it will be seen that nothing in the school curriculum has a closer contact with life. While few people are called upon to use draughtsmanship to any extent, all are called upon to exercise choice between what is good and what is less good in matters of shape and colour and craftsmanship, and to take action, either as individuals or as members of the community, which will affect their environment. The choice of clothes, house, furniture, arrangement of furniture, and the decoration of a room, all call for discriminating judgment.

As a member of the community, the individual is called upon to exercise his judgment in matters concerned with public building, town planning, and the preservation of all that has beauty and character in his neighbourhood and in the countryside. The individual, of course, has little opportunity to exercise his influence directly in some of these matters, but a well informed and well disposed public opinion is a potent force. It has been said that a nation gets the art that it deserves. On the whole this is probably true, and so it is therefore important that the public opinion of the future in these matters shall be rightly formed in our schools today. With these considerations in mind it is possible to determine the place of Art and Craft in the education of the young.

6. The educational value of art and craft.—It is clear that training in draughtsmanship, although it may still be of value as a means to an end, is not a sufficient end in itself. The love of drawing, painting, and making things seems to be instinctive in every normal child. By such means he expresses ideas about the things which surround him, long before he can use the written word, and this outlet for his lively imagination must be fostered and developed to the full. The spontaneity, the freshness and vigour which are characteristic of the free expression of young children's drawing and painting should be recognised as of greater importance than an imitative accuracy, but it should equally be recognised that for the normal child it is as natural to make progress towards adult standards in the language of drawing as in the written word.

Imagination and the strengthening of the creative impulse may be fostered just as fully through craft work as by drawing and picture making : indeed some children will find greater satisfaction and more profit through handling other tools and material than pencil, brush and paper. The teacher should find time for discussion, for consideration of examples of the art and craftsmanship, hand or machine, not only of the past but of the present. For this purpose pictures and illustrations may be used when original works are not available, as they seldom will be. This method of teaching will not be confined to the study of museum pieces, but will deal with contemporary building and articles of everyday use. As a background to these more positive influences which are brought to bear on the child's development, there will be those which may be considered as more incidental but none the less very important, the influence of the environment provided by the class room, the school and its surroundings, and the active part which the children are called upon to take in creating that environment.

To sum up, it may be said that the purpose of including instruction in Art and Craft in the education of the child is, twofold :—

> (1) to encourage the child's natural impulse to give visible form to his ideas and to develop in him the power to do this with courage, sincerity and vividness ;
>
> (2) to make him actively aware of what is beautiful in nature and art and what is fine and honest in craftsmanship.

7. Some considerations governing choice of method.—These are the aims towards which the methods of teaching will be directed. But there are many ways of reaching the same end, and the teacher's choice of method—apart from fundamental matters

f technique—will be determined by a variety of considerations. Among these will be his own individual
interests and special aptitudes, the accommodation
and equipment of the school, the type of locality,
and the potential help of other institutions, such as Art
Schools, Museums and Galleries, and, most important
of all, the varying characteristics and abilities of his
pupils. For this reason a rigid and uniform scheme
of work is obviously undesirable.

8. Stages in the teaching of art and craft.—In
Art and Craft no less than in other branches of school-
work it is important that from the Infant to the
Junior School stage, and from the Junior to the Senior
School stage, development should be continuous and
without any sudden deflection or interruption of the
course. If anywhere a change in the method of approach
is justified on the ground of a change in the child's way
of looking at things, it is at the beginning of the Senior
School stage, or at about the age of 11.

Up to that time, if there is no unwise interference,
most children pass through stages which show a steady
development of knowledge, a growing power to form and
retain a visual image, and an increasingly vivid and
lively use of such images. It would be misleading to
say that the change in a child's attitude to drawing
comes at any definite age ; children do not conform to
rule so readily, but it appears to be generally true that,
after the age of eleven, most children become more
conscious of the exact appearance of the things which
surround them, and more ready to compare their own
representation of an object with its actual appearance   In
the same way they pass through the stages of developing
more and more muscular control, more and more skill
and inventiveness in construction and design, until the
time comes when they wish to achieve something that
is comparable to the craftsmanship of adults.

II. ART AND HANDWORK AT THE INFANT SCHOOL STAGE

A. DRAWING AND PAINTING

9. Drawing in the Infant School.—Teachers o Infants have long been aware that it is natural for th normal child to use drawing as a means of expressio and for many years drawing has had a clearly recognise place in many of the activities of the Infant Schoo It should be realised, however, that the use of drawin as a language, as a sort of picture-writing with whic to express ideas, is only one aspect of the artistic develop ment of young children. Even at this stage the children natural love of colour may be stimulated, and the sense of pattern developed, while they may be encourage to take an active part in the decoration and arrangemer of the school room.

The child's drawing begins with meaningless scribbl but these marks, whether by accident or by desig soon begin to assume forms to which names are give For the most part the earliest drawings of this typ are formalised pictures of the human figure. Late symbols representing houses, engines, trees, and an mals, appear. In the early stages, one symbol ma often be used to represent all animals ; later, additio or alterations are made to differentiate between variou animals.

It is generally agreed that the free drawing of childre before school age is almost entirely drawing fro memory and remains so during the early years of schoo life, although exceptions to this generalisation may b found. It is of little use to ask a child of Infant Schoo age to draw an object from sight. To do so, he has t face a complex problem, and the fact that he may nc be conscious of the processes through which he has t go does not make the task easier. He has to envisag the new form, to analyse it, to form a mental pictur of each part that is being drawn, and to go through what may be completely new manual movements in transferring it to paper. In drawing from memory the child is using mental pictures which have already been formed and probably used before, either wholly or in part ; for in representing new forms he usually adapts and adds fresh features to symbols which he has used before.

With the general mental development of the child come clearer and better defined mental pictures and a greater power of analysis and co-ordination between eye and hand, with a corresponding movement towards a more realistic treatment. As the child's store of visual images is constantly being enriched by new experience, he becomes more and more able to differentiate between various shapes in his drawings. Even when young children are attempting to draw from sight, their drawings usually record what they know rather than what they see. Children's drawings of houses, showing not only three sides of the houses but all their contents, are examples of this characteristic.

It has been said that such early drawing has little in common with art, since it lacks conscious arrangement of the symbols used. But if in so occupying himself a child is seeking to represent his experiences, is struggling towards a more adequate way of expression, and is using his imagination in the arrangement of the formalised shapes he employs, then he is following the impulses that are the basis of all true art. Not that children's drawings can be called works of art : such works can only be the product of experiences of life richer and deeper than those of a child. It is possible, indeed, to exaggerate the intrinsic value of children's drawings, but scarcely possible to exaggerate the charm and spontaneity of the best work of this kind.

In the Infant School, then, the teacher's part is one of sympathetic encouragement rather than direct teaching, but if she is to be ready with the right kind of encouragement, and to know when to give it, she must give some time to the study of the drawings of the individual children in her charge. It is realised that this is not an easy thing to do in large classes, but it is vital to any real progress.

10. The growth of observation in Infants' drawing.
—As the children reach the upper classes of the Infant School, some of their pictures will show greater powers of observation ; the content will be richer, and the pictorial form more complex. It is well at this stage deliberately to direct the children's attention to the interesting and colourful things about them, either by describing familiar scenes to them, or by suggesting for their observation subjects which are familiar to them, before asking them to make a picture. Some children have such lively and active imaginations that they are never at a loss for subjects to draw and paint. Such children may very well be allowed to choose their own subjects ; but not all can do without some external stimulus. It will be found that some subjects have a common appeal for the majority of children in a class, and individuality will then show itself in the variety of ways in which the same subject will be tackled by different children.

In the attempt to " develop imagination," there has been a tendency to choose subjects which project the child's mind into a world of fantasy. Fairies and gnomes have been too frequently used as the main source of inspiration for imaginative work. Unfortunately, when asked to depict a fairy, the child has no visual image based on experience and inevitably falls back on memory of " picture book " fairies. As the artist of the picture book suffers from the same disability as the child, the result can only be a repetition of the popular version of the conventional fairy. As a general rule, it is desirable to choose subjects which are within the personal experience of the children : though it is not suggested that subjects should never be set which introduce elements outside the child's experience. Some of the most delightful drawings and paintings done by children have had biblical or historical subjects for their themes, but here, although the background or the costumes may have been inspired by pictures seen at one time or another, the people and the situations portrayed are real to the child and are often treated with a charming naivety and simplicity.

Naturally the children's individual interests should be studied and encouraged. The boy who likes to watch trains should be encouraged to make pictures of them. Many children enjoy making a series of pictures of the various incidents in a connected story, and the drawings made by a number of children may be mounted to make a picture book, whether they illustrate a story, or an experience which they have enjoyed together, or which has been vividly described, such as, for example, a visit to a farm or to the Zoo.

II. The development of design in the work of young children.—The drawings of young children suggest that most of them have an instinctive feeling for pattern, but conscious recognition of design or composition comes considerably later than narrative drawing in the child's development, though many children at this stage will enjoy inventing patterns that involve the use of colour.

These patterns may be built up from pieces of coloured paper, or from beads of various shapes, or may be carried out boldly with pastel or with a large brush and water-colour, on large pieces of paper. It may help the children to feel the rhythmic quality of pattern if the movements of the hand in making these large scale designs are sometimes related to other kinds of activity.

The beat of music, or of marching feet, will help to suggest pattern rhythm, and the child who has enjoyed rhythmic exercises is likely to have an added feeling for the rhythmic arrangement of shapes and colour which is fundamental to good pattern.

Coloured paper may be cut into various simple shapes and moved about on a background of paper until the child feels satisfied with the pattern which has been built up. This is an approach to pattern from a different angle, and the method will also be found very helpful in dealing with pictorial as well as with abstract pattern. Usually children realise the pattern made by their pictures more easily when dealing with the simple, bold shapes, which they cut from paper and arrange in this way, than when drawing with the pencil. But there is no end to the media which may be used in making simple patterns.

12. The teacher's function in regard to art in the Infant School.—There is no place for the specialist art teacher in the Infant School. The teacher's function here is not to show the children how to draw, but to give them guidance, and for this she need not be highly qualified as a practitioner, provided that she has sympathy, understanding, imagination and a love of beautiful things. The child should be free to use his own symbols and, if he is not hampered by imposed standards, these symbols will develop as his mind becomes fuller. He is constantly meeting fresh experiences and storing his imagination, not only with fantasy, but with memories of everyday occurrences, and it is the incidents of everyday life that are the real stimulus to imagination, and that form the inspiration of the pictures which most children enjoy making.

It is possible for the teacher to do much by suggestion and encouragement to stimulate ideas. Thus she may direct the children's attention to things worth studying,

—trees or clouds, for instance, or the effects of the wind, —so that their visualisation may be clearer and more ively. She will observe carefully the way in which he children set about their drawing. No doubt most of them will quite naturally or by imitation handle he pastel, brush, or crayon easily and effectively, out at times it may be necessary to correct certain aulty ways of manipulation, which, if left alone, might be difficult to alter later on.

13. Some suggestions on the choice of materials. —It is important, at this early stage especially, that drawings and paintings should be made on a large scale. Bold, vigorous movements of the hand and arm should be ncouraged, and these are impossible when small pieces of paper and finely pointed tools are used.

The use of large sheets of paper undoubtedly raises erious difficulties in crowded classrooms provided with desks which are not suitable for drawing, but these difficulties are being successfully overcome in many chools. Sheets of ply-wood or stout millboard, with a spring clip to hold the paper, form excellent substitutes or drawing-boards. Powder or tempera colour, which an be obtained in tins ready for use, is comparatively cheap and may, therefore, be supplied to the children n the generous quantities which are necessary if large cale work is to be carried on.

B. HANDWORK

14. Handwork in the Infant School.—Handwork occupies an important place in the Infant School. It hould not be treated as an isolated subject, nor ndeed as a subject at all, but it should give eality to the general activities of the school. In the very early stages one of the most valuable forms of andwork for children is to be found in the performance of everyday duties, such as watering plants, attending to flowers and flower pots, arranging things in the room, playing with and stacking away toys, and putting on their own clothes.

The children should have full opportunities for gaining experience in handling the ordinary material that normally surround them and should, in this way, learn something about what can and what cannot be done with them.

Freedom of manipulation in a number of media is desirable, and the teacher may profitably suggest methods of using these media and new ideas of construction.

During the early days of childhood attempts at developing muscular control should be mainly concerned with the larger muscles : fine work with the hands and fingers should not be expected. Such informal work does not imply a lack of progress ; for the teacher will be fully occupied in helping the child to overcome difficulties as they occur. This is the stage when experience is gained in meeting and handling materials and in acquiring technique of a simple kind, and the children should have a rich field from which to choose. They will rarely need formal directions, since the child will find greater scope in experimenting with toys and improvised models of his own invention than in making things to the teacher's design and measurements.

15. Modelling and its uses.—Modelling provides most valuable experience at all stages of a child's development, not only as a means to fuller understanding of the shapes with which he is dealing, but as a means of expression. Children seem to get a special satisfaction from working in three dimensions. When modelling is used as a means to a fuller understanding of the appearance of things, it is sometimes helpful to relate it to the two-dimensional drawing, but at this stage, it will most often be used as a means of expressing ideas of things imagined. Undoubtedly clay is the best material for the purpose ; its cheapness makes it possible to provide each child with a reasonably large quantity and to throw it away when it has become soiled. Much of the modelling done in the schools is dull and spiritless because the children have insufficient material to make any real freedom of treatment possible. It is realised, however, that there are disadvantages in the use of clay in the classroom. It may be messy, and many teachers have abandoned its use for this reason.

III. THE JUNIOR SCHOOL STAGE

A. DRAWING AND PAINTING

16. The transition to the Junior School.—There should be no abrupt change in the methods of teaching when children pass from the Infant to the Junior School. In their drawing and painting, courage, freedom and a lively imagination are still more important than technical accomplishment.

At this stage, a series of exercises, however carefully planned, showing how things should be drawn, often gives the child the impression that his spontaneous efforts are not acceptable : such help may result in making him afraid to commit himself, so that his drawing becomes stereotyped and lacking in individuality. It is the teacher's part to provide suitable materials through which the child can express his ideas with reasonable hope of success, and to help him to see with steadily increasing power the things that he wishes to draw. Even when provided with materials, many children will need the help of suggestion before their ideas can be brought together into pictorial form, but they should be free to accept or reject the suggestions that are made.

In the Junior School it is possible to introduce the first stages of practice in Lettering. The making of free rhythmic patterns with crayon, charcoal, or brush, filled in with washes of colour, will be followed by the making of printed patterns by means of simple printing processes, e.g. printing from potato, stick, or rubber cuts, and these exercises in pattern-making will be linked with the simple craft operations which will be carried on throughout the course.

Even with children under the age of eleven early experiments in pattern-making may be applied to practical ends. Attractive drop-curtains and back-cloths may be made for model theatres and puppet-shows, dolls' houses may be decorated, and patterned papers may be made for the picture-books in which they bring together their pictorial drawings, while children of nine or ten will probably be making use of simple patterns in stitchery and in weaving.

17. What the art course in the Junior School may do for the child.—The child who is given the right experience and the right training in art will, as he progresses through the Junior School, acquire increased facility in the manipulation of the pencil or brush, and increased power of representing on paper what he has in mind ; he will have developed skill and taste in the arrangement of colour and form and have become more vividly aware of what he sees around him.

B. HANDWORK

18. Gradual development based on interest.—In the teaching of handwork also it is important that there should be continuity from the Infant School stage when the child enters the Junior School. Much of what is now done will be directed by the child's own interests, but it should constantly be borne in mind that the child should be learning the right and proper use of materials. Thus, things should not be constructed in paper that are better made in cardboard, or in raffia that would be better made in wool.

The child in the Junior School soon takes a pleasure in making things that he can use. He will put a great deal of work into anything that helps him in his play or in his school interests. It must be remembered that the desire to make things is at the root of all craftsmanship, and unless the teacher is continually giving the children some stimulus to make things the teaching may become formal and a distaste for work may develop.

19. Types of work suitable for juniors.— Children at this stage begin to show a real interest in the traditional crafts : Needlework, Pottery, Weaving, Bookcrafts, and the simple Woodwork involved in making toys. It is the teacher's task to see that the work that is undertaken is well within the power of the children and, while there should be no over-emphasis in the matter of technique, children must not be left to flounder aimlessly for lack of guidance, nor should slovenly work be tolerated. Most children will like to know the best methods of doing things, and it will be necessary to teach certain traditional methods, so that simple technique may be acquired and mastery over simple tools may be gained. As the junior course proceeds there will naturally be a narrower range of materials used, because the children will show a preference for dealing with the more resistant materials, and will tend consequently to discard other materials. At the same time they will realise the need for working with greater precision, and for measuring with a reasonable degree of accuracy. It is not too soon to make a beginning in one of the traditional crafts.

The expression of ideas in a wide variety of media is generally considered to be best associated with the illustration of Geography, History and Literature. Excellent opportunities are afforded in communal work, where the best individual efforts are combined to make a well-constructed and pleasing whole. At this stage children will be allowed considerable freedom in the selection of the things they wish to make and the formal side will not be emphasised, but work clearly beyond their capacity should be discouraged and they should not be left entirely to their own devices as this brings disappointment. The discriminating teacher will welcome the opportunity, however, of giving guidance at the right moment in the selection of material and the methods of construction, sometimes to a whole class, sometimes to individuals. Later in the course there will be lessons in which the teacher gives definite instruction to the class as a whole. It is hardly necessary to emphasise the importance of associating the art work with the handwork activities throughout the course.

20. The organisation of the course ; equipment ; use of staff.—Whether the work which is attempted is connected with the expression of ideas, the illustration of lessons in other subjects, or practice in the fundamentals of a traditional craft, the competence of the teacher will determine the progress that is made and the standard that is reached. No course is likely to be satisfactory unless there is a progressive scheme and the difficulties of the children are adequately dealt with as they naturally occur. While some class lessons will be necessary, there will be many occasions when the class will be split up into groups, so that the children may receive more individual help than is possible in a class lesson. It is not assumed that on these occasions all the pupils are necessarily engaged in craft work. It is the common practice now in well-equipped Junior Schools to provide a " practical " room with adequate floor space, and with tables, chairs or stools, sink, water supply and ample storage.

In the teaching of the traditional crafts much of the apparatus can be made in the school, as, for example, sewing-frames for bookbinding and simple looms for weaving. Such apparatus should be well made and its making will provide sound training in adaptability and resource. The children have in fact reached the stage at which they can make really useful articles of various kinds ; and it is in this way that their desire is strengthened to make things which serve their purpose and the satisfaction is gained that comes from doing things well.

While the Junior Schools may be better served by the appointment of general rather than specialist teachers, there are obvious advantages in making the best use of the special gifts and interests of the various members of the staff. This is especially true of craft teaching in the upper classes of the Junior School. Whenever the organisation of the School permits of some interchange of class teachers, full advantage should be taken of their special knowledge and skill.

21. What the handwork course in the Junior School may do for the child.—At the end of the course, whatever particular form it may have taken, the children should have developed greater muscular control than they had at the beginning and should in consequence be able to deal with more resistant materials. They should have learnt to use a wider range of tools and to work with greater precision. They should have acquired some skill in measurement and construction and should have begun to appreciate the value of careful workmanship.

IV. THE SENIOR SCHOOL STAGE

22. The unity of art.—Recognition of the fundamental unity of Art, whether it is expressed by means of brush and pencil or through some form of handicraft, is essential, especially in the Senior School. The association of the Art teaching with the Craft work in the school

should help teachers and children to realise that Art
is not an isolated subject in the curriculum but has
a bearing on the work and life of the school as a whole,
and also on many aspects of everyday life outside its
walls.

The growing public appreciation, however, of the
value of instruction in craft work should not lead to
undue neglect of drawing and painting ; there will be
many children in the Senior School who will continue
to find great pleasure in draughtsmanship of all kinds,
and even those who find greater satisfaction in craft
work will discover that increased skill in drawing is a
powerful factor in developing those qualities which make
for fine design in craft.

A. DRAWING AND PAINTING

(i) *Self-expression*

23. Self-expression through drawing and painting.
—The attitude of most children to drawing and painting
undergoes a change in the period between the ages of
nine and twelve. They begin to be more interested in
the impressions made on them by external things than
in their own visual images. But this change is usually
a gradual one and there should be no sudden break
in the methods of teaching. Certainly there is no
justification for the abandonment of expressive or
imaginative drawing and painting. No teacher would
think of equipping children with the vocabulary of
a language, a knowledge of its grammar, and the
ability to make the symbols used in writing it, and
then withhold all opportunity for the expression of
ideas by the use of it. Yet it is still possible to
find schools where the whole time given by the older
children to drawing is spent in acquiring knowledge
of the appearance of things and the technique of
draughtsmanship, without making any use of this
knowledge to express ideas. Some teachers, on the other

hand, have taken the view that at no period of the child's school life should any instruction be given which will equip it with a knowledge of technique approaching that of the adult. While it is true that work of very great interest has been done by children taught by those who hold this point of view, there appears to be a desire, even among teachers in countries where the most modern experimental methods have been adopted, to secure a reasonable balance between the acquisition of knowledge and skill and their use in the expression of ideas. This is not the place to make a critical comparison of various methods, but it seems reasonable to suppose that there will be some analogy between the normal child's progress towards adult conceptions and adult technique in graphic art and its progress in the use of the written word. Pretentiousness, self-consciousness and unintelligent imitation are to be avoided in both these means of expression, but few teachers would be prepared to withhold all formal teaching in the study of written and spoken language. Naivety is only a virtue when it is sincere. What is sometimes praised as naivety in the work of an older child may be either an indication of retarded development or an especially objectionable form of insincerity.

It is certainly desirable that the child should be free to use its own language of expression in its own way without the imposition of adult standards by the teacher, but teachers should not have too great a fear of influencing the child. The teacher is not dealing with virgin soil. The average child has been subjected to many influences, good, bad and indifferent, before it comes into contact with the teacher. The child is influenced quite as much indirectly as directly, and often a teacher who carefully avoids actively influencing the child, does in fact exercise an unconscious influence by his or her preferences. The child has an uncanny gift for discovering what the teacher admires.

If, however, representational or imitative drawing and painting is to have its place in the scheme of instruction, the teacher should be sure that it is given at the right time and for the right reason, and that the objects used for study are suitable, and such as will excite the child's interest. Ability to represent faithfully and objectively the whole or a part of something seen may be of great value in connexion with many subjects of the curriculum, especially Nature Study and Science. There are occasions when a child draws an object in order to become better acquainted with its external qualities and to represent these qualities, or the more important of them, quite dispassionately, just as there are occasions when he seeks to express what that object means to him personally.

(ii) *Representational drawing*

24. Representational drawing considered as a means of acquiring knowledge and skill.—Some teachers hold the view that the right time for acquiring technique comes when it is clear that the child finds that his expression of ideas is hampered by his inability to depict a shape in a way which satisfies his growing realisation of the appearance of things, and that he should then be encouraged to study that shape in its simple basic form, and to draw it not only from one but from several points of view. These drawings should not be laborious examples of complete representation, but rather take the form of quickly made notes of the essentials. There is no doubt that most children gain a more comprehensive knowledge of the shape studied if they are allowed to handle the object, and, if it is a complex one, to study its construction and the working of any movable parts.

It is clear that the use of such a method, excellent as no doubt it is, is bound to be subject to the limitation of teaching conditions. Large classes and cramped quarters will make its adoption difficult, and many teachers may still find it necessary to use methods less individual in character.

Some teachers who have to teach large classes feel that they can make the acquisition of knowledge reasonable and interesting to the children if the object or group of objects studied is used for a definite purpose in a later lesson. If this is done, the children should be encouraged to look upon the knowledge they have gained as suggesting ideas rather than demanding realistic reproduction, and they should be free to use any convention they wish, either of shape or colour, in making their design. It is very desirable that the children should be able to handle the objects and take an active part in their arrangement, but, again, the use of this method is affected by the size of classes and exigencies of accommodation. Even when children are making drawings or paintings from the actual objects, their imagination should have free play in their portrayal of these objects.

25. Representational drawing considered as an aid to the appreciation of form and colour.—

Representational drawing may be considered as a means not only of acquiring knowledge, but also of developing a more sensitive appreciation of form, colour, texture, and pattern. This appreciation will come first through the teacher's choice of objects and secondly by his asking the pupils to compare shapes and to discuss them, in relation to other shapes and to their surroundings. It is as absurd to ask children to imitate poor, mean, and characterless shapes, and meretricious pattern, as it would be to ask them to sing inferior music or recite inferior verse. If a part of the lesson is given to discussion and comparison of such qualities as shape, colour, construction, or texture, and if all these qualities are considered in relation to fitness for purpose representational drawing may be one of the most useful aids to the development of the power to choose between what is good and what is less good—one of the most important aims the teacher has in view. If the children also take a share in the grouping and arrangement of the objects under discussion, they are exercising their imagination by doing what they will be called upon to do in everyday life, that is to say by designing with actual things rather than with abstract shapes on paper.

The provision of objects worthy of study is a matter of selection rather than cost. They can be found in the kitchen and the workshop, in fact wherever the use clearly dictates the form. This is not to say that objects which have other qualities should be excluded. The texture and colour of a textile or a piece of pottery may not vitally affect its usefulness, but may be well worth study for its intrinsic beauty ; the effect of light on shape and surface, the modification of colour caused by reflection, and the effect of balance in grouping, are all points of interest for study and discussion.

26. The drawing of plants and flowers, and their decorative treatment.—Representational drawing should by no means be limited to the drawing of inanimate objects. Children are interested in living and growing things. Flowers, leaves and berries have long formed subjects for drawing and painting, but too often little has been done to help the children to see the characteristic growth, form and colour of the various plants studied, the individual beauty which is so often a result of their fitness for their particular struggle for existence. A twig broken from a tree may be beautiful in its detail, but seldom gives any conception of the magnificence of the tree from which it comes. It will not always be easy for children to draw from the growing tree, but even in large towns it will usually be possible for children to make rapid notes in parks and gardens, which they can use when drawing and painting from memory in the classroom. Sometimes it is possible to provide plants growing in pots : the child need not necessarily draw the whole plant, but the part which is drawn will be seen in relation to the plant as a whole. When the drawings from plants and flowers are made with a view to filling a certain space in a pleasing manner the children are called upon to think of those questions of proportion, of spacing and distribution, which are some of the problems of the designer. Incidentally, in connexion with the teaching of nature drawing, it is desirable to stress the need for care and economy in the collection of specimens, so that the study of nature does not lead to the despoiling of the countryside.

27. Representational drawing and imagination.— Children will enjoy drawing one another, especially when engaged in the familiar activities of the school, the home and the street : they will enjoy drawing other things that appeal to them—animals, buildings, ships, motor cars, or aeroplanes.

It may be said that some of these cannot be subjects for representational drawing, because they cannot be studied in the school room, but a drawing from memory may be a representational drawing. It is not unusual for teachers to speak of any drawing which has not been made from sight as an imaginative drawing, but this is not necessarily a correct description. A memory drawing in which an attempt is made to give an accurate representation of an object or a scene need not make any demands on the imagination. If, however, the elements of such a drawing are visualised in such a way as to produce pattern, or express an emotional experience, imagination has played a part.

The teacher should foster the child's desire to arrange the elements of an exercise in picture making in such a way as to make a pleasing arrangement. The imposition of any formal rules of composition is, of course, most undesirable ; but inspiration may be found in the study of good examples of pattern in nature, in the various crafts, and in fine works of art. At a time also when children are drawing and painting flowers, the teacher may show them fine examples of the decorative treatment of plants and flowers, such as reproductions of Chinese and Japanese treatments of these subjects, or our own beautiful XVIII Century English Herbals. Imitation of such examples should, of course, be strongly discouraged, but to withhold from the children the pleasure and profit to be gained from the study of great works of art and craft for fear that they will imitate them is to carry caution too far. Children will often be found to have an instinctive sense of design of which they themselves are scarcely aware, and the skilful teacher will develop this characteristic without allowing their ideas to become stereotyped. Drawing from memory, which comes so naturally to the young child, should be encouraged throughout the whole period of school life. The ability to represent things seen depends more on the power to form and to retain a clear visual image than on manual dexterity, and a lively imagination depends for its expression on the richness and clarity of the store of visual images. The child draws only that part of an object of which it has a more or less clearly defined visual image, and the growth of its powers of draughtsmanship is very much in proportion to the growth of the power to form and retain such images. Much of the memory training will be incidental, the teacher encouraging the children to draw from objects or scenes studied sometime previously, inside the classroom or in their homes, in the streets or elsewhere. Some of the difficulties of overcrowded classrooms, with the consequent difficulties of giving a clear view of an object, will be minimised if the pupils are trained to depend less on sight and more on memory.

(iii) *Training in colour*

28. The " sense of colour."—Very diverse opinions
are held by teachers as to the best method of developing
the child's " sense of colour." There is little doubt
of the importance of its place in any system of art
training. The reaction of young children to the stimulus
of bright colours is evident to all ; but this instinctive
emotional reaction will not give them the capacity to use
colour with judgment. In one way or another, the power
both to enjoy and to use colour with understanding
as well as feeling should be developed.

It has been found that Infants, if given a set of colours,
will often produce paintings which are surprisingly
good from the point of view of " colour," without
having had any colour training. This would seem to
suggest that many very young children are naturally
endowed with a " colour sense," and that it might be
advisable to consider whether theoretical instruction
is necessary at any stage of the child's training. Many
teachers, indeed, hold that the formal teaching of colour
on a scientific basis, even at later stages, is a barrier
to the free use of colour which they hold to be an imperative necessity to the child. They prefer to leave
the child entirely free in its selection and in its arrangement, leading it through its own experiments towards
a use of colour which will be personal and expressive,
and there is no doubt that some of the most stimulating
and interesting work seen in schools has been the result
of this way of teaching. It must be recognised, however,
that the children's choice is bound to be limited by the
materials provided, and that their arrangement of colour
can scarcely escape the influence of their environment,
their proneness to imitation of others, and the teacher's
predilections.

Other teachers prefer to give progressive exercises
in the use of colour. They argue that the child

should be trained to make a discriminating use of colour, based on knowledge, from the earliest stages of school life, starting with a restricted field, which progressively widens, and that the range of colours used should conform to a scientific theory. One advantage of such a system is that it provides a standard nomenclature for colour, thus simplifying teaching and discussion. It is claimed also that it removes many of the difficulties of dealing with design in relation to certain of the crafts, since it makes it possible to supply materials, such as wool, silk, and cotton, in colours standardised in accordance with the same colour system. The danger of attempting to train the " colour sense " by formulating rules is that it may be thought possible to provide a recipe for good colour. Reaction to colour is so personal that it is very difficult, if not impossible, to define " good " colour, and it is certain that no system of training will result in a person who is insensitive to colour becoming a good colourist, any more than a person who has no ear for music can become a good musician. This does not mean that ability to appreciate colour, even in unpromising pupils, cannot be brought out by skilful teaching. Nature may be used as a source of inspiration : the children may study plants and flowers, butterflies, feathers and so on, with a view to making some simple analysis of the colours found and the proportions in which they appear, and the result of their analyses may form the basis of further experiment in the use of colour. Later, works of art and examples of craft may be studied in the same manner.

B. CRAFT WORK

29. The importance of craft work at the Senior School stage.—Handwork and craftwork will form an important part of the curriculum for all types of children in the Senior School. It cannot be too strongly emphasised that the brighter children need this type of activity just as much as those of lower mental capacity.

The acquired skill with the consequent mastery of materials should now be applied systematically to one or more of the traditional crafts, such as Woodwork, Metalwork, Needlework, Weaving, Bookcrafts, the Domestic crafts and Gardening. Both the technical and the cultural aspects will be borne in mind, and there should be no hard and fast line of demarcation between art and craftwork. The articles that are made should be of the right material, fit for their purpose, of sound construction, good proportion and pleasing finish. Stimulating and effective teaching, with appropriate apparatus, should develop in the children the power to make things which give lasting pleasure to use and to see. In such work they will find, later on, occupations for their leisure-time, and through it will be the better able to appreciate good design and sound workmanship.

Effective teaching should lead boys and girls to realise and appreciate the value of good craftsmanship, and their standard of taste should be raised through their own work as well as by examples around them, which should have been carefully chosen by the teacher.

A simple reference library as a source of ideas and information is a necessity, and visits to works, exhibitions, and museums, can be of great value.

(i) *Some general principles relating to craftwork.*

30. The transition to the Senior School.—The improved facilities for art and crafts in the Junior School have already been noted. An even more generous provision is now made in Senior Schools. In addition to the rooms for Woodwork, Metalwork and Housecraft, special rooms are being provided and equipped for art and crafts. The term " centre " is fast disappearing, and the new conditions have led to a realisation that handwork must be an integral part of the school course.

Under these conditions schools are able to give adequate instruction to all types of pupils.

It will be realised that the training in the Junior School has been a general training in handiness. The child has been encouraged to explore the possibilities and limitations of the materials he has been using, and to consider his reactions to these materials. What he has been gradually getting is a generalised aptitude, and not a specialised skill in any one direction or in any one material.

In the Senior School the pupil will in the main, pursue one definite craft. With boys this will usually, for various reasons, be Woodwork, while girls will naturally find their interests in the crafts of the home such as Needlework.

An increasing amount of time is now being devoted to art and craft work in the majority of schools. The crafts which have been begun in the Junior School stage will be continued on progressive lines in the Senior School. The interest and confidence which have been established in the Junior School will be carried further, and a higher standard of technique will be expected while emphasis will be laid on good design and good finish.

The effect of the occasional very fine piece of work that is executed in school should not be overlooked ; it extends far beyond the child who is responsible for it. A single achievement of this kind may well play its part in raising the standard of work normally done in a particular school. One has only to observe a boy handling a really well-made article to see his joy in the fineness of the work, and his growing appreciation of the beauty of form.

All schools will not do the same type of work. Some may wish to make articles that will be useful in the garden or for poultry-keeping, others, where a strong Science bias exists, may make a good deal of Science apparatus, though the majority will probably concentrate on cabinet-making. Whatever line of development is followed, it is essential that the fundamental technique should be soundly taught.

31. Systematic training in crafts and development of standards of taste.—The close association between the technical and the cultural aspects of Art and Craft training should be maintained. The experience of recent years in the development of constructional work, planned in accordance with the principles of true craftsmanship, has shown that children in the Senior Schools are capable of producing work of high quality, provided that they are guided by a teacher who is master of his craft and skilful in the art of teaching. If what has been done in the previous stages is consolidated and the technical basis at this stage is sound, it should be possible to reach a high standard.

Such a course of training on the lines indicated above naturally aims at inculcating a respect for, and an appreciation of, all that is fine and honest in craftsmanship and design, and a distaste for mean, ugly and insincere work. This systematic training in traditional crafts, such as those already mentioned, should lead, on the one hand, to the acquisition of greater skill in sound construction and the right use of materials and, on the other hand, to a keen sense of what is and what is not worthy of admiration.

Through the use of the lantern and the epidiascope, through visits to museums and through specimens placed on view in the classroom and craftrooms, much can be done to secure a standard of taste that will influence children in their outlook on what surrounds them, whether in the home, street, village, town, or countryside.

32. Need of using all available skill in the staff.— It is obvious, that in a Senior School a high standard of work cannot be expected unless the teachers have some measure of ability as practitioners, and it is very desirable that the organisation of the staff should be sufficiently fluid to bring all the available skill to bear on the teaching of Art and Craft. Even when the teaching is in the hands of specialist teachers, the services of other members of the staff, who may have special gifts as practising craftsmen, should be used as fully as the organisation of the school permits, while the specialist teachers of Art and Craft will often benefit by taking part in the teaching of other subjects.

33. The allocation of time.—It is not proposed to suggest any definite allocation of time to Art and Craft, but it should be clearly understood that, while a reasonable balance should be held between the various branches of what is taught, there is no reason why the period nominally set aside for art teaching should always be spent in drawing and painting, and the period allocated to craft teaching entirely given to the manual operations involved in the various crafts. The total time allocated to Art and Craft should be used to the best advantage.

It will strengthen the feeling that their work is real if the children are encouraged to carry it through in a reasonable time. While the time factor should not in any way dominate, it is not without importance in the training of senior pupils.

34. Differences of ability and how they can be met.—One of the important results of reorganisation of schools has been to emphasise the need for discrimination in the curriculum for the various types of ability in children. As in other subjects so in Art and Craft the needs and capacities of the children must be taken into account. Many Senior Schools are large enough to allow for effective classification and differentiation, and teachers thus have the opportunity for devising appropriate schemes of instruction for the less able children. Sufficient experience will have been gained of the capacity of these children in the previous stages to give an indication of what treatment will be most suitable for them in the Senior School course.

With the slower pupils it will often be sufficient to allow more time to complete their work ; with others defects in observational powers and a lack of manipulative skill will necessitate work of a simpler nature. The maintenance of interest is essential for them all, so that a careful selection of " projects " that make an appeal to them is desirable.

35. Accommodation and equipment.—While it is obvious that work of the highest standard can only be expected where satisfactory accommodation and equipment are provided, it is possible to teach art and craft successfully in schools which have no accommodation beyond the ordinary classroom, provided that some form of flat table is provided and adequate provision is made for the storage of equipment and work in progress. If it can possibly be arranged, a classroom should be set aside for this purpose and the place of the desks should be taken by tables and chairs. In some schools portable table-tops are used, supported on trestles which can, when desired, serve as easels. The equipment needed for most of the crafts is not extensive, and much of it can be made by the children themselves, if they are able to use woodworking tools. In Woodwork itself, for instance, while adequate equipment is, of course, necessary, much can be done to show that it is possible to use a limited tool supply to the best advantage, so that the boys may see that they can continue the work as a hobby in later years, and may be encouraged to acquire for themselves small kits of tools for use at home in their spare time, and as the foundation of a larger collection for use when they have left school. For the same reason it is useful to get them to make for their own use bench hooks, shooting boards and other appliances, and to encourage resourcefulness in the improvisation of equipment such as cramps, where there is any shortage in the supply.

36. Handwork and the use of leisure.—Whereas handwork is included in the Junior School curriculum because doing is often the best way of learning, in the Senior School the teacher must have his eye on the after-life of the pupils, and handwork should be taught and encouraged as a pursuit for leisure. Many schools are providing facilities for voluntary work outside school hours, and craftwork is a valuable adjunct to many leisure time pursuits which are begun in school days and continued as hobbies in later life. Effective teaching with appropriate apparatus of the kind that the child can obtain for himself will do much to aid this development. Some schools, too, have found that Craft Guilds provide a valuable stimulus.

(ii) *Design and the crafts*

37. The making of designs and patterns.—The kind of teaching that holds a reasonable balance between the acquisition of knowledge and skill and their use in expressive drawing and painting, will probably ensure that many children will continue to enjoy picture making ; nevertheless it is very desirable that children should not be encouraged to think of Art as concerned only with designs made on canvas or paper and used for decoration. The patterns made by the younger children may have no immediate purpose except to give pleasure, but the pleasure which comes from the orderly and rhythmic arrangement of shapes and colours should soon lead to a study of design in relation to craftwork. It is possible, however, to secure this relation between theory and practice from almost the first exercises, and in very simple ways.

There has been much confusion of thought as to what is implied by the term " design." By some people design has been thought to mean "ornament," by others to mean the use of the pencil or brush to fill a space with an arrangement of shapes and colours. It should be clear, however, that design is fundamental, and that fitness for purpose, the right use of tools and materials and the production of something worth living with are all considerations which have to be borne in mind by the designer. Surface decoration, if any be required, is only one factor in the whole problem and can only be considered in relation to the whole.

38. The first steps in crafts involving the use of patterns.

—As soon as the first fundamental exercises in pattern making have been done, the children, having made patterns with the brush or crayon or with cut paper, using the simple shapes with which they are familiar, such as the straight line, the spot, simple curves and other shapes, can soon be led to see the waste of time involved in the repetition of the pattern units by hand. It is not a big step to the devising of various means of reproducing the units, by cutting the patterns in such materials as are suitable for the purpose of making a die or stamp. They are faced then with a choice of material, whether potato, wood, lino, rubber, or cork, and also with a choice of tools, and the pattern they make will be affected by the limitations of the materials and tools which they choose. They will soon discover that it is possible to cut patterns in linoleum blocks which cannot be cut so conveniently in potato ; that prints made from potato cuts have a characteristic quality compared with prints made from a lino block, and that this quality is one that may be very desirable for certain purposes. They will discover that knife and gouge have each its proper use in cutting blocks for pattern making, so that even in this very elementary craft there is a strong element of choice. However elementary may be this attempt to make the best use of materials and tools and to bring out their characteristic qualities, the pupil has been placed on the right road to an understanding of designing in the material. These blocks may be used for the production of patterned papers, for which there are many practical uses, as, for example, in book-binding ; later they may be used in fabric-printing, when other and more complex problems will have to be solved, e.g. the choice of fabrics, the use of dyes, and the methods of printing and fixing, all of which afford valuable experience.

(iii) *The choice of crafts*

39. Principles which should determine the choice —It is realised that conditions governing the supply of materials have had a considerable effect in determining the choice of crafts to be taught in Elementary Schools, often with the unfortunate result that the choice has been determined or limited by the cheapness of the material used, or the saleability of the article made.

The operations involved should at all stages be of such a character as to make it possible for the pupil to reach a good standard of craftsmanship : it is better to make a simple thing well than to make a complex thing badly.

The craft chosen should afford opportunity for sound craftsmanship.   This can only result from good material used to the best advantage, from sound construction and from the proper use of tools.   When, through the imagination of the designer, all these factors are brought into a right relation, further study of the craft will provide clear opportunities for progressive development. Fundamentally, the problem of the architect who designs a building, or of the designer who plans a complex piece of machinery, and that of the child who cuts a lino block, weaves a scarf or binds a book, are the same; the difference is only one of degree.   From this it follows that a training in good craftsmanship, even of the simplest kind, is a training in the appreciation of good design in a very wide sense.

When judged by the standards indicated above, many of the rather trivial occupations which have been taught in Elementary Schools will be seen to have little value. Fortunately, there are enough crafts providing the right kind of experience, which have not only a tradition behind them owing to their association with the history of human progress, but also a reality because of their place in the everyday life of the present time.

Space will not allow of more than a few general remarks about each of them. While a text book dealing with methods of art teaching in general may be of doubtful value, a book which describes the operations involved in a craft, gives some account of its historical development, and is well supplied with illustrations of really good examples of craftsmanship, may be very helpful both to teacher and pupils.

40. The traditional crafts.—The traditional crafts to which these older children will now be introduced will make considerably more demands not only upon their ability to use their hands but also upon their ability to use their wits, than the simpler work which they did in the Junior School. Such crafts as Woodwork, Metalwork, Weaving, and Pottery, are crafts with a long tradition behind them and they all have a well-developed technique. No one can become really adept at any of these crafts without in some way having mastered its technique, and it is clearly necessary at the Senior School stage to give some definitely formal instruction. The extent to which this is done will vary from craft to craft, but it is obviously unwise to stress it to such a degree as to discourage the child. The teacher will rather encourage his pupil to attempt such work as will lead the pupil to see for himself the reason for acquiring a real technique and therefore to submit willingly to the necessary routine, because he can appreciate the purpose behind it. In Woodwork, for example, a boy must learn how to make the basic joints if he is ever to make anything worthy of the craft. In Metalwork there are various tool processes demanding great care and accuracy, and these processes, while they can be most boring and discouraging if taught unintelligently, can, on the other hand, become really interesting, if approached in the right spirit. The same remark is largely true also of such crafts as Weaving and Pottery. In all these crafts the approach to the technique should be a purposeful one. A boy or girl who is encouraged to look ahead will see the purpose of learning the technique, and will be inspired by the vision of coming achievement, so that present difficulties will be no great obstacle. When the crafts are approached in this spirit, older pupils are often willing to put in a great deal of hard work in order to master a technique which they realise is necessary, if they are to achieve what they wish to accomplish.

(iv) Some of the more important crafts

41. Needlework.—Needlework* as a craft has immense educational possibilities on account both of its constructive and of its decorative qualities. On the constructive side it includes a study of the varied and interesting ways in which a length of material can be so cut and stitched and arranged as to form serviceable and pleasing garments. The craft here is usefully allied to both weaving and knitting, by which material is actually produced and its varying qualities made apparent.

The making up of material, in general, involves a wide range of processes varying in difficulty from the simple operation of hemming a handkerchief to the

---

* Needlework is dealt with more fully in Chapter VIII of this Handbook.

most advanced forms of tailoring. A girl can only
master such processes as are within her powers, and
careful thought is necessary on the part of the teacher
to devise a method of approach to the craft and to
select processes which are compatible with the age,
proficiency and outlook of children.

Needlework will not have its full appeal unless construction, measurement and fitting are studied in
relation to stitchery both by hand and machine, and
unless these aspects of the craft are illuminated by a consideration of the quality and character of the material
used. Needlework can be a very dull business, if the
craft is limited, on the one hand, to calculations and
drafting and measurement and, on the other, to the
acquirement of proficiency in stitchery, or if it is shorn
of its interesting possibilities for design in colour and
shape.

In addition to the art of constructing garments, and
closely allied to it, is embroidery, which will include
designing not merely in stitches overlaid upon material,
but in the varying qualities and textures of materials
applied in some considered form.

In a school, something must be selected from this
important craft that will be within the children's power
both to master and to express. Generally speaking,
the work should aim at giving them sufficient skill to
use the craft for the practical purpose of making simple
garments and household necessities, and mending them
when worn, and also to experience the pleasure of
expressing their own interests and taste in design.

42. Weaving.—Weaving is one of the oldest crafts,
and it always has been and still is among the most
important. The fact that the hand-loom has very
largely passed out of use in industry does not lessen
the value of the craft as a means to the end the teacher
has in view.

Hand-loom weaving gives almost unlimited scope for experiments in colour changes and varied textures. The character of woven patterns can be very charming, even when worked on the simplest of looms and within the strict limitations imposed by warp and weft.

It has also the advantages that material of a high standard of craftsmanship and of an eminently useful type may be woven on looms of very simple construction, such as can be made in the school by the pupils themselves. This craft also provides for progressive development, from the use of simple looms suitable for children in Infant Schools or Junior Schools to the use of the table-looms or foot-power looms in the top classes of Senior Schools.

At this later stage, when the use of the foot-,or table-,loom is reached, care should be taken to provide a loom that is accurately made of well seasoned wood. The use of metal should be avoided, as far as possible, since it is liable to rust. The loom should be of such a width that it can be used by children without undue strain. A table-loom is of advantage in that it takes up no floor space, and, if a good type is chosen, it will do all that a foot-loom can do, and with greater ease in the setting up.

It is important that the children should learn to use the right kind of yarn for warp and weft, and experiments can be tried in the growing and use of flax.

At some time, spinning might be practised, with progressive treatment from the use of a home-made spindle to the use of the wheel; while experiments in the preparation of wool from the fleece and in the use of natural dyes will be found to be of great value. The children can be encouraged to make every use of local resources, and to construct their own booklets with pictures, diagrams, notes and records. It is possible in this way to find a real centre of interest for the children, and in some cases to revive interest in local occupations of the past, or to make the life of a modern mill take on a new significance.

43. Book production.—Book production includes all the processes concerned with making, preserving, and decorating, printed or pictorial records. These processes, some of which in themselves are crafts, are brought into close relationship one with another, and are made real and purposeful, when they are employed to achieve a common aim, the making of a book. Thus, the children may be engaged not only in the actual business of binding books, but in lettering and writing, designing the layout of pages, making illustrations by pencil, pen or brush, making lino- or wood-cut prints, making patterns for " end papers " and designs for covers in paper or other material, and, if the equipment is available, typography. Here they find opportunities for selection and arrangement of colour and material, inventiveness in the making of patterns and designs and for the exercise of real craftsmanship. Unless it is associated with other crafts and made real and purposeful in the manner indicated above, the practice of bookbinding is apt to resolve itself into a series of graded exercises demanding neatness and precision, ingenuity in using waste material, or arithmetical calculation.

For success in this branch of craftwork skill must be acquired in certain basic operations : cutting, folding, pasting, covering, hinging, stitching, and pressing. To these may be added the making of potato-cuts, lino- and wood-blocks for use in decoration, tooling or printing of cloth, and blind or gilt tooling of leather. Where the work is sufficiently advanced, the children will be capable of single-section and multi-section binding, case-binding, and quarter, half, and full binding.

Admirable typographical work, in which good design has shown itself in the beautiful lay-out of a printed page, is being accomplished in a good many schools and its inclusion has been fully justified where type setting and printing constitute a valuable part of a course of work in book production. The success of this work, however, depends on the use of a good type and machine for printing, and the cost of the equipment may prohibit its general introduction in schools.

44. Lettering.—Although mentioned as one of the crafts comprised within the general title of Book-production, Lettering is so important that it is desirable to deal with it separately and in rather more detail.

Training in the appreciation of good lettering is very desirable as a part of every school course. Contemporary lettering owes much to the Roman alphabet and designers of type have been influenced by the Roman letter, particularly in matters of shape and proportion. Photographs or reproductions of the Roman and other good alphabets are available, and it is advisable to have a range of good examples at hand for display in the classroom. Much of the modification which the Roman letter has undergone is due to the influence of the pen-made letter. The study and practice of the written letter are therefore of especial value, apart from the fact that pen lettering bears a closer relationship to ordinary handwriting than does that made by the pencil or brush. Children should be encouraged to acquire a formal book hand, written with metal pens (usually known as " one-stroke " pens). At the same time they may tackle simple pen-made capitals, but it is only at a later stage that they will have enough subtlety of discrimination to learn to draw the Roman and other alphabets.

Children should be dissuaded from the all too prevalent practice of spurious decoration. A piece of good lettering is beautiful because of the perfection of the forms, the spacing and the layout or arrangement, and no amount of so-called decoration added to lettering which does not already possess these qualities will make it appear beautiful. Children may be expected to acquire a certain standard of taste that will enable them to discriminate between good and bad printing and will awaken their interest in the many and varied examples of lettering which they see every day.

45. Fabric-printing.—The experience which can be gained by children in printing patterned papers from blocks made of potato, lino, wood or other material may lead to the more complex problems which have to be mastered in the block printing of fabrics. Not only does the cutting of the block for the new purpose present a fresh problem,—for it must be made suitable for printing a surface of a kind very different from that of the paper which the children have used in the past,—but the actual operation of printing requires a higher degree of dexterity and judgment, which can only come with practice and intelligent forethought. There are available fabric-printing inks which are reasonably permanent and which do not stiffen the material unduly. Experiments may be carried out in the use and fixing of dyes, where accommodation and equipment make this possible, and where the teacher has had some experience of this branch of the craft. There is no reason to think that fabric-printing makes undue demands on the children's skill. It has produced results which are quite remarkable, not only in Senior but also in Junior Schools, where some of the most interesting work has been done.

The process known as " screen-printing " provides another practical method by which fabric printing may be carried out.

46. Pottery.—Few crafts provide so rich a background of tradition as Pottery, and it is certainly one of the most valuable in providing a well balanced training in skill and in promoting appreciation of form, colour and texture. While, however, most schools can provide for some elementary experience of the craft, few are able to provide the complete equipment which is necessary in order to get the best results.

For schools which possess suitable rooms and equipment pottery offers a field for experiment which, for diversity and educative value, perhaps has no superior among the crafts. So far as concerns equipment, the main expense involved is in the provision of a kiln for firing the ware. Apart from this, the essential tools and apparatus for pottery making may be acquired for a very small sum, or they can quite readily be made in the school workshop. The difficulty of firing the ware may sometimes be overcome by co-operation with Art Schools, many of which are equipped with pottery kilns ; or alternatively it is possible to construct for a few pounds a satisfactory kiln of a type that is capable of meeting the normal requirements of a school.

A throwing-wheel is clearly a desirable piece of equipment for a pottery class, but it is not essential that one should be provided at the outset, as there are many kinds of pottery which do not require its use. Indeed, in view of the fact that the throwing-wheel can only be used by one pupil at a time the instructor must necessarily rely largely upon such methods as pressing, tile making, slab building, coiling and casting, all of which are standard processes of pottery making and are well within the capacity of the average child ; moreover, they are admirably adapted for class work.

47. Woodwork and Metalwork.—Although Woodwork and Metalwork are the most expensive in equipment of the crafts and require specially furnished rooms of their own, they are rightly the crafts most universally taught to the older boys in Elementary Schools. The materials employed enter into the construction of very many of the articles in common use in daily life ; they offer just enough resistance to cutting and shaping to make suitable demands on the muscular control of boys of this age; they call for the skilled use of a variety of tools; and they involve a wide range of technical processes, which can be so graded as to produce a progressive course of instruction. Though it is possible to reach a level of accomplishment which is satisfactory in itself at each stage of such a course, there is no upper limit of achievement, however long a boy may remain at school. Moreover, what he has learned in school, whether much or little, will be of the greatest value to him in after life, whatever his occupation may be. The value of general handiness needs no emphasis, but, if the course has been rightly conceived, it will do more than produce this quality. It will give a boy an insight into the construction of many things and help him to understand why they are made as they are; it will enable him to appreciate good craftsmanship in wood and metal and thus add variety to his interests; it will help him later to select, for his own home, articles that are well constructed and well designed; and, to some at least, it will give the power to design and make many articles which demand a high standard of craftsmanship.

Among all the crafts, Woodwork and Metalwork may claim pre-eminence not only for the range of beautiful objects that can be made and the variety of processes involved, but also for the degree of accuracy necessary in working the material employed. An error of $\frac{1}{16}$th of an inch in a woodwork joint, or of $\frac{1}{100}$th of an inch in a metalwork fitting, results in a misfit which is easily perceived by the pupil responsible. He does not need to have the error shown to him by his teacher. To perceive an error without having it pointed out by the teacher is the best way for a boy to learn the value of accuracy; to make a thing accurately and to know that it has been made accurately will give him self-respect as a craftsman.

48. Woodwork.—(a) *Successive stages of the work.*—The peculiar qualities of wood have led to fixed design in the traditional three main tools,—the saw, the plane and the chisel ; and the shape and form of these tools in turn have given rise to a definite technique. It is therefore of considerable importance that, if a reasonably high standard of craftsmanship is to be reached in school, the necessity for concentration on tool manipulation in the early stages of Woodwork should be realised.

It is idle to expect, however, that the power of cutting and shaping accurately in wood can be attained by the boy without a definite training in technique. He must gain a mastery over the tools he uses, and the teacher must demonstrate how they should be used. But such instruction should be limited, as far as possible, to the early part of the course, where, if it is given systematically on the right lines, the boys can acquire sufficient familiarity with the necessary processes, the correct use of the tools and the making of the common joints, in a very few months. As soon as this necessary technical skill has been acquired, it is desirable that it should be applied to some useful end, and some teachers, even in the early stages, prefer to arrange for small useful articles to be made which give practice in the processes that have to be taught.

The next step is to enlarge the scope of the instruction so that articles can be made which will serve some definite purpose in connexion with the school or the home. Individual needs and interests can now be considered, and the boys can play some part in designing the things they make. As they become more self-reliant they may rightly be allowed greater latitude, so that finally there will be considerable variety in the type of work done, not only by one boy and another, but even by one school and another.

In some schools opportunities are afforded for the girls to receive instruction in Woodwork. Much of this work is still in the experimental stage, but the results so far are encouraging.

(b) *Design in Woodwork.*—The wise teacher does not expect a developed taste in his pupils. It is part of his business to ensure that they receive the right sort of impressions, and look at and study the right sort of articles. Their early attempts at design should be discussed with the teacher and modified for one good reason or another. The particular proportions of a rectangle for instance, or the particular sweep of a curve, should be criticised by reference to some other piece of work which has been accepted as in good taste ; and the arrangement of colour and tone and the modification of outline should be considered in relation to the particular woods used. In this way the boys will gradually develop their own standards in Design, selecting this quality and rejecting that, and so expressing in some measure their own individuality and their own individual tastes.

Work which is inspired by ideas such as these may quite fairly be described as creative. Its quality will depend largely on the teacher's own background. A teacher who takes advantage of every opportunity that offers itself of seeing exhibitions of good craftsmanship and who makes a habit of studying good publications on design will have his mind stored with ideas through which he may stimulate his boys to turn out pleasing specimens of craftsmanship.

49. Woodwork : some practical details.—(a) *Choice of woods ; importance of good finish.*—Whatever is made should be soundly constructed and as well finished as the nature of the object requires in each case. Even if the course consists of no more than " rural carpentry," pride of workmanship should be evident and the objects made should be shaped true and made weather-proof where necessary by creosoting or painting.

Articles made in deal or white wood, which form part of every course, should bear the mark of accurate cutting and careful planing and, when their purpose demands it, should be suitably treated with paint, varnish or cellulose.

At least some experience with hard woods is, however, desirable for every boy and it is here that most scope will be found for accuracy and good finish. Care should be taken in the selection of the milder forms of hard woods, such as Japanese oak and straight-grained mahogany, and the quality should be as good as can be afforded. Though hard woods are more expensive than soft woods, well-finished articles made of the former take a considerable time to construct, and the average cost of timber over a year will probably not be found to be unduly increased by the inclusion of hard woods.

When an article is completed, it should be " finished," so as to stand the handling it is likely to get. The " finish " will depend on the nature of the wood and the purpose which the article made is intended to serve. Opinion differs as to the advisability of using veneer ; French polishing may sometimes be appropriate or even indispensable, but for most work polishing with linseed oil and wax will be sufficient.

(b) *Sharpening the tools.*—It is clearly most important that tools should be kept sharp and in good condition, so that no time is wasted during the lessons. If the boys are trained to sharpen the tools themselves, they will be better able to recognise when they are in good condition and to take proper care of tools of their own. The ability to sharpen tools can only be acquired gradually ; most teachers, therefore, keep a small stock of old tools on which beginners can practise so as to avoid damage to those in general use.

(c) *Working Drawings.*—It is not necessary for the boys to make drawings of their work in the early stages of the course. The main use of the workshop is for practical work. In some schools the drawings are done in the classroom, and, as a rule, the boys are taught to read drawings before they attempt to make them. Full-size drawings are helpful. There is no need to teach " oblique " or " isometric " projections at any stage.

.Towards the end of the course the boys should be able to make and read simple working drawings, as well as " blue prints," such as are used by workmen. It is suggested that the recommendations of the British Standards Institution on drawing should be adopted.

(d) *Notes and Records.*—Short talks and informal discussions will be found useful at all times, but much time can be saved if cyclostyled notes and instructions are freely used. The boys should keep notes in folders or note-books in which they make simple sketches of the objects constructed, and enter the quantity and cost of the material used, the time spent on the job and such other points as may be relevant. The information thus recorded will, amongst other uses, be found valuable as data for exercises in the Mathematics lessons. In addition, the teacher will probably find it necessary to adopt some system for recording the work done by each boy in his class so that the time factor may be watched and a comprehensive course ensured for all.

(e) *Books and illustrations.*—It need hardly be said that the workshop for woodwork or metalwork should be well arranged and tidy. Suitable illustrations should be displayed on the walls, in frames made by the boys, and some space should be set aside for the exhibition from time to time of really good specimens of work. It should also contain a small reference library of carefully chosen books and periodicals.

50. Metalwork.—Metalwork is a craft that is gaining popularity in the schools for many reasons.

The material used is one in which the craftsmen of every period have delighted to work. It is common and cheap, and from it are made a great many articles in daily use. Through practice in the craft a boy acquires general handiness and facility in the use of tools, and the power of working to fairly fine limits.

While in the graphic arts it is possible to allow very considerable freedom,—for pencil marks can be removed, and paint can be washed out,—with metalwork every tool takes its toll and no mark can be removed. Hence the worker in metal cannot like the artist change his method of approach as he goes on, but must be at pains to execute what is already a clear conception in his mind.

Metalworking processes cover a wide range and therefore naturally lend themselves to schemes of various types. The two main branches of metalwork now taught in schools may be described as :

(*a*) Formal Metalwork—in materials such as iron, steel, and brass.

(*b*) Constructive Hammered Metalwork—usually in copper.

(a) *Formal Metalwork.*—This term is intended to cover a wide range of processes such as filing, fitting, turning, tapping, drilling, soldering and brazing, which are needed in the making of a large variety of appliances and articles. Here again as in woodwork, on account of the resistance of the material used, definitely formal teaching is needed if the work is to be successfully done. A sound foundation in fundamental processes must be established before the attempt is made to specialise in any particular direction.

The possibilities in metalwork are many and varied. In some schools the course has centred round the making of simple tools, covering all the fundamental processes and demanding a reasonably high standard of accuracy. A boy who is given possession of the tools he has made may well be inclined to add to his collection later on and to devote some of his leisure time to metalwork as a hobby. In other schools the boys have made the majority of their garden implements and tools, and have found in this work scope for considerable ingenuity in adapting and modifying to their own use types of the things they see around them.

In some schemes, again, a useful course has been found in the making of mathematical apparatus, such as plane tables, theodolites, angle-meters, or clinometers, for use in surveying ; while in others it is based on the making of much of the science apparatus, e.g. appliances for registering or measuring heat, a model of a water circulation system, or various types of electrical gear and wireless appliances.

(b) *Constructive Hammered Metalwork.*—Hammered metalwork introduces a boy to a wide range of processes which he is unlikely to learn in other ways and which may be very useful to him in later life. It is an attractive craft, providing scope for some individuality in design and affording the pleasure that comes from making really useful things. The beauty of the objects made depends on their form and workmanship rather than on any extraneous decoration, e.g. by repoussé tool marks, a process which should be discouraged. Since the articles made are raised from sheet metal, usually copper and occasionally gilding metal, they are essentially hollow ware, ranging from simple ash trays to large trays, pin and flower bowls, cups and vases, sports trophies and so on.

The woodwork or metalwork shop is the most convenient room for this craft, but it may be done in the craft-room or an ordinary classroom if there are facilities for annealing and soldering. The work, however, tends to be noisy, and for this reason arrangements must be made to prevent the disturbance of neighbouring classes. It is usual to draw on paper a careful representation of the articles to be made, since once they are raised into shape the form cannot be altered. The copper or gilding metal is carefully cleaned, and the blemishes are stoned out. The metal is then marked out to shape and worked to form, the joints being hard soldered and soft soldered. It is pickled at every stage to clean it and the final planishing must be done with mirror-bright hammers and stakes.

Some of the tools required may be made by the boys for themselves and it is often found convenient to delay the introduction of hammered metalwork until the boys have done some formal metalwork.

(iv) *Some applications of school Woodwork and Metalwork*

51. Repairs and the making of equipment and apparatus.—(a) *Repairs.*—Since much of the handwork of the home consists in executing repairs, the school course should, whenever possible, afford boys practice in such jobs as the repair of furniture, garden equipment and science apparatus.

(b) *Making of equipment and apparatus.*—Part of the time allocated to Woodwork and Metalwork may well be devoted to the making of equipment, for use in some of the crafts,* such as a loom or a printing-press, and of apparatus needed for practical Science, Gardening and various school activities.

Sometimes the apparatus may most conveniently be made in one of the Craft rooms or in the Science laboratory, and at other times in the workshop itself,

---

* *See* Sections 19, 34 and 56 of this Chapter.

but in any case the teacher responsible for Woodwork and Metalwork should advise as to constructional details and as to the selection of boys capable of undertaking the work.

(c) *Larger* " *projects.*"—Some schools have found it possible to carry out more ambitious projects such as the construction of a small sports pavilion or the complete furnishing of a room in the model flat which sometimes forms part of the accommodation for House-craft for girls in the same school.

52. Handicraft in rural schools.—The rural school presents a somewhat different problem from that of the town school. Some rural schools in unreorganised areas have to be content at present with accommodation and equipment for handicraft which are not quite of the same standard as that commonly found in urban areas, and the work attempted has necessarily to be of a simpler character and more restricted in range. This is a condition, however, which is rapidly passing. The rural school, indeed, has an advantage in finding opportunities, that do not always exist in town schools, of applying its handicraft to many real needs, which may not arise in urban communities, e.g., in connexion with the implements required for the cottage, the home or the farm. For these it may often be necessary to use materials that are ready to hand and to improvise. But, though the materials used will often be rough, a boy who has been trained in the basic processes will suffer no undue handicap.

At all stages of the course there is a wealth of objects to which these processes can be applied, from the simple garden label (suitably painted and lettered) or the seed-box to the wheel-barrow or the greenhouse. In schools where small livestock is kept the range of useful objects that may be made is considerably widened. It would include such things, for instance, as hutches, bee-hives, coops, trap-nests or bins and fowl-houses.

Even with a limited equipment much profitable work may also be done in metal, either used in conjunction with wood, or alone, e.g., in the making of certain garden tools such as hoes, rakes, mechanical seeders, tree-pruners ; latches for gates, garden rollers from strip-iron and old oil drums filled with concrete, markers for tennis courts, apparatus for weather observations such as sunshine recorders and anemometers. Still other materials may sometimes be used with advantage, e.g., cement for making steps for the rock-garden or ponds for water plants, bird baths and pedestals for sundials, etc. Occasionally opportunities may arise for little jobs in brickwork or stonework, or in thatching. In the country repair-work is almost as important as new construction, and considerable ingenuity may often be called for in making good some defective piece of equipment about the school or brought from home. In some schools cobbling has been taught with successful results and this craft is equally applicable to urban schools of certain types.

The increasing tendency to concentrate Senior scholars in larger numbers in Area Rural Schools has made it possible to provide generously for the school garden, with its appurtenances of sheds for the storage of tools and crops, cold frames and greenhouses, potting and repair sheds ; and the conception of the outdoor accommodation of the rural school as an estate for the development and management of which the scholars are responsible is growing. Some schools have even found it possible to teach the principles of the petrol engine and to utilise it in various ways. In all this work there is ample scope for the exercise of craft skill and many schools have been quick to seize their opportunities.

V. FACILITIES FOR ART AND CRAFT

53. Use of the ordinary classroom for art and craft lessons.—If the school has a specially equipped Art room, the work of the Art teacher is greatly facilitated, but if the only available accommodation for Art and Craft teaching is a classroom which is used for general purposes, some adaptation of existing conditions must be made. For the Art lessons, the most suitable classroom furniture has been found to be flat-topped tables with chairs, for some kind of rearrangement is then possible for the Art lessons. The children should preferably use drawing boards (or a suitable substitute such as ply-board or heavy millboard), either resting on their knees in the most comfortable position for drawing, or merely to supply a better surface than the desk itself often provides. It will be found possible, with movable tables, to place those children who are actually drawing from objects so that the light falls from the left. If the classroom equipment is difficult to move, it will be wise to adapt the scheme of instruction to the conditions and reduce drawing from sight to a minimum, training the children to rely on memory as much as possible.

For Craft teaching in the ordinary classroom, some kind of bench is almost a necessity, although surprising results are secured in schools where ordinary desks only are available. A fixed bench running along a wall under the main window will be found to be of great assistance, and has the advantage of economising space. As an alternative, one or two trestle tables of a portable type will be found useful. In classroom conditions it is advisable to allow the children to carry on a variety of work so that both desks and benches are in use at the same time.

54. Materials and equipment in art and craft.—As far as actual materials for drawing are concerned, experience has shown that children of all ages are more

encouraged to produce " live " and vigorous work if
they have opportunities for working on a large scale,
whereas small pieces of paper often result in timid work.
Loose paper is preferable to drawing books which are
not only inconvenient to use, but tend to standardise
the size and type of drawing. Children should be given
sheets of paper as large as can be easily dealt with
on their desks or tables, and the provision of large
sheets of paper need not entail additional expense.
Kitchen lining paper (20″ × 25″ at 5½d. per quire) or
grey sugar paper (20″ × 25″ at 3s. 4d. per ream) are
both excellent for the purpose, especially when charcoal
or soft crayon is used as a drawing tool. It is good
for the children to form a habit of storing their drawings
neatly and in the order in which they are made, and
for this purpose portfolios can be constructed as part
of their work.

Water colour is the most appropriate and attractive
medium for general purposes for children of any age,
but many of the small water colour boxes often provided
are not altogether suitable. It is usually better to
select a few colours, for if these are skilfully chosen
an almost infinite range of colour becomes possible.
For some purposes, such as pattern making, or for
covering large areas, paste or powder colours will be found
useful and economical. They may be used as an opaque
colour or as a transparent wash. A brush which has no
elasticity is useless as a drawing tool ; obviously a sable
brush is the best tool, but the cost is prohibitive. A
good substitute may be found in large cheap hog hair
fitches, especially for work on a large scale. Provision
should be made for the mixing of colours. Plain, white
glazed tiles are extremely convenient for this purpose
and take up little storage space when not in use.

Clay for modelling is cheap, and with occasional
attention it will keep in good condition for a long time
if kept in galvanised tins with tight fitting lids.

Materials for the various crafts are too numerous and varied to make detailed suggestions possible : they should be of as good quality as possible, and all materials which imitate others should be excluded. It is unreasonable to expect children to form high standards of craftsmanship if the material they are given to use is shoddy and inferior, or if they are taught to use cheap fabrics which ape those which are more durable.

Much of the equipment for weaving, book-production, and other crafts, may be made in school, and the pupils gain a great deal in knowledge of a craft when this is done. The ingenuity shown by teachers and pupils in the use of waste material and in the invention and improvement of apparatus is remarkable, and wherever this is found, there also is something of the true tradition of craftsmanship.

VI. THE INFLUENCE OF ENVIRONMENT IN ART TRAINING

55. Some general considerations.—Though the importance of environment during the impressionable period of the child's school life is now fully recognised, it is not always regarded as one of the practical problems of teaching. But it is obviously absurd to attempt to develop a sensitiveness to form and colour in a room which is a negation of all that Art stands for. It is true that some of the adverse conditions to be found in schools may seem beyond the power of the teacher to remedy : the architectural style, or lack of it, of the building in which he teaches must be accepted. Sometimes, too, his opinion has not been asked in the matter of colour schemes for the interior decoration of the school. There is no doubt, however, that teachers are now consulted on such questions much more frequently than in the past, and when re-decoration of the premises is proposed the Art Teacher should take this opportunity of giving practical consideration to the colour schemes most suitable for the various rooms, having regard to their lighting, aspect, proportions and purpose.

Lightness and gaiety of colour are a great asset to a schoolroom, and the idea which still persists that neutral tints of rather a depressing quality are necessary in an Art room or any other schoolroom is a very unfortunate one. It is true that, if pictures are to hang in the room, it is well to avoid too positive a colouring for their background, but the colour may still be lively and stimulating. The woodwork in a classroom often provides surfaces which may suitably be painted in bright colours. It is often considered desirable that the lower part of the wall of the rooms or corridors should be darker in colour in order that marks, which will almost inevitably be made, should be less apparent. There is no need, however, for this darker tint to be dull and heavy. Of two colours that are of the same tone, one may be dull and heavy, the other full of vitality : both serve the purpose of protection equally well, but there is a great difference in their effect on the people who spend many hours a week in contact with them.

56. The environment of the art room.—There is no doubt that the provision of a specially designed Art room, or even a classroom set aside for the purpose of teaching Art, has a marked influence on the teaching of the subject. The Art room should be the centre of all the Art and Craft activities of the school. Especially where Craft teaching is well-developed, it is a great gain to have the equipment ready for use at all times, so that, where the time-table permits, children may have free access to it in order to carry on a piece of work.

The walls of the Art room should not be crowded with pictures and illustrations, for it is well to give the children an opportunity to appreciate the restful effect of large, clear, well-proportioned spaces. A few pictures at a time should be used as decoration, and these should be chosen for their well marked decorative qualities, and should be sufficiently large to do justice to those qualities. In addition, two or three imperial frames of narrow wood, fitted with movable backs of ply-wood, may be hung permanently on the walls, and used to display illustrations for lessons or to illustrate various aspects of design and craftsmanship. Examples such as the extremely valuable series of post cards in black and white and colour published by the British Museum, the Victoria and Albert Museum, the National Gallery, etc., provide at small cost a great range of subjects which may be displayed in this way. When children have little opportunity to visit museums and art galleries, these small reproductions offer a wide field for discussion, not only of pictures, drawings, engravings and sculpture, but of manuscript, pottery, furniture, fabrics and other examples of craftsmanship. It will be unfortunate, however, if this study is limited to the examples of traditional art and craftsmanship stored in museums and galleries ; illustrations of local examples will also be of great interest. Nor is it sufficient to consider the work of the past. It is equally important that the art, the architecture and the craftsmanship of the present should be considered and discussed. Photographs and illustrations of representative work of the present time, of building, of town planning, of furniture, fabrics, ships and motor cars, of the best examples of those things which make up our everyday surroundings, should be collected for the same purpose. It may be possible then to help the children to see the vital connexion of art with everyday life, and to realise that design is not limited by fixed principles invented in past ages, but is a living force sensitively reflecting the changes in the social and economic background of the time, and governed by the new materials, the new methods of manufacture, and the new standards of every period.

57. The environment of the classroom.—The great majority of teachers, however, will still be teaching in schools which are not provided with a room set aside as an Art room, and will have to ensure that the ordinary classroom provides an environment which is as inspiring as circumstances permit. This may not be an easy task in some schools, but much may be done in a simple and practical way. Pictures which do not serve a useful purpose or have lost their original interest should be taken down ; in fact, it is not a bad thing to clear the whole of the wall space periodically and start again with a definite scheme in view. Some of the diagrams, maps and illustrations which are arranged indiscriminately on the walls may well be a necessary part of the teaching equipment, but they should only be displayed where they are of most effective use, and they must be kept in neat and workmanlike order, if they are not to offend the eye. Those which are not of immediate use are best kept in folders, where they will be preserved from dust and other damage. One or two pictures, if they are worthy of a place as decoration, may then be hung with due regard to their decorative effect in relation to the whole wall space. It will be better to leave the walls bare than to hang inferior or faded pictures. A well proportioned clear space has great value in a scheme of decoration. It is taken for granted that the pictures will be hung where they can be seen by the children to the best advantage.

School furniture often makes it difficult to secure an orderly arrangement of a room. Fixed cupboards running along the base of the wall and rising to a height which children can reach, usually present a satisfactory appearance, but where cupboards of varying heights and shapes have been added as required, merely to provide additional shelf space, it is not easy to make a pleasant arrangement. Their uneven heights break the areas of wall space in a meaningless way and the

ense of unity in the room is often lost. Sometimes it is
possible, however, to group these cupboards together
so as to make one unified mass which is not unpleasing,
especially if they are painted the same colour and shade
as the lower part of the walls.

Many teachers encourage the children to take an
active part in the orderly arrangement of the room and
in its decoration. The arrangement of flowers, apparatus, pictures, etc. should be considered as practical
experiments in design, often far more valuable and
intelligible to the pupils than many more theoretical
exercises on paper. Where lettering is taught, and few
schools can afford to omit this valuable training, school
notices provide many opportunities for its practice.
The consideration of orderly arrangement should extend
beyond the limits of the classroom to the corridors,
the cloakroom and the playground. If good habits are
consistently inculcated and use made of baskets for
litter in school and playground, the countryside will
need less protection.

58. The environment of the locality.—Children are
usually encouraged to study the history, the geography
and the literature of their locality. They should also
be aware of the architectural treasures and fine examples
of craftsmanship, both of the past and the present, which
their own neighbourhood possesses. The teacher should
encourage the children's natural interest in their surroundings, in the life of the farm, the local industries,
the beauty of the countryside, the sea shore or the
street, and thus stimulate interests and pleasures which
will probably last into adult life. These scenes of everyday life are the natural subjects for drawing and painting
and when the child intends to make a picture he studies
his material with a new intensity and becomes aware
of things in a much more complete sense.

Where the school is in one of the larger towns, it may be possible for the pupils to see good examples of modern building, and of design based on the use of modern materials and modern methods of construction. Girls will need little encouragement to discuss the use of colour, line and material in clothes and to make some critical study of furniture and articles of everyday use. Visits to museums and picture galleries provide most valuable opportunities for widening the children's interest and experience, but unless they are very carefully organised they will probably be ineffective. Indeed, any attempts to develop an appreciation of Art will certainly fail, if they take the form of aimless or ill-directed study. Experience has shown, however, that if a wide view of Art is taken, it is quite possible to give children a real interest in well designed things, and to help them to form an honest first-hand opinion about a work of art. Whether their conclusions are right or not will always be a matter of opinion, but it is at least possible to encourage them to be sincere. It is hoped too that the art training will lead to a real enjoyment of the English landscape and to the respect for its amenities which springs from a sincere appreciation of beauty. The preservation of the countryside will never be secured by the threat of legal penalties : people will not respect that for which they have no personal appreciation. The future of the countryside depends on the public opinion which is developing in our schools today.

It is scarcely necessary to point out that the Art teaching which is limited in its scope to classroom exercises is a poor thing, and may produce little of lasting value. There may on the other hand be many Art lessons which have a permanent influence on the outlook of the pupils in which possibly no actual drawing has been done but a real contact with life has been made.

CHAPTER VIII

NEEDLEWORK

*

I. SOME GENERAL CONSIDERATIONS

1. The place of Needlework in the school generally.—Needlework* occupies a place of traditional importance in girls' schools, due originally to the position held by women as the makers and menders of the clothes of the household. This position has, in recent years, been somewhat shaken owing to the enormous increase of machine-made goods, both stitched and woven, which the trade produces at a cheap rate. On this account Needlework in school has lost what association it may ever have had with domestic drudgery, and is free to flourish as a fine constructive and decorative craft on its own merits. The products of this craft form part of the texture of daily life ; and this adds to the significance and interest of the craft which, for girls arriving at the stage of adolescence, provides not only an outlet for their natural taste and their desire to be well dressed, but also the discipline of good workmanship.

---

* The position of Needlework among the arts and the crafts in general is dealt with in Chapter VII, section 41, of this Handbook. Teachers of Needlework will find it useful to study also the preceding sections of that chapter, in which are discussed the principles underlying the teaching of art and craft.

Needlework, like all other crafts, has particular qualities of its own shared by no other craft : from the simple use of a needle and thread to join or adorn material, a wide range of processes has been developed such as cutting, manipulating, and sewing material in order to produce new forms. These processes reveal incidentally almost limitless possibilities of design in line, colour and the interplay of textures.

2. Needlework not a suitable activity for young children.—At the Nursery and Infant School stages of a child's education Needlework is not an appropriate exercise because the craft has too rigid a technique to be suitable for immature hands and eyes. In fact, even in Junior Schools care should be taken to ensure that children do not, for long periods, do work demanding close concentration or involving excessive eye strain. None the less, much goes on in the daily work and life of Nursery and Infant Schools which is invaluable as a basis for later exercises in Needlework. In the daily training in clean and orderly habits, the care of possessions, the use of simple tools and utensils, the manipulation of varied materials, and in the pleasure derived from gay colours and interesting shapes, lie the beginnings of craftsmanship.

II. THE JUNIOR SCHOOL STAGE

3. The conditions for a successful beginning.— It is generally recognised that exercises which involve actual needlework should be deferred until the Junior School age is reached, and, even then, the tools and materials for the early stages of the craft should be very carefully selected to suit the hands, eyes and understanding of the children. Needles should have eyes large enough to be threaded easily, but should be sufficiently short for small fingers to control ; thread should be smooth in texture and of a colour that is in clear contrast to the material on which it is worked ; materials should be soft but firm in texture, so that they do not offer unnecessary difficulty in manipulation, and strongly striped and checked materials should be avoided, in order to prevent strain on the eyes. Further, the children should not attempt types of work which involve processes too difficult for them to complete unaided, for they should gradually acquire the sense of power and constructive ability which grows with independent skill.

Briefly, the successful beginning of Needlework depends mainly on two things : skill and understanding. The children should learn how to use a needle in the right way, gaining gradually a more marked rhythm of movement by sewing with the thimble finger avoiding the bad habit of pushing the needle into the material with thumb and forefinger : for it is harmful to allow children to adopt a faulty technique.

4. The work should have a definite meaning for the children.—The kind of exercises which children attempt at early stages must be sufficiently interesting to appeal to them, and so selected that they are within their power to carry out. It is not enough that the children's part in the work should be limited to sewing : the processes of planning, measuring, cutting and fixing are all part of the craft, and the child's individual contribution in the matter of colour or pattern will add greatly to the value of any exercise.

It will probably be found that the most productive and educative exercises in needlework will arise, in the Junior School stage, in connexion with other activities, for the children will have more pleasure, and progress more rapidly, when making things for their home or their school, or for use in their own dramatic plays, games or projects, than when doing work which has no clearly defined meaning for them. In the same way, if children have a real purpose before them in making something, they will understand how important it is to preserve their work in good condition. Thus clean hands, careful folding, and suitable storage, will become matters of personal responsibility rather than mere classroom rules. In order to assist in this side of the work, the girls should be equipped with an apron or pinafore, a sewing bag or other means for keeping work clean, flat and uncreased between lesson periods, and the proper supply of thimble, scissors, tape measure, needle-book and pin-cushion.

5. First lessons in Stitchery.—The actual stitchery done by Juniors should be watched carefully by the teacher. She should see not only that the children are making genuine progress, but also that their progress is appropriate to the stage of development which they have reached. In the early stages the stitches will be irregular, for only as the eye begins to judge distances and muscular control develops, will evenly spaced sewing become possible. A system known sometimes as " decorative stitchery " is often adopted in Junior Schools in order to teach simple stitches which are easy to see and at the same time compose a pleasing pattern in colour. This twofold purpose will however be missed if the stitches used are of no value constructively, either because they are too large or are merely imposed as a decoration on the top of other stitches. The method of teaching sewing to Juniors should be based on common sense, with the recognition that coloured stitches are easy to see and pleasant to look at, but that for the sake of learning the craft all the ordinary simple stitches in common use are the most valuable ones to practise. If these stitches can be combined to form a pattern, the early exercises will be more interesting than the dull repetition of practice specimens.

6. Knitting.—The craft of knitting, like the early stages of weaving, may well find its beginnings in the Junior School, but care should be taken to ensure that it has purpose and interest, and does not degenerate into a merely mechanical occupation. There is no necessity to labour over specimen work, for a variety of small and useful articles can be made as a result of well graded teaching. As with the early exercises in sewing, the choice of tools for beginners is important. Needles should be neither too thick nor too long, and steel needles should not be used at all until some skill in knitting has been acquired.

III. THE SENIOR SCHOOL STAGE

7. The aim of the course.—In a Senior School it will not as a rule be necessary to have recourse to special devices in order to help children to realise the practical use of Needlework. By the age of 11 girls will be familiar with the simpler processes in sewing and knitting and they are reaching the age at which the value of Needlework in everyday life as a constructive and decorative craft is readily appreciated. The important thing for the teacher at this stage is to plan a really practical scheme of work by means of which she will aim at teaching the craft progressively, so that the girls make use of the knowledge they already possess and add to it gradually by definite stages. Emphasis on independent work is as important here as in the Junior School for it will be impossible to ensure that girls really understand new stitches and processes if they only do a small part of the work which the teacher has planned. Again, little advance will be made unless the tools and materials are suitable for the stage of progress the children have reached, and the interest will not be genuine nor the possibility of the craft fully realised, unless the girls themselves have some outlet for their own taste and invention.

8. Schemes of work.—A good course in Needle-work in a Senior School should aim at the following wide range of interest and skill :—

(*a*) A knowledge of the appropriate tools and their use, and due understanding of differences in the texture and manipulation of various materials.

(*b*) Proficiency in stitchery both for purposes of construction and decoration.

(*c*) Some understanding of the simpler ways of planning, and of cutting out materials, to make garments and of the relation of these operations to measuring and fitting.

(*d*) A knowledge of simple ways of mending, renovating and reconstructing garments.

(*e*) Skill and construction in knitting.

Throughout the course there should be an appreciation of the part played by colour, texture and shape in designing for Needlework of any kind.

9. Tools and Materials.—The right selection and manipulation of the tools used in Needlework is an important part of the craft, and should form the subject of definite teaching. The relation of the size of the needle and the thickness and tension of the thread to the character of the stitch and the quality of the material is one of the fundamental elements in Needlework, which girls should learn gradually to appreciate for themselves. This knowledge forms the basis of good technique, and is equally applicable to hand sewing and to machine sewing. The working and care of a sewing machine should certainly form a part of the course for older girls, and the study should include a considera-tion of the appropriate choice between machine and hand sewing in any piece of work. It should be realised that accurate fixing and careful tacking are necessary for good machining, and that correct technique is better than speed. The first practice should be on long stretches of material to avoid constant stopping, turning and starting. Failing other material, useful practice in machining can be obtained by stitching a newspaper with an unthreaded needle and this can be followed by stitching on appropriate articles such as dusters and pillow-cases.

Every opportunity should be used to give experience in understanding the differences in the texture, colour and pattern of materials. In making garments, the suitability or unsuitability for their purpose of materials of varying width and texture is an important factor ; while in decorative needlework the varying qualities of fabrics of all kinds are of no less interest. The study of materials may well include some investigation into their sources, as well as the history of manufactured fabrics. Strength, warmth, durability, and suitability for laundering, are all qualities of material which are of interest to a needlewoman. Closely related to this study is the craft of hand weaving, providing an opportunity for experience in the actual construction of materials, and unlimited possibilities for creative design. By experiments in cutting patterns in blocks or dies and printing them on material an introduction to the craft of fabric-printing and the uses of printed material may be made. The making of designs by applying one fabric on another or by embroidery opens out another field of interest in connexion with materials.

The value of some such creative work in colour and pattern by means of materials cannot be over-estimated, as it is in this way, rather than by exercises entirely restricted to drawing and painting, that some understanding of the qualities of design can be developed.

10. Stitchery and Processes.—It may be assumed that the main basic stitches required in needlework will be known by the time the Senior School is reached, but the girls' natural growth, both physical and mental, will demand a somewhat different approach to this part of the craft. Practice, however, will be necessary in order to obtain regularity and rhythm in sewing, to gain proficiency in handling materials so as to produce a workmanlike result. A certain doubt exists as to the value of learning stitches and processes which are not needed in the prevailing fashion in clothes, such, for instance, as the making of button-holes. But it is not difficult to recognise what, in general, are the fundamental processes in needlework as applied in the making of garments; for instance, it is clearly important to understand the various ways of dealing with fulness of material, and with raw edges; methods of making and finishing an opening, and of fastening; what can be done with material cut on the cross, and so on. The aim should be to give girls some solid foundation of knowledge and technique on which they may work later on.

In addition to using stitches, in making garments, girls should have the pleasure of experimenting with a number of new stitches which can be combined in various ways, and in a variety of threads, to form part of a design for embroidery.

11. Construction of garments : use of needlework patterns : cutting out.—From the early stages of teaching constructive needlework, the business of planning, measuring and cutting should form part of the practical work. Junior children can take simple measurements with tape measures, do easy calculations, make simple flat patterns and cut them out in paper before using material. For example, in the construction of a book cover or a bag for a brush and comb, the children should begin by measuring the dimensions of the book or the brush, and should note carefully the appearance of the cover or the bag when laid out flat before further construction takes place.

From simple beginnings such as this the older girls may be taught by progressive stages to see the relation between a flat pattern for a garment and the shape of the human form for which it is designed. Opinions will differ as to the advisability of taking pattern drafting with the girls, but it will probably add to their general understanding of a bought flat pattern if they have made some attempt, by modelling or paper folding, to relate the parts of the pattern to the human shape. If this is coupled with as much experience as possible in measuring and fitting, the girls will gain an appreciation of line and form, and be able to use bought patterns intelligently. It may generally be said that if girls know from experience how a pattern is obtained they are better able to make what alterations and adjustments are necessary in using bought patterns. They will understand, too, how variations can be made on a foundation pattern or how a pattern can be altered to suit a particular wearer's taste. They should be trained to consider the design of a garment as a whole, thinking out where necessary openings can best be placed, the best means of fastening, and the finish of neck and sleeves. Any personal and individual notes of decoration should be planned to form an essential part of the design for the garment.

Two main points should be emphasised : the *purpose* should decide the choice of material, and the *material* should influence the design and the choice of the processes and stitches.

It is clearly very important that, in spite of classroom difficulties, girls should learn to plan and cut out materials. Only by constant practice in identifying the parts of a pattern, laying them correctly and economically in material and actually cutting, can they acquire the confidence which will enable them to make use of their experience when deprived of the teacher's help.

12. Repairs and renovation.—In the Senior School the girls' increasing proficiency in handling tools and materials, and their knowledge of construction make it possible to give valuable teaching in the matter of repairs and renovation. As a foundation for this Juniors can be trained to adopt the right attitude to repairs by learning, for instance, to replace worn stitches on a hem or the seam of a frock, or to fasten broken tags on coats, or to sew on buttons.

This punctilious attention to "running repairs" should be carried on in the Senior School, and girls should be encouraged to mend torn button holes and pockets, repair gloves, replace hat linings, and all similar matters to which the self-respecting person attends.

This elementary work is little more than a matter of discipline, but it is not so easy to collect sufficient material for lessons on more advanced forms of renovation. It should, however, be regarded as a matter of great importance that girls should learn how to deal neatly with necessary household repairs, and they can at any rate start with those that the school itself provides from the Housecraft room, the canteen, or the staff rooms. In household mending it is useful to know when the use of the sewing machine is permissible or even desirable.

Darning should be taught as far as possible on actual stockings, socks, or similar knitted or woven materials, and followed at a later stage by the darning of table and house linen. Probably the best method of arranging for a suitable supply of material for darning practice is to assign this type of work to groups of girls rather than to the whole class. The same may be said of learning patching, for this is most satisfactory when practised on actual garments rather than on specimens, and it will usually be difficult to secure a large supply. Whatever methods of patching and renewing small sections of a garment are taught should be closely related to principles of construction.

If the girls are to be given instruction in the renovation of partly worn or out-of-date garments, they will appreciate this type of work most at the end of their school course. This is difficult work for girls of school age, as it demands a considerable degree of skill and some knowledge of dressmaking, and it is often too difficult for girls to tackle satisfactorily. To be able, however, to deal with alterations in garments is of great service, especially in connexion with the use of ready-made garments, and if the girls are sufficiently skilful to undertake it they will find it a valuable part of their course. Garments which are to be renovated should first be unpicked, then cleaned or washed and pressed ; this may usefully be carried out in Housecraft lessons.

13. Knitting.—In knitting, Juniors usually make rapid progress, acquiring such mastery over the elementary processes that the chief business of the Senior School is to give further practice, until the girls knit evenly and rhythmically and can undertake more advanced work. From a relatively early age they should learn to work from printed or written directions. While the elements of knitting are still being learnt, a fair amount of time must be given to it, but once this is accomplished the work tends to become mechanical, and it is undesirable to spend much time on it in school hours.

IV. THE ORGANISATION OF NEEDLEWORK

14. Responsibility for the teaching.—Where several members of a school Staff share the teaching in Needlework there should clearly be close co-operation between them, and it is generally desirable, in the interests of continuity, that one member of the staff should be responsible for the general oversight and co-ordination of the teaching. This, together with a carefully planned scheme, should make it possible to ensure progression in the course, and to prevent unnecessary repetition or omissions.

15. Length of lesson period, and class organisation.—With Needlework, as with any other craft, the length of period in the time-table is a serious consideration. In Junior Schools the normal lesson period may be long enough, but with Senior girls, an arrangement of the available time with a view to securing a longer working period is desirable and will generally produce a more practical output and considerably greater interest. Where the school organisation allows of it, the re-classification of girls in groups for Needlework lessons, so that work can be planned to suit their ability, is often found very successful. Even if this is impossible, it is important to grade the work to meet the needs of individual girls in a class, while not diverging too widely from the main scheme in operation.

16. Methods of teaching.—The teacher of Needlework should make use of various methods of teaching the subject, for all have their particular uses. There is need for class teaching, group teaching, and individual teaching ; often the need for all three will arise in a single lesson.

Class teaching, to be successful, requires carefully planned illustrative material, large scale diagrams, and working specimens for actual demonstration. The display of examples of stitches, or of a finished garment, will give a useful stimulus to the work. Group teaching will be useful in such exercises as cutting out material, when obviously the teacher cannot supervise more than a small number at one time. It is also a useful way of dealing with difficulties or mistakes which are common in the work of a number of girls in a class.

Community or co-operative work will provide other opportunities for group teaching and for the production of larger pieces of work than an individual worker can manage. Such work should be carried out on a design which has been discussed by the group as a whole.

17. The work of nervous and backward girls.—

The needlework lesson will call for careful watching, by the teacher, of the posture and expression of the children, since the effort to carry out work which is beyond their powers may lead to nervous strain. Processes which require the manipulation of small or delicate tools, such as a fine steel knitting needle, depend on a neuro-muscular co-ordination which no effort of will can sustain if the eye and the hand have not reached the necessary stage of development. Very tight sewing or knitting may be distress signals, not wilful faults, and the observant teacher will act upon such indications of the varying needs of her class.

It is of great importance, too, to plan work very carefully for the less intelligent pupils. Girls who are backward in their school work sometimes obtain proficiency in stitching by hand or machine, but find difficulty in constructive or inventive work of any kind. The teacher should ensure that, because of this, such girls are not relegated to purely mechanical work, but should give them opportunities of attempting very simple planning, cutting and fixing, and decorative work which will make an appeal through colour and pattern.

18. Text-books and records.—A good supply of

text-books and interesting books of reference in Needlework and allied crafts should be available in the Senior School. They are valuable for the teachers' use, and the girls should learn to consult them. It is also desirable that the girls should keep records of their own work, showing stitches learnt, patterns used, cost of materials bought, all of which will form a useful guide for future reference.

19. Tests.—It is both salutary and encouraging to set tests of skill and ability at intervals during the course. The tests bring to light general weaknesses and show the teacher the outstanding merits or faults in the work of individuals, and often are the only means of discovering how far the girls are able to work independently.

20. Material for use.—A responsibility rests with the teacher in the matter of the supply of material for Needlework lessons, and this responsibility is not merely connected with the need for selling the finished work. By means of the fabrics, wools, cottons, silks and other materials for use in the learning of this craft, the children will be gaining their earliest experience in colour and form, and in many cases they will be attempting to create satisfactory designs from material which has in the first place been selected by someone else, and may be uninteresting in colour and limited in range. It is usually possible, by exercising care and discrimination, to provide children with material to work with which is pleasing and inspiring, and in view of the very marked effect this may have, the effort is surely worth while.

CHAPTER IX

HOUSECRAFT

I. SOME GENERAL CONSIDERATIONS

1. The beginnings of housecraft.—The practice of the arts of home life does not, by any means, have its beginnings in the Senior School. If his first introduction to school is in a Nursery School, a child experiences there the advantages of fresh air, regular habits, food and sleep ; he learns to keep himself neat and clean, and to understand the necessity for co-operation and unselfishness if his life as one of a group of people is to be happy. In addition to these general forms of social training he takes his part, in so far as he is able, in serving and clearing away meals, learns to carry plates and use utensils, to brush the floor and fold a cloth. The practice of these simple achievements is carried further in the Infants' School in the arrangements for the mid-morning lunch and in the care for the order and beauty of the classroom. Here too a child makes his first attempts at handling materials, folding, cutting, tying and modelling. These social activities are often combined by the child himself in dramatic play in which he pictures himself as the centre of a household, cleaning, laying meals, looking after children, and generally experimenting in the domestic arts.

The Junior School carries on these various activities, giving a child further experience in materials and tools, and widening his responsibility for keeping order both in his own person and the school, and satisfying his pleasure in games and plays.

2. Housecraft in the Senior School.—As the child of the Junior School grows towards adolescence, the activities which have hitherto satisfied his play interests assume a different significance. The " make believe " character of these activities fades, and the child begins, on the one hand, to take an enjoyable part in games demanding skill and co-operation, and, on the other, to practise crafts which produce real things and supply actual necessities. A sense of reality may now be said to inspire the practical work of the school, for children are reaching the age when they can appreciate the difference between good and bad workmanship, or technique in relation to purpose, to understand the part played by the creative crafts in life, and to show keen preferences for colours and shapes.

3. The Senior School environment.—This emphasis on reality forms the keynote of the Senior School, and with it comes the necessity for space in which, on the foundation of social training already given, and the general educational activities of the Infant and Junior School a more direct training for life may be given. The ordinary school classroom imposes too great a restriction on such training, and to remove it to a separate building tends to divorce it from the other parts of the curriculum. The modern school building has therefore acquired important additional facilities specially designed for practical purposes, and aims also at giving the children the experience of surroundings which are well-ordered and made attractive both indoors and out-of-doors. Man's need for food, shelter and clothing, and his desire for order, cleanliness and beauty lie behind those parts of a child's training which deal with cookery and dietetics, the crafts of the needle, the handling of wood and metal, the care of a garden and the practice of hygiene, laundrywork and housewifery. The study of colour and design naturally plays an important part in the making of a home, while to its proper conduct belongs the humane consideration of the care of infants and of the sick and injured. These pursuits cannot be separated from scientific knowledge, which is vital to the study of the health, diet, clothing, equipment and labour-saving mechanism of a modern home.

As far as possible, therefore, the domestic arts and crafts should not be regarded as a number of isolated subjects to be followed as a matter of routine, but, rather, they should combine to form both a reality and an ideal in the child's mind. To this end it is of the utmost importance that the aims and principles of these very practical activities should be actually demonstrated in the school itself, which should be clean, orderly and attractive and provide an environment which the children are proud to maintain.

4. The scope of housecraft.—Enough has been said to emphasise the importance of regarding the domestic crafts as part of a wide course of practical training in which the various elements are drawn together by a common purpose into a complete whole. For the sake of convenience these parts must be considered separately, and the present section deals more particularly with Cookery, Laundrywork and Housewifery, often combined under the composite title " Housecraft ".

Housecraft is, from one point of view, a matter of practical proficiency which is attained by repetition of processes until good performance has become so much a matter of habit as to be almost automatic. This gives prominence at the outset to the activity aspect and subordinates the relevant theory. With younger children, theory detached from practice has little meaning, but, as they grow older, girls will make better use of their proficiency, if they understand the principles on which the processes are based and learn to use this theoretical knowledge to enable them to approach unfamiliar problems with confidence. As the course progresses practice and relevant theory may be dealt with at each stage, and at the end of the course it should be possible for the girls to work more independently and less by imitation, basing their work upon principles which they understand. In this way they should leave school with a body of experiences which not only provide a working knowledge of the various necessary processes, but also some understanding of the fundamentals of good housecraft. Such girls can be said to be really skilled in this group of crafts.

II. THE ORGANISATION OF HOUSECRAFT

5. The age of beginning.—One of the problems connected with the organisation of Housecraft is to decide at what stage in the girl's school life it is advisable to begin, and how to plan the work most wisely and economically in the time available. As a general rule, a girl entering a Senior School is too undeveloped to do effective practical Housecraft, and the postponement of the practice to a rather later stage has an added advantage in the fact that the girls bring to it a quicker understanding of its meaning and a more marked interest in home life. If the work is begun in the early stages of the Senior School, it should be sufficiently attractive to capture a young girl's interest; it should aim at developing sensible habits of work and learning the correct use of tools and utensils. Possibly at this stage a shorter lesson than is practicable later on may be found satisfactory.

6. Length of course and session.—Differentiation in the type of work and allocation of time are essential to suit the needs of girls of varying ability; indeed, from a teacher's point of view, it is advisable to admit some flexibility in the length of period at all stages of the Housecraft course. Not only must the age and skill of pupils be considered, but the very varying facilities of the schools. It is clear, too, that quite different purposes are served by the whole and the half-day's sessions, and this purpose should be the deciding factor in planning the length of period. The shorter period is suitable for specific instruction and practice, the longer period, approximating more nearly to the conditions of a home, provides opportunity for the organisation and carrying out of the variety of duties which constitute a day's work. Taking the same logical standpoint, it is evident that, if a course in Housecraft is to have its full educational value, it should be continuous throughout the girls' school life, so that they may see some progression in the scheme and enjoy their increasing independence.

The best results of Housecraft teaching are usually obtained when the girls who form a group for Housecraft are drawn from the same class in the school. This principle should, if possible, be maintained till the leaving age. Specially interesting work and visits can be planned for the older girls in their last term at school, the arrangements for which will be complicated, if younger and less experienced pupils are mixed with the same group.

III. CONTENT OF A SCHOOL COURSE IN HOUSECRAFT

7. The main aim : to set a higher standard of home life.—In any practical work it should be remembered that the acquisition of skill is a slow process, and much slower with some children than others, and that the mastery of a limited syllabus is more satisfactory than a superficial acquaintance with an extended scheme. In planning a course in Housecraft it is convenient to decide what processes in ordinary household work every girl should be able to carry out, and how much of the theory behind it she may be expected to understand. An outline of the necessary daily work connected with a small home will furnish the best basis for such a scheme. Possibly many girls derive their earliest ideas of Housecraft from household drudgery in difficult conditions, and the school will aim at setting them a higher standard of home life in conditions that provide a practical illustration of the way in which this standard can be achieved.

8. The introductory stage : the practice of the common round of home duties.—A girl should begin by learning to carry out as well as possible all those ordinary duties which she might reasonably be expected to perform at home, so as to give her from the first a high standard of personal hygiene and simple healthy living. These duties include keeping her own person in scrupulous order, learning to do well such elementary processes as cleaning shoes, making beds, washing hairbrushes, washing and ironing handkerchiefs, cleaning silver, cutting bread and butter and making tea. In planning this preliminary work it is always important to remember the particular outlook and rather limited skill of the younger girls, and to select duties which it is within their power to carry out effectively. Even at this stage the work can be used not merely to provide disciplinary exercises, but in order to give the first thoughtful approach to larger problems such as the causes and removal of dirt, the variety of agents for cleansing, the care of implements and utensils, and the satisfaction derived from order and beauty.

9. The intermediate stage : a graded scheme of cookery and laundrywork, based on the normal work of the home.—This introductory work should be followed by a graded scheme in cookery and laundry-work, still closely related to the life of a home, but aiming at the development both of skill and of such an attitude to the work as will make for orderly habits and the intelligent use of time and material. This can only be achieved if, at all stages, the work is suited to the capacity and understanding of the girls, and if there is a reasonable amount of revision and sufficient progression to allow for a proper development.

In planning this intermediate stage of the course the normal work of a house will again provide the essential basis. The processes involved in a family wash will include practice in all the ordinary washing processes, and give opportunity for acquiring the technique of ironing and finishing and the pleasure of wearing clean, well laundered garments. In cookery, the fundamental processes such as boiling, steaming and baking which all occur in simple meals, will suggest the necessary scheme. Progress will inevitably be slow, for each of the activities will involve fresh instruction, practice in using implements, an understanding of the use and care of ovens, stoves, boilers and other parts of the equipment of the kitchen. The girls should become accustomed to looking at their work as a series of household jobs, rather than as an isolated school lesson, practising not only the processes involved in a specific kind of exercise, but giving attention as well to the planning of time in relation to other duties, to preparation and clearing up, and to the business-like use of instructions and recipes.

10. The final stage : independent management of a day's work in a home.—The final stage of work in Housecraft will give opportunities for assembling the parts of the foregoing course, and give the girls the interest of planning and carrying out independently the combined work of a house. The fact must not be overlooked that some of the less able pupils may find this kind of work too difficult, and for them interest must be maintained in more extensive practice of the simpler things till they have the satisfaction of doing them easily and well. But the majority of the Senior School pupils will have, before they leave, this interesting experience, and approach the problem of managing a day's work in a home, putting into practice the various parts of the instruction which their course has been comprised. It is at this stage that the school will most appropriately insert some sensible instruction in the care of young children, which will thus take its proper place as part of the natural interest and duty of a home rather than form a separate class-room topic.

IV. METHODS OF APPROACH

11. Arrangement of the courses with regard to local conditions.—One of the first responsibilities of the Housecraft teacher is the business of grading and arranging the work. This arrangement should be based on a number of important considerations.

The general plan for a year or a term must be decided upon, and due regard should be given to the requirements of the seasons ; for instance, the period of fruit bottling, the interests of Christmas or the needs of school functions. The conditions and neighbourhood of the school must also affect the type of course which is carried on. For instance, where gardening is taken in a school, attention will be given to the cooking and preservation of fruit and vegetables in their seasons, and useful experimental work can be done, for example, in cooking different varieties of potatoes and root vegetables. In rural schools, particularly, economic biology, the effect of sunshine on food stuffs and other interesting investigations may well be included. Where, on the other hand the school is situated in a congested city, industrial town or mining village, it is clear that the scheme must be of a different character, and the emphasis will be laid on problems which will be only too obvious to need specific reference here.

In order that the schemes shall be really practical, therefore, the homes, interests and needs of the children must be an important consideration, and the scheme should reflect the careful thought which the teacher has given to it.

12. Arrangement of the work according to its difficulties.—Apart from the neighbourhood and the seasons, the work must be graded according to the difficulty it presents, not only in understanding the processes, but in actual manipulation. To take a single example, the making of a good cornflour mould is a more complicated process than the preparation of a rice pudding, yet both are sometimes taken together with inexperienced pupils because the ingredients are similar. The good teacher is the one who recognises these grades of difficulty and can plan a course which will lead her pupils slowly from one stage to another.

Similarly there is an art in associating in the children's minds causes and results which are alike, so that each lesson and exercise is not an isolated experience but adds some new element to already familiar knowledge. Much of the scientific exactness which the teacher gives to the planning of the work will be lost upon her pupils in the early stages, but as they progress they will realise that their proficiency has grown out of the ordered association of ideas.

13. Procedure in housecraft lessons.—Lessons in Housecraft were at one time invariably conducted on the same plan, that is, a preliminary demonstration by the teacher followed by practice in the same piece of work by the class. At the present time by no means all work in Housecraft follows this procedure, and much encouraging progress is being made on more liberal and independent lines. Following some definite and systematic preliminary practice in handling tools and materials, it is possible to allow girls to carry out assignments of work, preparing and arranging their day's programme in accordance with written instructions, and by discussion with the teachers, and finding out the necessary procedure for themselves from carefully tabulated directions. This plan, which is capable of many variations, demands the utmost attention and concentration on the part of the pupils, and undoubtedly gives valuable training in self-reliance and judgment.

It cannot however be denied that practical demonstration by the teacher is a necessary feature of all Housecraft courses, whether it is given regularly or periodically. A good demonstration teaches correct manipulation, gives visual instruction by showing the class not only each stage of the process but also the finished result. The teacher who carries out, before an audience in a certain time and to a high standard, the process she is teaching, keeps up her own technique and has material for reference, when she criticises the girls' work.

Girls who are used to working independently, and have reached a fairly advanced stage of proficiency, will experience the same sense of confidence if they, too, have occasional opportunities of preparing and giving a demonstration for the rest of the class.

14. Revision lessons and tests of progress.—The function of revision lessons is to review and relate previous lessons from a fresh aspect, consolidating knowledge, removing misconceptions, and generally strengthening weak places before proceeding with new work. Such lessons should give practice in variations of a familiar process, and generally develop confidence and speed.

The difference between revision lessons of this kind and tests to ascertain the proficiency and progress of a class should be emphasised. The teacher will have opportunities, when testing the class, of noticing methods, choice and correct use of utensils, economy of time and material, and the power to produce a finished result. It is usually advisable to test a small group rather than the whole class, and the results should be fully criticised. The advantages of having an examiner who is not the class teacher should sometimes be considered, and it is occasionally possible for teachers to exchange classes for this purpose.

15. Pupils' records of work.—It is not always possible for the members of a Housecraft group to remain together throughout school life, and so it is important that each girl should keep some kind of record of her work. This need not be very full but should show exactly what practical work she has done and possibly a summary of criticisms given by the teacher.

At one time notebooks were regarded as the girl's text-book made by herself as the course proceeded and designed to last for future years. To this end, notes were often dictated or written on the blackboard and carefully copied by the girls, little or no individual effort being involved. Much of this laborious work is now replaced by the use of text-books, and notebooks are more generally used for notes made by the girls as records of their lessons or their reading, or for answers to questions set by the teacher.

In addition to the use of text-books, recipes or notes on methods of work can be duplicated by the teacher for the use of the class. These can be pasted into note-books, or, better still, incorporated in loose-leaf files, additional notes or illustrations added by the girls providing their own individual contribution. Newspapers and magazines provide excellent illustrations. Often the records and recipes that are produced in this way are not only invaluable in organising individual work but also form collections that are worth preserving.

Some children of limited general ability will find the practical work as much as they can accomplish, and for these the minimum amount of written work, in the form of copying from the printed page or memorising by reading from simply written books or studying simple illustrations, will be sufficient. Written work has a definite place in the Housecraft class, but too great insistence on it creates a dislike in the case of the child who has been discouraged throughout his whole school life by failure on the academic side. On the other hand, patient training in the written expression of methods of work often awakens an idea of the connexion between speech and action which, with encouragement, gives confidence to the backward child.

The increasing use of text-books, books of reference and periodicals in general school work should give a lead to the Housecraft teacher, and there is no need for detailed discussion of their use here.

V. SOME OF THE WIDER ASPECTS OF HOUSECRAFT

16. The need for taking a broad view of the training.—It has been emphasised throughout that Housecraft is essentially a practical activity and that proficiency in the craft should be the main aim of a course. But the educational value of the work will be much strengthened by some knowledge of the scientific and aesthetic values which it possesses.

The responsibility for this is not, of course, borne by the Housecraft teacher alone, but is shared by the teachers of Science, Hygiene, Art, Geography, and by other members of the staff. Any method of approach will be informal and incidental, though some definite formulation at the end of the course may be possible and advisable for those girls who seem equal to making it.

A. COOKERY

17. Choice and price of food stuffs.—The choice and price of food stuffs will be dealt with, from the earliest lessons, by practical observation and the selection of materials used for practice work. The difference between fresh and preserved fruits, vegetables and meat, the appearance and price of joints of meat, expensive and cheaper cuts, kinds of cheese, standard brown and white flours, will be dealt with informally as occasion arises. During the shopping, which is part of the course, prices will be noted, with seasonal and local variations. At each stage, the cost of dishes and of whole meals will be worked out, so that the girls gradually gain an idea of relative prices and are prepared to make family budgets at a later stage. Home-made foods should be compared with those supplied in the shops, not only from the costing standpoint, but as regards ingredients and freshness.

18. Knowledge of food values.—The cost of food is only one factor in choosing suitable meals, and the relative value of different foods in a diet must be generally considered from the beginning. The value of such foods as milk, butter, eggs, bread, meat and vegetables should be broadly compared and their functions indicated : always using simple terms and appealing to the children's general knowledge.

Children can understand such terms as bone-making, body-building, heat-giving, power-giving, but chemical terms convey little or nothing in the early stages, and should only be introduced when the more able girls can relate them to their work in Science.

Experiments to show the physical reaction of ingredients to cooking operations may be performed either in the Science laboratory or the Housecraft room, but elaborate chemical tests particularly of a quantitative character are as a rule unnecessary and misleading. Continuous practice will lead the girls to associate a food not only with its main dietetic value but with its price and the correct method of cooking it. The study of food values and prices will enable them to construct menus, first for a day and then for a week, at the lowest cost consistent with adequate nutritive value. The relative amount of food stuffs needed per person can be found from tables, and standard rations can be memorised.

When the girls understand what is meant by a minimum diet, they can suggest variations in it and, working in groups, prepare and serve illustrative dishes for typical meals. The arrangement, too, of the midday school dinner, whether served in a hall or canteen or eaten by the Housecraft class only, is the most telling example of practical food values.

If girls have learned to choose, buy, cook, and serve well balanced meals for their own consumption and to criticise their own work with discrimination they will be the better equipped for the management of a home.

19. Some factors that promote nutrition.—Much more than cookery is involved in the consideration of nutrition. The girls at all stages of the course should realise the importance of regularity and punctuality in serving meals, quietness and good manners at table, and of pleasant surroundings. Where meals are served in school and visitors entertained, much can be done to obtain the right attitude and, where girls help with Nursery Classes, their own early training is revived. In addition, such topics as the value of rest after meals, influence of fatigue on appetite, the variation of diet in summer and winter will all form a basis for useful discussion.

The most lasting results will be obtained where a body of knowledge has been built up on the practice of good economical cookery. Isolated lessons on vegetarianism and similar deviations from normal diet have little value. Such topics should be dealt with incidentally.

B. LAUNDRYWORK

20. The science of laundrywork.—In dealing with the theoretical side of laundrywork, close co-operation with the courses in Needlework and in Science will develop a critical attitude to the composition of materials used in ready-made clothing and their reaction to washing processes. The various ingredients used in laundrywork should be studied experimentally and their physical reactions observed. Hardness of the water supplied, quality of soap, value of washing powder and similar commercial productions, cost of materials for washing day are only some of the subjects which may profitably be discussed.

Chemical formulae are generally out of place, but cost and quality of materials should be carefully considered in a practical way. The amount and cost of soap used for each class, for example, may be recorded, and teacher and girls will secure economy by careful checking of stores and price.

The changing conditions in housing, particularly in the increase of flat-dwellings, the limitation of drying facilities, and the difficulties involved in open-air drying, are all important aspects of home laundrywork. The use of public wash-houses, the selection and preparation of articles sent to trade laundries and the treatment of semi-finished work, are subjects for consideration in laundry lessons.

C. HOME MANAGEMENT

21. The need for co-ordinating " housewifery ", cookery and laundrywork.—The somewhat narrow conception of " housewifery " as a course of instruction in cleaning and other household duties, distinct from cookery and laundrywork, has now been replaced by a broader idea of the scope of Housecraft as a whole. Since the premises specially designed for practical work in the newer schools provide many opportunities for this wider scheme of household management, it is no longer appropriate to consider the duties of house-work apart from their association with other practical domestic activities. The harmonious working of a house depends upon good organisation, suitable conditions, and technical skill, and a course in housecraft must include some guidance in these matters as well as giving practical instruction in cookery and laundrywork. If a broad view is taken of the course, all the elements of home-making will, it is hoped, fit into their places in the scheme. The practice of healthy living has been indicated and practised through instruction in Hygiene ; the girls have received some instruction in the care of young children ; Science has illuminated everyday phenomena and the wonderful domestic equipment of today, which is so often accepted without question. Experience gained in the arts and crafts has shown that colour, harmony, and the individual expression of ideas play a vivid part in the life of a home. In addition to acquiring these elements, the home-maker should realise that rest and food, cleanliness and colour, exercise and recreation all affect the running of the household, and an attempt should be made by teacher and pupils to formulate plans, by which these can be secured with the least strain to the worker and the utmost benefit to the family.

22. Planning and preparation of the work.— The " housewifery " side of the work will not therefore consist solely of a separate study of methods of cleaning, examples of household needlework, and similar domestic duties. The high ideal of creating better citizens and better homes should inspire the whole course. This ideal can only be realised by the constant practice of relating one piece of work to another. From planning the work of a morning, or a week or a year, the girls may develop an intelligent interest in the planning of a house. The elementary calculation of the cost of a single meal will lead naturally to estimating the cost of running the meals of a household or a weekly budget, or considering the relative advantages of using coal, gas, electricity or oil. This general aspect of housewifery should not consist purely of talks or lectures on the part of the teacher. An understanding of good housewifery can only be achieved by practical experience. This emphasises first of all the orderly and reasonable preparation and organisation of the girls' own work, the use of a time-table thoughtfully compiled by themselves, the realisation that carelessness and unpunctuality actually lead to unnecessary labour, and the value of economy which grows from the elimination of waste of all kinds. In addition the girls should, if possible, have opportunities of making and creating things to add beauty or comfort to the home, and discover how these may best be kept in good order and repair.

23. The study of modern developments in House-craft.—Following the suggestion that actual experience is of the greatest practical value, there should be opportunities during the course for seeing examples of the most recent experiments and achievements in home-making, furnishing and equipment. To the perusal of books, papers and catalogues may occasionally be added visits to good housing estates or exhibitions. Interest may well be aroused in the supply of water, food, fuel, and the production of articles in daily use, and this active interest may lead girls to feel that unsatisfactory home conditions are not inevitable but can be improved with knowledge and skill.

Modern mechanical appliances can be more easily used and explained at school under skilled direction than in later years without assistance, and the acquisition of a working knowledge of labour-saving equipment should form part of a Housecraft course wherever possible. The girls should be trained, before using any apparatus for the first time, to study the directions issued with it and to follow them carefully step by step. Safety rules should be enforced, and responsibility for seeing that taps and switches are turned off when necessary should become a regular habit.

24. The use of additional accommodation for housecraft in the school.—Special accommodation designed to give more meaning to the Housecraft of a school is now provided in many areas. A suite of small rooms consisting of bedroom, sitting-room, bathroom and perhaps a small kitchen is sometimes provided in addition to the Housecraft rooms, in order to familiarise the girls with the common problems of a small house. In some cases a house on a separate site, is taken, and this provides for the additional and more intensive study of home management with a smaller group of pupils than is usual in the Housecraft room. Both types of accommodation are designed to give reality to the practice and, where they are not available, it is most important to make up for their absence by eliminating as far as possible the school atmosphere, so that the girls may still associate their work with the requirements of a home.

This accommodation, which is usually in the school itself, but sometimes in a house specially rented for the purpose, is intended not only to increase the facilities for training in Housecraft but also to enrich the general life of the school.

This means that the additional rooms, if provided, should be regarded as an integral part of the school and should be in constant use for purposes that arise naturally out of the life of the school itself. Every school will find its own ways of employing these rooms. They may, for instance, serve as a quiet place for the use of some of the older girls, or as a means of dispensing school hospitality on occasion.

CHAPTER X

GARDENING AND OTHER RURAL ACTIVITIES

I.—GARDENING

I. SOME GENERAL CONSIDERATIONS

I. Gardening as a school activity.—Gardening as a form of school craft is now well established, and it is generally recognised that some provision for it is as desirable in towns as in the country. In the rural school it may be regarded as the key activity, for it is more closely related than any other school activity to the life and work of the countryside and lends reality and purpose to other practical subjects, particularly to the wood and the metal crafts and to science. There is in fact little in the curriculum of the country school which cannot with advantage find some point of contact with, or some practical application in, the gardening course.

Although gardening does not occupy the same pivotal position in the education of town children, it is specially desirable for them because it is an open-air occupation and brings them into direct contact with nature. Again, it is as valuable for girls as for boys, and there is no reason why the former should not take a full share in the work, if the soil is not too heavy and the tools are suitable in size. When it is not possible for the girls to take the full course in gardening, they should, at least, be made responsible for the care of some of the flower beds and borders.

Gardening demands skill in the use of a variety of tools and the intelligent application of that skill to different tillage operations. In learning to raise and tend plants and to wait patiently for results, the pupils get to know something of their needs and uses and of their infinite variety and beauty. As the course proceeds they begin to see, too, that everything they and their fellows do helps towards the realisation of a carefully planned scheme.

2. The garden as a school amenity.—The ideal setting for a school, whether Infant School, Junior School or Senior School, is a garden. In the selection and lay-out of new sites the conception should be the school estate of which the garden is an important part, beautiful and at the same time an integral part of the school life. Much of the charm and joy of the garden will depend upon the variety and arrangement of its features and their blending to form a harmonious whole. The garden should be regarded as belonging to the entire school and all pupils ought to have some direct interest, some work to do in it, and so share both the enjoyment of its amenities and the responsibility for its upkeep. Thus it becomes a place of pleasurable resort in which all may take a pride. These advantages are less easily secured when the garden is not part of the school site : for not only is the continuous observation which is so valuable a part of the school training seriously curtailed, but a detached garden makes very little contribution to the amenities of the school. Whenever possible, a long narrow site should be avoided. Such a site is difficult to lay out effectively so as to form an attractive and natural setting for the school.

3. The nature of the garden.—Any aspect is suitable for the school garden, though it is well to avoid a prominent slope to the north, on which the land is likely to be cold and the crops late. Warm slopes to the south are suitable for early crops. If the slope is considerable, the terracing that may be necessary to prevent heavy rains from washing away the soil offers scope for attractive planning.

A windswept site requires a shield. This may be a hedge or a belt of quickly growing trees which may need some protection until established. When fully grown either will break the wind, add variety to the lay-out of the garden and afford useful data for observations on the effect of a wind break on growth and soil temperature.

A deep loam is undoubtedly the best soil for a school garden, but almost any soil can be made reasonably satisfactory by tillage and manuring. If there is any alternative, a really stiff clay or land which is heavily shaded by trees is to be avoided. Land which is liable to be water-logged is quite unsuitable for most purposes, unless it can be drained easily.

The size of the garden depends not only upon the number of pupils but also upon the kinds of work attempted. The more intensive the cultivation the smaller is the amount of ground needed per pupil. All gardens must, however, be large enough to provide adequate opportunity for practical work by all the pupils engaged. No hard and fast rule can be laid down ; but, where gardening is a part of the school course, there should generally be not less than half an acre of garden for a single-stream Senior School and at least an acre for a two-stream or larger school. Considerably larger areas will be required where it is intended to develop such special features as a permanent fruit plantation, plots for growing large quantities of vegetables for the school canteen, plots for farm crops, or grassland for manurial experiments. Separate provision of land should be made for any small live-stock kept.

For an unreorganised rural school of about 100 children a minimum area of a quarter of an acre is required for the satisfactory development of a comprehensive course of gardening. Quite a small garden can be made to serve a useful purpose in providing training in flower cultivation and producing varied material for Nature Study.

4. The planning and lay-out of the School garden. —In laying out the garden provision should be made for progressive training in the cultivation of vegetables, flowers and fruit. Skilful planning will be required to ensure this training and, at the same time, to provide attractive features such as a lawn, a pool, a rockery, a pergola, or groups of ornamental shrubs. Such features should be treated boldly, each being suitably merged into its surroundings and, when necessary, so arranged as to break monotony and prevent incongruous groupings. It is useful to include in the plan an assembly point, where the children can be called together for short talks and discussions on problems that arise. This should be easily accessible from every part of the garden and should constitute its natural centre and be set off by some of its most decorative features.

Any attempt to adopt throughout a particular area a standardised type of garden is to be deprecated. The lay-out of the garden will naturally embody the teacher's and often the children's, ideas and have a character of its own. It should not be fixed once and for all. Need for change will arise from time to time and the teacher should lay his plans in advance so that any changes that are made shall in no way lessen the attractiveness of the garden as a whole : they will in fact form part of the pupils' training in the orderly development of a garden.

The main paths should be of permanent construction, and should vary in their width according to the size of the garden. A large garden requires a wide main path which, if suitably flanked by flowers or bushes, gives it character and distinction. Seats may be provided here and there so that pupils and visitors may enjoy the garden at their ease.

Permanent paths should be properly made and finished off with a suitable surface. Unless the soil is fairly porous, it may be necessary to drain the path by digging a trench down the middle and filling it with stones or brick rubble. Gravel makes a satisfactory surface, but ashes generally give an unsightly patchy surface and should not be used unless they are perfectly homogeneous. Edgings of various kinds serve to keep soil off the path. They should be unobtrusive and should not be allowed to become permanently infested by weeds. Grass paths are attractive if well made and kept mown and edged, but are unsuited for heavy traffic.

Although it is undesirable to divide the garden into a large number of small plots separated by narrow paths, some temporary paths are necessary. These should be made of trodden earth, so that they can be periodically dug over and kept clean. Their surface should be level and their edges neatly and accurately cut.

5. The teacher of gardening.—The staff of a Senior School where gardening is taught may be expected to include a master or mistress with special qualifications for teaching the subject. It is clearly desirable that the head teacher of an unreorganised rural school, or a member of the assistant staff, should also be qualified. But a teacher who, though lacking special qualifications, is interested in gardening, has a practical knowledge of it and is convinced of its value, is likely to achieve success if he is prepared to equip himself further by such means as courses organised by Local Authorities and advice from expert organisers. No keen teacher of gardening, however well qualified, will neglect to take advantage of any source of new ideas and knowledge within his reach.

The many points of contact between gardening and the rest of the school curriculum may again be emphasised and the mutual co-operation of all members of the staff to make the most of these contacts may be taken for granted.

II. THE COURSE OF INSTRUCTION IN GARDENING

A. THE SCOPE OF SCHOOL GARDENING

6. The cultivation of vegetables.—It will be clear from what has already been said that the school garden should be much more than a vegetable allotment. Nevertheless, the cultivation of vegetables is an essential part of school garden practice and gains in interest and value from being associated with other forms of cultivation.

To begin with, pupils will concentrate on a few crops, in general those commonly grown in a cottage garden or allotment. In doing so they will learn to prepare seed beds, to sow seeds, to carry out the subsequent treatment suited to the requirements of each crop and to understand a simple rotation. Later more intensive cultivation and a much wider range of crops will be undertaken.

At this stage growing for succession should have an important place in the course; and the pupils should learn how to prolong the season of growth of particular crops, e.g. peas, beans or brassicas. Inter-cropping and catch cropping will also be practised and the pupils will realise that the fertility of the land must be maintained since the ground is never free of crops for long and is often bearing two crops at the same time. They will understand, too, that such culture requires a very different rotation from the simple type followed in their first year. Clearly work of this intensive kind cannot be carried out on small individual plots. Communal cultivation on one or more large plots is necessary.

The cultivation of the less commonly grown vegetables, such as artichokes, asparagus, celery, endive, salsify, seakale and spinach, and of such herbs as thyme, sage, parsley, mint, balm, sorrel, should also be included.

7. The cultivation of flowers.—Flowers play an important part in the making of an attractive garden, and it should be recognised that sound craftsmanship can be taught as well through the growing of flowers as through the growing of vegetables. The raising of annuals from seeds and the different methods of propagating herbaceous plants and shrubs present a wide range of operations of varying difficulty. The consideration of colour, of colour blending, of the sizes of plants and their times of flowering, and of massing for effect, is essential to the making of a beautiful garden. The growing of plants for cut flowers and simple experiments in plant breeding may also be undertaken. Work on this scale obviously requires considerable space and equipment for propagation.

It is not always realised that the fertility of the flower beds must be maintained by suitable manuring. Neglect of this important matter inevitably means disappointing results.

A lawn, of fine grass, should be laid down wherever space permits. It should be kept free from weeds and closely cut and neatly edged. Frequent cutting and judicious rolling will do much to produce a fine sward. Weeds such as daisies, plantains and " self-heal " should be eradicated. Periodical treatment with sulphate of ammonia or lawn sand will kill or discourage weeds and promote the growth of grass. An occasional dressing during the winter of finely divided leaf mould will restore soil fertility which tends to be lowered by constant mowing and the removal of grass cuttings.

8. The cultivation of fruit.—It is essential that provision should be made in every garden for some training in fruit growing. In some areas this may well be one of the main features of the gardening. Much of the most instructive part of fruit culture occurs in the nursery-garden stage. The school fruit plot, once it is established, should, therefore, at all times illustrate the progressive stages of the tree or bush from propagation to the mature fruiting condition. If there is sufficient space, a small orchard or fruit plantation of mature trees should also be gradually planted. On no account, however, must the formative stages of the work be crowded out. There must always be the nursery. When there is insufficient space to provide an orchard plot, closely trained forms such as cordons and espaliers may be grown on part of the vegetable garden ; but it cannot be too strongly emphasised that the planting of standard and half-standard trees on a vegetable plot is undesirable.

Cuttings of red and black currants and gooseberries should be taken and planted each year. At the end of five years there will be a series of bushes showing each stage from the cutting to the fruiting bush and illustrating the pruning required to train a bush in such a way as to produce the best results. After this the oldest bushes should be removed each year in order to make room for younger ones and so preserve a succession of stages.

The culture of fruit trees should begin with the formation of stool beds, which, if large enough, will provide abundant material for budding and grafting in the nursery beds. There ought to be sufficient stocks to supply every member of the class with two or more for budding or grafting. In general, named stocks, e.g. East Malling Types II and IX, are the most suitable for apples, quince stocks for pears, and Pershore stocks for plums. With these, as with bush fruits, the progressive stages of development should always be shown in the nursery plot. In a large garden different forms of training, bush, cordon, and espalier, may well be exemplified.

Space should also be found for strawberries and raspberries, while loganberries and similar hybrids yield acceptable fruit and are useful for covering a fence or making a break between one part of the garden and another.

9. Some general points connected with the cultivation of vegetables, flowers and fruit.—Every garden should have at least one frame and a whole range of frames may be needed in gardens where it is intended that the older pupils should carry out an extensive programme of winter work with vegetables and salads and propagation from cuttings. The management of frames is an important part of their training and adequate facilities should be provided for it. Given frames and sufficient stable manure, hot-bed culture may also be undertaken and the pupils taught how to temper fresh manure, to build and consolidate the heap and to attend to watering and ventilating it.

Pests and diseases of plants observed in the garden must be investigated immediately and dealt with in the appropriate manner. The winter washing of fruit trees should be the regular practice, while grease banding and spring spraying are also desirable.

As a rule, only named varieties of vegetables, flowers and fruits should be grown, and these, as well as any ornamental shrubs, should be clearly labelled, so that the pupils may become familiar with the names of the plants they cultivate and learn as far as possible to recognise characteristics which distinguish one variety from another.   The garden exists for the benefit of the whole school, and it becomes a much more interesting and educative place if plants are labelled, so that the children can find out the names of the plants for themselves.

The common weeds should be known by sight, their habits studied, and the best ways of getting rid of them discussed and practised.

Useful work may be done in the way of testing samples of seeds for purity and germination.

10. Economics of the garden.—The primary object of school gardening is not the production of food.   Food is, however, produced and must not be wasted.   There is no reason why some or all of the vegetables and some of the flowers and fruit should not be sold, but no gardening teacher should ever have to feel that, for the purpose of recovering the whole or even a large part of the expenses, the course of instruction is restricted to the growing of produce that will sell readily.   Nor should the teacher have to provide seeds and manures and take the produce.   Any profits from sales should normally be expended on further development of the garden.

It has been found possible in some schools to establish delightful gardens, with all the variety needed for progressive work and at the same time to make a speciality of certain crops which bring in considerable revenue. These are often flowers which command a relatively high price when well grown.   Supplies of fresh fruit and vegetables for use in the school cookery room or canteen should be obtained from the garden and charged or allowed for at a fair figure.

Pupils should keep accounts of receipts and expenditure for the garden as a whole or for the production of some particular crop. These accounts will not be comparable with those of a commercial garden, but they will impress the facts that there is a financial aspect of gardening and that waste and carelessness are expensive.

B. THE PLANNING OF THE SCHOOL COURSE

11. Planning ahead essential.—Planning for the future is essential in all gardening, and the plans that are made should be understood by the pupils as well as the teacher. Land must often be prepared or plants raised months in advance of requirements ; and developments such as a progressive course of fruit culture call for plans extending several years ahead. If the right time for sowing or planting is missed, it may be necessary to wait nearly a year before the opportunity again occurs. Plans set out on paper may not always be exactly followed in practice, but to try to work without them is to court failure.

It is clearly more difficult to organise progressive instruction in the unreorganised school, with one gardening class drawn from three age groups, than in the large senior school where there is a class or more than a class in each group. In the former the planning of the garden will naturally be simpler and the older pupils may share indirectly in the training of the beginners. In such schools group work is usually possible, and the first year pupils should be taught to carry out by themselves simple operations, in order that the teacher may be sometimes free to give special instruction in more advanced work to groups of older pupils. It is most important that each group or class should have its own sphere of operations, apart of course from such permanent features as the orchard, flower borders and lawn in which all share.

It has already been stated that gardening may properly be regarded as the key outdoor activity of a rural school. Adequate time should therefore be given to its practice. Not less than two hours per week throughout the year, exclusive of the time allotted to the associated course in Science, should be allowed for a course of instruction of the kind outlined above. It is general experience that pupils enjoy gardening and that many of them willingly undertake voluntary work out of school-hours in term time and during holidays.

12. Progressive courses of instruction.—It should not be difficult to select from the wide range of vegetable, flower, and fruit cultivation outlined above the content of a progressive syllabus extending over three or four years and showing clearly the work allotted to the different age groups.

The first year courses should provide for instruction in tillage operations, in the preparation of seed beds, and in the growing of the commoner vegetables and flowers. In carrying out the various operations involved the pupils will learn the correct use of tools, gain experience of, and share in, ordinary garden routine, and become familiar with simple rotations. They will also observe some of the work done by their seniors.

The second year course, in addition to the more advanced vegetable culture indicated earlier in this chapter, might include the main part of flower propagation, the laying-out of flower beds and borders, and the planting and pruning of roses and flowering shrubs, together with preliminary training in the use of frames and the management of the fruit plot.

Greater responsibility in all directions should be assumed in the third and fourth years when the work will normally include the charge of frames or the fruit plot, various experiments, and the cultivation of special crops and flowers. The pupils may now be expected to keep a watchful eye on the whole of the garden and to be ready to report or to deal with any matter that needs attention.

It is clear that it will not be possible to include in every garden all the features suggested earlier in this chapter and that it may, indeed, not be desirable, even if it were possible, to carry out in all schools the wide range of work outlined above.

C. WORK IN THE SCHOOL GARDEN

13. The handling of the tools.—The correct handling of tools should be taught from the very first, if the best results are to be secured with the minimum effort. Pupils should know the use of each tool, how to handle it properly and the reason for handling it in a particular way. To obtain the best effects, the tools must be large enough for thorough work and suited in size to the physique of those using them. Nevertheless they must be real tools and not mere playthings.

14. Tillage operations.—The pupils should have sufficient practice in simple digging, and in trenching, when the ground is suitable and the operation necessary. They must recognise the difference between soil and subsoil and know why each should normally be kept in its place. They should learn the use of fork and rake in preparing seed beds and understand the need for suitable consolidation of the soil while preserving a loose surface. They should also learn to use the line and hoe, rake or spade, in preparing straight drills of correct depth, to sow neither too thickly nor too thinly, to single plants in good time and in the right way, to transplant properly, and to use the hoe in surface cultivation. In effect, the pupils should acquire skill in the use of a variety of tools and learn to take pride in work done well and in workmanlike style.

Careful supervision is required and the pupils should be trained to observe closely, to report matters that need attention, to ask questions and to look for information in books, and to be generally resourceful, handy and self-reliant.

The teacher should always make it clear that the operations in the garden and those on the farm are applications of the same principle. Thus digging may be compared with ploughing, and the use of fork, cultivator and rake in preparing a garden seed-bed with the use of cultivator, harrow and roller in the preparations of a field for sowing. These and similar comparisons with farm practice will acquire more reality through visits to farms, orchards and market gardens. Gardening, then becomes the means of acquiring a steadily growing insight into some of the activities in which many of the pupils will play a part later on.

15. The use of manures.—It is essential that the soil should be maintained in good condition. For good tilth and fertility it must contain a fair amount of decayed organic matter, some of which will be supplied from the compost heap that should be found in every garden. But, when available, farmyard or stable manure will be the chief material used. If enough of this is not obtainable, a portion of the garden can be set aside each year for green manuring, and a succession of such crops as vetches, rye, rape or mustard grown and dug in.

The special needs of different crops should be studied and supplied by means of artificial fertilisers. The characteristics and uses of the common nitrogenous, phosphatic, and potash fertilisers should be considered and as far as possible demonstrated.

The soil must never be allowed to become deficient in lime. Its condition should be discovered by means of a simple soil testing outfit, involving the use of a universal indicator. The mechanical improvement of a clay soil due to the flocculating action of lime can easily be demonstrated by suitable means.

The manurial treatment of the garden should be compared with that of a neighbouring farm or market garden. Complete manuring for potatoes or mangolds, the application of superphosphate to promote root action and of basic slag to improve grass herbage are examples of the kind of practice to which attention may well be given.

D. EQUIPMENT AND SUPPLIES

16. Tools required.—A minimum schedule of tools will include :—

> *spades and forks*—as many altogether as the number of pupils in a gardening class. (For heavy land there should be more forks than spades) ;

> *hoes*—one for each pupil, at least half being Dutch hoes ;

> *rakes and cultivators*—half as many altogether as the number of pupils in the class ;

> a large *hay-rake* is most useful for securing a level surface on a large bed ;

> *trowels and weeders*—one for each pupil in the class ;

> *wheelbarrows*—one for a medium-sized garden, two for a garden that exceeds half an acre ;

> two long *garden-lines* and several short ones ; several *dibbers* ;

> a *mower*, and *edging shears* for grass paths or lawn, and *hedge-shears* ;

pruning and budding knives—at least two of each for a class of twenty; one pair of *secateurs*, preferably of the Rolcut pattern;

one *sprayer* if fruit is cultivated;

a set of *scales and weights;* a *spring balance;* a *measuring tape.*

17. The tool-shed.—The tools must be kept in good order. Toolsheds should therefore be large enough to be fitted with racks on which the tools can be neatly and conveniently stored. The best type is one with a good window, a bench below it and sufficient floor space to shelter a class in bad weather. It is invaluable for potting, drying, sorting and storing of seeds, and for assembling a class for discussions and making notes. When the school is without a workshop, the toolshed should be equipped with a carpenter's bench and set of tools.

The importance of frames has already been mentioned. A greenhouse, which may be erected by the pupils, is a valuable adjunct in gardens where tomato-growing, or the cultivation of chrysanthemums and similar flowers or propagation on a large scale is undertaken.

18. Seeds.—Seeds should be of satisfactory quality and in sufficient variety and should be available some time before they are needed for sowing. The teacher of gardening should be as free as possible to make his own choice of seeds. It is well worth while to provide the senior gardening pupils with seedsmen's catalogues in the winter and to give them good practice in working out schemes of sowing for the ensuing season, after taking into account the past cropping, the system of rotation, and times of sowing and harvesting.

A piece of ground should be set aside for the saving of seeds, in particular those of the biennial vegetables.

The seeds saved may not always be very valuable, but the practice enables pupils to follow the complete life-histories of a number of plants.

When a new garden is started an initial supply of ornamental shrubs, fruit stocks and cuttings should be provided. The stock subsequently required can then be obtained by propagation.

19. The keeping of garden records.—Pupils should be trained to make concise records of their work in the garden—e.g. the operations necessary for the cultivation of a particular crop, observations on its growth, or the grafting and subsequent development of an apple stock. Observations that have to be recorded regularly are for that reason the more likely to be accurate. The records ought to be so arranged that reference can quickly be made to any particular topic. Hence they are best kept in a loose-leaf notebook, where they can be filed according to subject, additional pages being inserted, when necessary, in their proper sequence. Pupils will then possess a valuable record of the whole of their gardening course. A mere diary in which the entries are not classified and indexed is almost useless.

Careful sketches or diagrams, properly annotated, and graphs are often a good form of record. Newspaper cuttings may sometimes be filed with the records, but the teacher must be careful to see that they are well selected. The laborious copying of letter-press and drawings from the blackboard or from books is usually a waste of time, and may indeed result in failure by the pupil to look attentively at real things. Some of the most valuable records are those of experiments and observations extending over a series of years and preserved for reference by successive classes.

20. The reference library.—It is important that the pupils should realise the help to be gained from books about gardening and, in country districts at least, about the whole range of rural pursuits. A reference library of books and periodicals on gardening, of illustrated catalogues issued by leading firms of seedsmen and nurserymen, and of the bound volumes of leaflets and some of the pamphlets and bulletins issued by the Ministry of Agriculture and Fisheries, is an essential. The Science library of the school will no doubt include books about insects, birds and other living creatures. The pupils should be encouraged to consult these books for information on specific aspects of their work, and use them freely in connexion with their observations in the garden.

E. THE SCIENCE OF THE GARDEN

21. The science and gardening courses should be complementary.—Science courses in country schools include, as a rule, a simple study of air, water and soil, and of plant and animal life, in addition to an elementary treatment of heat, electricity, and mechanics, and thus deal with the more important principles underlying farm and garden practice. The master or mistress who takes the Science is accustomed to draw freely upon the outdoor work for illustrations. Similarly, the teacher who takes the gardening has many opportunities of supplementing classroom teaching; and it is most important that, when the Science and the Gardening are in different hands, the two teachers should co-operate closely, in order that the courses may be complementary in the fullest sense of the term.

Pupils should be trained to observe closely and systematically in the garden. They should note the relation of soil conditions to weather; the effect of varying soil conditions, of warmth, moisture, aspect, and of the relative amounts of light and shade, upon sowing, rate of germination, thinning, transplanting and character of growth; and the effect of manurial treatment, hoeing, and watering, on the growth of plants and on their yield. A great part of the value of the gardening course is lost if it fails to make the pupils quick to see and eager to inquire. With minds thus alert they can, with advantage, carry out carefully planned out-door experiments. These should bear upon garden practice, have a simple and clear aim, and be likely to give definite results. Conflicting factors should be eliminated or allowed for ; the space devoted to experiments should be reasonably large ; and the preparation and setting out should be done with care. Observation should be accurate, frequent, and regular, and careful records should be made of what has been observed.

22. Types of experimental work.—The following may serve to indicate the type of problem which may be investigated experimentally : the depths of sowing of different seeds ; the results of early and of late thinning ; the effects of transplanting at various distances apart ; the influence of hoeing upon a growing crop ; the effects of shade, shelter, or invading tree roots ; the effects of simple manurial treatment ; variety trials ; the effect of stocks on scions ; and the methods of dealing with pests and diseases. Whenever possible, advice should be obtained from the nearest Agricultural or Horticultural College about the planning and arrangement of experiments. The interest and value of such work will be greatly increased if the same experiment or set of experiments can be carried out, under expert supervision in a number of schools in a particular district.

II.—THE KEEPING OF SMALL LIVESTOCK AND ALLIED ACTIVITIES

I. SOME GENERAL CONSIDERATIONS

23. The keeping of small livestock as part of the practical training in a country school.—Teachers with experience in the keeping of small livestock are agreed that the work makes a strong appeal to the many children who are naturally interested in animals and that, when it is combined with gardening and handicraft, the whole forms a broad course of practical education specially suited to the setting and to the needs of the country school. The marked increase in recent years of work of this kind, and the facilities which the new Senior Schools offer for it, make it desirable to outline its possibilities and to indicate how it may best be developed and extended.

At the outset it should be realised that the instruction is not intended to be vocational ; nor should it consist solely of a series of classroom lessons. It is impossible, in the limited time available, for children to acquire a high degree of craft skill or to gain a detailed knowledge of every process. On the other hand, experience has shown that many boys and girls in country schools can become familiar with a wide range of sound practice, particularly in bee-keeping and poultry-keeping, and, as a result of their experience and the science teaching associated with it, gain an intelligent understanding of some of the more important principles underlying the life and work of the country-side. The training may also lead to hobbies of lasting interest and value. Finally, children are quick to appreciate the fact that, under satisfactory conditions and with proper care, the keeping of small livestock may be made to pay.

The most suitable activities are bee-keeping, poultry-husbandry, the keeping of rabbits, and dairying. It is not suggested that many schools will attempt all these or that the entire work connected with dairying, for example, can be carried out satisfactorily on the school premises. The best plan in the case of other livestock such as pigs and goats, which are sometimes kept at school, is undoubtedly to encourage the pupils to form Young Farmers' Clubs and keep the animals at home. It is not, therefore, proposed to include any further reference to these in this chapter.

24. Desirable conditions.—Provided that the school has a garden in which a quiet corner sheltered from north and east winds can be found for one or more hives bee-keeping is quite practicable. An orchard in which the hives can be set to face south-east is probably one of the best places. Care must, however, be taken to find a site where the hives will not directly abut on a path which is frequently used by the children.

Although, under the " intensive " system, poultry can be kept quite satisfactorily in a corner of the school garden, it is better, wherever possible, to reserve for the purpose a small paddock or part of a meadow. It is essential, too, that the area should be adequate. Thus, an area of 20 sq. yds. per bird is suggested, when poultry are to be kept on the " semi-intensive " system. A south or south-east aspect is to be preferred, so that the birds may get ample sunlight ; but shade from excessive sun and protection from strong winds must also be considered in connexion with the choice of site.

Adequate provision must be made for the storage of food stuffs and of the appliances and equipment when not in use.

25. Housing and appliances.—The housing for the school livestock should, whenever possible, be made by the children. Thus, when poultry are kept, visits might be paid to up-to-date farms in the district for the purpose of examining and measuring suitable types of houses. Plans can then be drawn and estimates made as to the quantity and cost of the necessary materials. The actual construction and erection involve the consideration of stresses and strains ; the effective use of several kinds of joints ; the hanging of doors and windows ; protection against wind and rain ; provision for lighting and ventilation ; food and water supplies and finally, the actual work of building on the selected site. Some Education Authorities provide one house as a model, which the boys can copy if more are required. While this arrangement doubtless makes it easier to get poultry-keeping started in the first instance, the value of the training is materially increased if all houses and appliances are made by the children themselves. The planning and making of a poultry house give children an insight into the purposes of its various parts, which they cannot get from lessons.

Most of the appliances connected with poultry-keeping and bee-keeping such as coops, mash hoppers, water stands, brooders, houses, hives, observation hives, brood boxes, clearer boards, frames and feeders can be made in the school workshops. Similarly, veils, quilts and covers may form part of the needlework.

26. Experience necessary for teaching.—It is desirable that the master or mistress undertaking the instruction should have had some previous training in the subject or at least possess some knowledge of it as well as practical experience and skill. A keen interest in country life and close contact with it in childhood and youth will often prove a satisfactory starting point. It is not, however, unusual for the necessary knowledge and experience to be gradually acquired by keenly interested teachers who take up the work on appointment to country schools and make a start by attending short courses or reading about the subject and paying visits to well-managed poultry farms and apiaries. Valuable advice and information can usually be obtained from farmers and bee-keepers, as well as from County Agricultural Organisers, whose active help should be enlisted from the outset. Wherever possible, too, arrangements should be made for periodical visits by the county experts.

Before undertaking any branch of small livestock keeping teachers should consult the bulletins and leaflets issued by the Ministry of Agriculture, together with some of the numerous inexpensive books which deal with the practical side of the work. A selection of these should be available in the school library for the children to refer to.

27. Range and scope of the work.—Teachers are advised to start bee-keeping or poultry-keeping on a small scale, with one stock of bees, for instance, or a pen of about a dozen birds. This provision is sufficient for showing most of the common operations and for illustrating essential principles ; and many teachers may not wish to exceed it. Schools with suitable facilities or with teachers specially interested in either bees or poultry will naturally extend their stocks, so as to provide a wider training, and this deserves encouragement. On the other hand, if the school is to set, as it should, a high standard in the details of practical management, it is imperative that the stock carried should never be greater than can be effectively dealt with by the children. The main purpose of the training will be defeated if the hives, houses and appliances are not kept perfectly clean, if the bees and birds do not receive regular and proper attention, or if the demands made by routine operations on the children's time prevent them from receiving the necessary training in scientific principles.

For success in the work, theory must be closely linked throughout with practice ; and, just as with other forms of Practical Instruction, some of the most effective teaching will take the form of incidental talks and discussions during routine operations and the demonstration of new ideas or processes.

28. Links with other subjects.—Brief reference may be made here to the use to which outdoor work of this kind can be put in classroom teaching. The Science master or mistress will doubtless be quick to seize on many of the outdoor operations for the illustration of scientific principles. Similarly, sound practice in any form of livestock keeping is based on the elementary rules of hygiene ; and the penalty, which seldom fails to follow any neglect of these, is usually sufficiently swift and real to carry conviction. The measurements and calculations connected with the construction of bee hives and poultry houses, the purchase of food stuffs, the mixing of rations for growing, laying and fattening birds, and the keeping of accounts and records of all kinds, provide invaluable data for practical arithmetic. There are many other ways in which the work may be called upon to lend reality to classroom teaching, though care should be taken to avoid forced or unnatural correlation.

As with Gardening, the records kept should be restricted mainly to simple accounts of the work done and the observations made. All essential figures relating to housing, current costs, yields and receipts, should be recorded in tabular and graphical form.

29. Care of livestock when the school is closed.— The care of livestock during week-ends and holidays is undoubtedly a difficulty which may even cause some schools to hesitate to undertake work of this kind ; but the difficulty is not so great as is sometimes alleged. In most schools there are children with homes nearby, who can be relied on to tend the animals at such times ; and usually it is possible for the livestock club to make some small payments for their services. It is a good plan to arrange for some experienced poultry farmer or bee-keeper, who is interested in the school, to pay periodical visits during the longer holidays and, if necessary, to report any signs of neglect to the teacher.

II. POULTRY-KEEPING

30. How to begin.—Poultry-keeping is probably the most suitable form of livestock work for the older boys and girls in country schools. It offers a fairly wide range of daily or seasonal activities connected with cleaning, feeding, watering, breeding, hatching, rearing, fattening and preparing table birds for market.

Teachers proposing to begin poultry-keeping are advised to get into touch with local experts from whom valuable advice and assistance can be obtained.

When the time comes to provide housing, visits should be paid by the class to one or more farms with up-to-date equipment, and measurements and sketches should be made. The Ministry of Agriculture's pamphlet on *The Housing of Poultry* (Bulletin No. 56) might also be consulted and the plans in it studied.

31. Housing the poultry.—In deciding the type and size of house to be adopted various factors will have to be taken into consideration, as, for instance, the condition and aspect of the site, the size of the unit, and the system to be followed. Usually one of the " semi-intensive " types of houses with space for about 20 birds will be found best suited for beginners. The necessity for ample floor space will be appreciated, when it is remembered that the house must serve as an exercise ground in bad weather, as well as a place for roosting and egg laying. It should also be high enough to ensure good ventilation and plenty of head room for the pupils when engaged in cleaning it out. It should have a floor space of three square feet per bird : if a larger floor space can be allowed, all the better. The children are quite capable, under the teacher's direction, of building the sections, bolting them together and making all the necessary fitments, perches and perch sockets, dropping boards, nest boxes, trap nests, and hoppers. Given sufficient ground, other types of housing will doubtless be designed and built, if only for instructional and experimental purposes, as the teaching develops.

It will be found useful to divide the ground for each pen into two runs' and to place the house so that the runs can be used alternately. This arrangement gives time for the grass to recover after each period of use and so lessens the risk of disease due to the ground becoming foul. A cinder or asphalt path to ensure a clean access to the house is desirable.

32. Choice of breed.—The nature of the actual start will depend partly on the season and partly on the funds available. Three or four sittings of eggs may be bought and broody hens borrowed or hired to hatch them ; or a dozen three month old pullets may be bought, or, again, the school may start with a breeding pen of its own, say a cockerel and six hens. The first plan is perhaps the most interesting, but it must be remembered that, for the beginner, the rearing of chicks is probably more difficult than any other branch of poultry-keeping. Whichever method is adopted, careful enquiries should be made as to the pedigree, egg records and robustness of the vendor's stock and the measures, such as blood testing, which he has taken to ensure a clean bill of health. The choice of breed will be conditioned to some extent by the soil, aspect and accommodation, and on this point advice will doubtless be sought from experienced breeders in the district. It should perhaps be stressed here that in egg-production strain is of very great importance, and that loyalty to one breed over a period of years is essential.

33. Routine practical work.—It is expected that the majority of the older boys and girls will share in routine practical work, and that for this they will normally be divided into weekly rotas, each rota being under the charge of a leader who is responsible for seeing that the directions for watering, feeding, cleaning and general attention are carried out satisfactorily. Copies of the detailed written instructions should be posted in the classroom and food-shed and it should be made clear to the class that cleanliness, regular feeding and clean water are essential for success in poultry-keeping.

A selection must be made from the many food mixtures in common use, and this is a point on which the advice of the County expert may well be sought. If the school has more than one pen of birds, experiments can be made with different rations and the results noted. The importance of good grass on the runs and of a supply of grit and oyster shell or limestone should be stressed.

From the point of view of egg production it is advisable that birds should not normally be retained beyond the second year, and arrangements must accordingly be made to replace the older birds every year. While it is a growing practice in the industry to leave breeding to the specialist, in school work the older pupils should gain as wide experience as possible. The greatest care must be taken in the selection of eggs for hatching. Birds of known pedigree and of sound constitution must always be used for breeding. In order to introduce fresh blood, it is advisable to go outside at least every two years for a cockerel or one sitting of eggs. Where the number of new birds required each year is small, it will usually be found most convenient to hatch them under broody hens in coops placed in shelter. A number of schools, however, possess incubators, and, when greater numbers of chicks have to be reared and conditions are satisfactory, it will be better to make use of these. The subsequent rearing, particularly of artificially hatched chicks, is a matter involving regular attention if losses are to be avoided; and it is this side of school poultry-keeping with which most difficulty is experienced. For successful rearing the chicks should be kept on a separate range which can be changed from year to year.

The fattening of cockerels as well as of older birds enables the children to gain a further insight into food values and to become familiar with the preparation of table birds for market.   In some schools the production of table poultry may occupy a more prominent part in the work, and the pupils consequently gain experience of the breeds most suited for the purpose.

34. Science teaching and poultry-keeping.—Poultry-keeping offers abundant material for good biological teaching in connexion with housing, feeding, breeding, hatching, rearing and general management, while a simple study of the structure of the fowl and the egg and of the early development of the chick makes a very valuable addition to any biology course.

Given a successful start, development will depend on the enthusiasm of the teacher and pupils and the amount of time available.   There are many directions in which the work may be developed without materially increasing the stock, e.g. experiments in connexion with breeding and crossing ; artificial incubation and rearing ; and trials of different types of houses and food mixtures, and of fresh breeds.   There are schools, too, in which, for various reasons, poultry-keeping may be the main out-door activity.   In such schools expansion should be gradual, and it must never be forgotten that nothing in livestock keeping is so certain of retribution as overcrowding and dirty housing.

III. BEE-KEEPING

35. Bee-keeping a specialised craft.—Although bee-keeping is an excellent subject for inclusion in the curriculum of a rural school where conditions are suitable, a course in it should not on this account be lightly embarked upon, for, the lore of the craft being specialised and so to speak " peculiar," it is not every man's hobby.

In fact one of the first requisites is that the teacher himself should be a keen and knowing bee-keeper; for on him will depend the success of the course.

Another important point to keep in mind is that, while a course in Bee-keeping may be rich in educational value to all the boys and girls in a class, the actual handling of the bees in and around the hive should be a purely voluntary exercise so far as the pupils are concerned.

36. How to begin.—It will be advisable to begin bee-keeping, as has already been suggested, with one or two hives. This number is adequate for giving the pupils some knowledge of the rudiments of the subject, and in many schools it may never be desirable or necessary to increase it. In other schools, however, bee-keeping may be one of the main features of the rural work, and a dozen or more hives may be kept going, the various processes involved in building up the hives and stocking them and in the production of honey and by-products being dealt with in some detail.

It is advisable to begin in a modest way with a double-walled hive, built to take the British standard frame. Although more troublesome to construct than the simpler single-walled variety, this type of hive has the advantages of having air space completely surrounding the brood chamber. If it seems desirable to extend the scope of the course by having a number of hives, one or two of single-walled type may usefully be installed for comparison.

37. Acquiring the stock.—Circumstances and available money will usually decide whether the hive is to be stocked by means of a colony of bees, a nucleus, or a swarm. If sufficient funds are available it will probably be found best to purchase a colony of bees, for, barring accidents, a surplus of honey will normally be ensured in the first year; and the early enthusiasm of the young bee-keepers will not be damped by a tedious wait for results. Buying a nucleus is a less costly method, but only sufficient skill and knowledge can ensure a surplus of honey before the end of the year. A more generally satisfactory method for school purposes is to stock the first hive from a swarm, for, although a surplus the first year is very problematical, the method has the advantage that swarms will probably be obtainable free of charge from local bee-keepers interested in the rural activities of the school.

38. Scope and character of the work.—Bee-keeping as a practical training does not require the kind of regular attention and rota work that are necessary in poultry or rabbit keeping ; and the fact that only incidental attention is necessary, especially during the summer, simplifies the problem of tending the hives during the holiday season. The pupils should be carefully instructed in the care of the swarm, in winter feeding and attention, and in the various methods and devices used to increase the production of honey and the size of the colonies of bees. Bee-keeping is an excellent example of an activity in which success can be assured only by attention to the minutest details.

In schools in which bee-keeping is a special feature considerable attention is naturally paid to such processes as the extraction of honey and beeswax. Some schools indeed possess their own extractors. The activity can in this way be linked up with the Housecraft instruction, particularly in relation to the extraction, straining, bottling and grading of honey, the packing for sale, and the making of syrup, candy and furniture cream.

39. Science teaching and bee-keeping.—The subject will not attain its proper objective in the curriculum unless the various routine processes involved, too often taught as mere rule of thumb methods, find meaning and reason through the study of the biology of the bee, with all that this implies. As careful and detailed a study of the anatomy of the bee as accommodation and equipment will permit should be made in the laboratory or classroom, special attention being given to the structures which have special significance for the course in hand—pollen basket, legs, tongue, spiracles, tracheæ, wax pocket, and sting. The functions of the various parts should be considered, even if only theoretically : for instance, the tracheæ, the mechanism of respiration, are of special importance on account of their liability in certain conditions to become blocked up by mites, giving rise to Isle of Wight disease. A good compound microscope will be found useful in studying the structure of the bee and in examining tracheæ for mites. When this is not available a micro-projector will, for teaching purposes at least, form a good substitute. A simple dissecting microscope, such as can easily be made in school, will be found invaluable in investigating the general structure of the insect.

A detailed study should next be made of its life-history, the difference in the life cycles of queens, workers, and drones being carefully noted. A study of the individual insect leads naturally to some consideration of the internal economy of the hive itself, and of the respective contributions which the three kinds of bees make to the life of the whole community. The communal life of the bee can be followed by means of an observation hive, which should be part of the standard equipment of every school which has bee-keeping in its curriculum. This hive may well be installed inside the school buildings, with an aperture to permit of the passage of bees to and from the open air. Quite apart from instruction in bee-keeping, a hive of this kind is a valuable addition to the equipment for biology teaching in any school. Attention should be drawn to the interesting biological phenomenon of swarming, and to the fact that the masses of bees thus sent adrift to fend for themselves form organised and complete communities.

Any study of the biology of bees would be incomplete without some knowledge of the flowers from which the nectar is gathered. This implies examination and identification of the flora of the countryside with special reference to the activities of bees and cross pollination. Where a microscope is available a study of the pollen of the predominant wild and cultivated flowers will form an interesting adjunct to the study of the insects themselves.

IV. RABBIT-KEEPING

40. Value and scope of the work as a school activity.—Rabbit-keeping is easily begun and entails a relatively small initial outlay : it can also be easily continued by a pupil when he leaves school. There is no need for elaborate accommodation, and much of the food will consist of the surplus green stuff of the garden. Of late years rabbit keeping in this country has become more important, partly because of the increased consumption of hutch-bred rabbits and partly on account of the demand for pelts and Angora wool. School rabbit-keeping may therefore be of some influence in suggesting profitable side-line occupations for leisure and home industries for children and parents.

In the classroom, good use may be made of rabbit-keeping in connexion with the study of biology and hygiene. The work also has undoubted possibilities on the practical side : the pupils, in addition to making hutches, nest boxes, exhibition boxes, and crates and boxes for the despatch of pelts and carcases to market, can take part in dressing skins, making rabbit fur garments, and, if Angoras are kept, hand spinning of the wool.

For guidance on details of housing, feeding and general routine teachers should consult the Ministry of

Agriculture's Bulletin (No. 50) on *Rabbit-keeping*, along with other books, and pay visits to well-established studs.

41. Choice of breed.—The choice of breed will depend to some extent on the personal preference of the beginner. A visit to a show where rabbits are exhibited is perhaps the best way to become acquainted with the characteristics of the various breeds.

Each established breed of rabbit has its specialist club which fixes standards and aims at fostering the breed and helping the breeder. The beginner will find it sound policy to join the club catering for his particular breed and to make his start with stock purchased from a member of the Club. One, or at the most two, good does should be purchased and mated at the vendor's rabbitry. The initial capital should be invested in one good doe rather than in several moderate ones. With careful attention rabbits increase rapidly and the provision of accommodation for young stock is generally the most serious housing problem to solve. The size of the stud should be kept well within bounds, and on no account should more rabbits be kept than can be provided regularly with green food or roots.

V. DAIRYING

42. Scope of the work.—Because of its importance among rural industries, dairying may fittingly find a place in the curriculum of the country school. In addition, the wide use of milk and its value as a food make it highly desirable to include some instruction on it in every school. The extension of milk consumption by children under the " Milk in School " Scheme supplies an added argument for this, and provides many opportunities for incidental teaching.

Any instruction undertaken may be expected to vary considerably in scope, even in country schools. In most it will naturally be concerned mainly with the value of milk as a food, the necessity of keeping the supply pure, and ways and means of ensuring this, particularly in the handling and treatment of milk during distribution and in the home.

In country schools this course will often be followed by lessons on clean milk production, supplemented by visits to carefully selected farms. With a view to stressing still further the importance of absolute cleanliness at every stage in the production and handling of milk and its products, and, it may well be, with the purpose of stimulating deeper interest in the work, Education Authorities and teachers in dairying areas may quite naturally wish to extend the teaching to include demonstrations of clean milk production and of butter and cheese making and to arrange for some of the older children to take an active part in the work.

There is a real need for good practice in the handling of the school milk supply, and such practice, combined with very simple incidental teaching throughout the earlier stages of school life, probably forms the best introduction to more definite instruction in the Senior School. Even in the case of Senior School children some teachers may consider it undesirable to do more than continue or slightly extend this teaching, particularly as some instruction is included in the Housecraft course.

As the most important part of any simple course of instruction on milk is concerned largely with its liability to contamination and the steps necessary to prevent this, the teaching may best be linked up with Science and included as part of biology. The ordinary equipment of the Science laboratory will usually be found adequate for the necessary demonstrations and practical work.

43. Planning the course of instruction.—In planning a general course of this kind the teacher will normally make arrangements for a simple study of milk and its products (including the treatment of their composition in so far as this is necessary to throw light on their keeping qualities and handling) ; " clean " and " dirty " milk ; natural and artificial souring ; simple methods for preventing the increase of or for destroying bacteria in milk, e.g. cooling, pasteurisation and sterilisation and the treatment of dishes and utensils in which the milk is kept. The study of bacteria and moulds, including the growing of cultures on nutritive media and simple experiments in controlling their growth which will normally accompany this side of the work should prove of great value in connexion with the housecraft and hygiene teaching. The question of pathogenic bacteria in milk requires careful treatment by the teacher, who must be careful not to lay undue emphasis on this topic.

Instruction in clean milk production will involve additional lessons on such topics as cowsheds and, in particular, their lighting, ventilation and cleaning ; the methods adopted for the cleaning and sterilising of milk utensils, including milking machinery ; the preparation of the cows and other steps to be taken by milkers prior to milking ; the treatment of the first drawn milk ; the precautions taken to prevent pollution from the air ; cooling ; and the subsequent handling in the dairy prior to distribution. Visits to examine cowsheds and to watch all operations will be necessary. With a view to making the teaching still more effective teachers may arrange for some practical work by the children, e.g. actual practice in cleaning the milk pails, grooming the cows and washing down their flanks, washing the udder, and even milking. Such work should not as a rule amount to more than the practice necessary to impress the pupils with the need for absolute cleanliness at every stage in the production of milk.

44. Butter and cheese making.—Practical work in connexion with butter making and cheese making involves a supply of relatively expensive apparatus and appliances. As the equipment is needed in any one school for a very short time only each year and few teachers are as yet qualified to undertake the instruction, the Education Authorities who have developed work of this kind usually employ peripatetic instructresses. This arrangement works quite well with small groups of children, and is probably the best way of meeting the problem. It should be understood, however, that, although lessons on butter and cheese making may be specially appropriate for selected children in a dairying district, practical instruction of this kind is less valuable educationally for most children than the more general course of instruction in the handling of milk.

CHAPTER XI

ENGLISH LANGUAGE AND LITERATURE

SUMMARY OF CONTENTS

I. GENERAL CONSIDERATIONS

1. General aims of English teaching.—In no other subject of the curriculum is it so difficult to define the immediate aims of the teaching. In English the teacher has several tasks to perform, all inter-related and all vital. "Language is a skill, an art, a feeling, and a doing:" and in language the selected experience of mankind is concentrated for our delight and instruction. We may perhaps distinguish four main phases of the child's relationship to language. There is a certain practical control of words and phrases that must be learnt, there is a capacity for reacting to the meanings of words, to their intellectual and emotional associations, which must be acquired ; there is the power to organise words for the purposes of self-expression to be taught ; and there is the experience of the best kinds of self-expression, of literature, to be gained.

2. Responsibility of the whole school staff.—It is, of course, the business of the whole school to forward the child's mastery of language, for this is the medium by which he is to be educated and by which he will further his education. In particular, it is the responsibility of the School in general to make him lively and exact and fluent in speech, to insist that any written expression of his shall convey the thought with accuracy and orderliness. It is not so much that the English will benefit if, for example, the Science teacher does this. It is rather that the Science teacher cannot teach his own subject effectively unless this insistence constantly accompanies his teaching. The study of any book is necessarily a language lesson : and, if this is duly remembered in the earlier and middle stages, the older pupils will be fitter to cope with the difficulties of their more advanced work. The children should be required to do much more than make brief answers to questions. They should be encouraged to restate in words of their own the substance of what they have read and, with the teacher's help, to turn it over in their minds until they apprehend its meaning completely. For this both oral and written exercises will be needed. Apparent failure when the work in various subjects comes to be tested is often due to the ill-defined impressions the children have received from what they have heard or read. It should be remembered how many expressions, even in books specially written for children, are vague and abstract. With these principles and admonitions in mind, every teacher in the school will do much to further and strengthen the child's control of words.

3. The special responsibility of the teacher of English.—Like every other teacher, the teacher of English must have these aims constantly in view, though at times his treatment of specific aspects may be more formal. But he has the particular duty of introducing children to the world of Literature and of enriching thereby their experience of life through that broad and lively discipline which their discovery of books will afford them. The teaching of English, however, includes more than this, for children need opportunities for putting into appropriate language their own thoughts and experiences, and in this part of their English work it has been found that their own outlook upon life, their knowledge gained in school, and their interests and hobbies, afford the most natural material for such practice in the art of expression. In these two ways they will thus acquire not only some acquaintance with good literature of a type suitable to their age, but also some standards of judgment and appreciation which may stand them in good stead in later life.

The virtual disappearance of illiteracy has resulted in the production of a mass of reading material which appeals almost exclusively to cheap sentiment and facile emotion, which neither has, nor claims to have any literary value, and which is concerned above all things to spare the reader any exercise of thought. It is certainly true, on the other hand, that good books of every kind were never before so inexpensive and universally accessible as now ; and the existence side by side of these two fields of literature creates the present problem with which the teacher of English is inevitably concerned. In view of the comparatively early age at which children finish the Elementary School course, it would be unreasonable to blame the school if, later on, they yield overmuch to an appetite which is easily, and may be dangerously, satisfied. But something, and in the hands of a good teacher a great deal, can be done towards leading them to prefer the better to the worse and towards instilling into them certain standards of taste which may last. It behoves the teacher of English to further this aim by every means in his power.

Literary education is, after all, a systematic attempt to build up a sense of values, to persuade the mind to accept certain types of experience which are of cultural and personal significance ; it is a method of retaining in activity our traditional and characteristic modes of feeling and thinking that have given our civilisation its distinctive flavour and direction, but which are in danger of disappearing under the conditions of modern life.

Such broad considerations as these may, at first sight, seem remote from the practical issues of the classroom, but in reality they can never be irrelevant to the teacher of English. In a modern civilised community it is his privilege and his responsibility to educate minds into toughness and sensitivity, to train children to think hard and clearly and, at the same time, to recognise and enjoy, so far as children may, some of the finest and deepest experiences of humanity. Only if these aims are vigorously pursued can our society keep its sanity and wholeness.

4. What may be achieved by the end of the Elementary School course.—How far can these views be practically related to the task of teaching ? An obvious starting point is to ask how far we may reasonably expect to have progressed by the time the child leaves the Senior School. The answer need not imply that in the English lessons we are trying to teach a large number of separate capacities with separate techniques. If a teacher attempts to apportion his time rigidly between Reading, Recitation, Spelling, and the like, he will certainly not travel so far or so happily as he might do. Systematic planning of work there must be, but it need not follow

the lead of an obsolete and over-classified time-table.
But if we have a full sense of the needs of the community
and the needs of the child our demands will take shape
somewhat like this. The child should be able to express
himself sensibly on plain matters in sound and un-
self-conscious speech ; he should be able to arrange a
variety of ideas on the subjects he has been taught and
on matters of common interest into orderly and effective
written form, however briefly ; he should be skilful
in apprehending the spoken and written thoughts of
other people, responsive to the beauty of appropriate
poetry and prose, interested in human beings, in their
motives and actions, able to appreciate his surroundings
with discrimination, and familiar in some measure with
the great ideals, beliefs, and standards of conduct, which
give life and spirit to the society in which we live.

5. The approach adopted in this chapter.—It will
be convenient to approach under separate headings the
problems of English teaching in the Infant School, the
Junior School and the Senior School. Naturally very
closely related issues have to be discussed at each stage
of the Elementary School course, and a full grasp of
the whole process of English instruction throughout
school life is indispensable to an understanding of the
difficulties of any stage ; but these divisions correspond
to real phases in the development of the child's mind,
and, consequently, in his relationship to the written
and spoken word. At each stage a rough distinction may
be made between English as Understanding and English
as Expression, intimately connected with each other
though these processes must in fact be. Understanding
will include not only the intellectual comprehension of
spoken and written language, but also some responsive-
ness to feelings and experiences expressed in words,
and will involve the acquisition of an effective vocabulary
through listening and reading, the receiving and using

new ideas and interests, and the general intellectual nd emotional awareness of life which language and terature exist mainly to create. Expression will omprise training, not merely in the respective techniques f speaking and writing but also in the adequate and rdered expression of ideas in either medium. English, a short, is on the one side listening and reading, on the ther side speaking and writing ; and each of these groups f activities will call for separate consideration.

II. ENGLISH IN THE INFANT SCHOOL
A.—UNDERSTANDING

6. Understanding and Conversation.—The first sk in English in the Infant School is to promote understanding. No unreal separation is here suggested. a the first years of school life the greater part f the teaching is English teaching ; the enlargement f the child's ideas is inseparably bound up with the cquisition of new words and expressions. Opportunities r talking should, accordingly, not be restricted to a w so-called conversation lessons ; on the contrary, ost of the school hours should be devoted—above all ith the youngest children—to informal conversation etween teacher and pupils. Such conversation will ise naturally, when the children have overcome their rst feeling of shyness, on an unending variety of topics -themselves, their homes, the schoolroom and its ntents, the occupations in which they are engaged the moment, and so forth. It should follow a natural, it a pre-arranged, course, and the more reticent as well the more talkative children should be drawn in. hildren should be encouraged to ask questions from the rst, since their interests and needs will thus be more sily recognised.

7. The material to be studied.—The means by which ildren are introduced to new ideas and activities, that their desire to talk and ask questions is aroused,

are of great importance. Pictures and picture-book
appeal most readily, and much use should also be mad
of nursery rhymes, poems, fairy-tales, and folk-lore an
other stories. These should be told or read to th
class by the teacher and it will not matter if the meanin
of occasional words or phrases is unknown to the childre
If the rhyme or story deals in the main with an experienc
which the children can appreciate, there is no need t
break the unity of the impression by overmuch explana
tion of details. The desire to avoid difficulties
language should not lead teachers to choose poem
songs and stories devoid of literary merit and lackin
the qualities of vigorous rhythm and diction whic
appeal to young children.

Some stories must be read, others may be rea
and others must be told. When, for example, the lang
age of the story is the great part of its effect, it wou
be a mistake to tell it from memory. But in rece
years there appears to have been some decay in t
ability of teachers to tell stories to children, though the
are happily signs of a revival of interest in this art. T
replacement of good story-telling by the reading
stories from children's reading books is not to be w
comed. A list of stories derived from good writer
and graded as to type, content, complexity, and vocab
lary, should be in the syllabus of every Infant School.

**8. The teacher's language and the child's vocab
lary.**—The language used by the teacher herself is of gre
importance, and should be a stimulus and an examp
to the child. She will, for example, carefully avo
watering down everything that she says into the " bab
language " that is sometimes thought suitable. T
vocabulary of a normal child of five is far more extensi
than is commonly supposed. The experienced teach
knows how to ask questions that require more than o
word in answer, and, equally important, how to increa

the children's understanding of and command over language by deliberately introducing and explaining new words. System and foresight are of great value here. A wide vocabulary cannot be imposed on the child, but, if the course planned for the year is thoughtfully examined, it should be possible to construct a list of words and phrases, arising naturally from the child's school life, which should be known by the end of the year.

9. The beginnings of dramatic activity.—When the class have heard a story or poem, it may be repeated or retold by individual children. The interval between hearing it and reproducing it will vary according to their age and capacity, and the repetition will take different forms. For nursery rhymes and poems it will consist of exact reproduction of the words of the teacher. At first the reproduction of stories will also be largely a repetition of what the teacher has said. At a later stage, e.g. by the age of six or seven years, the child may be allowed to vary the expression for himself. Dramatisation, which is discussed below, is of great assistance. There are other possible methods by which the child may be trained in the understanding and control of language, e.g. guessing games in which children are called upon to describe things without actually naming them and to identify things described by other children.

10. First steps in learning to read.—Various methods of teaching the child to read have achieved popularity at different times. At present there appears to be a tendency for " phonic methods " to be reinforced by the ' look-and-say " methods and, on general grounds, this seems to be a reasonable approach. Much can be learned also from the " sentence method," though it is doubtful whether the exclusive use of this system can be generally successful. Probably the child will learn to read by a combination of all three methods. He may start by learning the names of his companions

through seeing them in bold letters on bags, lockers, etc
He may learn the names of objects from labels or h
may in the same way learn short sentences such a
" This is a door," in order to give him a stock of name
of things, and other short sentences designed to giv
him the words for various types of activity. He ma
even learn the titles of pictures on the walls, o
find out words by reading a nursery rhyme whic
he already knows by heart. But he will not lear
the sounds of letters until he knows a fair numbe
of words by sight and until he has had som
preparatory speech training. Learning to use th
instrument must never be entirely separated from th
enjoyment of its use : and he will not read a book unti
it conveys some meaning to him, while the first book
that he reads will ring the changes on sentences c
phrases rather than on individual words.

11. Individual and group methods in reading.—

After only a few months the children will be found t
vary greatly in their power of reading, owing to difference
in natural quickness and in home influence. The metho
of breaking up a class into suitably graded section
has by now established itself. The most forwar
children are classed in a separate section, promotio
to which is treated as a reward. They are encourage
to help each other, and to note the words which the
have failed to recognise, with a view to asking the teache
about them afterwards. In many Infant Schools i
which individual methods are applied with succes
the quicker children really teach themselves to reac
They are given a start by being taught a certain numbe
of easy words, and then, with the help of such apparatu
as pictures of unmistakable objects with the nam
first attached and afterwards separated, or boxes c
letters or words, they prepare themselves for readir
primers and story books.

B.—EXPRESSION

(i) TRAINING IN SPEECH

12. Some criteria of oral expression.—In the good Infant School with its activity and lack of constraint, the oral expression of the children may be expected to display four characteristics. It will be alive : the pupils in expressing themselves will feel that they are expressing something that is of significance and interest to them. It will be clear : clearness of expression develops with clearness of thought ; the two are mutually interdependent and none of the school's work can be effective without them. It will be expressive : it will not only be full of the children's own ideas and interests, but the children will have the power to use those modulations of voice and those forms of language by which feelings are normally conveyed. It will have an element of beauty : even small children appreciate rhythm and the charm of words and take a real delight in good speech. It would be idle to pretend that these things are often found together. But they are found together when the full opportunities of English training in the Infant School are clearly realised and seized.

13. The importance of spontaneity.—The wise teacher will understand in the first place that nothing must be done to suppress the child's natural spontaneity of speech. Common faults of expression will, of course, be corrected, such, for example, as the colloquial misuse of grammatical agreements. If the child is familiarised regularly and frequently with the correct form used in a context which he is unlikely to forget, and if a few minutes' daily practice is given, much can be achieved. But good speech is much more than a passively accepted familiarity with the correct conventions. It consists also of good vocalisation, clearness of idea, continuity of thought, and cheerful self-reliance. These things are intimately bound up with what we have called under-standing. But the teacher must deliberately set herself to foster their development.

14. Training in articulation and pronunciation.— Poor vocalisation and faulty utterance spring from two main errors : (*a*) indistinctness of articulation—the sounds of which a word is composed not being definitely produced ; and (*b*) incorrectness of pronunciation—the wrong sound being made instead of the right one. In most cases the training depends almost entirely on conscious or unconscious imitation of the teacher, who should therefore be especially on her guard against falling into habits of slipshod and indistinct speaking, or of artificial and strained intonation. It is important that every teacher should know how the individual sounds should be articulated. Thus equipped, she can do much, provided that her aim is restricted to overcoming obvious and childish difficulties of speech and to securing clearness of articulation ; and provided also that every precaution is taken with nervous children who may be likely to become stammerers.

Attention should be paid especially to initial and final consonants. Some warning may even now be needed against setting up false standards of correctness in speech.

15. Confidence and freedom in self-expression.— But the most vital thing of all is that the young child should move in an environment of easy, pleasant and continuous speech. He should be encouraged to reproduce what he has heard and read. When he is giving his impression of some experience he should not be interrupted, except indeed for the correction of some glaring vulgarism. His understanding of English should be based on stories and poems that are rhythmic, simple and graceful. It should be realised that there is an art of listening, in which training is possible. Every new experience should be followed by an enlargement of the child's vocabulary. Particularly in dramatic activity the child will find a joyful game in which he is almost unconsciously trained in all the virtues of effective expression. Perhaps the best starting point for drama in the Infant School is the use of simple occupational mimes. This can be followed by the acting of familiar stories in which one or two of the characters speak. By the time he leaves this stage of his school career the child should have acted frequently in suitable classroom plays. There is no need for these plays to be childish and sentimental affairs. Many teachers may prefer to dramatise the well-known children's stories—often highly dramatic in content— by themselves. But the language should be straight-forward and expressive : the characters should know *why* they behave and speak as they do. There should be much preliminary discussion and reading before the play is actually rendered in front of the rest of the class. In all modes of expression the children must be encouraged to gain and retain self-confidence.

(ii) TRAINING IN WRITING

16. First steps in learning to write.—While this broader English training is being carried on, the children will at the same time be acquiring manual skill, and learning to make letters and reproduce words in writing. Certain principles laid down in Chapter II of this Handbook, regarding the first stage of learning to write, need perhaps some elaboration here.

In the first place, it was said that in its beginning writing should always have meaning for the children, and that the symbols used should resemble those they have been accustomed to see in print. Young children can have little need to record or communicate anything in writing ; but, just as they like to draw their experience of the world, so do they like to reproduce the forms of printed words they are able to recognise and name. In other words, writing is essentially the converse of reading. Where the formal teaching of writing is postponed as suggested until the second year in the Infant School, i.e. until the children are about six years of age, there will be little need of special devices such as sandpaper letters, since the various forms of hand-training already given and the greater power of hand-control of the six-year old will make it easier for him to imitate the forms of letters.

Definite teaching will be necessary in order to ensure the right sequence of strokes, and a continuous striving towards regularity of size, shape and spacing. Various tools and materials should be available for use, and the progress from chalk to soft pencil, and thence to broad pen, should be a matter for the individual, not for the class. Nor need these tools be mutually exclusive ; adults use pencils as often as pens. The size of letters should be determined by the kind of tool chosen and by the relative ease in writing, i.e. by the physiological mechanism of the writer. It is time to abandon the traditional requirement of large writing from small hands wielding fine pencils. For young children ordinary exercise books should be halved in width, in order to obviate the need for spacing lines. With paper 3" to 4" wide they are able to maintain a reasonable straightness of line, and regularity in spacing is better and more permanently achieved through gradual training than through the use of guide-lines.

The second principle laid down is that children should write with reasonable speed. It is possible for children of six to write fairly quickly—seven words a minute—if their tools are smooth and no artificial requirements are imposed ; but, with unsuitable pens and the interruption caused by having to touch this line and that, their rate may easily be slowed down to 35 letters in half-an-hour.

With the statement that children should be able to spell correctly words with which they are familiar, a new aspect of writing is introduced, The usual custom in Infant Schools is to limit the exercise of writing almost entirely to the careful imitation of the forms of letters and words. Even in formal practice, however, children welcome the opportunity of independent effort in reproduction from memory as a prelude to correction by copying. As they become proficient enough to use these remembered forms in carrying out various wider activities, some help in spelling may occasionally be necessary ; but the need will arise naturally and the help be purely incidental. Children who find exceptional difficulty in spelling may first be given boxes of letters with which to make their words, so that they are not confronted with the double task of reproducing the forms of letters as well as their order in the word.

17. The first beginnings of written expression.—

No form of written composition belongs properly to the Infant School, but many children at this stage enjoy putting simple ideas of their own on paper and of course they should be encouraged to do so. As far as possible, children at this stage should write nothing that is without meaning or interest to them. They can answer simple questions in words taken from their reading-books, and they can transcribe words and sentences which are of value to them in developing understanding, and with which they are familiar. But if their powers of lively comprehension and confident and easy speech have been effectively developed in the Infant School, and if they have mastered some of the preliminary difficulties of handwriting there, their written composition in the Junior School can be made adequate and vigorous.

III. ENGLISH IN THE JUNIOR SCHOOL

A.—UNDERSTANDING

18. The Aims of the English teaching in the Junior School.—It is the task of the Junior School to ensure that by the age of 11 normal children have become acquainted with a fair amount of literature, in prose and verse, such as appeals naturally to boys and girls, have enjoyed it and know something about it ; and that they should also have acquired some proficiency in understanding and using the language. Thus, they should be able to understand what is said to them and to give relevant answers to questions when the subject-matter they are studying is discussed ; they should have mastered the mechanical difficulties of reading sufficiently to grasp the content of a not too difficult book, passage, or sentence, and to discuss the ideas it contains ; they should, as a result of their training, have some power of continuous and lively speech, and be able to take part in simple classroom plays without being self-conscious, and read aloud or recite expressively and with clear articulation ; they should be capable of writing a few lines of simple narrative and description and of expressing intelligibly their own thoughts on matters of common interest. In training the children to attain this standard there will, of course, be no sudden break with the methods of the Infant School. Conversation, narration, dramatisation, reading aloud,—all these will play a large part in the work, especially during the earlier stages. No doubt the time available for practising these various sides of spoken language will diminish as the claims of written English become more insistent. None the less, during the greater part of the Junior School stage at any rate, the emphasis will be on the oral aspects of language in the widest sense of the term.

19. The Teaching of Reading.—A number of children, on account of natural dullness or irregular attendance, or from other causes, will come up to the Junior School more or less backward in reading. It is accordingly important that teachers of at any rate the lowest classes in a Junior School should be acquainted with methods of teaching Infants to read and with methods for dealing with the reading difficulties of backward children.

The large size of the classes in many schools renders it difficult to give each child the necessary amount of practice. The plan of breaking up the class into sections for reading and allowing the better readers to work by themselves is now generally practised, and should be adopted with increasing frequency as the children grow older. It makes considerable demands on the skill and resource of the teacher, for he must possess not merely the ability to ascertain by judicious questions where help is needed, but also the power—which is one infallible sign of a real teacher—of perceiving, as it were instinctively, when a child is working, and when he is merely idling with eyes fixed on his book. It is true that at first a great deal of practice in reading aloud will be necessary, especially with less proficient pupils, in order to correct mispronunciation of words and to secure reasonable fluency. But silent reading for " content " is equally important ; and it should on no account be supposed that reading of this kind is something of which only older children are capable.

It is essential that almost from the earliest stage children should be taught to make the phrase and not the word the unit of reading. Every care should be taken to prevent the reading practice taking the form of a monotonous droning of apparently unrelated words. Such a performance is still too common, and, when it becomes a habit, is most difficult to eradicate, sometimes persisting even high up in the Senior School.

It is also to be hoped that the type of lesson will now at length disappear which consists solely of setting child after child, often in a large class, to read aloud a few lines in turn without previous preparation, while the rest of the class are required to follow word by word. The emphatic warning against it contained in the last edition of this *Handbook of Suggestions* must be repeated.

20. Reading aloud.—" Reading aloud " should mean the practising by the children, under the guidance of the teacher, of the clear and effective rendering of a paragraph, story, or poem : or it should mean the reading to the class of something likely to interest them by children who have previously prepared carefully what they are going to read, if possible with the help of the teacher : or again, it should mean the reading by the teacher to the class of some carefully chosen passage, which, if he has a high conception of what the art of reading aloud really is, he will find it necessary to prepare beforehand. The children should be encouraged to criticise and discuss one another's performances ; but it is the teacher's standard which will be the chief factor in determining the quality of the reading aloud in his class.

The essential quality which should be secured in reading is clearness of utterance. The reader should be easily audible to all who are supposed to be listening to him ; the class will often close their books while a passage of any length is being read, and be trained to attend carefully. Next, he should read with sufficient fluency to keep the listeners' attention. Further he should read with expression. Expression should not be thought of as something which is to be brought into the reading after a certain stage of mechanical proficiency has been reached. If children understand, as they should, the meaning of what they read, they will read with expression, modulating their voices naturally and throwing the accent on the key word of the phrase or clause. The teacher should not tolerate, much less require, exaggerated or affected " expression," nor give such merely mechanical rules as " Raise the voice at a comma." The children should not be allowed to suppose that their pauses should be entirely regulated by the punctuation marks ; they should consider for themselves how each sentence may be most effectively phrased. The teacher will find himself better able to criticise the reading, especially from the point of view of clearness of articulation, if he does not always follow it in his own book. Otherwise, he may often be led to pass over faults, e.g. mumbling or slurring of sounds, which could not have escaped his notice had he been entirely dependent for knowledge of what was being read on the child's own rendering.

21. The content of reading.—The nature of the material offered to children for their reading and understanding is of vital importance in the Junior School. Their books will include fiction, and, especially as the children grow older, simple books of travel, hobbies, and other kinds of information, which appeal directly to their interests. They should not be too difficult, for the children must be encouraged to gain confidence in reading by themselves. There will also be books of graduated prose extracts from good authors. These extracts should be of interest and significance in themselves, long enough to provide genuine matter for a lesson's work, and free from an elaborate accompaniment of exercises and questions which are either irrelevant to the context and do not contribute anything towards a fuller understanding of its meaning, or are of a kind that any competent teacher can compose for himself with direct reference to his own method of teaching. To their poetry further reference will be made later, but it is to be hoped that, among the stories which the children will hear or read, there will be included those old stories—whether from the Old Testament, the Ballads, or the Arthurian Legends—which are part of our national heritage.

22. English in relation to other subjects.—The pervading importance of English in the Junior School hardly needs emphasis. It is difficult to keep the teaching of English, History, Geography and Nature Study apart in their early stages. Careful co-operative planning is clearly necessary in order that work may not be inappropriately arranged. It is a matter of real importance, for example, that children should not be given too many written exercises in successive lessons. Their written work at this stage should be the short and refreshing expression of an untired mind. Again, historical stories may well form the basis of some of the written work in English. It may be worth while to illustrate the vital connexion of the teaching of English with that of Arithmetic. Many children find arithmetical problems difficult simply because they cannot read the sentence : it may demand far closer attention and more exact realisation of meaning than is usually expected from them in reading. Consider the following :—" A man who walks four miles an hour starts at 8 a.m. on a journey of 29 miles. If he rests twice for twenty minutes at a time, when will he arrive ? " The Arithmetic is easy, but several distinct facts have to be separately realised and their bearing on the matter considered. It is primarily a matter of understanding language.

23.—Development of the child's vocabulary.—The children will, to a varying extent, gradually increase their command of language by speaking, reading, and writing, in the ordinary way. But it appears that some form of practice more definitely directed to increasing their stock of words will be desirable, at least in the earlier stages. It has already been suggested that the

Infants' teachers should begin this process, and it should be continued in the Junior School. Needless to say, it will not be a matter of learning lists of words which are unrelated to one another, or meaningless to the children. At the earliest stages of the Junior School the words will generally be associated with things —with the contents of a room, a shop, a school ; with pictures and with common objects of many kinds ; with the material dealt with in the Nature Study, History, and Geography lessons ; and with the Handwork done and the models made. Progress will be, broadly speaking, from the concrete to the abstract. " Word chains " and other games in which one word suggests another, may be of value if not overdone. Advantage will, of course, be frequently taken of the reading lesson for relating one word to another, either by association or by contrast.

24. The choice of reading matter and its treatment in class.—As the children grow older, this form of language training will probably become more definitely based on some reading lessons of a more intensive type, and possibly, for the cleverer children, with the close study of a short and not too difficult piece of English prose. As soon as the meaning of the whole has been grasped and, very likely, reproduced more or less in the children's own words, they will go on to details, and study the words, phrases, and sentences, with an increasing degree of exactness. Work of this kind will not only be directed to increasing the child's mastery of language, but will serve as a centre for the widening of his range of information and experience. It is important that the extracts studied should be selected with this end in view. Will this interest the children and, at the same time, afford a genuine opportunity for enlarging their experience ? Mere tit-bits of information are not required, but glimpses of the way in which people live, think, and behave. It is not necessary

that all the passages should be " literary," but at least
they should be good of their kind, soundly written
well-ordered, and fit material for language study that
is not merely grammatical. The children should be en
couraged to ask and answer questions about them
and not merely to accept slavishly the authority of the
written word.

25. Learning to study with the aid of books.—Even
in the Junior School, it is probable that far more could
be done in the way of teaching children to find out
simple things for themselves from books. The habit
of using books for purposes of reference or search is a
study habit of supreme importance, and teachers will
readily think of many exercises, oral and written, by
which this can be developed. Such exercises in the
Junior School should be short, simple, direct, and well
suited to the books used. They cannot, as a rule, be
extemporised in class.

**26. Poetry at the Junior School stage and its
treatment.**—Poetry will not be the least important part
of the English work in the Junior School. The essential
thing to keep in mind, especially at this stage, is that
poetry should be a source of genuine enjoyment to the
children no less than to the teacher. The children's
enjoyment will be greatest when the poetry chosen :

> (1) reflects experiences which they themselves
> have had or can readily understand ;

> (2) deals with matters which appeal to children
> between 7 and 11, such as stirring or unusual events,
> the simpler kinds of clash of character, or even
> humour of a primitive sort associated with any
> form of incongruity ;

> (3) has a rhythm which is lively and emphatic,
> and a diction which attracts them through its force-
> fulness, or some striking combination of sounds or
> even a play upon words.

ORDER FORM

for Government Publications of the United Kingdom

To.................................... Date....................................

....

....

....

Please supply me with copies of the following :—

Number
of copies

Price.

£   s.   d.

....

....

....

....

....

....

....

....

I enclose remittance value £   : s. d. to cover cost and
postage. (Any sum sent in excess of the correct amount
will be refunded.)

*Please
write
clearly*

Name...

Address...

....

....

(35824) Wt. 33800/842 50,000 2/37 Hw. G.383

[OVER

This does not mean that Junior School children are insensitive to genuine poetry or that they should never be given it. But their appreciation of poetry of the highest quality will be all the more genuine and sincere if their approach to it has been through verse which appeals to their natural interests. There is abundance of verse which of its kind is first rate, not only by well-known writers of the past, but also by poets of the present day. The child—and this warning cannot be stated too emphatically—does not require verse which is written down to his supposed intellectual level and written especially for school use.

The child at the Junior School stage is by nature neither introspective nor reflective and does not take kindly to the bookish study of poetry. He wants to be up and doing, and to savour the rhythm, the language and the sentiment of the poetry he likes through active forms of expression : reading it aloud, saying it aloud, chanting it in chorus or even dramatising it ; he may even be impelled by his enjoyment of it to compose verse of his own. This will do more to awaken his power of appreciation than either the mere compulsory committing to memory of poems considered good for him, or the elaborate study of the printed word. Embarrassing questions asked about a child's personal reactions to the sentiments and phraseology of the poem do more harm than good. To ask a child to consider objectively a line or a phrase—in regard to its sound or meaning—is useful ; but to ask him to explain how he feels in regard to a particular passage is calculated to breed hypocrisy and sentimentality.

It must not, however, be supposed that the Junior School child's acquaintance with poetry should be a mere matter of vocalisation, or that he is likely to appreciate it properly without the example and help of the teacher. Before the children deal with a poem themselves, the teacher should introduce it to them in the most effective manner : first, by calling up in their minds the appropriate set of ideas and the accompanying mood, and secondly, by reading the poem aloud so that, to the best of his ability, he brings out its particular qualities.

The more the children like a poem, the more they will, as a rule, wish to know about it, in regard not so much to the particular words used as to the situations which form its subject-matter. Thus the teacher would be justified, provided always that the children's response is real, in telling them something about the background of the poem, the motive or the circumstances which prompted it, or anything relating to rhythm or language which is likely to increase their interest in the poem. He will find that, if he can get them to discuss the poem with him, they will often ask questions or express opinions which will give him a useful lead.

If the teaching in the Junior School has been successful, it will be found that the children not only like their poetry, and, to some extent, understand it, but also know a good deal of it by heart.

In the past there has undoubtedly been a tendency to make children remember too much verse and enjoy too little. But, though memorisation is not the sole function of the approach to poetry at this age, the young child's active memory may well be stored with fine and gracious fragments of poetry and prose. These should be carefully selected, although the children may sometimes be asked to memorise something they choose for themselves from their anthologies. Pieces so committed to memory should be frequently revised. Children should be encouraged to get the sense of the whole before they start to memorise, and should try to commit to memory passages of a reasonable length rather than a few words or a line at a time.

B.—EXPRESSION

(i) TRAINING IN SPEECH

27. The broader conception of Speech Training.—
It is hardly necessary to emphasise the social as well as the
educational importance of effective training in the proper
use and comprehension of language.   No school can
be held entirely responsible for the speech of children
attending it, which may be more or less strongly influenced for good or bad by factors beyond its control.
None the less, teachers do in fact provide a model for
the speech of children during their most impressionable
years.   Good speech, like good behaviour, is best learnt
naturally and indirectly in a good school.   Most lessons,
too, will assist in the purpose of speech training and will
afford practice in speech—whether it be talking about
something that the children have read or are going to
write about, describing something before them in a
Nature Study lesson, explaining " How it works " or
" How it is done," or shewing how to perform some
process in Mathematics.

28. Training in Articulation.—Speech Training in
the narrower sense, begun in the Infant School, should
be continued in the Junior School.   It should be continued, if for no other reason, because endless friction
and waste of time are caused in school by inaudible
answering.   The first essential of speech is clarity :
the basis of clear speaking is precise articulation, which
can only be secured by careful training.   A knowledge
of how the individual sounds should be articulated is
not difficult for the teacher to acquire, and he cannot
easily improve the indistinct speech of the children,
if he is without this knowledge.   Tone in speech can
also be trained.   The aim should be to secure clear and
pleasant speech, irrespective of dialect : whatever dialect
a person may be speaking, he can learn to articulate

clearly and with good quality of tone. A short daily practice is necessary for the purpose of acquiring clearness in speaking and a consciousness of what good speech is. When the oral work that is being attempted is formal in character, more attention can clearly be given to speech than when it is oral work demanding thought and expression of self. But this practice will be of little value, if, when once begun, it is not continued. This is one of the many matters in which co-operation between the Junior and the Senior School is necessary.

29. Opportunities for Speech Training.—Almost every lesson, however, will afford opportunities for developing the children's power of clear and connected speech. As the child grows older he should be expected, in giving an account of anything he has done, heard, or learnt, to speak for a longer time than is usual in an Infants' class. The best way to make sure of improvement is to encourage the child to give a full and connected account of what he has read or been told, and, so far as possible, to avoid concluding the recapitulation or revision of reading or other lessons by a series of questions requiring merely a word or clause in reply. It is difficult to give each pupil sufficient practice in continuous oral statement, but if full advantage is taken of the countless opportunities for the practice of speech that arise much can be done. There are many ways in which the teacher can supplement the usual methods of speech training. Particular children may occasionally tell a story or speak on a suitable subject. When a book is being read by a class or group working together, the children may be called upon, at the conclusion of a paragraph or chapter, to state what they have gathered from it. In general, it may be stated that English lessons should invariably give opportunity and encouragement for discussion, the statement of agreement and disagreement, the asking of questions by the children, and constructive digression by the teacher. English in all its aspects will be most successfully taught in an atmosphere of sensible, friendly and co-operative discussion.

30. Dramatic Activity.—(a) *The function of dramatic activity.*—In recent years there has been a notable growth of interest in dramatic activity in the school, and it is certain that drama is a most effective method for improving the clarity and fluency of children's speech. It should be realised, however, that drama is also a good deal more than this. In the school it may perhaps be appropriately defined as a training, a study, and an art. It is an excellent discipline in speech, poise and self-confidence. It affords remarkable opportunities for active literary study : and it is a natural and effective mode of artistic expression for children. In the Junior School the miming and dramatisation begun in the Infant School should be continued. Volumes of plays may afford material for classroom production. The mere reading of parts round the class has nothing to recommend it. However simple the play may be it should always be prepared—an attempt should be made to understand the characters, the movements, the situations ; it may be produced in the Hall or an empty classroom or even in a clear space in front of the class ; a really active and stage-like reading should be given ; and it should be criticised, the rest of the class being encouraged to comment on the representation and its meaning. Dramatic activity should never be confined to the more capable or histrionically gifted members of the class. It is particularly useful in " bringing out " the dull boy.

(b) *The choice of material.*—The same principles that dictate our choice of poetry in the Junior School may govern also our selection of plays for class use. They should not be too obviously written down to children, they should be free from the vices of artificiality and sentimentality, they should deal with characters who are of real interest in situations that afford material for discussion, and they should be written in language that has at least the merits of simplicity and forcefulness. It is evident that work of this kind needs careful planning. It must never be allowed to degenerate into noisy reading by a few and partial inattention by the many. A tradition of brisk and workmanlike dramatic lessons must be created. The division of the class into teams is an expedient which must often be employed, so that each child may get a chance.

(c) *Dramatic activity in the classroom.*—The intensive study of dramatic literature has no place in the Junior School, but it should not be forgotten that dramatisation —i.e. the creation of plays by the class from non-dramatic material—is an excellent exercise in written and spoken expression, of which children can see the intention and into which they throw themselves with understanding and enthusiasm. There is much suitable material in ballads, short narrative poems, and familiar stories. There should always be plenty of discussion beforehand. The teacher should not ask too much in the way of constructive genius from the children, but he will realise that he can teach them simple elements of craftsmanship that will prevent dramatisation from becoming merely the manufacturing of dialogue.

Besides promoting classroom plays and dramatisation the keen English teacher will want to try his hand occasionally at dramatic production on a large scale. In a good school play many energies and talents are called into service, the children taste the joys of personal achievement, and added colour and life are given to the work of the school. The teacher can easily make himself acquainted with good, simple books on producing, staging and lighting. It goes without saying that the aim will be to create a final product that is joyful and stimulating to children, not necessarily impressive to the adult onlooker : and if the teacher is an enthusiast, he will not be too easily satisfied.

31. The problem of dialect.—Indistinctness of utterance, in children who are physically capable of speaking distinctly, ought not to be excused on any grounds. It is due chiefly to laziness in the use of the speech organs. But training in pronunciation presents certain special difficulties. It may be taken for granted that the school should ensure, so far as it can, that its pupils leave it able to make themselves understood in any part of the country to which they may go ; and it is a motive to which the teacher can appeal at the proper time.

" Standard English " need not be interpreted in a narrow and pedantic sense. But the English to be aimed at should be at any rate a kind of English which both in idioms and in pronunciation is generally intelligible, and in pronunciation approximates to that which is used, though with many permissible if small variations, by educated persons. In matters such as accentuation and " quantity " the teacher is bound to be dogmatic ; he cannot but insist, for example, upon the sounding of consonants which are dropped in blurred and slovenly speech.

But in various parts of the country dialects are spoken which differ materially from Standard English in pronunciation and also in form. Some of these dialects have a history and associations which entitle them to respect ; others are regarded, not always on logical grounds, as debased and reprehensible. Teachers should not consider themselves in any sense called upon to extirpate a genuine local dialect. Yet experience shows that it is not impossible to encourage, at least for public occasions, a pronunciation in which variations from the normal are diminished.

So much the school must no doubt endeavour to do. Its success will depend upon the extent to which the teacher—assuming him to have no special knowledge of phonetics—can acquaint himself with the characters of the sounds in dialect and in Standard English respectively and with the manner in which they are produced, and upon his skill in getting his pupils to realise these differences themselves. The result will no doubt be that the children will become what is rather loosely called " bilingual." But a teacher with an interest in the subject may well go further and encourage the children to take a pride in their dialect, thus rendering them consciously " bilingual." He might encourage them occasionally to speak their dialect in school, to recite in it, to act in it, and to compare it deliberately with Standard English. Such a procedure, in skilled hands, could hardly fail to increase their interest in language, and their command over it ; it is, in fact, by no means difficult to interest children in the study of sounds and idioms. But, since methods of this kind postulate a certain development of linguistic consciousness, they had perhaps better be postponed until the Senior School is reached. All attempts to correct dialectical peculiarities, as well as other peculiarities, too early, will be almost certain to have a depressing effect upon a child's power of speech, an effect which must be carefully avoided. Teachers should encourage the children to speak their dialect freely and boldly in the Infant School and in the earlier stages of the Junior School, and then build upon that.

32. The content of English for the backward child.—The methods to be adopted for children who are naturally dull and backward have not yet been adequately explored, and there is abundant room for experiment. Speech will obviously be of more importance here than with normal children ; inability to speak with any confidence is probably a contributory cause of backwardness. It seems that these children require more stimulating oral teaching and practice and less writing than normal children ; that they should have more stories read or told to them ; that the teaching should be mainly based on their own experience and on things that they have seen, done, or made ; and that no opportunity should be lost of illustrating it from the commonest matters of daily life. With them, even more than with normal children, training in speech and writing will mean training them to fit the appropriate words to a situation that they have experienced directly ; and to devise exercises to this end will be a chief part of the skill of the teacher. In reading, a supply of easy and interesting story books should be available. If the text is too difficult, the beginning of the paragraph, or even of the sentence, will be forgotten before the end is reached, and confidence—a very important thing—will be lost.

33. The importance of naturalness in children's speech.—There remain certain difficult problems in connexion with the guidance and development of language in school. Problems of this kind call for a clear realisation on the part of the teacher of the different forms which spoken language may assume. There is, for example, language which embodies a direct reaction to a subject or a situation and is a spontaneous expression of feeling or thought. Such language is not necessarily subject to the grammatical rules that are appropriate when exact and reasoned statement is called for. If the teaching is directed entirely to securing a " correct " use of language it is very easy to suppress in young children free and natural modes of expression, a result which would be very undesirable. On the other hand, the children's speech may show, in more or less abundance, elements which cannot be regarded in this light, which are hardly spontaneous, and are not vivid in expression—tricks of speech, in fact, which are generally held to be vulgarisms. To correct these, without unduly depressing the children's native powers of speech, is a task which will make considerable demands on the teacher's taste and skill.

(ii) TRAINING IN WRITING

34. Differences between spoken and written English.—In considering how to introduce young children to written composition, the teacher would do well to ponder the differences between written and spoken language. Some apology may be needed for calling attention to a few fundamental considerations about this. Speech, it should be remembered, is informal, elliptical, aided by facial expression and vocal intonation; writing is, by comparison, formal, consecutive and ordered ; the mental attitudes which underlie and accompany speaking and writing respectively are not the same ; when we talk in the ordinary way, it is not formal prose that we speak ; the language of conversation should on no account be regarded as an inferior kind of prose. In the earlier stages the children will write more or less as they speak, but, as they progress towards written composition in the real sense, they will have to learn conventions which do not come naturally to them. " Composition " will have been practised in the Infant School through oral methods mainly. If the children have been trained to speak continuously, they will find it easier to express and arrange their ideas in writing. The transition from oral work to written work may be a difficult matter, and, where direct instruction of this kind seems called for, skilled teaching may be necessary to avoid artificiality. It may be assisted by various devices, e.g. by the teacher's writing on the blackboard to the children's dictation an unpunctuated version of a story which they have learned and then, by comparison with the original, breaking it up into sentences. This is a method which is obviously capable of many variations.

35. The treatment of written composition.—On arrival at the Junior School the pupils will begin, no doubt, to write short and simple exercises of various types. But this is not a process which need be hurried ; written composition is generally begun too soon and practised too often. Too much of it should not be required until the children can write easily in the mechanical sense, and long exercises should not be demanded.

It would be unreasonable to say that children should not begin to express themselves in writing until they feel the need to do so ; many would not feel any such need until too late. But the suggestion does contain this truth, that children should feel that what they write has some point and purpose ; they should not be set to write on topics quite unconnected with anything that they have been doing, seeing, reading or discussing. If the material that they read matures into active dis-cussion lessons, the transition to brief written exercises will be natural and easy. They can answer briefly in writing questions about the meaning of what they have read. They can be asked to deduce something further from a passage that they have been discussing and to express it in a sentence. They can deny statements in their reading and find a reason for doing so. They can begin the practice of dramatisation by writing out the dialogue implicit in a brief episode of a story. Exer-cises artificially contrived to illustrate mistakes should be avoided. If the oral basis of the child's written work is fully maintained, the distinction between free composition and assisted composition becomes somewhat unreal. Opportunities for writing will arise out of the work of the class. The more independent kind of child will give a touch of originality to what he writes ; the slower child will be content with recapitulating and

arranging ideas which have already been discussed, sometimes even writing these out under the teacher's guidance;
the cleverer child will be given occasional openings
for more definitely original work like story-writing,
but this will not be the regular field for written activity.
There must, of course, be sectionising, in order that
the written work shall not demand too much or too little.

36. Formal training in written expression.—Most
of the capacity to write English in an ordered form and
according to the accepted conventions is derived from
familiarity with books and from the practice of moder-
ately formal and continuous speech. But some direct
teaching will save time and repeated explanations.
There will be abundant practice, for example, in the use
of the full stop and the capital letter, and later on in
the use of the relative pronoun and of the inverted
relative, of quotation marks and question marks.
Such practice need not be purely formal, or without
its element of fun or provocation to thought. It should
never become merely tedious and it should progress by
single steps. It is closely related to the question of the
teacher's correction. This should be directed to substance as well as to form ; it should deal with statements
of fact, with matters of taste, and with the sense of
orderliness. Where it is concerned with grammar and
construction, it will not overwhelm the child with details,
but will emphasise particular errors at a particular time.

The formal English practice indicated above will take
account, no doubt, of the difficulties and lapses which
the written work of the class exhibits. With regard to
the children's own diction in the wider sense, the
teacher may find dealing with it a task of some delicacy.
He will avoid trying to force it too much into a conventional mould ; he will welcome any instance of
vigour and originality in expression, even if it be not
technically correct, and he will be chary of condemning
language because it savours of colloquial speech. The

children will learn in time when such language is suitable and when it is not ; and they will come to realise that what may be appropriate in writing a dialogue or a conversation would be inappropriate in a piece of straightforward composition.

37. Spelling.—A certain amount of spelling drill is probably necessary in the Junior School : but such drill should be, as far as possible, individual. It is a waste of time to keep calling on good spellers to spell words in which they are not liable to make mistakes. The teacher's task is to devise means for helping each child to master his own peculiar difficulties, and the best guide in selecting the words which he should be taught to spell is to be found in his own written exercises. The children should be taught at an early stage to verify the spelling of the words they use, for a large number of spelling mistakes are due to carelessness rather than ignorance and occur in common and simple words, often because they are mispronounced.

The more closely spelling is connected with composition, and composition with reading, the more effectively will children be taught to spell. Opportunities for incidental teaching will constantly occur and a good teacher will have no difficulty in making this apparently incidental teaching genuinely systematic, while he avoids the dangers of boredom and inattention produced by the old formal lesson in spelling. Little is to be gained from oral spelling lessons. It is a good plan for the children occasionally to make a special study of the spelling of the words on a particular page which is to form the basis of an exercise in composition, so that they may train themselves to retain mental pictures of words and be able to visualise them easily. It cannot be emphasised too strongly that to spend time in early years on the spelling of words which the child will not use, if at all, for some years to come, is wasted labour.

38. Dictation.—Dictation has long occupied a place of some importance in the traditional scheme of English instruction. It is still frequently allotted a prominent position in the time-table. As a regular and definite constituent of the teaching of English it is to be deprecated. It is a convenient method of testing spellings that have already been committed to memory, although it is of no value in the direct teaching of spelling. For young children it is useful in providing practice in the correct writing of words that they already know. Modifications of the traditional form of dictation can occasionally be used for training in careful listening, in getting the real gist and argument from a spoken passage.

39. Grammar in the Junior School.—It is only by direct contact with the spoken and written language that the teaching of Grammar can be redeemed from the unreality and sterility which have so often accompanied its teaching in the past. It must be recognised that there are many children in the Elementary Schools for whom Grammar is the least suitable and useful part of their training in the use of the mother tongue. In the Junior School the study of Grammar, in any case, has only a small place. The child may well become familiar with some of the simpler grammatical terms, but this does not imply the mere memorising of a set of definitions. Any exercises that may be given will be all the more effective if they are not merely grammatical, but are concerned with meaning as well as with form. There is no need whatever for a separate Grammar lesson in the Junior School, and very little need for written grammatical exercises.

40. Handwriting : the development of a "cursive" hand.—As writing becomes purely automatic and therefore swifter there is a natural tendency to run on between combinations of letters so that no time may be lost in

he pursuit of the hurrying thought. This tendency
hould be looked for and guided, and simple combinations
nd slight modifications of form suggested, so that the
hild gradually acquires a cursive hand based on the
imple forms he has already acquired. With most
hildren the change begins to appear somewhere about
ine or ten years of age, but children who find difficulty
1 the simpler form of writing will not do any better if
orced to adopt the more difficult. Backward children
vho show a fairly satisfactory and pleasing print-script
1ay fall still farther behind in their written exercises
: the change to a cursive hand absorbs an unreasonable
mount of attention and energy.

If for any reason the school makes a point of teaching
 particular style of writing other than that based upon
rint-script, intensive practice in the last year is likely
o prove more effective, because more consciously
ollowed, than weekly writing periods for several years
eforehand. In any case no style should be taught
vhich involves an emphasis upon meaningless strokes,
.g. joins and introductions, to the disadvantage of
ignificant forms. Moreover, for many purposes, such
s the writing of lists and notices, headings, mapping
tc., print-script should continue to be practised side
y side with cursive script. For capital letters in com-
ination with cursive writing, too, print forms are
ar less subject to degeneration than the elaborate
ourishes in which some schools take great pride.

IV. ENGLISH IN THE SENIOR SCHOOL

A.—UNDERSTANDING

**41. The importance of choosing the right kind of
eading-matter.**—By the time the child reaches the
enior School he should as a rule have mastered the
nechanical difficulties of reading. It is, as we have
een, the teacher's task first of all to awaken in these

children an understanding of their environment, parti
cularly when it seeks to affect them through the writte
word. The Senior School course should include a
approach to a wide variety of reading-matter, carefull
selected and sensibly arranged. The basis of the wor
in the understanding of language will be the discussio
lesson. Suitable passages will be read in class an
subjected to a thoughtful and critical examinatio
by the class and the teacher. An examination of th
kind will be concerned with meaning, with structu
and with feeling. The passages chosen will probab
be taken from a suitable " reader " of some sort ; the
should be, like the passages studied in the Junior Schoo
aspects of human experience, within the child's gras
but not written down to him, containing matter wortl
of thought and discussion, and unembarrassed by t
many editorial aids.

42. The place of independent reading.—In tl
Senior School many books will be read, and they may we
be read for different purposes. The teacher will mal
himself responsible for some oversight of the chil
independent reading. He may issue library lists an
discuss them, keep some record of what the child
reading, and occasionally ask him questions or set hi
written compositions upon this material. It would
foolish to attempt to impose any kind of artificial adu
standard of literary values upon the child, but it
equally foolish to hope for much in the way of critic
development in the child's mind if his independe
reading is cut off entirely from his work in school.

43. Systematic training in study.—It is, of cours
important that children should develop some defini
capacity for reading for information before th
leave the Senior School. The teacher will take trou
to see that the English course systematically furthe
this end. There should be a class, or school, libra

which contains works of reference, some at least of which are not specifically designed for use by children. Pupils should be encouraged to find the requisite information for such purposes as writing an essay or giving a brief discourse to the class. The use of a dictionary should be a recognised part of English study. More reciprocity might well exist between the teacher of English and the teachers of other subjects. Books of common interest might be read in whole or in part by arrangement with the Geography teacher, the History teacher and the Science teacher. The teacher should endeavour to impress upon his pupils some conception of the *usefulness* of books for many practical purposes of life. Reading of this kind should always be tested by question and discussion or by some kind of written exercise. The use of other sources of information, such as the newspaper, should find some place in the preparation of the child for the understanding of the complexities of his environment.

44. Libraries and their use.—The provision of adequate school libraries is a matter of importance. Much is already being done in this way, e.g. by providing circulating libraries for schools in rural as well as urban districts. None the less, far too many schools are still to be found where there are not enough library books ; where there are not enough shelves for what books there are, and where, in the absence of a special room, there is no classroom allocated for the purpose of a library.

As has already been suggested, school libraries should not consist wholly of story-books, though there must indeed be a supply of such books if the pupils are to be encouraged to read as copiously as is desirable. They must also cater for the numerous boys and girls who have an interest in plants and animals, aeroplanes, ships, steam engines and railways, motor-cars, photography, wireless telegraphy, architecture, pictures, games, scout-lore, arts and crafts, or whatever it may be. Books of reference, such as almanacs and encyclopædias, and a first-rate English dictionary, should be included ; and the provision of some newspapers and magazines (which need not be absolutely up-to-date) is desirable also. In choosing books of the character indicated above, it may often be desirable to choose those not designed by their authors for use as school books. The management of the library should as far as possible be entrusted to individual pupils, who would be responsible for looking after the books generally and keeping the catalogue up-to-date.

Efforts are now generally made to bring schools into close touch with public libraries, where they exist, by means of co-operation between the librarians and the teachers. The assistance of librarians in giving help and advice to young readers is often of great value. It has sometimes been found possible to arrange for school classes to do some of their work in the reference room of public libraries—an excellent plan. One particular recommendation was made in the last issue of this *Handbook of Suggestions,* and may be repeated : Local Authorities can afford much assistance to teachers by forming libraries at convenient centres from which they can borrow books, and in which they can see specimens of school books.

45. The wider aims of the Senior School child's reading.—Reading for information is one aspect of the work in the understanding of language which should face the child in the Senior School. He will also have to read for something more than information, however valuable and interesting ; he will read for some familiarity with the experience which finds expression in literature, for imaginative contact with the lives of others, for the acquisition of a set of values which will stand him in good stead in the world of books and in the wider world in which his life must be lived, and, incidentally for the enjoyment of what is well written. The supervision of this reading is a difficult task. It is easy for the teacher to attempt too much, and it is a matter for great regret if the teacher attempts too little.

In the discussion of poems a wider vocabulary will be used and perception of somewhat more subtle characteristics be expected. In the last year in the Senior School, poems more definitely concerned with simple views of life, man, and society, may reasonably be introduced and discussed. The method of comparison of one poem with another will prove very useful at this stage. It is natural that the teacher should find work of this kind difficult; but if he begins this task willingly, he will not easily be turned back.

46. The study of prose fiction.—The study of prose fiction has always held some place in the teaching of English and there are excellent reasons for this. The novel is the one form of literature with which we may be certain the vast majority of the children who leave Elementary Schools will continue to maintain familiarity. It is a form of literature which appeals very naturally and easily to the child with his intense love of story and action. The teacher should realise that the mere reading of a novel, in class or out of it, coupled with an occasional question about the progress of the story, is not the sum of the possibilities of this phase of literary teaching. Attention should be directed to the author's use of words and to the kind of experience and outlook that is expressed therein. The novel should form the centre of discussion-lessons much as poetry does. Codes of human behaviour, diverse facets of man's experience, and the intimacies of character, are topics readily extracted from a good novel. Effective teaching with its centre in prose fiction would be much easier and commoner if the work were adequately planned, and the novel carefully examined and divided into sections before its reading was begun.

47. Poetry in the Senior School.—In the section on poetry in the Junior School, emphasis was laid upon the importance of the child's approaching poetry through the gateway of his natural interests. In the Senior School the same vital principle must be observed, but it will be realised that the child's interests have broadened and that it is now possible to undertake more in the way of simple reflection upon and criticism of the verses studied. In the discussion of poems a wider vocabulary will be used and somewhat more subtle perceptions of differences in feeling and treatment between one poem and another may reasonably be expected. The study of poetry should not be neglected because it is difficult, or because there are dangers of sentimentality and insincerity in the attempt to develop anything in the nature of " appreciation."

The poems to be studied should be carefully chosen. They will include narrative, lyric, dramatic, and simple satiric pieces, dealing with material that can be brought within the child's comprehension. The teacher may well attempt to build up the background of the poem by illustration and description before any attempt at discussion is begun. The imagery of the poem may be examined and its structure, rhythm and meaning studied by the teacher and the class. The poetry lesson should, in fact, be a real attempt at the understanding of language in its most concentrated and evocative form. It should not degenerate into the observation of metrical tricks and niceties, into a suggested and insincere appreciation, or merely into the committing of a number of lines to memory. This, of course, does not mean that it is any less important a part of the teaching in the Senior School than it is in the Junior School to ensure that the children are learning by heart some memorable poetry.

In many schools the children are encouraged to make their own attempts at verse composition. It is clear that they find real pleasure in this method of expressing their experiences and that, by so doing, they have in addition increased their power of appreciating the poetry they study.

B.—EXPRESSION

(i) TRAINING IN SPEECH

48. Further development of the child's vocabulary. —To ensure real understanding of relevant literary material is one main objective which the English teacher in the Senior School will set before himself. He will also seek to carry further the capacities for spoken and written expression to which reference was made when the work of the Junior School was under discussion. In the Senior School the teacher will find plenty of occasions for the exercise of tact and skill in dealing with certain wider aspects of the children's speech. He will, for example, seek to encourage their power of vigorous and racy expression. He will realise that even slang has its place, and will try and get them to understand what that place is. In so doing, he will have frequent occasion to remind himself that language is the creation of the many and not of the few ; that it takes all sorts of people to make a language ; that it is from the speech, not so much of the study, as of the street, the factory, and the field, that language is vitalised and recruited ; and that the broad processes of linguistic change operate in their own way, resisting all attempts to regulate them by authority. But it is of no use pretending that this aspect of the subject, regarded from the point of view of the school, is not one of great difficulty, and one upon which it is almost impossible to offer definite suggestions.

49. Encouragement of clear speech.—There is, however, a tendency in children as they grow older to speak less clearly and less coherently, a tendency which is perhaps more marked with boys than girls. A training in clear articulation and in the quality of the speaking voice is as essential at the Senior stage as it is earlier, and therefore should not be dropped. The principles which should underlie the training are the same as those for the Junior School ; and the desire to speak well can be stimulated through verse-speaking, dramatic work and class discussions.

50. Reading aloud.—Mention has already been made of the " reading lesson " in which a passage is read and discussed with a view to the understanding of its content. There will be room also for a reading lesson for the purpose of training in reading aloud, about which a few words may be said. Two faults which should especially be avoided are artificial modulation of the voice without due regard to the meaning, and exaggeration of emphasis. The pupils should realise that their object must be to reveal by their reading the full meaning of the author. The niceties of rendering may now be carefully studied, and in this connexion it should be remembered that punctuation is a guide to the eye rather than to the voice. Such points should be discussed as where breath should be taken and pauses made ; the best way to phrase a sentence ; and the effect of changes of emphasis, tone, and speed. Suitable poems should still be occasionally memorised and recited. The reading aloud of poetry should receive careful attention.

51. Dramatic activity and dramatic literature.—Something has already been said of the function of drama in the Junior School. In the Senior School dramatic activity should be vigorously continued Classroom productions, the dramatisation of longer stories or more complex ballads, discussion, criticism and school production, all have their place. At this stage the study of dramatic literature may also be considered. There are plays which have a traditional place in the classroom and, rightly studied, should continue to do so. Much of Shakespeare has a direct appeal to the young, who enjoy acting scenes from such plays as *A Midsummer Night's Dream*, *The Merchant of Venice*, *Macbeth*, and *Julius Caesar*.

52. Dialect and speech training.—The comments made on the problem of dialect in the Junior School may well be brought back into consideration here. Much depends on the particular environment of each school, but in areas where there is a vigorous local dialect some degree of bilingualism seems to be the likeliest solution. As the children grow older their linguistic sense will grow, and it will be the teacher's aim to foster this sense directly and indirectly. They will become more alive to the fact that language varies according to its purpose ; and they will gain more insight into the conventions which govern some of the most elementary of these differences, such as the difference between colloquial speech and more formal speech. It may again be emphasised that if all English lessons are lessons in which active understanding and continuous discussion are encouraged, the child's speech is more likely to progress soundly, than if much formal work is supplemented by some formal speech training.

(ii) TRAINING IN WRITING

53. Exercises in Composition and other forms of written work.—The written work in the Senior School should follow much the same principles as that set in the Junior School. It should never be remote from the child's experience. It should be definite and clear in intention. It should frequently be based on the child's reading. In the Senior School the elements of written composition will have to be studied more thoroughly than in the Junior School, with special reference to such matters as the sound choice of words, emphasis, variety in sentence structure, and paragraphing.

Descriptive exercises, concerned with familiar sights, scenes, objects, and processes, including operations done in the Practical Instruction and the Science rooms, should form a definite part of the work. The writing of letters dealing with the most ordinary occasions of life should of course be included. History, Geography, and Science lessons, at any rate in the later stages, will afford a training in answering questions briefly and to the point, a training of which it would be hard to exaggerate the practical importance ; and the teacher of English would do well to acquaint himself with what the children are doing in these subjects. Books read will also provide topics ; and exercises which involve obtaining information from more than one book will sometimes be set, at any rate to the cleverer children.

Nor should the written exercises be confined to " composition " so-called ; they should include practice, for example, in taking notes from a spoken discussion or from a wireless talk. The summarising of paragraphs may well be attempted ; but whether exercises in formal précis writing are possible for children up to the age of fourteen is more doubtful. Such exercises, if attempted at all, should only be attempted by the most advanced.

54. Opportunities for training in written expression provided by work in various subjects of the curriculum.—The extent to which written work done primarily for the purpose of History, Geography, or Science lessons might be accepted as part of the English work is a matter calling for serious consideration ; as suggested in the preceding paragraph, a mutual arrangement between the teachers concerned might do something to lessen the burden of written work all round. The work in the Science room and the Practical Instruction room will afford opportunities for the accurate description of processes. The work in Mathematics may also subserve the same purpose, and especially perhaps that in Elementary Geometry—e.g. a verbal or written description may be called for of how to bisect a line, or of how to construct an equilateral triangle. The essential part which comprehension of language may play in the solution of problems in Arithmetic has already been referred to in connexion with the Junior School. Good setting out of written work of every kind may be used to provide an elementary training, not only in exact thought, but in concise expression and the correct use of technical terms.

55. Some principles to be remembered in teaching Composition.—The teacher will not set too many long compositions of a more formal kind. Most exercises set for written work should be discussed generally in class before they are attempted. The reading of the child will constantly provide opportunities for written work, sometimes brief, sometimes more extensive. The importance of the capacity to develop an argument in writing will not be forgotten.

56. The Written Expression of the dull and backward child.—For the most backward anything like formal composition would be quite out of place. The aim of the teacher will be rather to get them to want to write, and to provide them with exercises in which they can see some purpose. Any interesting thing that they are doing or making may serve as a basis for simple written work. Notes can be made about games and school events, or a little newspaper can be compiled by the class. It is to be hoped, it may be added, that the backward classes in a school will be taken by the same teacher for at any rate all lessons that involve the use of books. Before they leave school, these children must have been trained in some of the most obvious and practical uses of language, e.g. they must have had some practice in understanding and transmitting simple instructions, verbal and written ; in taking down messages ; in interpreting some of the printed forms and instructions which they will deal with later ; in writing simple letters, postcards, and telegrams, for the ordinary purposes of daily life. All this may involve a good deal of sheer mechanical repetition, but it cannot be helped. Some elementary accomplishments of this character must be learned by as many children as possible before they go out into life.

57. The importance of truthfulness in composition. —Precision in writing rather than mere fluency should be aimed at, especially as the children grow older ; and the endeavour to secure it will provide a valuable discipline for the cleverer or more imaginative among them. The chief criterion by which the pupils' compositions will be judged will be their truthfulness in the widest sense—the truthfulness with which they record their experiences and impressions ; the accuracy with which they describe things or scenes ; and the honesty which they show in stating, when called upon to do so, what they really think or feel, and not what they imagine that they are called upon to think or feel. Truthfulness to observed fact and to impression is, after all, a virtue which can be cultivated at an early stage ; it is, moreover, the one quality which the humblest writer may possess in common with the greatest.

58. Correction and revision.—Ideally, no doubt, the best plan would be to go through each exercise with the child who wrote it ; and the value of this direct contact of mind with mind is so great that every effort should be made to secure it. But it must be admitted at once that in many schools this would be quite impracticable owing to the size of the classes, and the teacher will have to vary his methods according to the conditions. Mistakes made by several children in common can be dealt with collectively. At times a whole lesson may well be spent in hearing pieces of composition read aloud by their authors, and in making and inviting oral comments. Important principles as to the build and balance of sentences, variety or monotony of diction, and correctness of punctuation, can be illustrated in this way. The essential point, however, must be that the child should understand what is wrong and know how to correct it. This can never be secured if the teacher's revision goes no further than merely marking every mistake, without regard to its relative importance, and handing the exercise back without comment.

As regards the pupils' part, it would be neither desirable nor possible to ask them to rewrite every composition ; but sometimes they will be asked to write a rough draft, to correct that draft themselves, and then to produce a more finished composition for submission to the teacher. By this means they will realise that a piece of writing can be improved by further work upon it. As regards correction by the teacher, Senior and Junior School will no doubt agree upon a code of correction for elementary mistakes. Correction should be progressive ; the existence of a mistake in a line could be indicated by some mark, but the child could be left to find it out for himself. Above all, attention should not be confined to elementary blunders. The rewriting of a badly formed sentence may be more important still, and constructive criticism, alternative suggestions for wording, and so on, should be given. The teacher, again, might mark the exercises at different times for different purposes, the purpose being made clear to the class when the exercises are given back.

It is fully realised that this more thorough and constructive type of correction will impose a heavy burden on the teacher of a large class. This burden might to some extent be mitigated by more class discussion of the composition exercises themselves, and, possibly, through arrangement with other teachers, by fewer and shorter exercises being written in the time specifically allotted to English. But the whole matter must be regarded as a major problem of school work and organisation, and one that is well worthy of investigation over a wide field.

59. The Function of Grammar.

—There has been much controversy about the place of Grammar in the school, and it cannot be pretended that this controversy is finally settled. Certain guiding principles may, however, be suggested. Any grammatical work attempted should rather be done incidentally than in a definite period on the time-table. It should spring from reading or from composition and should not consist in formal exercises in the application of so-called " grammatical rules." By far the greater part of grammatical work should be oral. The teaching should be confined to essentials such as the differentiation of the various parts of speech, the recognition that clauses and phrases can stand in the same relationships to the rest of the sentence as individual words can, the difference between co-ordination and subordination, and simple functional analysis. Care should be taken to recognise idioms for what they are, and not to force them into supposed obedience to grammatical conventions. Such grammatical work as is introduced should arise naturally from actual speech, writing and reading in the work of the class, rather than consist of formal exercises in abstract grammar. Experience tends to show that such exercises have not much value for giving command of the native tongue, which comes rather through imitation and practice.

60. Handwriting.—Whatever may be the form of handwriting approved in any school, for the writer's sake it must be easy to write and, for the reader's, easy to read. For ease and speed of reading, writing must be plain, regular, and clearly laid out on the page, i.e. with adequate margins and spacing between the lines. Smooth paper and nibs that are not too fine are among the requisites. Printed lines impose a spacing which is often inappropriate to the size of individual handwriting, and in themselves interfere with the reader's vision. It is many years since children were taught to draw on squared paper ; but the art of writing has not yet escaped from lines.

Provided that the two essential qualities of handwriting—legibility and speed—are ensured, the particular style adopted is of little importance. Such children as make any frequent use of writing after leaving school will most probably change their style of writing for one reason or another during their adolescent years. What is important is to make clear to them the essential qualities common to all accepted styles.

V. CONTACT WITH A WIDER ENVIRONMENT

61. The teacher's knowledge of his pupils' contact with a wider environment out of school.—The child's contact with his wider environment is of vital importance to the English teacher, for it will form the focus of his teaching. He should know something of the cinema, of the films which the children see and of those which they ought to see. He should know something of the libraries, the museums and art galleries, the places of historical or of general interest, which can be utilised in the child's education. It is his task to broaden and deepen the child's understanding of life, and he cannot easily neglect these things.

Something, too, should be said of the place of wireless broadcasts in the English lesson. Here is an excellent opportunity for bringing the child into contact with new sources of ideas and experience, for training him to use a new cultural instrument which he may neglect if he is not trained, and for familiarising him with clear standardised English speech.

VI. CONCLUSION

62. The larger view of the English teacher's task.—It is evident that the task of the English teacher is no light one. It requires an interest in children, an interest in words, and an interest in the larger world. Specialised knowledge is of less importance than such interests as these, for they can easily flower into the relevant kind of knowledge, whereas knowledge without these interests can only succeed in imprisoning the child's vital and curious mind within a mesh of facts. With such interests and aims the English teacher in the Senior School should succeed in the essentials of his task : the training of a young citizen who can speak clearly and sensibly, who can write with order and expressiveness, who can find what he wants in books, who is alive to the fulness of words, and who confronts his environment with enjoyment, with self-reliance, and with an openness to new ideas and new experiences.

CHAPTER XII

HISTORY

I. SOME GENERAL CONSIDERATIONS

A. HISTORY AS A SCHOOL SUBJECT

I. The main aims of the teaching.—History is the story of the doings of human beings and the society in which they lived, and this story has to be told to children mostly under the age of 15. First-hand experience is obviously impossible for the child, who must depend upon his teacher or on books for his knowledge of facts and events and of the relations between them, which form the subject-matter of History. Many of the connecting links between past events are beyond the comprehension of any but the brighter children, and the notion, in particular, of communities or states acting as wholes is difficult for a child whose experience is limited to the comparatively narrow environment of his home and his school.

The story of things that have happened to human beings in the past is, however, of natural interest for children, if it is presented in a lively, vivid way with due regard to its proper setting in time and place.   We can, at least, ensure that they have in their minds a body of stories of notable events and people pictured against a background which, though it may be incomplete, is yet clear and true as far as it goes.   None the less, if History is to be to the child anything more than a succession of interesting stories, the teacher will have to present them in such a way as to help him to realise that the world is always changing—and not in a fortuitous way.   He can show how a particular event may influence many subsequent events, and he can let his pupil feel that some events are vastly more important than others.   It is from his History lessons that the child will come to learn that the present grows out of the past and conditions the future, and that what happens in one community may affect other communities.   Thus he will see that the story of England is not an isolated story, but is linked up with that of other parts of the world.   In this way, the teacher may arouse in his pupils, through a sense of its significance, a lasting interest in the past and a desire to extend their knowledge of History after they have left school, and he may hope that his teaching at school will lead them later to look on current events in their broader aspects and as affecting the lives and interests of others as well as their own.

2. The appeal to children's enthusiasms.—There is one aspect of History which is of first importance to the teacher.   From its study the mature reader may gain a wider intellectual outlook and a saner judgment, and these benefits in their degree may also accrue to older children.   For all children, however, history is pre-eminently of value as a stimulus to their imagination and as an appeal to their enthusiasms.   The content of the syllabus or of any lesson in it is of much less importance to children of this age, and especially to those who are slow to learn, than the spirit behind the teaching. History deals with true stories of real men and women, of actual communities and nations ; it is a record writ large of their influence for good or evil. There is no need for the teacher to turn his lessons into sermons ; still less should he encourage the children to sit in judgment on the great men and nations of the past. If he makes History living to the children, they will learn naturally in how many different ways the great figures of history have helped mankind, and by what sort of actions nations and individuals have earned the gratitude of posterity. Without any laboured exhortations they will feel the splendour of heroism, the worth of unselfishness and loyalty, and the meanness of cruelty and cowardice ; and the influence of their lessons in history will be at work long after the information imparted to them has been forgotten.

3. The need for careful selection of subject-matter. —In the treatment of a subject of which the range is so vast careful selection is all-important. The teacher's choice will, of course, be determined partly by his own interests and reading, but he should deal, first and foremost, only with what children can understand : with personal character and prowess, adventure, discovery, invention, and with the way in which men have lived and worked ; but with statutes only so far as their purport and meaning can be made plain to a child ; and with economic, political or religious conflict only so far as its main issues and results are necessary for an elementary understanding of great changes in national life and of the rights and duties of a citizen of today. It has always to be borne in mind that history is a continuous narrative of events and that the teaching should avoid the danger of leaving in the child's mind a series of isolated episodes.

4. Syllabuses should vary with the circumstances of the schools.—Schools, moreover, vary widely in their circumstances. In large schools, especially in those which draw their pupils from homes where reading is encouraged, where travelling is not unknown, and conditions are generally favourable, a more extended treatment of the subject will be possible than in those which enjoy fewer advantages. The suggestions that follow are intended to apply to their full extent only to schools where the work is done under generally favourable conditions. Indications are, however, given of the lines on which schools with special difficulties might proceed. It is not intended in these suggestions to recommend a definite course for general adoption as a whole, and History syllabuses, even for schools in similar circumstances, may properly vary according to the capacity and interests of the teacher. Each teacher should think out and frame his own scheme, having regard to the circumstances of his school, its environment, its staffing and internal organisation, and in some measure also to the books and the topics which most appeal to him.

B. READING THE ESSENTIAL FOUNDATION OF HISTORY TEACHING

5. The teacher's reading.—In History, perhaps more than in most studies, the teacher's own reading and his power to make judicious use of it are of the first importance, and many teachers with a special interest in the subject will naturally wish to get together little libraries of their own. While it is not difficult, even in the country, for teachers to obtain the books of reference they need, nevertheless, the teaching sometimes displays insufficient breadth of knowledge and therefore insufficient power of selecting such facts as give vividness, reality and historical balance to the story. The study of the writings of some of the great historians of the past such as Gibbon, Froude and Macaulay and of the best modern historical works dealing with the social and economic aspects of the subject, will give life and reality to the narrative of events, and enrich the presentation of them.

In the vast store-house of English literature the teacher may find inspiration; for the literature of any period is often the expression of the life and thought of that period. Readings from Chaucer and Piers Plowman, for example, are almost indispensable for a true appreciation of life in the later Middle Ages; Spenser and Shakespeare light up the Elizabethan period, Milton, Bunyan and Pepys the 17th Century; Addison, Steele and Boswell's Johnson the 18th Century; Cobbett and the great Victorian novelists the early 19th Century.

The continuous refreshment which the best literature may give will help teachers from day to day and year to year to clothe the dry bones of History with flesh and blood.

6. The children's reading.—(a) *Text-books and reference-books*.—As History offers exceptional opportunities for independent study on the part of children, the selection of a good text-book is of great importance. The best students' histories are too difficult for children, yet no book should be chosen for the senior classes which does not represent good historical scholarship. The language of the books chosen without being unduly childish, should be sufficiently simple and vivid to be followed by young pupils with interest and should not require too much verbal explanation by the teacher. The matter should be historically sound, the descriptions of important persons and events reasonably full; and the narrative, though brief, so presented as to impress the reader with a sense of its continuity.

In addition to text-books it would be well also, where possible, to provide for each school, or for a group of schools, a collection of good histories of different periods, monographs, biographies, etc., which would together cover the ground. Such books can, as a rule, be obtained from Public Libraries and, in rural areas, from County Libraries.

(b) *Library facilities.*—Most Public Libraries now offer special facilities for children. In many of them an arrangement has been made by which the children in the senior classes of the school have tickets entitling them to borrow a book. A list of suitable books is made by the teacher, and thus a kind of circulating library is started in school, which in course of time is replaced by another. Those teachers are particularly fortunate whose children have access to a special reading room in the Public Library. But no matter what reading the Public Library may offer, it does not remove the need for a historical section in the School Library.

(c) *The use of historical fiction.*—Every encouragement should be given to the children to read good historical fiction. There is scarcely an episode of importance, from the Roman Invasion onwards, which has not been dealt with by a writer of ability. A collection of such books, which should be of real literary merit, should be in every school library for the use of pupils as well as teachers; historical novels are, if possible, better read at home than at school, for the habit of reading at home for pleasure will strengthen the older pupils' power of independent study. It will help them to use books to good purpose in the classroom and to prepare many of their lessons for themselves with pleasure and with excellent effect upon their general education.

Among these books should be some from which the children should on occasion hear or read a story as it was told first-hand, especially when the writers are also excellent story-tellers.

C. THE SCHOOL COURSE

7. General arrangement of the school course.—
In the following pages the Junior School stage and the
Senior School stage are dealt with separately. It is
not suggested, however, that any definite break in the
course is to be desired for its own sake. Indeed, always
assuming that the teachers of the Junior School are left
free to choose the topics they are to handle, with the
tastes and interests of their children to guide them,
there is a great deal to be said for a close connexion
between the work of the Junior and Senior School, by
means of which the syllabus of the latter can be adjusted
to the foundations already laid.

In addition many schools contain a considerable proportion of children, whose mentality, even where they are
Seniors in point of age, makes necessary a very simple
treatment of the subject, little if at all in advance of that
suggested for Juniors.

II. THE JUNIOR SCHOOL STAGE

8. Aim of the work at this stage.—Though the
approach to the teaching of History in the Junior School
should be direct and simple, and though the most
natural methods of instruction may be expected to be
the most successful, it must not be thought that the
work done in this subject in these early years is not of
the greatest importance. Only in the hands of a teacher
who loses no chance of stimulating the natural interests
and curiosity of the children will a foundation be laid
on which the more advanced teaching of subsequent
years can be built to advantage. If, however, the
course is well arranged and well presented, the pupil,
by the age of 11, should have gained acquaintance with
some of the outstanding figures and types of history
in a rough chronological order, should have some idea

of the circumstances under which they lived, and should have begun to develop some curiosity as to their motives and aims.

9. The approach through stories.—It is specially important to remember the value of a successful appeal to the imagination of the young child. In all good History teaching such an appeal must play a great part, but here, where the children are young and the subject fresh, its value is perhaps greatest. Early impressions are of great importance and produce an attitude of mind which it is not easy to eradicate afterwards. Our own sense of values has been so moulded by our early training that we may easily go wrong in taking it for granted that the lessons of our childhood are the right ones for children of today.

Simple and attractive stories are the obvious means of arousing this interest in very young children and should form the main substance of the instruction. These stories need not be confined to any one country or to any one age. They should be so arranged as to introduce the child to a gallery of striking pictures drawn from the whole range of history. In addition to stories from the history of the British Isles, the course might well include some stories of the Bible lands, of the Siege of Troy, of Leonidas, Socrates and Alexander, Horatius and Hannibal, Roland and Charlemagne, Dante and Giotto, St. Louis, St. Francis of Assisi, William Tell, Joan of Arc, Columbus, Cartier and Cortez, as well as similarly outstanding characters of more modern times.

It is not difficult to find, in good literary form, stories of the Tale of Troy and the Odyssey; stories from Herodotus, Plutarch and Froissart; from the Sagas, the Arthurian cycle, the Arabian Nights, and so on, and whether the story lesson is labelled " Literature " or " History " is immaterial. The younger the children, the stronger should be the romantic element in the narrative ; and during the earlier years it may be inadvisable, even if it were possible, to distinguish between legend and history.   There is also force in the contention that to the child's mind it is the older part of the story which is the least complex and the most tinged with romance.   No doubt there are characters in comparatively modern history such as Florence Nightingale, Garibaldi and Livingstone whose stories can be made to appeal strongly to young children : and the teacher to whose taste these appeal will do well to include them. Nevertheless the balance of advantage under normal conditions probably lies with the heroes and heroines of the remoter past, and experience suggests that the child can often feel a deeper and a more personal interest in the story of Leonidas at Thermopylae, of Regulus returning to captivity at Carthage, of William falling as he landed at Pevensey, and in the doings of Marco Polo and of Joan of Arc, than in the incidents of more recent centuries.

10. Selection and grouping of the stories.— Each teacher will, no doubt, arrange his own scheme of stories largely according to his taste and the books at his disposal.   As regards the content of the scheme it will probably be best, at least in the initial stages, to deal mainly with personalities, but the interest most children naturally take in the accessories of a story can be used quite early to place each personality in something like its proper historical setting.   Stories which deal with typical or imaginary characters may also have a real value if they successfully bring out something of the life of the people rather than of their rulers.   As the top of the Junior School is reached, the subjects chosen for the stories will naturally be presented in a somewhat maturer way, and the satisfaction of the children's curiosity may transform the story imperceptibly into the history lesson.

In arranging the stories there may be real advantage in classifying them according to their character and content, while even at the outset it is wise to take them in such groups as will give them a certain unity of form and colour. These groups might illustrate certain great ideas or types of character, or might be based on place or nationality. Within the limits of the groups, however, it is probably wise to adhere fairly closely to a chronological arrangement, and whenever the arrangement of groups involves a serious breach of chronological sequence, the breach should be made very clear to the children.

Whatever decision the teacher may make on these points, it is essential that the work should be so planned, and so carried out in practice as to give the child's imagination plenty of scope, to let it receive vivid impressions of other ages in which manners, ideas and environment were very different from those of today.

11. Methods of instruction.—(a) *Reading, narration and discussion.*—The stories can be told to the children, and it is also an excellent, though much neglected, practice to read aloud to them well written tales. In any case, the children themselves should take an active part in the lesson, and not be merely passive listeners. Thus, they should be encouraged to ask questions ; it is a useful practice, if not carried to excess, to let them re-tell the stories which they have heard ; and when once the initial difficulties of composition have been overcome, they should attempt to write down their impressions of some simple scene or incident chosen from the narrative. When they can read with sufficient ease, they should often be set to read the story in the book by themselves, preferably before the lesson is given.

Nothing is so likely to deaden the interest of the child as the type of lesson still sometimes heard in which the children read aloud in turn from the class reader and the teacher follows with a running commentary.

(b) *Illustrations.*—Full scope should be given to the constructive powers of the children in making models to illustrate their stories. They should be encouraged to draw pictures and picture charts, and also, within suitable limits, to collect illustrations bearing on their work.

Pictures of historical interest are of real value, but it is not easy to arrange for their provision on a scale which gives every individual child adequate opportunity for reflection. Again, visits to places of historical interest in the immediate neighbourhood may prove stimulating.

(c) *Dramatisation.*—The children's expressive powers may also be exercised by dramatisation and the Juniors may well act their history stories as naturally as Infants act fairy tales. With the help of suitable pictures and contemporary illustrations shewing armour and dress, the class can co-operate with the teacher in arranging their own parts. They may thus learn something of the life and colour, speech and habits of the periods from which the scenes are taken. But a good deal of selection and preparation is necessary if this method is to yield its best results and give as many of the class as possible an opportunity to help.

III. THE SENIOR SCHOOL STAGE

A. SOME PRINCIPLES GOVERNING THE CHOICE OF SUBJECT-MATTER

12. Importance of not overloading the syllabus.— Assuming that the teaching in the Junior School has successfully followed the lines already indicated, the pupil's interest in History will have been stimulated by clear pictures of outstanding personalities and events. He has now come to an age when he can begin to study History as a connected story, in which there is a sequence of events together with a thread of development of which he may become conscious. There can be no greater mistake than to attempt so wide a survey that it is necessary to hurry in order to cover it in the time available, and that no time is left for anything but lists of names and events and generalisations for which the basis has to be taken largely for granted. It is of far more value to give the pupil so lively an interest in the study of History that he will welcome any opportunity to pursue it further, than to burden his memory with facts which can have little or no significance for him. One of the main causes why this purpose is too seldom achieved is the overloading of the syllabus and of the lesson in the attempt to make them complete and exhaustive rather than selective. Much that appears—and rightly appears—in the ordinary textbooks and is known to the adult student of History, is beyond the reach of children. It is forgotten that in the selection of personalities and events for study by his pupils, the important question for the teacher is " What are the essential incidents and personalities and the details associated with them that I must not omit ? ", and for the rest not " How much can I put in ? " but " How much can I leave out ? ". Significant detail should not be omitted from a mistaken desire for completeness. It must be frankly recognised that a good deal must be sacrificed, even of what may fairly be regarded as important and attractive to older students.

Much is frequently included in History syllabuses for children under fourteen years of age because it is felt that, in the absence of further education, many children will never have the chance of being introduced to such topics ; yet it is clear that matter introduced prematurely can be of no permanent value, and it is also clear that if further education were assured to these boys and girls much that the syllabuses contain could be more profitably and suitably dealt with at a later age.

13. What may be achieved by the end of the course.—When conditions are favourable, the child may perhaps be expected, by the time he leaves the Elementary School, to have some idea of the stage in world history at which British history begins ; of the peoples that were merged in the English nation ; of the main social and economic changes through which the country has passed in the last thousand years ; of the development of the national system of government ; of the growth of the Empire ; and of the present position of the British Commonwealth of Nations in the world. Above all, he should have begun to realise also that this story has some bearing on everyday life, and that the England of today and the British Commonwealth of Nations are the result of changes that can be traced through centuries.

This is the ideal, but it is recognised that to attain it fully may be beyond the reach of many schools. The variations in plan necessary in the case of classes where the children are of less capacity, must be left to the judgment of the teacher, and it is fully recognised that, for such children and in schools where conditions are difficult, a less extended but well-considered treatment of the subject may be all that is possible. In such cases it must be remembered that the maintenance of interest in the subject is the primary and all important consideration. To keep this alive it may well be desirable to shape the whole course substantially on the lines suggested for the Junior School, so that the pupil shall leave school with at least some knowledge of those outstanding characters in our national story whose names are commonplaces of our daily life and thought. Alternatively, it may be prudent to omit many topics, in themselves of great importance, in which the children can feel little interest, such as, for instance, industrial conditions when the school is deep in the country, or modern history outside Britain when they have little effective touch with the outside world. It is in cases like these that the interest in local and social history to which reference has already been made, may be expected to make a particularly strong appeal, where a wider and more general scheme would arouse comparatively little interest.

But whatever is selected and whatever is omitted the course should always be continued to modern times. Even in the smallest schools children should not spend two or more years on a single period, or leave school without a knowledge of events which have happened in their own life-time.

14. Topics selected should have significance to the school child.—Without limitation of topics to those which are of primary importance and interest to children, it is impossible to secure emphasis when emphasis is needed, or to find room for the detail necessary to create reasonably clear ideas and pictures. Children, also, need the picturesque element which appeals to the imagination and gives life and reality to persons and events. Whatever helps them to believe in the story and to see the actors in it as real men and women, is of value. Thus the personal appearance of great men, their characteristic action and bearing at decisive moments, and their recorded sayings, are all details ; yet in numerous cases they have stamped themselves on the popular imagination, and no wise teacher will omit them in a course of History for children.

The teacher's guiding principle will, therefore, be that the selected topic should be both of historical value and easily and naturally intelligible to the pupils. Children like to hear or read about the lives of great men and women. They can take the keenest interest in Archimedes and Caesar, in the heroes of Agincourt, in Drake and Raleigh, in Wolfe and Montcalm, and can appreciate much of what Alfred or Edward I, Chatham or Clive,

Blake or Nelson, Champlain or Cook, Wilberforce or Lincoln, Harvey or Lister or Pasteur achieved in their different ways. But they need not, indeed should not, be harassed with the details of the divorce of Henry VIII, or with the intrigues of Charles II's reign, or with the conflicts of political parties in the 18th or later centuries.

15. Value of social and local history.—Both social and local history, again, have a natural interest for children. Their curiosity is easily aroused by the story of changes in such matters of daily concern as houses and dress, food and means of transport, and they may be led on from these to some consideration of more difficult matters, such as changes in the condition of agriculture, trade, industry and war. Every child too should know something of the history of his own village, town or county, and local history will often supply excellent examples of changes in the mode and character of life at different epochs. Visits, too, where these are possible, to the actual scene of historic events or to the actual remains of times which have passed away are of great value in creating atmosphere and in making history live. But under normal conditions care must be taken lest the line of approach through social or local history tends to obliterate the great land-marks in history. Local history is perhaps better taught, not as a separate course, but by constant reference to the history of the locality as illustrations of the national story.

16. The value of some background of world history.—Whatever the topics selected for inclusion in the Senior School course, it is desirable that the teacher should so present them that his pupils can see them against a background of world history. Thus, the story of our kith and kin beyond the seas, of their settlements and struggles, of the great deeds they have accomplished, of the development of the lands in which they have settled, or which they have administered, should be presented as an important and integral part of the story of the British peoples as a whole. But even British history only becomes intelligible when the pupil realises its place in the story of the world. When dealing, therefore, with the history of the British Dominions and Colonies, the teacher will have abundant opportunity to bring home to his class the fact that they cannot learn British history without learning it as part of a larger whole, and that their sympathy and respect are due to other nations and races, with whom whether as allies or rivals, fellow-colonists, rulers or traders, Englishmen have had, and still have, so many dealings. A respect for other civilisations than that of Western Europe will best grow out of a knowledge, however small, of their history. Even to hear once that the Chinese were a cultured people when our ancestors were savages may exercise a lasting effect on the outlook of a child.

B. BRITISH HISTORY AS A PART OF WORLD HISTORY

17. Some ways of dealing with ancient history.— No course of History can be satisfactory that leaves the pupil with the impression that the story of the world began with Julius Cæsar's visits to Britain. To give an adequate picture of the history of the Ancient World is of course impossible, but since we all enjoy the fruits of ancient wisdom and civilisation, many teachers may think that we ought to know something of how these things came to be. Some teachers, accordingly, commence the course by making the Bible their main source for ancient history, adding such references to the ancient empires of Egypt, Assyria and Persia as are necessary. Other teachers make a practice of giving at a suitable stage in the school course, a very simple sketch of world history by means of biographical studies of outstanding figures, leading the pupil to see, not merely disconnected lives, but something of the character of the civilisations which they represent. The important thing in such teaching is to concentrate on those parts of the world's story from which modern civilisation can trace a direct descent, i.e. Palestine, Greece and Rome ; it is easy to waste time on stories of primitive man or to devote too much attention to stories of the Asiatic Empires and Egypt. But, through Ancient History rightly taught in biography and story and picture, the pupil may learn to recognise what we owe to Greece and Rome : the feeling for beauty and the beginnings of scientific thought and method, on the one hand, the spread of law and order, on the other ; and how the fusion of the two made western civilisation, as we know it, possible. Again, he may be shown how, as the Middle Ages drew to their close, renewed interest in the ancient Greeks and Romans altered the outlook of all western peoples, and how the university and the printing press passed on the inheritance.

In Ancient History, some of the more important stories of the ancient world which the pupils have learnt at the Junior School stage might be reviewed, and where possible a few lessons might be given on some of the main features of the early civilisations which those biographies and stories illustrate, especially where they bear on our own history.

18. Linking up British history with world history.—

Where a series of lessons on the Ancient World is given, it is usually followed by the topics chosen from British history with allusion to the concurrent stream of general history, and experience shows that this is a practicable plan of attacking the wider relations of History. Though time is seldom found for the systematic teaching of foreign or world history, the course should make it possible for children to see such parts of our own history as are parts of world movements in due proportion. For example, if such topics as the following are dealt with boldly and simply the children may be expected

to have a better understanding of our own history;
Britain as a province of the Roman Empire; the raid
and settlements of the Northmen; the Crusades, th
Renaissance and the Reformation; the expansion c
Europe overseas; the position of Spain under Philip I
of France under Louis XIV and Napoleon; the unif
cation of Germany and Italy; the development of th
United States of America; and the international growt
of modern industry and commerce.

19. The League of Nations.—If the teacher brings t
his work a broad conception of the treatment of th
history of Great Britain and the British Commonwealt
of Nations, dwelling not less upon the points of contac
between nations than upon the differences which hav
separated them, he will naturally wish that the childre
should learn something of the League of Nations an
of the ideals for which it stands. In most case:
opportunity will offer, not only in the History lessons
but at other times, for drawing attention to that for
of international co-operation which the League re
presents. It may be pointed out that in the moder
industrial world the increased communication betwee
nations, owing to improved methods of transport, th
economic interdependence of nations upon one anothe
and above all the vast scale and terrible machinery c
modern warfare, have made it necessary that the people
of the world should combine with their natural sens
of local patriotism a conception of their common interest
and duties.

This subject is dealt with more fully in the Appendi
at the end of this volume.

C. SOME EXAMPLES OF THE WAY IN WHICH THE SCHOO
COURSE MAY BE DEALT WITH

**20. The teacher should make his own selectio
of periods and topics.**—The teacher will naturally hin
self determine what period of History he will deal wit

at any particular stage and what topics he will include in his treatment of that period. Something has already been said as to the kind of selection that may be made from the field of Ancient History ; but it may be found useful to give some examples of the way in which a typical course in History may be handled in accordance with some of the principles mentioned in the opening sections of this chapter. These examples, however, are only intended to suggest a method of approach ; they are not offered as the basis of a school syllabus, nor is it to be expected that any one school could deal satisfactorily with all of them.

21. Early English History. — In Early English History, the period of Saxon and Danish invasions may be passed over briefly, the children's attention being drawn to a few outstanding figures such as St. Augustine, Bede, Alfred and St. Dunstan. In districts where local material in a form readily intelligible to children is available, somewhat extended treatment of the details of the period will readily suggest itself : for example, the visible traces of themselves which Celt, and Roman, Saxon and Dane have left in the names of places, remains of buildings and earthworks, roads, coins and pottery. Living witnesses to the story of those times can be found in the Celtic inhabitants and Celtic speech of Wales, and in the Saxon framework of our own language.

Maps are of special value in this connexion, and every teacher should be familiar with the publications of the Ordnance Office, particularly those maps and reproductions which have an obvious historical interest. All children should be familiarised in a simple way with places and with routes, and more advanced pupils should learn how the waterways helped, and forest, marsh, and highland impeded, the movements of bodies of men. Upon the map, when the story of the Roman occupation is being told, the pupils should mark the great military

posts of the Romans, and their important towns : e.g
London, Colchester, York, Chester, Lincoln, Bath
Silchester, etc. and the great Roman roads and wall
They should learn how the line of the Roman roads ca
be traced by place-names derived from the Latin *strata*
Stratford, Streetly, etc. They should learn that whe
a town or village ends in " ham " or " ton " or " burgh
it is of Saxon origin, and that " by " or " rigg " o
" thorpe " indicates a Danish settlement. They shoul
understand why such names occur frequently in certai
parts of England and are entirely absent in others.

22. The Middle Ages.—In the treatment of th
Middle Ages, outstanding features should be selecte
and illustrated by accounts of interesting and importar
personalities. Thus life in Norman times could b
illustrated by William I and Henry II ; the beginning
of Parliament by Simon de Montfort and Edward I
the story of the Church by Hildebrand, Becket, S
Francis and Wycliffe ; the wars of the Middle Age
including the Crusades and ideals of chivalry, by Richard
and the Black Prince ; the story of Wales and Scotlan
by Llewellyn, Wallace and Bruce ; the growth of know
ledge by Dante, Roger Bacon, Marco Polo, Prince Henr
of Portugal, and Caxton ; and the story of France b
St. Louis, Edward III, Henry V and Joan of Arc. Suc
a selection of topics, if treated with proper attention t
detail, would take up the time likely to be available fo
this period, and, with many classes, too great emphas
need not be laid on the thread of political continuit
connecting them.

Without any attempt to define precisely such term
as feudalism, the gild, the Church or the manor, it wi
frequently be possible to bring home to the children
minds by concrete examples, how these characterist
institutions of the Middle Ages influenced the lives an
actions of men of that day : what a prominent par

for example, the churchmen played in the making of history, how much power the ownership of land brought with it, and what life was like to the town dweller.

The names of streets, roads, buildings—e.g. Watling Street, Greyfriars, Friargate, Priory Lane, Abbey Street, Jury Street, Old Jewry, Old Bailey, Guildhall—should become names with meaning. Similarly, but far more important, the most striking differences from age to age in the style of architecture, such as the change from Norman to Early English, and in the methods of building, such as the change in the use of building material, can frequently be shown by local churches and other buildings. Some teachers devote a few lessons to two or three battles of decisive character, such as Hastings Sluys and Agincourt, which lend themselves to picturesque treatment, and help the children to understand how different warfare used to be, and how weapons, armour and transport have changed.

23. The Tudor Period.—In studying the Tudor Period and the Sixteenth Century, several lessons might with advantage be given to the life and work of Columbus, Vasco da Gama, Frobisher and other discoverers, and again the story of the Armada and of other famous exploits of Elizabethan sailors, and to the beginnings of the East India Company. The story of the Navy becomes of special interest and importance from the time of the Tudors. With the help of pictures the children will readily appreciate the contrast between the Spanish galleon and the " Great Harry " of Henry VIII—the first British battleship—or the " Sovereign of the Seas " of Charles I ; or again between the " Revenge " of Grenville and the " Revenge " of today.

It is probably not wise, under normal conditions, to devote much time to the Renaissance and the Reformation—both difficult—but the pupils can be helped to realise how in life and in literature, in art and architecture, no less than in discovery and religion, the Tudor period marks the beginning of modern history. The teacher might tell of Copernicus and Leonardo da Vinci, of Erasmus and Luther, More and Colet, as well as of Queen Mary, Queen Elizabeth and Mary Queen of Scots; and he will explain that the Reformation in England was only part of a general movement. That the position of the clergy was altered, that the monasteries were destroyed, that a service in English replaced a service in Latin, and that there were then—as there are now—different kinds of Protestants in England as well as elsewhere, are facts which a child can appreciate. But the theological discussions which accompanied these external changes must obviously be left untouched.

24. The XVIIth Century. — The constitutional struggle of the Seventeenth Century should be presented as simply as possible, and illustrated mainly by the careers of outstanding personalities like Hampden and Strafford. But there should be no attempt to teach the bewildering succession of Acts of Parliament, Remonstrances, Petitions, etc., which if not unintelligible, are at least wearisome to children. Some of the essential features of the Constitution under which we live are the direct result of the Revolution of 1688, and these should be made clear to the older pupils.

The history of the Civil War, however, presents peculiar opportunities for connecting local with national history, for it has left its traditions and associations in nearly every county. Events that happened in the neighbourhood of the school, the part played by the ancestors of local families, the material traces of the conflict which still remain, not only command a special interest in themselves, but add reality to the whole study. The London child should know how Charles was baffled at Brentford, and how the London trainbands held their own at Newbury. The west-country child should know the parts played by Bristol, Gloucester, Plymouth and Taunton. The East Anglian will be moved by the tragic story of Colchester, and he ought to understand why his own neighbourhood was happy in its general freedom from the incidents of war.

The beginnings of the British Empire in the Seventeenth and the first half of the Eighteenth Century—the story of the American Colonies, the early struggles of the East India Company, the settlements in Newfoundland and the capture of Jamaica—should receive due attention. Here the teacher will find great opportunities for an interesting treatment of Geography, for instance, by indicating the gradual penetration of the American continent from the French settlements in Canada and the English settlements in Virginia, Pennsylvania and New England, the Jesuit missionary stations on the Great Lakes, the explorations of La Salle and the founding of New Orleans, the line of frontier posts along the Alleghanies and the advance from West Virginia and Pennsylvania into Kentucky.

25. The XVIIIth Century.—The Eighteenth Century, which, for the purposes of this survey, may be regarded as commencing with the English Revolution and ending with the Congress of Vienna, is only too frequently dealt with in either a dull or else a one-sided manner. The dull way is to work chronologically through a series of wars, dealing mainly with their continental aspects; while the reaction from this method has led some teachers—and the writers of the text-books they follow— to lay such emphasis on industrial and mechanical development that the children have never heard of Marlborough, Chatham, Clive, Wellington and all the colourful story of the struggle with the French in America and India, with the French Revolution and the Saga of the Peninsular War. It should not be impossible to strike a balance between these two modes of approach.

Without neglecting to trace the great changes consequent upon the development of machinery and more intense methods of cultivation, usually summed up in the two dangerous catchwords—the " Industrial " and " Agrarian " Revolutions—one may well make the most of the vigorous and appealing personalities who, overseas, were laying the foundations of the British Commonwealth of Nations and those of other nations whom they were fighting. No child, anywhere, can be interested in the politics of the period, nor should this be expected of him. In a purely urban district, in which children do not know the difference between a plough and a harrow, the importance of Townshend, Jethro Tull and Bakewell, can with difficulty be appreciated ; in purely rural districts the inventions of Arkwright and Crompton offer similar difficulties of comprehension. Both these sides of Eighteenth Century development should indeed be touched upon : the town children should learn how it is that the landscape of England, which they see on their excursions, has taken its peculiar and characteristic aspect ; the country children should learn how and why the huge growth of towns, with the problems created for us by that growth, was the result of the inventions of the Eighteenth Century. But the detail should be adapted to the circumstances of the school.

In purely domestic history, the easier approach may be by means of topics, such as, " the change from the open field system to modern farming," or " the growth of the factory system ". In dealing with developments overseas, where the protagonists lend themselves to more picturesque treatment, the personal approach may be better : the stories of Marlborough, Clive, the elder Pitt, Wolfe, Captain Cook, Washington, Napoleon, Nelson, Wellington and his men, have, if properly treated, a strong appeal for children.

26. The history of recent times (1815 to the present day).—(a) *Difficulty of the period.*—This period is one of peculiar difficulty and should be taken towards the end of the school course, when the minds of the children are most mature. For though it deals with conditions which are similar to those with which the children are familiar, it involves the introduction of economic and political conceptions that are difficult for any child to grasp, important as their influence may well be on their later life.

While this period can never be made interesting when treated reign by reign, there are dangers in treating it by reference to isolated movements, such as " Social Reform," or " Progress of Science and Invention," if the children have an insufficient background of fact. This method leads to the accumulation of knowledge in watertight compartments, with a consequent loss of time sense and of understanding of gradual development.

(b) *History of the present day.*—The great importance of bringing the story down to the present day has already been pointed out and should need no emphasis. We have to deal with a generation of children born since the conclusion of the Great War, which tends to become for them a matter of legend. In presenting the history of the immediate past it is best that the controversial sides of questions closely connected with modern politics should not be stressed. On the other hand, it is perhaps equally inadvisable that these questions should be awkwardly shelved when the natural interests of the children bring them to the front. But if the History teacher deals with such topics he should remember that he has the responsibility of making it clear that every question has more than one side, and therefore that it is obligatory on him to see that no one side of any question is presented alone or in undue prominence.

(c) *The biographical method.*—Some teachers prefer to deal with movements through the lives of the men and women who played a principal part in them. Thus the story of the British Dominions is taught by the lives and deeds of early settlers, of explorers like Sturt and Eyre, of administrators and soldiers such as Gibbon Wakefield, Lawrence, Grey, Gordon, Kitchener, Roberts, Rhodes and Botha; social reform and the great struggle against slavery, which commences this period, through accounts of Clarkson, Wilberforce, Elizabeth Fry, Shaftesbury and General Booth; the progress of invention and science through the work of Stephenson, Edison, Marconi, Pasteur and Lister.

But such a method will probably be found to be inadequate in dealing with quite recent history, if only because of the obvious difficulty of dealing with the careers of men still alive; it is therefore necessary, in order to bring the story down to the present day, to devise methods of treating more recent events and movements which allude only incidentally to personalities.

(d) *Tracing local results of important changes.*—The results of great industrial and political changes, such as the increased use of machinery, the Reform Bills, the Factory and Education Acts, can often be made clear to the children by tracing the actual effect of such changes in their own town or locality. In this way they should learn something of the shifting of the great centres of industry and population from the east and south to the north and the reverse movement in recent times; of the connexion of their town or country with parliamentary institutions; of the contrast between life in a large manufacturing town of today and life at a time when most people lived in villages and market towns; of the conditions of industry before and after the great reforms of the Nineteenth Century.

(e) *Comparisons between the present and the past.*—It is specially necessary in this modern period, where the wealth of material is so great, that attention should be concentrated on the broadest and simplest aspects of the subject. Comparisons between the present and the past will frequently suggest themselves, and it is by the method of comparison rather than by set lessons or direct instruction that the foundations of intelligent citizenship can be best laid. Any attempt to deal elaborately with the parts of the British Constitution, the local government of the country, or the administration of justice, is wearisome and must be largely unintelligible to children.

Children can easily perceive how many of the institutions which they see around them have their roots in the past, and how often, though they are called by the old name, they fulfil new functions. Without any pretence of studying constitutional history in detail, they can be led to see—in fact they can often discover for themselves—that the powers of the monarch have altered in practice from time to time; that Parliament as set up by Edward I was composed of very different people, and was summoned for a very different purpose and in a very different way from the Parliament of today; that a sheriff in England was one thing in the Twelfth Century and is another in the Twentieth; that the custom of the judges going on assize dates back to Norman times; and that from first to last there has been continuous growth and development.

Social conditions lend themselves even more readily to this method of treatment. The teacher will be almost compelled to touch upon the differences between the present day and, for example, Tudor times, in such matters as the provision made for the infirm and aged, the mobility of labour, and the facilities for travel, especially by sea. The way, too, in which the progress of science has knit together not only single countries, but all parts of the modern world, is a striking and profoundly important fact which should be impressed upon the pupils.

(f) *The teaching of " citizenship."*—Considerations of this kind have led many teachers to believe that the history lessons provide the best medium in which to develop the beginnings of training in intelligent citizenship ; and there can be little doubt that, in the hands of skilful and broadminded teachers, lessons and discussions on current economic, political and social problems arising naturally from the History lessons and shown, as far as may be, in a historical setting, will do much to stimulate a thoughtful interest in current affairs and in the duties of citizenship.

Other teachers are, however, equally convinced that before children leave school, they should receive definite lessons and training in " Civics " or " Citizenship " or " Simple Economics," or as some prefer to call it " Current Topics." But most, if not all, of these teachers rely in the main on a historical treatment and, so long as they avoid troublesome details and keep their lessons, reading and discussions broad and full of human interest and practical application to everyday life, they achieve a real success in developing some measure of civic spirit.

D. SOME PRACTICAL CONSIDERATIONS

27. The history teacher.—It is of great advantage if the staff of a school includes some member who is specially interested in History, and who will therefore throw himself into the work with enthusiasm. Even where it is not possible to delegate to the specialist a very large share of actual teaching, he can be of great service in advising other teachers, in helping to draw up the syllabus, and in suggesting books for reading and reference and other aids to historical study.

28. Planning the syllabus.—However the syllabus may be arranged, it will be clear that, in most schools, it will not adhere strictly to either of the two plans which have been described as " periodic " or " concentric." There is no reason why the two plans should be mutually exclusive. But it is necessary to take care that no period shall be isolated, for History cannot be properly taught if it is merely cut up into convenient lengths and presented in detailed sections, which are not treated as component parts of a whole. Every era stands related to its predecessor and to the facts which encompass us today ; so that in a sense the teacher of a period is the teacher of the whole of history. It is, therefore, essential that there should be frequent reference, in the course of each year's work, to those earlier events which bear upon it, as well as illustration from the institutions and customs of today. Intelligent revision at regular intervals will of course form an essential part of the scheme ; but, even where the syllabus has been judiciously lightened, the amount of ground to be covered will remain so great that it is unlikely that room will be found in the normal school course for any regular recapitulation of the full story. Any time, however, that the child may have at his disposal after the completion of that course may be used very profitably for this purpose. In such a revision, however arranged, the connexion of present with past may be emphasised with particular effect and the chain of causation more fully emphasised.

29. The desirability of private study by the pupil.—Exposition by the teacher in vivid and simple language has its place in History teaching and may be more inspiring than any book. But if the teaching of History is to be worthy of its place in the school curriculum, occasions must be found for sustained effort on the pupils' part, and for real study and thought.

To create a fleeting impression is not enough. Something more is necessary. Essential facts should be learnt and regularly revised, and outstanding dates which serve as useful landmarks should be definitely memorised throughout the Senior School. And when the pupils have been trained to read a book, many teachers find it a good plan to throw on the class the responsibility for mastering the relevant chapters of the text-book, and to postpone the oral lesson until the pupils have first done their best to wrestle with difficulties and to assimilate the main points. A series of oral lessons, however brilliant and entertaining, cannot be expected to be more than evanescent, unless it is supported by solid study on the part of the pupil ; nor can any devices, however ingenious and attractive, be made an efficient substitute for hard work. Any attempt to teach History by reading the book aloud paragraph by paragraph will prove entirely ineffective. When the teacher has discovered how far the pupils understand what they have read, he will be able to illumine and supplement the book, by amplifying stories, opening up new ground, quoting some telling phrases associated with a person or event, and answering the children's questions.

30. Oral and written questions. Note-making.— It will, of course, be necessary for the teacher to test the children's ability to master the substance of their books by means of oral and written answers to questions and occasionally by longer compositions. The more advanced pupils may perhaps be systematically trained to make for themselves brief notes of summaries of lessons or chapters. At any rate, some of their written work should be illustrated by sketches, maps and pictures ; and it should be remembered that notes which are not clear in substance, and legible, and properly arranged fail in one of the main purposes for which they are intended, i.e. speedy revision.

31. The use of illustration.—Pictorial illustration, contemporary work especially, is indispensable in all stages of the teaching. Portraits of eminent persons, reproductions of old prints, documents and other famous records, such as the Bayeux tapestry, will often form the best means of representing social life and customs, pageants and battles, and the apparatus of husbandry, industry, trade and war. Some modern pictures of historic scenes may also be useful. Guidance as to the sources from which such illustrations may be obtained will be found in the excellent Leaflet No. 82 published by the Historical Association. Nor should it be overlooked that the bound volumes of the illustrated periodicals of the last fifty to one hundred years contain useful matter.

32. Films and wireless broadcasts.—The teacher will also consider how far the cinematograph film and the wireless broadcast can serve the aims of the teaching of History. Through these media representations of the past, of the daily life of the people, of their work and their recreations, of the great changes in industry and commerce can do much to help children to make pictures in their minds of what the past was really like. And, if the teaching of History is to touch events of the present day, teachers may find it useful to have at their disposal, as opportunity offers and as need arises, material presented by one, who is outside the school and who perhaps possesses greater knowledge of national and world affairs or greater power of impartial presentation.

33. Chronology.—Dates are an important means of tracing and fixing the course of events. For a time some teachers tried to do without them with the result that many children lost all sense of historical sequence. " The When, the Where and the Why " are the essential points in the study of History, and may be connected, in that order, with " the Who," which should take a leading place in the earliest stage.

With a view to giving the children clear ideas about dates and the duration of periods, it is a good practice to require them to construct time charts, on the principle of allotting equal spaces to equal intervals of time. As a rule, the more simple the time chart the more arresting and effective it is.* In addition to these time charts, which will normally be made in the children's note books, a general chart for the classroom wall is found useful by some teachers, especially if its illustrations are simple and striking.

34. The connexion of history with geography.—
Geography and History may often go hand-in-hand, to their mutual advantage, though the attempt to combine them in a single scheme is rarely successful. The influence of Geography, especially in its broader physical aspects, cannot be too strongly emphasised. For example, the pupil can be led to observe how the fertile river valleys of Egypt and Mesopotamia became the early homes of civilisation, how the sea has profoundly affected the life of Britain and Holland, and how the mountains dividing valley from valley were a determining factor in the development both of ancient Greece and of modern Switzerland. And Geography helps to explain the consequences to Great Britain of her insular position, of her nearness to Europe, of her long narrow shape and of the character of her seaboard, and of the discovery of America. It suggests why the Low Countries have so often been the seat of war and why British policy has always been concerned for the fate of this part of Europe.

In the same way, if the teaching of Geography is intelligent, much knowledge that is essential for a

---

* See pamphlet *Time Charts*, published by The Historical Association.

proper study of History can be acquired through it. Thus, in some schools the study of the geography of Asia includes elementary ideas about the rise and spread of Mohammedanism, with special reference to the numerous Mohammedan peoples living under the British flag. Moreover, to those teachers who are specially interested in world history, the connexion with Geography offers great attractions, for in Geography teachers have always aimed at some knowledge of the whole world, and if the History is more closely connected with the Geography, it tends also to become the history of the world.

The historical atlas should be constantly at hand, and the importance of rapid sketch-maps, in illustration of the history, drawn both by teachers and by children, should not be forgotten. Good historical maps will often be needed to show, for instance, the medieval trade routes, the early French and English colonies in North America, the gradual development of the British Commonwealth of Nations, and the vast scale of the Great War.

CHAPTER XIII

GEOGRAPHY

SUMMARY OF CONTENTS

I. SOME GENERAL CONSIDERATIONS

I. The aims of the teaching.—The claim of Geography to a place in the curriculum of the Elementary School is now generally recognised. Any exhaustive treatment of the subject must, indeed, be reserved for adult students, but even in its early stages it involves so many facts within the range of a child's experience, —such as, for instance, the varying altitude of the sun, the connexion between rainfall and certain winds, the crops in the fields, the colourful display of the grocer's or the fruiterer's shop,—that it provides frequent opportunities for encouraging children to reflect upon their immediate surroundings and to exercise their imagination about the world in which they live. If Geography be treated from the human standpoint, the child at school may be trained to realise how the conditions under which men live have helped to mould their lives and their activities. As he grows older, he may learn something of the relationships, commercial and cultural, which link his own district with other parts of his country, with the Empire and with the rest of the world and so be in a better position to understand the problems of peoples in lands other than his own.

A well planned course of Geography should, therefore, supply the pupil with a definite body of ordered facts, topographical, commercial, economic and scientific, that are part of the stock of information which members of a modern civilised community need for the understanding of current events. It should give him, also, some acquaintance with the more important geographical principles and some power of applying his knowledge of them, especially in regard to his own country and his own district. It should help him, further, to understand, and to be able to use, maps and diagrams illustrating such characteristics of any particular region as its physical features, its climate or its productions. Such a course should, finally, give the pupil some training in finding out for himself how and where to obtain information on geographical topics in which he is interested and in testing the truth of geographical statements.

2. The relation of geography to other subjects.—
It would be a great mistake to regard Geography as a self-contained subject and to ignore its wide and vital connexions with other branches of the curriculum. Thus, History cannot be studied without reference to Geography, just as many problems in Geography cannot be solved without reference to the facts of History. Geography involves calculations, practical measurements and the use of graphs, which constitute a valuable part of a child's training in Mathematics. The subject-matter of Natural Science—observations of changes in the weather and of phenomena in the garden and

experiments in physics and biology—all this contributes to the proper understanding of Geography. Conversely, questions dealing with the spread of plants and animals, and the incidence of certain diseases, such, for instance, as malaria, are generally unintelligible without some background of scientific knowledge. It should hardly be necessary to add that the teacher of Geography, no less than the teacher of any other subject, is a teacher of English both spoken and written.

3. The scope of the course.—The range of Geography is so wide that careful selection of matter for study is essential, and in framing a syllabus every teacher will have to ask himself what is best suited to the particular needs and resources of his school. The answer must depend partly on the district in which the school is situated, and on the circumstances of the children, but even more, perhaps, on the qualifications and experience of the teacher himself and his colleagues and the time allotted to the subject.

In the reorganised Senior School there is usually a specially-qualified teacher in charge, and in these schools it is possible to cover a good deal of ground, and to undertake some fairly advanced work, particularly with the brighter classes. In other schools where circumstances do not permit of specialisation or in which the teachers have not had the advantage of studying Geography in its modern developments under competent guidance, a less ambitious syllabus should be attempted. Some of the principles and methods described in this chapter may be unfamiliar ; and it is clear that a really comprehensive course can only be followed in a school where there is a competent specialist ; but many of the suggestions made in it, will, it is hoped, be of use in helping teachers to improve their lessons even on the most familiar topics, and in indicating possible lines of reading which they can follow up for themselves.

The importance indeed, of the teacher's own reading, can hardly be over-emphasised. Many of the children's misconceptions which arise in the later stages of the course may be traced back to early stories. The idea for example, which they get of Japan, as a land of flowers and jinrikishas is difficult to reconcile with her present position as a great industrial world power. For teachers of older children the need of a good geographical background is still greater. If they can make themselves conversant not only with the larger standard text-books and works of travel, but also with the modern development of trade and economic conditions, and if they have time and opportunity to investigate the geography of their own district, they will discover that the results of their studies are often as interesting to their scholars as to themselves. A knowledge of fiction which contains reliable pictures of foreign countries and peoples will help to give life and colour to the lessons.

Schemes of Geography appropriate to the various types of school will be discussed in later sections, but in preparing any syllabus care should be taken to give each stage a clear and definite aim and to adjust the material included to the time available.

4. The understanding of maps. — Whatever the course may be, it is clear that its success must depend largely on the power of the children to read and understand a map. Senior School children should not only have a clear idea of the position of the towns and districts with which they are dealing, and the power to find any place by means of the index of their atlases and the use of latitude and longitude, but they should also have the power to visualise to some extent the features represented by the map. In the early stages the use of picture and map in juxtaposition is valuable and in the later stages outdoor geography and school journeys may be used to give the child a real idea of the meaning of maps. The climate of a region should be expressed by the summer and winter conditions in both temperature and rainfall. These and other important points may be illustrated by maps specially constructed to bring out the particular features, by diagrams and pictures, and by specimens of the products of different countries. Some of these illustrations may be prepared by the teacher, others by selected children working in small groups. With the aid of his maps a child will readily learn the exact situations of the chief places in the country he is studying, and may discover for himself many of the causes which have brought about the growth of towns, or groups of towns, in certain positions. Throughout the course the children should be trained to make maps for themselves and in the later stages they should be able to draw rapidly and with reasonable accuracy sketch maps to illustrate the points of their lessons, such as the position of towns, the areas in which particular industries are carried on, etc. This subject is dealt with more fully in Section 25 below.

5. The importance of periodical tests. — The success of the Geography teaching must depend largely on the regular revision and testing of the work done, including any notes which have been given. Each teacher will no doubt devise the system which is most suitable to his own needs. " Slip testing " or the giving of a number of questions which demand short answers is of course a useful means of determining whether the children have remembered satisfactorily the salient points of what they have read. Full tests are, however, needed at intervals and these might well include some questions on locational geography : for instance, the children should be asked to fill in places or natural features on blank maps. They should be encouraged also to draw sketch maps, diagrams or graphs as answers to questions. Where written answers are demanded, they should normally be confined to one or two paragraphs. The essay type of question is generally unsuitable for children of this age.

II. THE INFANT SCHOOL STAGE

6. Children's early experiences of their immediate surroundings.—The formal teaching of Geography has no place in the education of little children, for, as such, it is not an interest or activity which falls within the compass of childhood. In the first years of school life the interests of young children lead them to pursue activities rather than subjects. In following their interests they gather information and experience which properly belongs to several subjects, and it has long been recognised that the study of nature, handwork and stories are the natural approaches to Geography. Such activities, based on the common experiences of life are all fresh and exciting to children of five and six. They take delight in observing sun and shadow and rain, the movements and habits of animals, the obvious effects of weather on plant, animal and human life. By practical experience, they learn the characteristics and behaviour of water, and of clay, sand and pebbles under varying conditions. They gain valuable experience from their interests in vehicles and transport of all kinds, in the work of men and women especially where it involves movement and construction and in the routine of the countryside, the seaside, the farm, street, and shop. The young child lives very close to his immediate surroundings which to him are never stale or dull ; the best introduction he can have to his later study of Geography is that he should become familiar with and knowledgeable about all that lies around him.

The teacher's part is to create an atmosphere in which the natural interests of the child are stimulated and encouraged, and to allow him all possible freedom to explore his immediate surroundings by practical handling and experimenting with material. When there are gaps in the normal environment, the teacher can occasionally supply phenomena and incidents of a supplementary kind, e.g., in the sand pit, school garden, " shopping corner," and playroom.

7. Stories should be selected with care.—The traditional practice of introducing Geography in the Infant School in the form of stories centring round " children of other lands " is of questionable educational value. Children of from 5 to 7 years of age are dominated by their own immediate surroundings, and whilst they can enjoy stories with plot and sequence, they are seldom able to create in imagination true pictures of what is widely different from their customary setting. Their experience is at this stage very limited, and it is normally beyond their capacity to envisage foreign peoples and foreign life with reality. Little children in our schools have practically no links or associations with diverse and varied life in icefield, prairie, desert or jungle, and if knowledge covering them is given prematurely, much of it becomes fantastic and unrelated to the world in which they live. It would appear to be better to reserve such subjects to the early years of the Junior School, when they can be attacked with freshness, with greater experience and imagination, and with the power to investigate through picture, globe, map and book. Not that all geographical stories are out of place in the Infant School or that all references to foreign lands and peoples should be suppressed. On the contrary, when children ask questions that arise naturally out of everyday events and interests, they may be simply answered.

Simple stories with a geographical background have their place in the Infant School, particularly when they are genuine stories with plot and sequence. Most children are interested in lions, elephants, camels, bears and can be made familiar with their forms and habits by pictorial illustration. These animals should be presented as living in their natural haunts in jungle, desert or forest ; but such details of environment will be far less complicated than in the case of stories of foreign peoples. Incidents of adventure, which do not require much background of knowledge for comprehension, are also excellent for children in their last year in the Infant School. They are usually interested in stories of travellers lost in desert or forest, of sailors shipwrecked on lonely islands, of heroism in the presence of great natural dangers such as earthquakes, floods and fires. When selected with care, many folk tales have considerable value, especially the folk tales of the more primitive peoples, such as animal stories beloved by negro peoples, and stories of Arabs and their horses ; for these have as their essence, not the differences of peoples in different parts of the world, but fundamental experiences which are common to the human race and familiar to us all.

III. THE JUNIOR SCHOOL STAGE

8. The work in the lower classes of the Junior School.—" Work in the primary school in Geography as in other subjects must be thought of in terms of activity and experience rather than of knowledge to be acquired and facts to be stored, though due regard should be paid to the stimulation of the imagination by vivid description. It follows then that the beginning of formal geography should be delayed to a later stage than has been common in the past*."

---

* Report of the Board's Consultative Committee on *The Primary School* (p. 171), printed and published by H.M. Stationery Office, London, 1931, price 2s. 6d.

The aims and methods in the lower classes of the Junior School, therefore, should not vary materially from those of the Infant School and the basis of the teaching should be the child's own environment. The child should be trained to observe with increasing accuracy and with fuller understanding the things which he sees on his way to school, on nature rambles and elsewhere. The windings of a stream, the goods displayed in the local shops, or the crops around the school can be used to implant geographical ideas. The simple weather records of the Infant School can be extended and the child can observe at first-hand the apparent motion of the sun and its increasing height in the heavens as summer approaches, cold and warm winds, the function of the weather vane, wet and dry weather, etc. In this way terms such as " hot " and " cold," " wet " and " dry," used in a geographical sense, are interpreted by the children in terms of what they have themselves seen and felt.

With these observations of local conditions should go the making of simple plans, first perhaps of the teacher's table or the classroom, and then of the school and its neighbourhood. In this way the conception of direction and the cardinal points will be introduced naturally, and simple questions of the configuration of the land may enter into the teaching. The use of pictures and maps of the same district placed side by side will enable the child to see more clearly the meaning of the conventional colouring and obtain a simple idea of scale. From this, the transition to the map of England, and thence to other maps on the same scale, is easy. Side by side with lessons in local geography there is scope in the lower class of the Junior School for the intelligent treatment of life in other lands. At this stage children possess a sufficient background of experience to enable them to imagine conditions they have not experienced and they will have acquired also some facility in reading. Moreover the growing ability to piece together facts acquired from different sources enables them to supplement class lessons with information gained for themselves from pictures, the globe, maps and books. At this stage, too, the geography of other lands and peoples may be made more interesting by the introduction of " project " work and other forms of corporate activity, since children of from 7 to 9 years of age will have acquired skill in the manipulation of materials which may properly be used for such purposes.

9. The beginning of definite geographical instruction.—In the upper classes of the Junior School the teaching of Geography as Geography should begin. It is not desirable to lay down any definite rule as to when the change should take place and it should in any case be gradual. With a bright class this more definite instruction might usefully begin after the age of 8, but in normal circumstances it would probably be advisable to defer the change until the children are from 9 to 10 years old.

There should be no abrupt transition to the work at this stage from that done in the lower classes. The interest of the child in his environment and his curiosity about foreign lands and peoples form the natural means of leading him from the district in which he lives into the wider world. At this age the collecting instinct is usually strong and children may be encouraged to form collections of pictures, labels, etc., which if well arranged are valuable aids to teaching.

The making of simple maps and plans is another means by which interest may be aroused. It is of the greatest importance that the habits of self-help learned in the Infant School should be fostered and the children encouraged to take a really active part in the lessons.

In the paragraphs which follow a list of topics suitable for children at this stage is given. The list is obviously beyond the power of any one school to attempt, but teachers may find in it suggestions which will be useful for their particular schools. It is important that the balance between the three aspects of the subject— local geography, the geography of the United Kingdom, and regional geography—should be preserved, but in other respects the teacher should be guided in his choice of topics by the capacity of the children, the position of the school and his own inclinations.

10. Local geography linked up with the study of the British Isles.—The lessons in local geography will be continued but on more systematic lines, and be more closely linked up with the surrounding district and finally with the British Isles as a whole. Taking as a basis the simpler maps of the earlier stages of the course, the children can begin by studying the local one-inch or six-inch Ordnance map and then go on to the map of Great Britain. The build of the country may be shown first by means of models and maps, but it must be remembered that the use of a model is to teach children to interpret maps and that once this power has been acquired, the model is unnecessary. Pictures and photographs, particularly photographs from the air, will be found of value in this connexion. The children will perceive the difference between the hilly west and the relatively flat east and that rainfall is frequently heavy in hilly districts. They will notice how the hills separate one part of the land from another, and consequently how important it is to find ways through. The winding courses of certain roads, railways, and canals thus become intelligible, and the teacher will have little difficulty in working out with his class the easiest route from place to place. Subsequent lessons may go on to show, in districts where the children are acquainted with similar conditions, how these conditions together with the varying height of the land affect plant and animal life, how wheat gives place to oats, arable land to pasture, cows to sheep, the partridge to the grouse. Next, the positions of the great coalfields can be mapped by the children and the country roughly divided into manufacturing and farming areas. The children should thus gain some definite knowledge of the positions and staple industries of the principal towns and of the various occupations followed in different parts of the country.

11. The beginnings of regional geography.—Children can be led to divide for themselves the world into regions according to the winter and summer conditions ; to mark off the surface of the earth into hot, warm, cool, and cold areas ; to realise how these areas lie more or less symmetrically on either side of the equator, and to understand how all these conditions affect the habits and occupations of the people living in one region or another. For this purpose the teacher may have to give more than one picture of any particular region. The tundras and steppes, for instance, should be described both in their winter and in their summer aspects, while in the hot areas contrasts should be drawn between hot wet and hot dry regions. At each stage the child's home conditions should be used as a standard of reference.

12. Trade routes.—It is natural to pass on next to the relations and intercourse between one nation and another, especially between ourselves and other peoples. It can be shown how the need for interchange of productions has led to the establishment of trade routes, and how the direction and nature of these have been determined largely by physical and climatic features. Children readily notice the names of distant places associated with articles of food and clothing,—Indian tea, Canterbury lamb, Canadian cheese, New Zealand butter, Australian fruit, Egyptian cotton,—and many important facts will come to light if these commodities are traced from producer to consumer. Every advantage, too, should be taken of events which are of sufficient general interest to give them a prominent place in the daily press, e.g. expeditions in little known regions, long journeys by motorcar and aeroplane or airship.

13. Rediscovering the world through stories of exploration.—During this stage the general arrangement of land and water over the earth's surface must be clearly visualised by the children. To help them to realise the relative positions and sizes of the great land masses, and the shape and extent of the intervening oceans, a good plan is to let them follow on the globe the journeys of such pioneers as Marco Polo, Vasco da Gama, Magellan, Drake and Franklin. From the difficulties and problems which confronted these early travellers the teacher can draw abundant material for instruction in a most interesting form. Various incidents in the story of exploration will call attention to the changing altitude in the noonday sun as the travellers proceeded northwards or southwards; others will bring home to the children how in the early days of sailing ships journeys were dependent upon the direction and strength of the prevailing winds in different parts of the world; how mountains and deserts stopped progress across the land; how difficulties arose through floods or drought. In fact, if he chooses his stories well, the teacher can in a sense lead his children to rediscover the world for themselves, giving them at the same time a correct idea of the general distribution of land and water, mountain and plain, wind and calm, rain and drought, over the world's surface. The experienced teacher will need no reminder that, over and above his actual teaching, the children must examine and compare instances for themselves. If they have been trained to associate cause and effect, the discovery of relations between simple sets of facts is well within their powers at this stage. They may be asked, for example, to explain why people who live in steppe-lands wander about from place to place ; why manufacturing areas are densely populated ; or why some parts of England have more rain than others.

14. What children should know at the end of the Junior School stage.—At the end of the Junior School course a child should have a good knowledge of the district in which he lives, its position, climate, neighbouring towns and villages and local industries. He should know the position of the main towns and industrial and farming areas of the British Isles and have a general acquaintance with the main regions of the world. In addition he should be able to use and understand the maps in his atlas.

IV. THE SENIOR SCHOOL STAGE

A. PLANNING THE COURSE

15. Some guiding principles.—The aims of Geography teaching in the Elementary School have been set out in the first section of this chapter and it is unnecessary here to do more than to refer to them. There are, however, certain main considerations in planning a course for Senior School children which require more detailed consideration.

It is neither possible nor desirable to suggest any form of typical course. The nature of the scheme must depend on the qualifications and tastes of the teacher and the circumstances of the school. It will depend, too, on the average length of time for which the children remain. It follows, therefore, that the schemes will vary greatly in different schools, but there are certain main principles which should underlie all schemes.

(i) *The scheme should be in two parts : the first to be completed by all pupils.*—It is of the greatest importance that the Geography scheme should be planned to provide a complete course for all children before they leave school. Various methods have been adopted to secure this end, but perhaps the most convenient way is to divide the scheme into two parts.

The first part of the course should be of such a length that the majority of children have time to complete it before they leave. This will entail a rigorous selection and the elimination of much which usually finds a place in a school course. Only the essential and most suggestive points can be dealt with and it is better to deal adequately with these than to attempt to cover a larger field in a more perfunctory manner.

The three main elements of the first part of the course should be the study of the main natural regions of the world, the study of the British Isles, and local geography.

The second part of the course should preferably be divided into self-contained sections, so as to allow the children who leave school during the last year to complete at least an entire section.

(ii) *Needs of the brighter and the slower pupil should be taken into account.*—The scheme should provide for the needs of both the brighter and the slower children. In large Senior Schools it will be found best to provide parallel courses :—a more advanced course which may give the pupil some insight into world problems and some conception of citizenship as a series of relations with fellow citizens and with foreigners and a simpler more concrete course for those who are unable to appreciate the more abstract aspects of the subject. In the latter course pictorial illustration and first hand vivid narrations will naturally play a large part.

In smaller schools where precise classification is impossible, the difficulty of the retarded child may be met by providing a graduated series of exercises.

The methods of instruction will differ materially from those appropriate to Juniors. In the Senior School the children should be trained to seek out information for themselves with the help of text and reference books and atlases and to state logically the result of their investigations either orally or in writing.

B. THE FIRST PART OF THE SENIOR SCHOOL COURSE

16. Geography of the world.—In dealing with the main natural regions of the world, as indeed throughout the course, the main emphasis of the instruction should be on the human rather than on the more purely scientific aspects of the subject. It follows, therefore, that physical geography, save in so far as it is necessary to understand the effect of relief on climate, vegetation, and man's activities, need not be stressed. Geology and the detailed explanations of the laws which govern climate and vegetation can also be omitted in view of the shortness of the time available. The importance of location on the earth's surface, the position of the natural regions selected as typical, and their climate including rainfall must be thoroughly known. The broad divisions of natural vegetation, the distribution of animals and cultivated plants, and the distribution of population, considered in relation to the causes which have brought it about—e.g. the presence of minerals, proximity to markets, the development of industries, etc.—should be dealt with.

At each stage of the course the teacher should determine what limited number of definite facts should be mastered by the children and kept present in their minds by regular revision.

At the conclusion of the course on natural regions children should be familiar with the world as a unity: with the "pattern" formed by the different regions and with the major geographical distributions of climate and vegetation which the "pattern" makes coherent and reasonable.

17. The British Isles.—The place at which the geography of the British Isles should be introduced and the method of treatment are matters for the teacher concerned. It may be taught concurrently with the essentials of world geography either in one lesson a week or one term a year, or it may follow the world geography. Many teachers find it convenient to begin with a preliminary survey and to end the course with a more intensive study including the place of Britain in the Commonwealth of Nations.

Whatever the plan adopted, it is advisable to make a new approach so that the study of the British Isles becomes a distinct and definite branch of the work and the lessons follow a different plan from that adopted in the Junior School.

The build of the country, the relations between build, climate and production must be studied anew or extensive lines, but it would appear that the industrial and commercial development of the British Isles might be approached through detailed and intensive studies of such industries and development as touch the lives and work of the children concerned. For example, the Coal Industry would form an interesting study in many areas especially if boys and girls were introduced to coal output figures in different fields, the destination of local exports, the use made of by-products, and the general characteristics of an extractive as compared with a manufacturing industry. In other areas detailed studies of transport, of population, of export and import trades might be more appropriate.

18. Local geography.—Local geography will form an integral part of the study of the British Isles. It may be regarded under two aspects—as an end in itself and as providing a standard of reference by which children can judge the conditions under which people in other lands live.

Under its first aspect, local geography may be used to give the children a real interest in the neighbourhood in which they live—the build of the country, the soil, the supplies of food and water, the occupations of the people and their connexion with the larger economic units.* Ideas of production, markets and the price of commodities may be introduced and by the intensive study of some local product or industry, e.g. sugar beet, the children can obtain at first hand an inkling of the working of some of the more important economic laws. The records of temperature and rainfall, etc., now kept in a more scientific form, provide a constant guide when dealing with the climates of other lands and should prevent the vague use of terms such as " cold," " wet," " hot," and " dry." There should be constant cross references from local circumstances to the conditions to be found elsewhere.

C. THE SECOND PART OF THE SENIOR SCHOOL COURSE

19. Choice of topics.—The second part of the course covering the last year should be supplementary to the study of the world in outline and the British Isles in some detail and should be planned to provide for the needs of those who may leave at intervals before the end of the school year. It will probably be convenient

---

* The maps produced by the Land Utilisation Survey are of great value in this connexion and teachers will find much of interest in *Village Survey Making*—(Board of Education, Educational Pamphlet No. 61, printed and published by H.M. Stationery Office, London, price 1s.) and in the *Land Utilisation Survey of Britain* 1931.

for the reasons given above to divide it into sections which will occupy a term or part of a term. It can thus be arranged that each child before he leaves will have completed, in addition to the main course, at least one definite piece of work. The choice of subjects for study in this part of the course will depend on the bent and capabilities of the teacher. Examples of the sort of topics which have been found in practice to be suitable are :—the physical aspects of Geography, economic Geography, historical Geography and regional studies.

20. Physical aspects of geography.—Some teachers have connected the study of home geography closely with natural science. Systematic records are kept of temperature, rainfall, the readings of the barometer, the directions of the winds, the hours of sunshine and the sun's altitude, and, near the sea, the periods and heights of tides. If the results are tabulated and compared with those of other years and with others obtained elsewhere, and the children are encouraged to draw conclusions from them, it is possible to lead up to a real, if elementary, understanding of such geographical terms as mean temperature, isotherms, depressions and anticyclones, and to some realisation of the movements of the earth, the effect of latitude on the length of the day, the variation in the times, height, and frequency of the tides. Other teachers without going deeply into science, have trained their pupils to make a systematic study of the school district in various ways. Maps have been made to show both local soils and the crops grown on them, field by field and year by year. Comparison of these with the contour and rainfall maps brings out the effects of altitude and weather on productions. In some cases attempts have been made to connect the natural features of a district with its geological history and structure

Clearly, however, it is, as a rule, only the rudiments of geology that can be introduced into the curriculum. Rather more can, however, be done in the case of schools in upland and highland and mining districts, or where rocks are exposed to view on the sides of valleys, in quarries or in sea cliffs or cuttings for roads and railways.

21. Economic aspects of geography.—This branch of Geography offers unlimited scope for interesting studies suitable for boys and girls in their last year at school. The production and supply of familiar commodities may be chosen for closer study e.g. wheat, timber, india-rubber, vegetable oils, temperate and tropical fruits. These may be most usefully treated in a descriptive way—for example, a study of the temperate grass-lands of the world will serve to bring out man's great activities in spreading the production of wheat. The topography of such areas may be studied in so far as it affects wheat production, the relative yields of different areas, methods of cultivation, climatic conditions most favourable to growth and ripening, transport of wheat from main producing areas, accessibility of sea ports, time taken in transport, dates of harvest and the possibility of regular supplies throughout the year. Equally valuable are simple studies of the ways in which different groups of people gain their livelihoods. The distribution of definite extractive industries like mining, fishing or forestry and the possibilities of their diminishing production over a period : the intensive study of a local machine industry from sources of supply of raw material to the distribution of the finished products : the different modes of transport and their geographical and economic significance ; all these have their place as possible lines of study for older children. Further suitable subjects will suggest themselves, e.g. studies of sparsely populated areas, the great cities of the world and their significance. The introduction

of economic geography usually involves the use of simple
statistics as a basis for descriptive and explanatory work.
Provided children possess a minimum of " key " knowledge, e.g. that they know what is meant by " one inch
of rain," and provided the figures used have real meaning
for them, statistics may be used as a basis for comparison,
and as a check upon hasty generalisation. Throughout
such studies it is essential to distinguish between what
is fact and what is inference.

22. Historical geography.—In a course of historical
geography might be included the search for new trade
routes to the East in the 15th century, an enterprise
which led to the crossing of the ocean, the exploration
of the coasts of Africa, and the discovery of the New
World, which altered the economic relations of Western
Europe and resulted in the change from land to sea
as the chief means of inter-communication.

Nor would any course of historical geography be
complete without reference to the expeditions organised
in modern times for the purposes of discovery—the
" Challenger " expedition, the voyage of the " Beagle,"
the various expeditions to the Arctic and Antarctic
regions and to the interiors of the great continents,
the attempts to climb Mt. Everest and explorations
in the Amazon basin. The development of air routes
might well be included.

Of great importance, also, as subjects for study are
the changes which followed the introduction of steam
and electrical power, and the progress of mechanical
invention in the XVIIIth, XIXth and XXth Centuries.
Among these changes were : (a) the shifting of manufacturing centres to the coalfields and with the development of electric power, their migration southwards ;
(b) the settlement of hitherto unexplored lands, largely
due to the increased demand for raw materials and

food supplies on the one hand and for fresh markets on the other ; and (c) the improvements in the standard of living due to the development of various industries such as the sugar trade of the West Indies, the transport of perishable produce made possible by the invention of refrigeration, and the changes of population and the growth of new industries and of new towns like Pittsburg or Middlesborough following upon the discovery of mineral wealth. It may also be shown how since the Great War the established commercial relations of the whole world have changed.

The results of many of these changes are especially apparent in such regions as the Low Countries, the Alpine area, eastern North America, Egypt, and Asia Minor. More recently changes have been brought about by such factors as the development of the use of water power and oil fuels as sources of energy and the exploitation of new deposits of iron and other ores. Studied in relation to recent historical changes, these form good subjects for older pupils.

23. Regional studies.—Another possibility is the more detailed study of selected regions, emphasis being laid on different aspects according to the character of the area selected. In areas with the Mediterranean type of climate the teacher will dwell upon its outstanding climatic features—winter rains and summer drought—and its characteristic flora of drought-resisting plants ; he will pass on to the land-locked position of the European area, with its peninsulas and islands ; showing how in early times communication was easy along the coasts, how the region became the cradle of important civilisations, how and why it partially declined in importance later on, and, later still, revived after the opening of the Suez Canal. He will then contrast these facts with the conditions of transport and the productions and inhabitants in similar areas in other continents.

The treatment of the Asiatic monsoon region will bring out the effects of the monsoons ; the connexion between river traffic, early settlements, and trade routes ; how the richness of the valleys attracted a dense population, and how the mixture of races to-day amongst the inhabitants represents successive waves of invaders anxious to seize so rich a prize. Reference should then be made to regions with a similar seasonal rainfall in N.E. Australia, E. and W. Africa, and their present stages of development, their population and history.

Areas without trees because of inadequate rainfall will serve to bring out man's activities in spreading the production of wheat and of meat and the limits set to this expansion by the cost of transport. On the other hand, in many areas of little rainfall, man has been entirely unsuccessful in making any general use of the land to produce any vegetation other than its native plants. The comparison of the different types of natives in these areas and their habits may form another topic for investigation.

D. DIFFERENT WORK FOR BRIGHTER AND SLOWER PUPILS

24. Adaptation of courses and methods to suit different degrees of capacity.—Experience has shown that the main difference between the brighter and the slower pupils lies in the greater power of the former to grasp relations between ideas. It follows, therefore, that an attempt to pass all children through a given course in the same way must lead to failure, and it is necessary to determine how best to provide for the needs of children of diverse capacity.

The subject is one which has not yet been fully explored and there still remains a fruitful field for investigation. It is clear, however, that a mere truncated edition of the course for the brighter children will not meet the needs of the less intelligent. The course for the latter should be simpler in outline and should be based as far as possible on the children's own experience. In the larger Senior Schools it is possible to arrange for this by means of parallel courses ; some suggestions for the use of smaller schools also are made below.

(i) *The more advanced course.*—In the more advanced course the aim will be to train the children to learn from books and atlases instead of relying only on the teacher's oral lessons. Indiscriminate reading, however, is likely to lead only to the acquisition of many unconnected facts, and the books for individual work should accordingly be carefully selected. Children can be set to find the information required to answer a definite question, and either write the answer or be questioned on the facts. Thus, they may be told to find out the months during which a crop in a chosen area passes through its various stages until it is used elsewhere, or to discover what new areas might produce certain raw materials and which of these would command cheap transport abroad. In all cases the ability to use information rather than its mere acquisition should be the aim of the course.

(ii) *The less advanced course.*—The aim of the instruction in the less advanced classes will be to give the children an interest in the life and occupations of the place in which they live and some appreciation of the outside world in relation to it. The methods adopted will be very different from those suitable for the advanced sections. Taking as a basis the children's own environment and experiences the teacher should endeavour by means of lively oral lessons and by reading vivid and well-chosen extracts to kindle the children's interest. Pictorial illustrations will play a large part and from selected pictures the children can be encouraged to find out points of resemblance or contrast. Simple, striking diagrams are useful and the making of simple maps to show the main areas of supply and the main centres of industry. The treatment of the subject matter should be as concrete as possible and the emphasis should always be laid on the human aspect.

(iii) *The course in small schools.*—In the smaller Senior Schools and particularly in the rural schools, the methods of differentiation suggested above are often found to be impracticable.

In such cases it may be necessary for the same oral lessons to be shared by all the children. It is, however, still possible to make a real differentiation in the work by grading the exercises which the children have to do. Exercises such as tracing the courses of main roads, railways or canals and the marking of areas in which the major industries are found are within the capacity of most children and would serve for the less advanced pupils. The brighter children as well as doing these exercises should be trained to seek out for themselves the reasons which led to the present state of things.

V. AIDS TO GEOGRAPHY TEACHING

25. Maps.—The purpose of a map is two-fold : the accurate recording of definite facts of position, distribution, and so on, and the presentation of such facts in a manner which enables them to be visualised.

(i) *At the Junior School stage.*—The first maps used should be those which the children make for themselves, either from direct observation of a part of their home district, or as the " free expression " of the setting of a geographical story. Children quickly accustom themselves to the idea of relative position, especially if they have before them at times a map spread horizontally, and with the north of the map pointing in a north direction. In the upper classes of the Junior School the use of maps forms an essential part of the course and the child should be led to understand that the map is but a larger representation of some part of the globe. No formal lessons should be given on projection, though the impossibility of putting on flat paper a true map of a curved surface may be pointed out. Wrong impressions as to size and direction which maps on Mercator's projection as well as on equal area projection may convey can be corrected simply and without reference to mathematics.

(ii) *At the Senior School stage.*—In the Senior School this use of maps should be developed, and special maps showing winds, rainfall, temperature, vegetation, mineral areas, etc., should be part of the ordinary apparatus of the geography lessons.

(a) *Special maps.*—Isothermal and isobaric lines should, however, be treated not as distinct entities, but as marking off areas having different conditions of temperature and pressure. Those selected for study should be carefully chosen for the purpose in view. In studying special maps it is natural to begin with maps of the school district and the home country.

(b) *Study of contour lines : use of models.*—Methods by which children can be introduced to the use of maps have been discussed in previous sections and it is unnecessary to refer to them again. In the Junior School the children will have become familiar with the meaning of " highland " and " lowland " and their representation on the map by special colours. They are now in a position to proceed with the more definite study of contour lines. One of the most effective methods is to place a model in water and to draw a line on the surface of the model along the edge of the water. By adding more and more water it will be possible to obtain a number of contour-lines at different levels. The use of models in the Senior School will serve to bring out clearly the meaning of such common terms as *land-relief, watershed, drainage-basin, scarp, gap, strait, fiord, drowned valley, shoal,* and to explain why, with contour-lines, the "Vs" point up, not down, the valleys, and how promontories and islands are really continuations of land-ridges. Once the children have grasped the idea of contour-lines and colour markings, they should apply their knowledge to Ordnance Survey* maps on various scales, especially those of districts known to them.

In making contour-maps it is not advisable always to choose the same set of contour-lines. A set of contours which brings out the characteristic features of South America may serve only to obscure those of Africa, and those appropriate to the structure of Wales may fail to illustrate the counties of the plain.

(c) *Transverse sections.*—Attention should be drawn to the fact that in transverse sections the vertical scale is always greatly exaggerated and the children should be shown the actual slope of any steep hill with which they may be familiar. The making of such sections will help to bring to light many interesting facts, such as the shallowness of certain parts of the ocean, especially where the great fisheries lie, and to show the relation of great oceanic depths to mountain heights. Even young children can obtain rough sections from their own models, but for more accurate work a contour-map is essential.

---

*Teachers will find much interesting and useful information concerning the Ordnance Survey maps of the United Kingdom in the books "*A Description of the Ordnance Survey Small Scale Maps,*" and "*A Description of the Ordnance Survey Large Scale Maps*" (price 8d. each, post free 10d., if ordered direct from the Ordnance Survey Office). Ordnance maps for school use can be bought cheaply in quantities on application to the Director-General, Ordnance Survey, Southampton.

(d) *Outline maps and sketch-maps.*—The practice of copying atlas maps has now, to a large extent, disappeared. Whatever slight educational value it may have, it is, in itself, of little use in Geography, but while this kind of map-drawing has gone, so, too, has the learning of maps, a fact which is much to be deplored. Some teachers supply their pupils with outline maps or allow them to make them for themselves by means of a " multiplier," or by tracing, or by the use of a cardboard template which the children have cut out. On these maps are represented such details as may be required for special purposes —physical features, rainfall, seasonal temperatures, vegetation, or distribution of products and manufactures.

The older children should have practice in drawing from memory, rapidly and with fair accuracy, sketch maps to illustrate special points and should be able to fill in outline maps correctly. Distances should be calculated from the scale to which a map is drawn, and, conversely, a scale should be constructed from given distances. Attention should be drawn to the value of the lines of latitude and longitude as a means of indicating world-position and of calculating distances and areas. By representing points of special interest, such as distribution of industries, positions of towns, roads, rivers and railways, and rainfall, on transparent or tracing paper (" butter paper " serves the purpose well and is cheap), a series of maps can be made which, by being superimposed on the physical map, will bring out the essential interdependence of geographical conditions.

(e) *Wall-maps.*—In purchasing wall-maps it should be remembered that the really necessary maps are those coloured to show land relief. Place-names and other details, such as political boundaries and railways, can always be obtained by the children from their own maps and atlases.

Children should also constantly compare the map with the globe. They should notice carefully a few meridians and parallels on both, e.g. the meridian of Greenwich, of Calcutta (roughly, 90° E.), of the " date-line " (180°), of New Orleans (90° W.), as well as the equator, the tropics, and the latitude of London and of their own school.

In the Senior School and perhaps in the upper class of the Junior School, the interpretation of the map may sometimes be linked with a school journey. If maps or sketches of the itinerary are first provided, and definite problems set, to be solved en route, school journeys enable the children to verify their own deductions, to understand their maps better, to prepare maps to scale from actual measurement, as well as to realise more clearly the working of cause and effect in local geography.

26. Atlases.—The selection of the atlas is important. Photo-relief maps, though representing a graphic representation of relief which is readily understood by young children, often exaggerate heights and do not give the definite information required when the children are working out problems and discovering for themselves such facts as the lines of water-sheds, the existence of passes, the relative gradients of hills, or the directions of roads or railways. For this purpose orographical, or " layer " maps, as they are sometimes called, are indispensable. For the older children the atlas also serves as a work of reference, and the information given on the maps should be as full as is consistent with clearness. Separate maps to show selected features will be prepared by the children themselves and from these all superfluous detail will be omitted. Every school atlas should contain an index and the children should be trained to use this with facility.

Valuable work can be done by inducing the older scholars to study suitable books with the help of their atlases, by setting them carefully prepared questions and exercises on what they have read and by encouraging discussions on any points of interest that arise at intervals.

27. The globe and its use.—No instruction in Geography can be really satisfactory which does not involve frequent reference to the globe, and every school should possess a globe, at least 12 inches in diameter. Some teachers find one on which outline and elevation are shown in colour most useful ; others prefer a black globe on which the outline of continents and some lines of latitude and longitude are faintly traced. Use of the globe is necessary in order to show the general distribution of land and water over the earth's surface, the comparative size of continents, and the world-position of any continent or other area under consideration. It will also serve to correct wrong ideas arising from the use of maps. Measurements of large distances should always be taken from the globe rather than from the map ; and if this is done, children will be able to appreciate such points as the advantages of " great-circle sailing."

The globe should be placed with its axis parallel to that of the earth. The inclination of the axis to the horizontal is then equal to the latitude and the axis points to the Pole Star. By repeated observations during the year of a globe thus arranged and placed in the sunlight, children will be able to understand why days are short in winter and long in summer, and to gain a clear idea of the variations in length of daylight in different parts of the world at different seasons. They will understand also, why the sun appears to rise and set at different points of the horizon during the year and how the sun's altitude varies at mid-day with the position, north or south of the equator, from which it is observed. With large classes some teachers prefer to use a number of small globes, so as to allow every child, or at least groups of two or three children, to observe such points as have just been mentioned for themselves. Rubber balls can be used for this purpose.

28. The use of geographical books.—During the first stage it is perhaps best not to use any geographical " reader " at all, unless an exception be made in the case of some of the profusely illustrated books published in recent years. Interest will be added to the lessons by the use of models and specimens, of coloured drawings and of good pictures or photographs of typical scenes. Later on, the illustration of geography may include the collection of picture postcards according to some definite principle, the use of lantern-slides, and an occasional visit to a really good exhibition.

Though it is doubtful whether young children learn much geography by reading aloud to their teacher, there is no reason why the teacher should not read aloud to them. This method of instruction has always played an important part in good home training. In schools it presents certain difficulties, but these should not deter teachers from giving it a trial. It is better to read descriptions than to give them, because the written narrative is more likely to be well-expressed, to be based on first-hand experience, and to suggest points for discussion between the teacher and the class.

When children can read with ease and understanding, they should be given books which contain vivid descriptions of places, peoples, animal and vegetable life. Such books, if not overloaded with details, will serve to supplement the oral teaching and the study of maps and atlases. In the highest classes of the Senior School children should have access to a number of books of this kind, some of which should be in the school library.

It is not necessary to read book after book from cover to cover. Some will repay careful reading, others will only be consulted for specific purposes, others again will be dipped into in order to supplement or confirm previous knowledge. This clearly depends upon what the teacher has in view and the stage which his children have reached. In the last year or two of school-life his duty is to guide and supervise their work rather than to teach by word of mouth, to devise and suggest problems or comparisons rather than to work them out. At this stage it is important that children should have reliable text-books, not " readers," from which to get their information ; these need not be large or expensive. Great care will be needed to secure that the exercises are presented in suitable sequence ; and more than one period may be required before any one problem of this type can be worked out. It is important that questions asked orally or in writing to test the children's work should not only be on matters of fact but, in the case of the brighter children, should involve comparisons with other facts or with other parts of the world.

29. Reference books.—It is perhaps out of place to speak of reference books in connexion with the Junior School, but even there collections of pictures and well-illustrated books are of great value. In Senior Schools the possession of a stock of reference books is essential, particularly for the brighter children. Too often the reference books found in the schools are limited to " specimen " copies and out-of-date works which have little bearing on the course which is being followed and in consequence are seldom consulted.

The list of reference books in Geography for use in a Senior School need not be long, but the books should be carefully chosen and housed in a position to which there is ready access during school hours. Among them should be found some larger atlases than those which are used in the ordinary school work. In addition to the 1″ and 6″ O.S. maps of the district which are used for class teaching, there should be copies of other types of Ordnance Maps for the district, Land Utilisation maps where available and sheets of the Ordnance and other maps, British and foreign, selected to show good examples of features of special geographical interest. Geological and historical maps should also form part of the stock.

General works of reference such as Whitaker's Almanack, collections of newspaper cuttings on points of geographical interest and newspaper supplements which deal with particular industries or countries should be included. Many useful publications can be obtained at the London Offices of the Dominions and their separate States and Provinces.

In addition, there should be some of the larger standard geographies and books of travel and description. It would be useful to include a small collection of stories and books of adventure in which the geographical setting is vividly and accurately drawn. Some of the annual publications such as the Statesmen's Year Book, Reports of the Ministries of Agriculture and of Mines, the Reports of the Overseas Trade Department and Statistical Abstracts issued by various Departments contain valuable information, but these are often too expensive to be kept up to date in a school library. It is, however, sometimes possible to obtain them for a time by arrangement with the Public Libraries which may also be able to supply books needed for special purposes, but not of sufficient general interest to warrant their purchase.

30. The geography room.—There are often difficulties in providing a special room for the teaching of Geography in Junior Schools, but there is no doubt that it is desirable to do so when it is possible.

Geographical pictures lose their interest when they form part of the decorations of a classroom and small exhibits of pictures and specimens bearing on the lessons taken excite the interest of the children when they are changed periodically. Much unnecessary carriage of maps, diagrams and pictures is also saved.

In the Senior Schools the need for a geography room is much greater and every effort should be made to set aside a room for the subject. It is of great importance that the children should be able to consult reference books, atlases, etc., during the course of their work and should have any apparatus they may require readily available.

One of the larger classrooms is most suitable for the purpose. A southern aspect and easy access to the playground facilitate the taking of observations. The room should be well lighted both by natural and artificial light so as to avoid eye strain when maps are used. Dark blinds should be fitted and a portion of the wall may be prepared to serve as a screen for the projection of pictures. Means should be provided by which a globe can be suspended and above and beside the blackboard map rails should be fitted. All spare wall space should have suitable panels for the exhibition of pictures, cuttings, etc.

Chairs and tables are preferable to desks for the children. There should be ample storage accommodation, including some nests of shallow drawers to take maps and plans and a cupboard sufficiently large to take rolled-up maps. One or two glass-topped specimen cases are desirable and a suitable library cupboard for reference books with a cupboard for instruments beneath. The wall maps should include world maps showing relief, climate, and the major natural regions. To these should be added the relief map of the county if available or the $\frac{1}{2}''$ O.S. map made up as a wall map.

31. Modern " mechanical aids ".—Both the lantern
and the epidiascope have begun to play an increasingly
important part in the teaching of geography. Of the
two, the latter is the more generally useful for school
purposes. An instrument capable of throwing images
both from solid objects and diagrams as well as from
lantern slides is of the greatest value. Teachers can
make transparencies of their own diagrams and other
illustrations, without undue difficulty. Where the
school possesses a cinematograph apparatus the film,
used under suitable conditions, will do much to give
life and reality to the instruction. There is now a good
stock of films which can be used in the teaching of geography, among which may be mentioned those supplied
by H.M. Post Office.

An increasing number of schools are now equipped
with wireless sets and with a skilful teacher the wireless
lessons may become a valuable part of the school's
geography teaching. It is possible to hear at first hand
vivid descriptions of the countries of which the children
are reading. With adequate preparation and following
up, these lessons may give a life and colour to the work
which is sometimes lacking.

32. Lectures.—It is sometimes possible to find a
member of the staff who is willing to lecture on some
point of the course in which he takes special interest.
Such lectures given at intervals may be very valuable
and are suitable, as are some of the methods mentioned
in the preceding section, for more than one class. The
school hall might be used for the purpose. There are
times, too, in large Senior Schools in which the same
ground has to be covered by parallel classes and it may
occasionally prove a saving of time and energy to give
the lesson to grouped classes rather than to each class
separately.

33. School journeys and educational visits.—

The importance of Local Geography has been emphasised in the earlier sections of this chapter and attention has been called to the necessity for first-hand observation on the part of the children. The school journey and the educational visit afford many opportunities for this type of work. If these visits are arranged to form a real part of the scheme and careful preparation is done, the children will be helped to notice interesting things and to record their observations. In this way the facts of Geography will become more real and the pupils may gain an interest which will serve them well in after life. Visits to factories and museums can be used with good effect and for schools in the neighbourhood of London the Imperial Institute offers many opportunities. The exhibition galleries are arranged in such a way as to present vivid pictures of the geography of the Empire as a whole and so to lead children to a better understanding of the Empire and its resources.

CHAPTER XIV

NATURE STUDY AND SCIENCE

I. SOME GENERAL CONSIDERATIONS

I. The general aims of science teaching.—The romance and wonder of Science make an especially strong appeal to the young and enhance their natural desire to get to know the world around them and to find an explanation of its phenomena. To observe carefully and dispassionately, to formulate one's observations in words or in other ways, and to make proper inferences from what has been observed, constitute a kind of experience in which all children should share. The child in the Elementary School cannot be expected to progress far in the more abstract regions of scientific thought or in the more technical applications of scientific method, but at any rate he can form some idea of what is involved in careful investigation and systematic relation of facts to principles, and principles to facts, if he is made acquainted with some examples of how the great pioneers of Science have attacked and solved their problems. Although he is not being trained as a scientist, he can, at least, be led to realise the important part played by Science in a modern community, can acquire some of the knowledge that will enable him to deal with its everyday applications, and can learn how human beings may live in a rational and healthy manner. Thus, through the study of nature, animate and inanimate, the school can do much to make richer and more significant its pupils' experience of life.

II. THE INFANT SCHOOL STAGE

2. Active experience rather than formal lessons.— The majority of normal children of 5–7 exhibit a lively curiosity in the world around them. The movements and sounds of animals, the bright colours, varied shapes and pleasant scents of flowers are a never failing source of interest and pleasure. Nor is their interest confined to natural phenomena : it is equally aroused by things that attract their attention by movement or by some unusual quality, such as mechanical toys, soap-bubbles and toy balloons, by motor-cars and trains.

A child's mental images, concepts and power of imagination grow out of what he sees, handles and does, and words mean little to him unless associated with active experience. It is the teacher's function to bring the children into contact with the right kinds of experience, to encourage them to observe, to experiment, to discover, to talk about their experience in a natural manner. The success with which this has been done will be shown by the readiness of the children to seek further knowledge. Such work is of most use to the children when it relates to their own environment and, needless to say, cannot be successfully carried out through formal lessons given at set periods.

3. Outdoor activities.—Observations can best be made where plants and animals are in their natural setting. In almost all districts there is a wealth of material at hand in lanes, fields, woods, streams, ponds and seashore, and even in the larger towns there are the public parks.

In towns the opportunities open to children for observing plants and animals are more limited. To substitute pictures or printed descriptions for the real things may not be without its value but can in no sense be regarded as a training in observation. On the other hand, in every town children have many opportunities of studying things which are of interest in themselves, such as the contents of shop-windows, traffic on river, road or rail and all the varied life of a busy modern community. The teacher can see to it that all this wealth of first-hand experience is not wasted.

A garden on the school premises is invaluable. Cultivation of plants, the planting of seeds, digging, watering have an immediate and never-failing appeal to quite young children; through these activities they acquire knowledge of seasonal changes and operations which will be put to fuller use later on. Little children are interested in plants which they can eat or flowers which they can use as decorations or gifts. The perennials should be hardy and suitable for inexperienced handling, and the annuals quick growing and brightly coloured. Where sufficient ground for a garden plot is not available successful work can be done with rock gardens in boxes placed against the wall of the playground, or with boxes on the window-sills or ledges. The children can bring the soil, prepare it, sow the seeds and care for the seedlings. Even in the centre of towns bulbs and such plants as catmint, candytuft, ten-weeks stock, nasturtiums, marigolds, pansies, geraniums, lobelia flourish well.

The making and stocking of a small pond, when practicable, forms a useful outside activity and will provide material for indoor observation. Bird-baths, bird-tables and nesting boxes will provide good opportunities for interesting observation: where bird-tables are used, it will be desirable to arrange for the feeding to continue on days when the school is closed.

4. Indoor activities.—If animals are kept, the teacher should encourage the right attitude towards living things by training the children to care for them, feed them and keep them clean. The children should examine the natural habitat and the artificial accommodation should resemble it as nearly as possible. Suitable activities will be found in the making of an aquarium, vivaria such as breeding cases for moths and butterflies, in the care of the animals in them, and in the tending and feeding of the school pets.

It is desirable that the classroom activities should be connected with the outdoor work ; they should include, for instance, observation of the germination of seeds similar to those planted in the garden. An indoor garden can be made in a large tray, lined with zinc, with a hole for drainage at one end. Plants, such as wheat, tomatoes, peas, maize, can quite well be grown in plant pots indoors. It is easy to arrange for each child to grow his own mustard, cress or grass.

Observations made by the children should be recorded daily at the time when they are made ; the records should be in pictorial form and not only of the plant and animal world, but also of changes in the weather.

The study of nature provides material for developing the children's powers of language and their observations should form the basis of the daily nature talk. They can be trained to describe what they have seen with some degree of accuracy and the widening field of knowledge will offer opportunities for extending their vocabulary.

Nature stories from the many suitable books now available will find a place, especially at times in winter when observation of natural phenomena is not possible.

Good use may also be made of photographs and other pictures, e.g. of animals which children have no opportunity of observing at first-hand themselves.

III. THE JUNIOR SCHOOL STAGE

5. The aims of the teaching at the Junior School stage.—The study of nature at the Junior School stage should develop naturally out of the activities and experiences at the Infant School stage, but it should take more definite form as the children's interests change and their experience widens. The main aim of the teaching, with children between the ages of 7 and 11 years, should be to keep alive and quicken the spirit of wonder and inquiry and to give it appropriate scope for activity.

The treatment of the work should be consciously designed not only to give the children opportunities of observing and of tending plants and animals with a view to their gaining at first-hand some knowledge of growth in nature, but also to foster their interest in the simpler phenomena of inanimate nature in earth, air and sky and in the mechanical appliances they meet with in everyday life. In this way they will come to have a foundation for the more systematic work in biological and physical science at the Senior School stage.

A special task of the Junior School is to satisfy a growing desire to construct. This can be met by giving them practical work to do in connexion with their first-hand observation of plant and animal life.

GENERAL CHARACTER OF THE COURSE

6. What may be achieved by the end of the course.—As a result of well directed observational studies the children should, by the time they leave the Junior School, have acquired a good background of knowledge.

The study of nature necessarily follows a seasonal course, but it is essential that progress should be secured from year to year and that the treatment of the subject should develop with the children's growing power of systematic thought. In the earlier stages the children should make straightforward observations and collect simple facts. Later, their observations should become more detailed and the facts collected should be related in the form of continuous studies. Towards the end of the Junior School course the children will begin to show interest in comparing and classifying and in experimenting with a clear purpose in view.

Simple experiments on breathing and burning, on the growth of plants in the absence of light and on the response to stimuli, on the absorption and giving off of water by plants, on the effects of rearing caterpillars in cages of different colours, are typical of the kind of work which can be carried out with simple apparatus.

In no part of the work is there more need for progressive training than in the making of records. As the Junior School course develops, the pictorial charts made at the Infant School stage should be supplemented and gradually replaced by individual notes, and by drawings of increasing accuracy. The children should also be able to present their weather observations and other continuous records in graphic form.

7. Outdoor activities.—(a) *Where there is a school garden.*—The most natural of all outdoor activities are those which have their centre in the school garden. No attempt should be made to run it on the lines usually followed by Seniors. The lay-out should aim at an attractive and conveniently arranged common garden with a generous grass plot. There should be opportunity for making a rockery, a good herbaceous border, and a shrubbery which will supply flowers throughout the year, a shallow pond, a bird bath, nesting boxes and feeding tables to provide for the care of the birds during severe weather. The children should not only set seeds and tend the various plants, but also take care of the grass borders, the paths and edgings, stake the plants in the herbaceous borders, hoe and remove the weeds. A knowledge of the plants at various seasons will be necessary to distinguish between flowers and weeds. Common vegetables and small bush fruit may be grown, but they should at this stage not be cultivated with the idea of producing a paying crop.

(b) *Where there is no school garden.*—If a school garden is not available, rock gardens in wall boxes, window boxes, indoor garden trays, plant pots and bowls will be found useful. Even a quite small garden-plot will provide opportunities for the pupils to learn at first-hand about nature and seasonal changes and to make a study of bees, moths, butterflies, snails and spiders. The top class may make observations of insects in their relation to flowers, and this will provide a basis for lessons on pollination in the Senior School. The older children may handle the soil and find out some of the simple facts regarding its physical characteristics. Observations can be made of the times taken for the germination of different kinds of seeds and of seeds in different atmospheric temperatures. Weather observations, too, should be made and recorded daily.

Many schools, however, do not possess even a small garden plot. In their case it will often be possible to provide a background for indoor work by seasonal nature walks, visits to parks and gardens or simple field work. If the neighbourhood of the school offers facilities for outdoor work, much can be done by the older children independently, given an initial plan and occasional class-lessons. With a large-scale Ordnance Survey map of the district available, the first steps of a " regional survey " can be made.

8. Indoor activities.—(a) *Work connected with the study of animate nature.*—The work of the classroom, which should supplement and in some cases replace outdoor activities, should consist mainly of more systematic studies of plant and animal life. Seeds may be germinated and bulbs and corms grown in such a way that the various stages of growth may be observed and life histories followed ; cacti and small rock plants can be grown in miniature gardens and water plants and mosses kept under suitable conditions ; a variety of decorative plants can be grown and propagated in pots and window boxes.

In the Junior School the " nature-table " with which the children have become familiar at the Infant School stage can now serve as a general record of the changing countryside, and provide a means for the continuous study of plants and animals under conditions favourable for observation.

The classroom will probably be found to be the best place for designing the garden, the drawing to scale of the plan of the lay-out, the calculation of quantities of seeds, plants, and tools needed and the working out of the cost of these.

(b) *Observation of animal life.*—As a rule, animal life makes a stronger appeal to children of Junior School age than does plant life ; in considering what kinds of animal life shall be kept the deciding factor should be whether or not the creatures can be kept in captivity in the classroom under natural and healthy conditions. One of the most obvious methods is to provide a simple aquarium. Several small aquaria are better than one large one : they are more easily kept ; if supplied with suitable pond weed and stocked with a few snails and crustaceans they will not need aeration ; and they allow for the segregation of rapacious animals. Aquaria should be shielded from strong sunlight and protected by a muslin cover from dust. They should be fitted up in early autumn and kept going all the year so that the habits of both plants and animals can be observed throughout the seasons.

Insects also can be readily kept under observation. A useful permanent cage can be made of a wooden framework with top and three sides made of perforated zinc and the front, which can be made to slide up and down, should be of glass. A movable zinc tray on the bottom makes cleaning easy. Such a design can be easily adapted and simplified, muslin being used instead of zinc and various transparent materials substituted for glass.

A wooden box with one side of glass and a cover of perforated zinc can be made into a temporary home for worms or snails.

The essentials of a vivarium for amphibians are water for swimming and a landing place providing cover.

(c) *Housing and feeding of animals at school.*—If small mammals are to be kept the teacher should be thoroughly conversant with modern hygienic methods of housing and correct methods of feeding. If the school premises afford sufficient space for keeping the animals under such conditions that they can have adequate light, air, warmth and exercise, rabbits or guinea-pigs can be kept and, when wanted in the classroom, transferred for the time being to a specially designed observation hutch. Mice require less space but it is advisable here also to have a permanent home, in which the animals can remain undisturbed, and an observation cage. The children should, in no circumstances, see animals kept in captivity in any but the best conditions.

The design and construction of bird tables and other accessories are suitable related activities.

The children should be encouraged to make simple insect cages, to fit up small aquaria and wormeries and to grow their own seeds and bulbs at home.

(d) *Children's Notes and illustrations.*—The teacher's responsibility, however, does not end with the provision of living and growing material, however excellent that may be. The children's observations need to be directed by questions and their experiences are incomplete if they do not express them in concrete form such as written notes or drawings. Modelling in suitable material is a useful aid to visualising form and structure and the making of notebooks and portfolios for nature records gives scope for other handwork activities.

9. The study of inanimate nature.—The course at the Junior School stage, especially in towns where the opportunities for the study of animate nature are often very limited, may include lessons on the simpler phenomena of inanimate nature. No attempt should be made to develop anything of the nature of a formal study of any particular branch of Science, and the aim will be not so much to explain phenomena as to awaken the children's interest in them and to develop their powers of observation and description. Such topics as soap-bubbles, images in mirrors, the effect of prisms on light, the action of a magnet and simple electrical phenomena appeal to children. Working models and toys provide the additional interest of movement, and the designing and construction of simple models is always attractive. A good basis for lessons at this stage is the curiosity of children as to "how it works."

The chief mistake made by teachers at this stage is to attempt to deal with abstract generalisations of Science in set lessons on such subjects as "the properties of matter," "solids, liquids, and gases," "the work of the leaf, root and stem." At no stage, and least of all in this stage, should generalisations be attempted unless they are founded on and justified by the children's own observations and experiences.

10. Other facilities for the study of nature in school.—Although direct contact with nature is the basis of all true nature study, the children's experiences need not be limited to what can be observed and discovered at first-hand. The Junior School should have its Natural History Library, consisting, for example, of reference books which the children can learn to consult, of readable books about plants and animals and of animal stories. It should also have its collection of pictorial illustrations.

Use should be made, where possible, of the optical lantern and micro-projector. Moreover, now that the resources of cinema and of broadcasting are becoming more and more readily available, there is room for experiment in the use of films and of wireless talks as a means of arousing the interest of the older children and stimulating them to further activities.

IV. THE SENIOR SCHOOL STAGE

A. PLANNING THE COURSE.

11. The special task of the Senior School.— The modern type of Senior School, free from cramping traditions and the necessity of preparing for examinations, offers an opportunity to develop Science teaching on fresh lines, to take what is suitable from old ideas and to experiment freely with new ones. Its task is not to begin the training of professional scientists, but to give the child some idea of the methods by which man has discovered so many of the laws of nature, of the immense power that these discoveries have put at his disposal, and the use to which he is putting his knowledge.

In selecting material for study and devising methods of treatment, it is necessary to consider both its effect on the child as an individual and its value to him as a member of society. As far as is possible under school conditions, the pupil should learn how scientists carry out their work.

He should " realise by what slow degrees accurate knowledge is won, the place of hypothesis, the need of caution in forming judgments, the necessity for experimental verification and for carefully weighing evidence."*

He should also gain some knowledge of how Science is transforming life in the home and world outside, and of the wealth, variety and inter-relations of living forms, both plant and animal, which surround him, and should make some study of the working of the human body and of the conditions for its healthy functioning. An attempt, too, should be made to create lasting interests by developing hobbies which will help to fill leisure time when school is left behind.

12. The teacher of science.—It is becoming more and more desirable that Science teaching should be in the hands of a teacher with adequate knowledge of Science ; for it is only those who have the necessary background who can teach this subject on broad lines. Now that rooms are available for the teaching of practical Science, the task of maintaining fittings, apparatus, stores, aquaria, accumulators, etc., in good order demands the presence of an expert. It is not, however, suggested that the teacher's academic training should be confined to Science, still less to one branch of Science, for he must not offer the children a course based solely on his own academic studies in Science, and he has constantly to bear in mind the relation of Science to other parts of the curriculum.

---

* P. 13, *Science in Senior Schools*, Board of Education, Educational Pamphlet, No. 89, printed and published by H.M. Stationery Office, London, 1932, price 1s. 3d.

13. Size of classes.—Much controversy ranges round the question whether Science should be taught to classes of 20 or of 40 children. The problem appears to be mainly one of space and supply of apparatus. It is clearly impossible to give successful laboratory work to 40 pupils in a crowded room with insufficient material, but, given a laboratory of some 960 square feet and enough apparatus, the task of supervising the work of 40 children does not appear to be beyond the capacity of a competent teacher. To divide a class into halves for a demonstration lesson involves a waste of the teacher's time, and is unnecessary.

14. Choice of subject matter.—Natural Science is so vast and so many branches have strong claims for inclusion in the course, that the task of selection is difficult. It is suggested that Biology and Physics, with the ancillary Chemistry, should form the foundation, material from other branches being included if time and circumstances permit.

(a) *Biology.*—The claim of Biology is unique in that man himself is one of the organisms formed of living material. The happiness and efficiency of the individual and through him of the community depend to a large extent on a knowledge of the laws of health, including an understanding of the nutritional values of foods. Biology offers unrivalled opportunities for continuance as a hobby after leaving school; the laboratory is at hand in the countryside, and the subject is so wide, that something new may be discovered by the humblest worker.

The foundation will have been laid in the Junior School, and the study of animate nature begun there should form the basis of the Senior School work. Further studies of the life-history and habits of a number of typical animals and plants should be made. The essential unity of all living matter and the inter-dependence of forms of living and non-living matter should be made clear. Observations can be linked with Physics and Chemistry when such characteristics of living creatures as movement, feeding, respiration and excretion are under consideration. Response to stimuli, growth, reproduction, home-making and progressive scales of animal and plant life should be dealt with from a comparative point of view. Communities such as those of bees, wasps and ants, associations between particular plants and animals and simple cases of symbiosis and parasitism may be included.

All this should lead up to an understanding of the working of the human body and the conditions for its healthy functioning. Such topics may be dealt with as studies of food (including milk), its nutritive values, its transport, preservation and the effects on it of cooking ; the laws of personal hygiene ; the maintenance of healthy surroundings and the control and prevention of disease.

(b) *Physics.*—Physics deals with certain fundamental generalisations which have to be taken into account in all branches of Science, and hence has a special claim for inclusion in the course. In home and at school, the modern boy and girl sees every day the practical applications of Science and should learn something of the physical principles underlying them.

The basis of the work may well be the conception of energy as something which may assume different forms,—heat, light, mechanical, electrical and chemical energy,—which has certain influences on living and non-living matter, and which can be measured, or bought and sold.

Simple working machines may be studied, from the point of view of efficiency and " mechanical advantage," and children should realise that no more can be got out of a machine than is put into it. The laws of reflection and refraction, as far as they are required in order to understand simple optical instruments, (including the eye), should be dealt with, and some study should be made of colour. The production, transfer and conserving of heat are matters of great practical importance, while electricity is entering more and more into daily life. The effects of the electric current, electro-magnetic induction, the means of production, the control and transfer of electricity and the simple properties of alternating current should be considered. The study of sound, though it can be developed in an interesting way in connexion with music, is apt to be neglected; the characteristics of notes, vibration, resonance, echoes, and organ pipes, all lend themselves to simple and striking experimental treatment.

(c) *Chemistry.*—Chemistry is of great importance in the arts and manufactures and, from many points of view, its study can be an excellent training in scientific method and habits of thought; but the chemistry of such familiar things as wood, bread, butter, is too complex for the Elementary School. The logical development of the Atomic Theory from an experimental basis requires far more time than can be given and is a very difficult study except for the more intelligent pupils. The study of chemistry, therefore, is best made ancillary to the work in biology and physics. For instance, when air and water are being studied their chemistry can be dealt with at the same time. Similarly, the study of carbon, carbon-dioxide, lime and chalk and certain salts can be taken in connexion with biology, as also can fermentation and digestion, if treated simply.

(d) *Astronomy.*—The study of the sky,—of age-long interest and importance to man,—has in a number of schools been made a valuable part of their work, though the difficulties are considerable, since observations must be made out of school hours and the time available is very restricted. The children can be taught to recognise the brighter stars and to study the motions of the planets and constellations, and should be encouraged to read some of the many good books that are now available.

(e) *Geology.*—The elements of Geology will probably be taken in connexion with Geography. Soil studies will find a place in the Science course, especially in rural areas, and the geological aspect of other topics should not be omitted. In mining areas, particularly, children should know something of the history and structure of the rocks and of the effects on them of earth movements and, in connexion with the physics and chemistry, of the devices which enable the minerals to be obtained with the maximum safety to the miners. In many areas the children can see how the physical nature of rocks affects the scenery, the soil and the communications, and how their chemical composition also affects the vegetation. The position of former land and seas can be deduced from the collection and simple classification of fossils ; in certain areas the effects of the great ice sheet can be traced ; a search of gravels may possibly result in the finding of implements and other relics of early man. Studies should as far as possible be out of doors. The Geological Survey maps and sections are of great help.

15. Principles governing the choice of subject-matter.—(a) *The teacher should work out his own ideas.*— Many factors have to be considered in selecting material for the Science course, and what is best for one school will not necessarily be so for another school. There is no royal road to the school study of Science, and each teacher must undertake the task of syllabus building for himself : there should be constant experiment with new topics and new methods. Though fruitful suggestions may be adopted from many sources, it is only possible for the course to be a living force in so far as it represents the working out of ideas which the teacher has made his own.

(b) *Influence of the environment on the course.*—The emphasis of the course must to a great extent depend on the character of the neighbourhood in which the school is situated, but there is no reason for the urban school to feel that it cannot do biological work. The special knowledge and interests of the teacher must perforce have their influence, but he should not hesitate to take up new studies ; if necessary, master and pupils should be learners together. In districts where the industries are predominantly chemical and the majority of the pupils enter these industries, more chemistry than suggested above may well be included.

(c) *Though based on the children's experience the course should not lack coherence.*—Though suggestions have been made as to the content of the course based on the customary division of Science into branches, it is not suggested that the actual teaching should be based on these divisions. The contact pupils have with their environment and the questions that arise spontaneously in their minds about the things around them should provide the starting point for the teaching ; their interest being gained from the beginning, they may then be led on to a recognition of the underlying general principles.

In such a method as this of planning the course to be followed there is a danger that the work may lack coherence ; if it is to be successful the teacher must have in his mind a definite aim and a clear idea of the fundamental principles that he hopes to explain to the children, and he must make a careful study of what interests the pupils in their environment. The topics have to be selected with skill, and those which are too difficult or complicated to be followed up with profit and those which do not illustrate fundamental principles should be excluded. Some examples of topics which have been successfully worked out are : Air, Water, Heating, Lighting and Water Supply of a House, Clothes, Colour, Bicycles, Clocks. The course should not be regarded as settled once for all but should be varied from time to time as experience suggests.

(d) *Work for less intelligent children.*—The range of ability in any age group is very wide ; the less intelligent children find it difficult to see relations even between things which they have themselves observed and very difficult to express their ideas in writing. They should, therefore, if possible, receive special treatment. For instance, their Science should be developed on the lines of practical projects such as gardening, the construction of simple pieces of apparatus, the wiring of an electric lamp holder, the overhauling or the fitting up of an electric bell or a simple telephone circuit. They are interested in dismantling and assembling objects in common use such as locks, taps, bicycle pumps and flash lamp batteries, and in the study of animals, especially their external features, their movements and their gradual development. To encourage the latter interest, it is well to give them special charge of aquaria and vivaria. They should not be expected to make the usual form of notes, but can draw sketches and with some help write a few short sentences summing up the results of their work.

B. METHODS OF DEALING WITH THE CONTENT OF THE COURSE

16. Various forms the work may take.—If the conception of treating Science as a single whole is accepted, it follows that all the work of a class, whatever branch of Science a particular lesson may deal with, should be in the hands of one teacher. This may sometimes mean that the teacher will himself have to study branches of Science with which his training has not made him familiar. In most large centres of population there are now facilities for further study, but where such opportunities are not available, there is no reason why class and teacher should not explore the new field of knowledge side by side. A teacher's work is not likely to be alive and stimulating unless he is constantly adding to his own stock of knowledge.

(a) *Lectures.*—Lectures, if the matter is such as appeals to children and is accompanied by suitable illustration, can do much to arouse interest in some of the wider aspects of Science, and have this advantage that they can include topics which are not readily dealt with through demonstration lessons or practical work.

(b) *Demonstrations.*—Demonstration lessons are a valuable element in the course. On the one hand, the teacher should undertake experiments, which though necessary for the logical development of the work are too difficult and dangerous for the children ; on the other hand, he will find that he can save much time by carrying out once and for all equally simple experiments, which there is no point in making every pupil do for himself. His demonstrations should set a standard of performance for the children to aim at ; they should be convincing, visible to the whole class and as simple as possible. When about to demonstrate before a class something he has not demonstrated before, he should rehearse his experiment beforehand.

(c) *Practical work.*—" Practical work " is an essential part of all Science teaching. The ideas which a child gets from doing things for himself become part of his mental equipment more completely than those he gains from seeing things done or hearing or reading about them. The duller children learn best through some form of activity, and this appears to be true of some of the more intelligent. The less able children, for instance, may well spend a good deal of time in the construction of very simple pieces of apparatus before they attempt to use them ; for the brighter children this will not be so necessary, since they will see for themselves what the apparatus is for, and how its construction is governed by its purpose.

Group work has its value in the development of the spirit of co-operation, but it also has its dangers and should not be used exclusively, as there is a tendency for one member of the group to do more than his fair share to the exclusion of the others.

It is unlikely that the supply of apparatus will be sufficient for all pupils to do the same experiment simultaneously, but arrangements can be made for a variety of experiments to be done in a lesson which all relate to the topic under consideration.

(d) *Discussions.*—When a particular topic has been studied in a series of lessons, it should then be discussed in class with a view to welding the work done into a coherent whole and to bringing out its relations with what has gone before. When a new topic is about to be introduced, the ground to be covered and the method of approach should form the subject matter of a discussion. It need hardly be said that these discussions will not only give good practice in oral expression, but also provide excellent opportunities for revision.

(e) *Records and notes made by pupils.*—Records are usually of two kinds : notes of demonstration lessons and accounts of the pupils' own experiments. The former serve as an aid and a stimulus to memory and can provide good training in summarising and selecting salient points ; hence they may be very brief and written merely in note form. The latter give the pupils practice in making accurate records for their own and others' information and should take the form of connected accounts of what they have done or observed, and what conclusions they have drawn.

Both types of notes should be written at once in their final form and valuable time should not be wasted in first making rough notes and then making a fair copy.

Over elaboration should be avoided, and sketches and diagrams, the object of which is to elucidate the text and to save lengthy description, should not become an end in themselves; they should never be mere copies of illustrations in books but should be made direct from the apparatus used or from the material studied.

The training of the children in making their own notes should be a gradual process. In very early stages, the teacher may give them models to imitate and as a next step the class may share in a combined effort. If cards containing directions for making observations or performing the experiments are used, these directions should not be copied by the children into their note books. If their study of Science is to have any permanent value, the knowledge they gain must become part of their mental equipment and readily available for use; it is not sufficient to have it safely stored away in a note book.

(f) *Out-of-school activities*.—The course should not include compulsory homework, but a number of activities may be encouraged on a voluntary basis. There are now many small books on Science which are written in an interesting way and which can be circulated round the class for home reading; these contain suggestions for things to be done and for simple pieces of apparatus to be made from materials which are readily available, and their use will expand the range of what can be done in school hours.

The habit of observation and skill in recording can be promoted if the children are encouraged to study the sky by day and by night and to carry out other simple studies including the continuous observation of a selected area. Home Gardening and Bee-keeping have proved to be of value in many schools. Science guilds and societies, the meetings of which may take the place of some of the ordinary lessons, will provide a fresh stimulus.

17. Aids to the teaching of Science.—(a) *The school garden and the greenhouse.*—The school garden and the school greenhouse, which have been dealt with in detail in another chapter of this Handbook, may be made the centre of much of the instruction in Science, for Gardening is essentially the putting of Science to practical uses. They will provide much of the material required for the biological work and are the right places for making experiments on the germination of seeds and the conditions of healthy growth and propagation. Parts of the garden may be laid out in such a way as to illustrate plant associations in different habitats.

(b) *Visits to works, museums and exhibitions ; nature rambles.*—One of the claims for the inclusion of Science in the curriculum is that in studying it the pupils are dealing with facts at first-hand. It is, therefore, essential that they should both become acquainted with the applications of Science in industry by visits to works and factories and come into contact with nature by studying in the field. Visits to museums and exhibitions have this value that they enable children to see collections and exhibits which are on a far wider scale than anything that is possible in the school.

Owing to the expense involved and the limited time available for them, these visits are so infrequent that it is essential, when they do occur, that the best possible use should be made of them. Careful preparation is required, if every advantage is to be taken of a visit, and it should be followed up by suitable exercises, oral and written accounts, answers to questions and a discussion, with a view to making the experience coherent and bringing out its bearing on the school course and on the life of the children.

(c) *Broadcast lessons.*—Broadcast talks by field naturalists have become popular in many schools. Such lessons, while they cannot take the place of the teacher, can be of great use in arousing the interest of the children, in suggesting fresh ideas, and new ways of treatment, and may result in new forms of activity and in first-hand investigation on their part.

(d) *Films.*—The use of films in teaching has been greatly hindered by the high cost of the apparatus required and by the unsuitable character of most of the films available, though these are now being rapidly improved. Their use makes it possible to widen the scope of the Science teaching and may also be justified as a means of rapid recapitulation. It should not, however, be forgotten that Science teaching should never depend on pictures when real things are available.

(e) *Epidiascope, micro-projector and optical lantern.*— For many demonstration lessons it is essential to have means for the optical projection of slides, diagrams and small pieces of apparatus ; and the epidiascope will serve to show any of these things. When enlarged images of small living creatures and microscopic structure have to be shown, the micro-projector, will provide the best means, as the teacher, when using it, can be certain that the pupils have seen what he wishes them to see. This cannot be ensured by the use of a microscope, and much time is lost if each child has to look in turn. An epidiascope and a micro-projector should be part of the equipment of every Senior School. A lantern is useful not only for showing slides but for many optical experiments, especially in dealing with colour. An arc lamp is a good source of ultra-violet light.

All these pieces of apparatus are expensive, but they can be improvised if good lenses can be obtained; a highly successful lantern can be made from a large tin, an episcope body from plywood, and, if an ordinary microscope is available, a 12-volt car head-lamp, suitably mounted, will provide the necessary illumination for micro-projection.

(f) *The science library.*—Even if the school has a room set apart for use as a library, the Science room should have a number of books kept in it so as to be available for immediate reference; some training in how to make the best use of these is essential. Standard books of reference are too highly technical and written in too difficult language for the majority of the children to be able to consult them with profit, but fortunately there are available many simple books which will help the pupils to identify all the common plants, insects, butterflies, etc., and to get information about them. There are, too, Science encyclopædias specially written for children, in which they can find the answers to most of the questions that arise in their minds. The story of Science, lives of great scientists and accounts of recent discoveries can all be had in a form which the pupil can follow, and there are innumerable books about Science suitable for general reading which will stimulate interest and a desire to learn more of the subject.

18. Relations of Science to other subjects of the curriculum.—(a) *Gardening and keeping livestock.*— These subjects are dealt with in detail in Chapter X of this Handbook. It is difficult to over estimate the help that can be given by them to the Science course. The children will be learning about the conditions for healthy growth and propagation and the application of Science to the needs of man. They will gain some ideas of Mechanics from the use of gardening tools and from the construction of suitable houses for the animals kept.

Many physical and chemical principles, too, will find illustration in the cultivation of the soil, etc. In the case of the less intelligent children gardening and the keeping of livestock in conjunction with handicraft may well form the basis of the Science teaching, where the school premises permit of the proper development of these activities.

(b) *Handicraft.*—This subject can be of direct help to the Science teaching, for some of the time available can be given to the construction of apparatus which may be put to good use in the room allocated to practical work in Science. Many children will find an added interest in making something they will use in another part of their school work. Apparatus-making may even be encouraged as a hobby.

On the other hand the children will do their woodwork and metalwork more intelligently if they understand the mechanical principles involved in the proper handling of the tools they employ and have some idea of the forces acting in the objects they construct.

(c) *English.*—Science should contribute much to the training in English. One of the chief difficulties children have in expressing themselves, orally or in writing, is their lack of experience and ideas. In their Science work they have done or observed something in an orderly sequence and should, therefore, have ideas to express and some notion of how to arrange them. They should be given frequent opportunities for this kind of expression and a high standard of accuracy should uniformly be expected in such work.

(d) *History.*—The Science teacher should have an extensive knowledge of the history of scientific discovery and of the development of scientific thought. It is of little value to teach the pupils the history of Science before they know something of Science itself, but every opportunity should be taken to vivify and humanise the work by the introduction of relevant historical and biographical details. An attempt to adopt an historical or biographical basis for the development of the teaching soon leads to difficulties, for in this way phenomena are likely to be encountered, before the children are ready to understand them. When so much that is fruitful has to be omitted for lack of time, there is no need to go over all the mistakes of the past and much time can be wasted on abandoned theories and out-worn terminology.

In the History lessons the social, economic and political effects of outstanding scientific discoveries should be traced.

(e) *Mathematics.*—Much of what was at one time regarded as suitable preliminary science in the way of practical measurements of length, area and volume is best done as Mathematics. It is an interesting fact that what is regarded by the child as intolerably dull Science is done with avidity in the Mathematics lessons. Where Mathematics is developed on practical lines much of the Mechanics can be included in the course. If outdoor exercises in surveying form part of the Mathematics course, lessons on the principles underlying the design of the optical square, optical angle-meter, hand level, sextant, and prismatic compass can be included in the Science course.

(f) *Geography.*—There is a very close connexion between Geography and Science, and the Geography teacher will be greatly helped, if the topics of Air and Water come at an early stage in the Science course. Care should be taken that the work in Geography and the work in Science do not overlap, as, for example, in meteorology, astronomy and geology. The elements of these branches of Science are probably best taught in connexion with Geography.

(g) *Housecraft.*—This subject has a relation to Science similar to that of Gardening, in that it is essentially an application of Science to human needs. Some physical and chemical principles can be studied in topics taken from the course of domestic training, but many of the materials used in the work are too complex in composition to be dealt with in the Science lessons. A girl's conception of Science should not be limited to the science of the dwelling house : there is a wide range of topics outside the province of Housecraft which should be included in the Science course.

V. FACILITIES FOR TEACHING SCIENCE

19. Size and lay-out of the science room.—The first essential for teaching Science is plenty of space ; a suitable room for classes of 40 is one 40 feet long by 24 feet wide, with a store room at one end, the full width of the laboratory and from 6 to 8 feet in depth, fitted with deep shelves on one long and one short wall.

The windows on the long corridor wall should not come below 7 feet from the floor ; on the other side they should come down to bench level. On this side a plain light wall bench, 2 feet wide, for the display of models, for projects which require to be left standing some time and for the support of aquaria, etc., may run practically the whole length of the laboratory. On the wall at the store-room end should be fixed the blackboard with the demonstration bench 10 feet long and 2 feet 3 inches wide placed 2 feet 6 inches in front of it. The opposite wall should have the carpenter's bench and cupboards placed along it, leaving the remaining wall for shelves and such pieces of apparatus as are best fixed to a vertical wall. No balance cases or bench are required, as spring balances should be used.

If no greenhouse is available, two windows which get some sun may be fitted with wardian cases. The lantern screen should be put across one corner and not in front of the blackboard. Wooden suspension beams 7 inches by 3 inches, in cross section, spaced at equal intervals, should pass the whole length of the laboratory and be bolted to the roof principals.

In the centre of the room can be placed four light plain benches 11 feet by 4 feet with their length at right angles to the demonstration bench.

20. Equipment of the science room.—(a) *Gas, water and electricity supply.*—Gas points should be laid on to the demonstration bench, but flexible tubing can be used to lead gas from floor points to the centre benches if it is desired not to fix these to the floor.

One sink should be fixed at each end of the long wall bench and one in the demonstration bench ; one wall sink should have a drainage board.

A power point is required on the demonstration bench and others for the use of the lantern and for obtaining a supply of current for rectification to charge storage cells and, when transformed to a low voltage (12 volts), for pupils' experiments. The low voltage supply can be fed to the benches by sections of cables running in slots in battens, lengths of these being joined end to end as required by 2 pin plugs and sockets. All windows should be fitted with light-excluding blinds.

(b) *Carpenter's bench.*—The bench provided for repair work, and for the construction of simple pieces of apparatus such as auxanometers, klinostats, transformers, etc., should have a flat top and be fitted with both wood and metal vices. A list of suitable tools and raw materials is given in an appendix to *Science in Senior Schools*. These should form a supply quite distinct from those provided for the handicraft room.

(c) *Aquaria.*—Many schools succeed in keeping large aquaria in a state of equilibrium by a suitable adjustment of plant and animal life, but now that means of aeration can be had at reasonable cost, it seems better to keep a number of small tanks, so that species likely to prey on others may be kept separate. Earthenware sinks have been found satisfactory, and have the merit of not admitting light at the sides. A frequent source of failure is allowing scraps of food to decay in the tanks.

(d) *Illustrations and models.*—The Science room should contain portraits of famous scientists and diagrams, pictures and models illustrating machines, life histories, manufacturing processes, etc. These should be frequently changed, only those connected with the work in progress remaining on exhibition ; otherwise they cease to arouse interest.

(e) *Safeguards in the laboratory.*—The teacher should know how to deal with the emergencies which are likely to arise in the Science room, and a fire extinguisher, a bucket of sand, blanket and a first-aid case should be readily accessible for immediate use ; dangerous substances should be kept locked up.

Rules for laboratory use which will reduce as far as possible the risk of accidents should be put up in a prominent place and the children should know these rules.

21. Schools with no science room.—Schools which have no Science room are greatly handicapped, since little individual work by the pupils is possible and most of the teaching must be by demonstration. Some practical work in biology can be done at ordinary desks, if hand lenses are available and the children can handle and observe specimens. The position can be improved if a room can be fitted with a demonstration table and one or two wardian cases. If no water supply is laid on to the room, the difficulty can be overcome by using buckets, and for gas can be substituted stoves burning paraffin under pressure.

CHAPTER XV

MATHEMATICS

I. SOME GENERAL CONSIDERATIONS

A. INTRODUCTORY

1. The threefold aim of mathematical instruction.—The teaching of Mathematics in the Elementary School has three main purposes : first, to help the child to form clear ideas about certain relations of number, time and space ; secondly, to make the more useful of these ideas firm and precise in his mind through practice in the appropriate calculations ; and thirdly, to enable him to apply the resulting mechanical skill intelligently, speedily and accurately in the solution of everyday problems.

The expert teacher who realises the threefold nature of his task will not fall into the common danger of over-emphasising the second of these three aims at the expense of the other two. He will naturally be pleased if his pupils can work with speed and accuracy the ordinary mechanical sums in the " four rules " and in money, weights and measures, but he will always feel that this sort of achievement may be somewhat barren if it cannot be turned to real use. If, however, his pupils, as a result of their mathematical training, have learnt to apply their text-book knowledge to practical problems, the teacher will have succeeded in the main purposes of his instruction.

A good deal of the mathematical teaching in schools, indeed, which has as its aim nothing but the cultivation of speed and accuracy in working sums of a mechanical type, cannot be justified even as a form of mental training ; for operations with numbers and quantities which cannot be applied to life-situations must be largely without meaning for many children who perform them. In the early stages, especially, teachers should restrict themselves to giving children facility only in such mathematical skills as they can use and see the point of using. Throughout the school course the speed and accuracy which will count for most in the long run will be that shown in work which has a direct application for the child who performs it.

2. The importance of making the work fit the capacity of the individual child.—Syllabuses of in-struction in mathematics are still very much under the influence of an older tradition. They need not only to be brought into closer relation with the requirements of today, but also to take more account of the natural proclivities of childhood. Mathematical conceptions are easier to understand and to apply when they arise out of the pupils' interests and experiences, and the duller the child the broader the concrete foundation should be. Present-day treatment is far too much influenced by the supposed needs of those who proceed to Secondary Schools. The wide differences in ability that occur within each age-group need to be more fully recognised. Where a two- or three-stream organisation exists, it is easier to arrange for alternative syllabuses. It is equally desirable, though perhaps not equally practicable, to do this in all schools.

There is probably no subject in which the requirement that the syllabus must be adapted to the interests and capacities of the children is so well recognised, though difficult to fulfil, as in Arithmetic. Not only do capacities and normal rates of progress differ widely, but the subject has a definite content which must be taught in a more or less definite order, and if progress is to be continuous, certain fundamental skills and certain essential kinds of knowledge must be acquired by each individual pupil at every stage of the course.

The usual Arithmetic course in most schools consists largely of short " sums " of which the pupil has to work out a large number one after another. If these " sums " are so difficult that he gets them wrong, his sense of failure rapidly grows, distaste for the subject inevitably follows, and in such circumstances he becomes un-teachable. It is essential therefore that the exercises should be so graded in difficulty that every child can enjoy the stimulus of success and of steady progress. He should, moreover, at each stage of the course see their bearing upon the practical problems of life.

B. ARITHMETIC AS A SUBJECT

3. The approach through children's games.—

Number relations are implicit in many children's games, for example, in counting-play, in scoring-games and games with numbered boards and dice, and in many of the occupations that they imitate from adult life: for example, shopping, weighing and measuring. Such games and occupations, if carefully selected and arranged, are valuable throughout the early stages, but most of all in the Infant School. They familiarise the child with numbers and with the common units of measure, and they import meaning and interest into Arithmetic by basing its conceptions on a wide range of experience. Some of them—for example, the scoring-games and shopping—involve much practice in the simpler arithmetical operations, and also have so obvious a meaning for the child as to provide him with a strong motive for success. Such meaningful practice shortens the labour of learning and leads to good habits of calculation.

Such familiar and interesting "make-believe" and "real-life" situations provide the best introduction both to pure Arithmetic and to problems. When John, for example, buys at the classroom shop, the class may be led to see that the problem is "What change should he get?" They may go on to describe in their own words concisely and accurately the transaction that takes place, and to say what particular arithmetical operation the transaction has called for. The skilful teacher, by varying the shopping situation, may lead up to a varied series of problems, graded in difficulty. The children will thus come to see how text-book problems arise and how to state them. By approaching problem-solving in this way thus early they learn to grasp the situation which the words of a problem represent

4. The approach through the use of apparatus.—

But there comes a time when the very wealth and variety

of these games may make abstraction difficult and may obscure the essential character of the operations involved. Arithmetic as such soon advances beyond their range, and the foundation for its more systematic procedure is needed. This should be provided for by formal practical exercises in calculating with the help of simple objects like balls and counters. Formal practical work of this kind with simplified material is a stage half way between the fully concrete situation of the game and the abstract sum. By using apparatus to help him in his calculation the pupil comes to *see*, in both senses of the word, what the operations mean : e.g. how the operation required for " 27 plus 6 " may be derived from the simpler calculation of " 7 plus 6," or why six-eighths is the same as three-quarters.

Apparatus, however, may do harm if it is of the wrong kind. Apparatus, for example, that involves the moving about of objects one by one, tends to fix the low level habit of counting, if it is kept up too long, and to obscure the essential character of the higher level habits of addition, multiplication, etc. Apparatus may also do harm, if its use by individual children continues too long. If pupils are taught that it is more " grown-up " to work without apparatus, even when they have it, the teacher will soon discover when it may be withdrawn. Long after this, however, the teacher who can use skilfully one or two types of standard apparatus, e.g. the ball-frame, will find them useful in removing difficulties of understanding, especially those of children who may be relatively backward.

C. THREE ESSENTIAL STAGES IN THE TREATMENT OF ANY ARITHMETICAL TOPIC

5. Practical and oral work : mechanical work ; problem work.—The justification for ordered and systematic instruction in Mathematics, whether in Arithmetic, Algebra or Geometry, is that it enables the pupil to make faster progress than he otherwise might in acquiring the technique needed for the solution of the practical problems encountered in everyday life which call for the application of mathematical knowledge. The teaching, in particular, of any arithmetical topic or process in school should proceed by three clearly-marked stages. First, by way of introduction, should come practical and oral work designed to give meaning to, and create interest in, the new arithmetical conception—through deriving it from the child's own experience—and to give him confidence in dealing with it by first establishing in his mind correct notions of the numerical and quantitative relations involved in the operation. Next should follow " mechanical " work, the purpose of which is to help the child to form the mental habits in which skill in computation is rooted, so that he may be able to perform both speedily and accurately the particular arithmetical operations required. Finally, there should be problem-work : when the necessary skill has been acquired by each pupil, he will naturally apply it to solving the kind of problems which rendered it necessary for him to acquire it. Thus the treatment of each topic will end, as it began, by giving the pupil practical experience in dealing with situations which have meaning for him.

In applying the principles here indicated, however, the teacher should be on his guard against adopting any stereotyped procedure which is followed rigidly, either within the compass of a single lesson or over a series of lessons. In proceeding, too, from one stage to the next in his teaching of any particular topic or process, he should aim at preserving a proper balance as regards the time devoted to the various stages. He should not, for instance, give to mechanical work a disproportionate amount of the time at his disposal, nor should he make the fundamental mistake of deferring all practice in problem-solving until after the mechanical rules laid down in his class syllabus have been completely learnt. Above all, he should in this matter bear in mind the individual needs of his pupils, and should differentiate the syllabus so that he need not hurry the slower, or keep back the brighter workers among them.

(i) *Arousing interest through preliminary practical work.*

6. The importance of introducing a new topic in arithmetic by means of practical and oral work.— The importance of the introductory practical and oral work of the first of the three steps in teaching an arithmetical process lies in the fact that the child can learn to understand the meaning of numerical conceptions and operations by working exercises with small numbers and familiar quantities only. To increase the size and complexity of the numbers used is to demand greater skill in computation, but often, with young children, serves only to obscure the meaning of what is done. Facility in dealing with a new conception grows slowly, and is often reached only after long familiarity. Such familiarity is best acquired through oral work and the solution of a wide variety of simple problems involving quite small numbers and including as many as possible that are derived from the child's own experience.

(ii) *Developing mechanical skill.*

7. The amount of mechanical work usually done should be reduced.—To allow of a properly balanced course of instruction, the range and the amount of mechanical work usually attempted, especially in the Junior School, must be reduced,—for many of the children, if not for most. This may be effected by postponing the teaching of the more difficult " rules " or by restricting the exercises set to give practice in them to examples involving small numbers. It is usually a waste of time to teach a mathematical process or technique to a child, unless he is likely to acquire a reasonable degree of skill in using it before he leaves the class in which it is taught. The duller child, in particular, must not only have his knowledge of forms of numerical calculation related more directly and more extensively to his own everyday experiences, but he needs more practice in applying to quite simple life-situations such mechanical skill as he acquires.

8. Memorisation of tables essential.—At every stage of the school course, however, certain essential habits must be acquired as a foundation for further work. For example, the fundamental tables—addition–and–subtraction, multiplication–and–division—present the results of the preliminary oral and practical work in systematic arrangement and they derive their meaning from it. Their items must all be memorised, for they form the basis of the mechanical work which follows. The pupil must quite early be able to add any two numbers less than ten, for practically every lesson involves many of these operations. If he fails to learn the tables properly, i.e. to give the result automatically, without intermediate steps and without stopping to think, or if he fails to master them at the right time, he is hampered in all subsequent work and wastes, in the course of his school life, far more time than their accurate memorisation would have required.

9. Arithmetical " rules ".—The mechanical rules of written arithmetic are primarily devices for adding, subtracting, multiplying, or dividing quantities that are too large or too complex to be dealt with mentally. If the child were supplied with actual machines, to do the work of these rules automatically, his power of attacking problems would hardly suffer. Indeed it might be increased. The written rules, in fact, are best regarded as forms of mental technique or as complex habits to be formed. To teach them successfully means that the child will acquire, with the least expenditure of time and energy, such a degree of speed and accuracy that they can be readily applied.

It is often contended that the child should learn these rules intelligently. If this means that he should be able to recognise the kind of problem situation that leads to them, it is true. If it means that he should grasp the full logic of, say, the subtraction rule at the age when it is commonly learned, it is certainly untrue. Some insight into the logic may facilitate memory and computation and may therefore be desirable. This aspect, however, should not be over emphasised.

10. How to secure economy of time and effort in mechanical work.

—The importance of economising time and effort in mechanical work has already been stressed. The following suggestions have this end in view :—

(a) *Methods should be standardised.*—This should be done, if not throughout a district, then at least throughout the group of schools contributory to a given Senior School. The method of procedure should be quickly reduced to a final and simple form, (e.g. in dealing with " 36—17," the child might say, almost from the start, " seven from sixteen, nine ; two from three, one,") avoiding unnecessary statements. " Crutches " if used at all, should be discarded before they become fixed habits. The writing of " carried " figures, for example, is probably best not taught at all, at any rate with normal children.

(b) *A definite standard of accuracy should be aimed at.*—For every rule the teacher should have in mind a standard of working accuracy which each child should reach before passing on to another. Any such standard, e.g. three right out of four is more quickly reached with short " sums." The fewer figures and operations involved the smaller the chance of going wrong. This implies that exercises of smaller number range should be used with the duller children.

(c) *Excessive mechanical work should be avoided.* The amount of mechanical work to be covered at any stage should not be so great as to upset the balance of the syllabus. A suggested minimum syllabus for normal children is given in Chapter II of the Board's pamphlet *Senior School Mathematics.* Further economy of time and effort may be secured by avoiding alternative methods, or by reducing the number range, as suggested above.

(d) *Mechanical drill directed to a specific purpose is valuable.*—Much time may be saved if the mental habits that each new rule implies are considered separately, and special oral drills are devised when needed. Short division by six (for example, $351 \div 6$) requires, (1) a familiarity with the division aspect of the table of sixes even when the table is known, (2) the ability to deal with exercises like $35 \div 6$, and to " carry " the remainder, (3) the ability to take 48 from 51, (4) the ability to set down neatly. Any one of these may require special attention. Again, in fixing the rule for multiplication by decimals only one new habit is required,— that of placing the point. This may be quickly established by specially devised oral work.

In short, mechanical drill work should be purposeful. It is sometimes claimed that the mere indiscriminate working of long " sums " may increase accuracy, but even if this were true the method would be wasteful of time.

(e) *Brisk working promotes accuracy.*—Accuracy grows more quickly when reasonable speed is demanded. For exercises requiring thought procedure may be leisurely, but in mechanical exercises brisk working should be encouraged.

(f) *Unnecessary written work to be avoided.*—There is no need for a child to write down every exercise that he attacks. Cards with half-a-dozen mechanical sums, so constructed that the card can be laid on the paper and the answers written beneath may save much time, especially if a standard answer card is used which can be laid on the child's book.

(iii) *Applying skill to the working of problems*

II. Mechanical practice valuable only in so far as it gives power to solve real problems.—The teacher should see that the children understand that they are not doing mechanical arithmetic merely for the sake of getting sums right, stimulating and satisfying as that will always be. Mechanical practice should be taken for the same reason as practice with a new stitch in needlework, or fielding practice in cricket, i.e. in order that the skill acquired may be used, while it is still fresh, in coping with the difficulties of a real situation. In other words, the teacher will not take the point of view that instruction in arithmetic must inevitably take the form of : (a) teaching the bare skills and (b) looking round subsequently for sums in books that test the ability to apply the skills acquired. Rather, he should take the view that in approaching any new range of work, whether it be vulgar fractions, or proportion, or simple interest, his first task is to interest his pupils in a variety of easy problems, involving such small numbers and such simple quantities that written computation is not required.

Only when familiarity with new conceptions has been gained in this way will it be necessary to consider what mechanical rules and what formal written procedure need to be taught in order that problems involving bigger numbers and more complex quantities may be introduced. Though this formal instruction may cover a series of lessons, its ultimate purpose and justification should be borne clearly in mind all the time.

If the introductory work is well done, the primary notions and operations will be derived from the child's experience. Practice in solving a wide variety of problems that can be treated orally will help to strengthen the relation between experience and arithmetical operation. But when the child has learnt the mechanical rules, i.e. acquired the skill to handle larger numbers and quantities, the range of application of what he has learnt will be increased. He will not only be in a position to attack the traditional text-book problem, in which the data are selected and marshalled for him, but will be ready to meet a wider range of real life exercises. This kind of practical work is fully discussed in *Senior School Mathematics*. Simple forms of it are appropriate to all stages.

12. Problem work : some principles to be observed.—A problem is an exercise that contains an element of novelty. In the time available only a few methods of calculation can be standardised, i.e. converted into mental habits, and these enable the pupil to attack only a small proportion of the exercises that he meets. For the remainder he must be able to modify or combine methods as circumstances demand, or to devise new ones.

Problem-solving cannot be taught as rules are taught. The traditional method of dividing problems into types and teaching a standard method for each type has but a limited value in view of the large number of types. Training children to solve problems is in essence training them to meet and surmount difficulties for themselves, and the best training is the kind of teaching that grades difficulties so that the pupil can surmount them, and presents them in such a way that he has to do his own thinking.

But although problem solving cannot be directly taught certain suggestions for handling problems are worth bearing in mind :—

(a) *The pupil must face the problem unaided.* To remove the new difficulties in advance, e.g. by suggesting the method to be used, is to destroy the essence of the problem, and reduce the exercises to mechanical work.

(b) *Problems must be easy.*—This means that they must be such as the pupil can tackle unaided with some chance of success. The view sometimes expressed that backward children cannot do problems—(which implies that they are learning what they cannot apply)—really means that most text-book problems are too difficult for them. The experimental grading of problems in order of difficulty has hardly been begun.

(c) *Approach through real-life situations.*—Problems are best approached through " real-life " situations, as already indicated. " Real - life " problems may be supplemented by varied oral exercises in which the answer only is written down. These may be introduced at an early stage, and up to the end of the Junior School backward children will hardly go beyond this type.

(d) *Language used should be simple.*—Young children commonly fail with text-book problems, because they cannot read them, i.e. because they are unable to realise the exact situation that the words describe. In order to minimise this difficulty problems should deal with familiar and interesting situations. They should be expressed in short, crisp sentences and in simple language.

(e) *Demonstration better than verbal explanation.*— Children will grasp a situation more easily, if the training begins with problems involving such simple numbers that practical apparatus can be used to illustrate the operations. For example the pupil, when he first meets such a question as " How many quarts in five gallons ? ", can easily be shown that five groups of four are involved and that multiplication is indicated. Demonstration where practicable is to be preferred to verbal explanation. If, at a later stage, pupils attempt to solve a problem by multiplying when they should divide, or fail to understand what the remainder stands for, they will often surmount the difficulty at once if the problem is restated with the simplest numbers and demonstrated with actual objects. But this difficulty should rarely arise, if care is taken from the start to link process with objective demonstration and with verbal statement.

(f) *Full comprehension of the meaning of the problem the first essential.*—When written problems, involving several steps and the use of large numbers, are introduced, the teaching should not be directed primarily to suggesting the method by which they can be solved, but rather to training children to ask themselves what is given and what is required, to note what units are employed, to use diagrams when possible and, in general, to analyse the problem in such a way that the meaning will become clear. If children have been systematically trained, as they should be, to see how problems arise out of real-life situations, they will find the written problem much easier to understand.

D. MENTAL ARITHMETIC

13. The uses of mental work in Arithmetic.—

" Mental " Arithmetic includes all exercises in which pen or pencil is not used, except perhaps to record the answer. Much of the Arithmetic of everyday life is " mental " in this sense. The value of such work, provided that the exercises are chosen to serve a definite purpose, has been stressed throughout this chapter. Its main purposes will be :—(a) to give practice in solving a wide variety of problems, with or without the help of apparatus ; (b) to give brisk drill in specific habits (e.g. in addition of fractions, changing the subject of a formula) or in the tables themselves ; (c) to revise : e.g. a test might be given to discover, by means of a few very simple exercises, how much a class has remembered of the rules for operations with decimals or for finding the areas of plane figures.

Certain short cuts in computation may usefully be introduced through mental work. Only a few of these short cuts are important, e.g. the rules for finding the cost of a dozen articles, or for multiplying by twenty-five.

Few text-books contain enough exercises in " Mental Arithmetic " ; still fewer provide purposeful exercises of all types. For some purposes, e.g. brisk drill work, the exercises are best devised by the teacher who knows the needs of the class ; but most teachers need a supplementary source-book for mental work. If ample exercises of this type are available, one section of a class can be set down to " mental work " by themselves. Even where classes are taught as a whole, there are many types of example which the child needs to read as well as to hear ; some require the *numbers* only to be written on the blackboard.

Finally, it is well to remember that, although the use of pen and pencil in ordinary written work makes thought clearer by necessitating its clear exposition, the rule " Show your working " may easily lead to mental slackness. The complementary rule " Never do work on paper that can be done mentally " often needs to be emphasised ; the bright child may often be set to do mentally as many as he can of an ordinary set of exercises.

E. ORGANISATION OF THE SCHOOL COURSE

14. Individual work and group work both essential.—In some schools, provision is made for differences of ability by allowing each pupil to proceed at his own pace. In Arithmetic, where it is of special importance that the pupil shall surmount his own difficulties, there will always be much individual work. Teaching which relies solely upon it, however, misses the great stimulus and value of oral group work. A group which is put on to individual work, before sufficient group instruction has been given, will be in danger of making many mistakes. The teacher will be hard put to it to keep pace with the corrections and the pupil, through repetition of errors, will contract bad habits that are difficult to eradicate. Moreover, the method, if carried on throughout the Junior School results in a truncated course for all but the best children.

15. Adapting the course to the children's capacity.—Where numbers admit of it, the course should be planned on the basis of the " two-stream " or " three-stream " classification which the Hadow reorganisation makes possible. There may be then a minimum syllabus, in which each major topic will be completed by all normal children at about the same age. There may also be a supplementary course with extra rules, larger numbers and more difficult problems, enough to provide ample work for the brightest children ; on the other hand, there may be a few for whom the minimum will be too much. Many schools are not large enough to allow the classes to be organised in separate streams. Where it is possible at least for each age-group to have a teacher of its own, differences of ability can be met without much difficulty by sectional treatment, though to ensure adequate oral teaching the number of sections should not be too large. In such circumstances the supplementary course might be designed to enable the brighter children to work largely by themselves.

In a small school, where each teacher is responsible for more than one age-group, it is very difficult to allow for differences of ability as well as of age. If the age range is very wide, several sections may be necessary ; but multiplication of the groups often leads to the neglect of one or other of them and to the cutting down of necessary oral work. For practical work such as measurement or out-of-door surveying it may be necessary to take the whole class together, but the tasks allotted to the children should be graded according to their ability. In very small schools it may be a useful plan to set a bright child occasionally to supervise the work of a small group which is less advanced or to arrange for children to work in pairs.

In any case, the syllabus must be considerably simplified in the school where children of a wide age range are taught by one teacher.

16. A course should not be on rigid lines : it should be modified to meet individual needs.— But, although forethought and planning are necessary, it cannot be too strongly emphasised that the most suitable course for any given class cannot be laid down in advance, even by teachers who know the children, and still less by text-book writers who do not. Real success is only possible when the teacher is on the alert to notice where modification is needed and is resourceful in supplying it. He must distinguish between failures that are due to misunderstanding, to lack of skill, or to carelessness, and treat them differently; note children who habitually get their sums wrong and modify their course before they become discouraged; see that the brightest ones are kept on the stretch and fully employed; devise exercises that arise out of the children's special interests and prescribe drills calculated to help them to remove bad habits and to master essential forms of skill.

17. How a text-book should be used.—Text-books should not be followed too closely, nor should they be changed too often. The teacher will do well to note in an interleaved copy the modifications that experience suggests to him. He may note, for example, which exercises may be omitted; record additions that he has to make; note which exercises prove difficult and which easy, where difficulties of language occur and where alternative methods may be employed, where rough estimates or checks may be profitably employed, and where short cuts may be looked for from the brighter children. If experience is gathered and recorded in this way, especially when children's books are being corrected, the second passage through the course will be far more profitable than the first.

18. Methods of correcting written work.—Correcting the pupils' written work—i.e. indicating their mistakes by means of signs or marks—has two primary uses. It enables the teacher to profit by experience, as suggested above, and it brings home to the pupil where he stands. The correction must be thorough, if interest is to be sustained, and if the teacher is to discover the sources of error in the pupil's work. Correction, however, in the sense of putting right what is wrong, is mainly the pupil's business. Different types of error need different treatment which will depend upon the diagnosis, and this should be indicated in the marking: an error in reasoning may necessitate further teaching before correction by the pupil ; inaccuracy may be due to ignorance of tables, or to bad setting down, or merely to general slackness or to a casual slip. It may be unwise to insist on the reworking of an exercise just because of a single slip.

19. Value of short methods : Estimating and proving.—The brighter children should be kept on the alert for short cuts and alternative methods. All pupils should often be required to make preliminary estimates of results. Many teachers show the children how to " prove " their sums and frequently require them to do so. The use of a book in which some exercises are starred to indicate that estimates should be made or the best method sought, is a stimulating device. Very few short cuts are of such general application that they should be specifically taught. Moreover specific teaching rarely ensures that they will be used at the appropriate occasion. Discussion of short methods has little effect on subsequent work unless, by the " starring " or some other device, the habit of looking for opportunities is continually encouraged. The more backward children should be taught standardised methods, and will rarely be able to depart from them.

F. INCLUSION IN THE COURSE OF OTHER FORMS OF MATHEMATICS

20. Possible lines of development.—The Board's pamphlet *Senior School Mathematics* describes in some detail the forms of mathematical training other than Arithmetic that may be included in the Elementary School course.

The practical activities of the Infant and Junior Schools will extend the child's familiarity with size, shape, and direction. The Junior School teacher may do much to facilitate the growth of geometrical notions, which is necessarily slow, and to link them to correct description. In the Senior School such activities as Practical Surveying, Practical Drawing in connection with Bookcraft, Woodwork, and other forms of craft-work will develop these notions and make them more explicit. It should be the aim of the teacher of Mathematics to bring home to the pupils the geometrical facts and principles involved in these practical activities through discussion and by means of supplementary exercises, and so enable them to acquire a working knowledge of some of the more important generalisations of geometry.

Other forms of mathematical work that Senior Schools can profitably introduce are the reading and drawing of graphs (for which also a foundation may be laid in the Junior School stage); generalised Arithmetic, especially the construction and use of formulae; and, where conditions are suitable, the use of logarithm tables and an introductory course of Mechanics.

II. THE INFANT SCHOOL STAGE

21. The aims of number teaching in Infant Schools. —The aim of the Infant School should be to organise an environment in which the orderly development of children's early ideas of number and his experiences of measurable quantities etc. can take place most easily. It is particularly important that the training which is concerned with the enumeration of objects and with the understanding of the simple numerical relationships arising out of it, should be accompanied by the introduction of situations in which the child meets with the commoner measures of money, weight, length, and capacity. A zeal for number analysis on the part of the teacher may lead to a rapid development in the Infant School child's ideas of number and numerical relations ; but the ability to deal with numbers will not in itself help a child to understand what is meant by 2 lbs. of butter, a yard of dress material, half-a-pint of milk, or a 10s. 0d. note.

Instruction in number should, therefore, have, as its objective, a development of ability, suited to the capacity of the child, not only in counting and number analysis, but also in dealing intelligently with the simplest common quantities. Even before they begin to attend school, children have acquired some experience of number, distance, shape, size, weight and money. The extent and clearness of this knowledge will vary considerably with home conditions, but the children will probably have in their vocabulary some general terms associated with quantity such as " little," " high," " heavy," etc. and some of the number names.

22. The approach to number teaching through various activities.

—When children enter school they should not at first be expected to make any change in the ways by which they normally acquire number knowledge. Their environment should, however, be more stimulating and the teacher should from time to time draw attention to the quantitative side of their experiences and take steps to systematise what they are learning. She will, for example, make use of the traditional counting rhymes, games, and songs for teaching the number names and she will introduce occupations such as bead threading, which gives opportunities for counting, and the handling of objects designed to bring out differences of size and shape. Children enjoy counting and no special setting is required for a great part of the early teaching in enumeration. The child may count the buttons on his coat, he may play the make-believe games of laying plates for six and he will hear stories such as that of the three bears with their bowls of differing size. His rhythmic activities and his handwork will also add to his experiences of numbers and quantities. He will throughout be increasing his power to describe what he does in appropriate language.

23. Learning to count. Use of number patterns before figures are taught.—In learning to count, the child first meets a number, say *four*, as one of an invariable sequence of words (*one, two, three, four* etc.). He also learns to associate the words, one by one, with a series of objects, touching or pointing out these as he does so. The abandonment of this habit later on marks a definite stage of progress. He also learns to associate the words *three, four* with the numbers of objects in a group rather than with those counted third and fourth.

It is at this stage that some teachers introduce orderly arrangements of dots to represent the numbers in easily recognisable patterns, such as $\vdots$ for *five*. Practice in recognising such patterns and counting the dots adds to the range of number activities and may be made a useful preliminary to the teaching of figures. Figures themselves add nothing to the understanding of numbers and they should, therefore, not be taught until the children can make confident use of the sounded names corresponding to them.

24. The introductory step in the teaching of number operations.—At a later stage, when introducing simple operations, the teacher will be well-advised to display the same caution in teaching the symbols for adding, subtracting, and so on. The first essential is that the operation itself should be understood in a sufficient number of situations to give it generality. Adding must be associated not only with counting the total of two or more groups of balls, counters or dots, but with groups of all sorts of things in a great variety of circumstances. Again, subtracting may be associated either with the comparison of groups of objects or with removing a smaller group from a larger one.

It will be wise for the teacher to see that the children are able to perform such operations with a variety of actual objects, and to describe what they do, before she gives them exercises, for example, with counters, in which the only variety is the changing of the numbers involved. Thus, while he is still at the stage of learning what subtraction means, a child will say " I threw 5 balls into the basket and Jack threw in 2, so I threw in 3 more balls than Jack." Or, " I had 5 biscuits and gave Jack 2, so I have 3 left for myself." Later he will become interested in trying out the operation of subtraction with a great variety of numbers and should then proceed to memorise the addition-and-subtraction table. But the preliminary work done with the aid of objects and the practice in describing what he does will help to lay the foundation of an intelligent use of this table, and the child's actual experience will help him in constructing the table itself. A child is more likely to remember that his score of 5 was 3 more than Jack's 2 than he is to recall items of a series of routine exercise with counters. Moreover, in his eagerness to get at the answer to a little sum arising out of some game the child will tend to discard unnecessary aids to calculation.

25. Practice in simple operations with a variety of numbers.—Skilful teachers have devised numerous ways of giving children plenty of practice in doing sums of graded difficulty. The use of apparatus sometimes adds the play element to the working of a sum ; beads, cards or dominoes may also be used to represent the numbers concerned. Number patterns are particularly

helpful when a number has to be broken into its component parts, e.g. the removal of 3 dots from the 7 exhibited thus ∴∴ clearly leaves 4 dots ∴∴, though this is less obvious if the pattern ∴∴ be used for 7.

In using apparatus for this purpose it should be borne in mind that memorising the fundamental tables has to be completed early in the Junior School and that a habit of counting or of using other aids to finding out the answer should not be associated with calculations of which the results are already confidently known. The practice of visualising numbers and that of " building up tens " may retard memorisation, if they are adopted habitually instead of as helpful or explanatory stages. On the other hand, the importance of groupings in tens and in twelves justifies an early teaching of the composition of both these numbers in the informal stages of building up the complete addition table. The children will co-operate in the right use of apparatus if encouraged to approach little sums in an attitude of experimentation or with a desire to reach results quickly and accurately ; sometimes the one and sometimes the other of these attitudes is appropriate to their stage of progress. The dangers of over-dependence on apparatus have been dealt with above in Section 4, page 502.

The range of operations to be dealt with in a practical manner will not necessarily be restricted to addition and subtraction. For a small range of numbers the children may learn to deal with all the four fundamental operations even if they do not get to the stage of making symbolic statements of their results.

26. Range of numbers for which automatic knowledge can be expected.—There will probably be wide differences amongst children, who have reached the end of the Infant School stage, in the sureness of their knowledge of the addition-and-subtraction table ; but normal children should be able to deal practically and orally with all sorts of operations involving numbers not greater than 12 with certainty and rapidity, i.e. without stopping to think. They may not, however, be so sure of the composition of numbers between 12 and 20. With children whose development is retarded, more time must be allowed for fundamental ideas to take root. If such children pass on too quickly to the symbolic statement of little sums, or even to formal practice with counters, they may for a time give the appearance of keeping up with their fellows, but they will pass from stage to stage without forming the mental habits which the graded exercises are designed to foster. Their attainments when they proceed to the Junior School stage will be superficial and their condition much inferior to that of a backward child whose experiences of number have been arranged to suit his stage of development.

27. Counting and notation.—Counting should be extended beyond the range of numbers commonly used by children and they should be encouraged to count in groups as well as in ones, (e.g. they might count the children in a class as they sit in twos, the panes in the window, or the milk bottles in their crates). Children should also practise counting backwards in ones and naming in order the odd as well as the even numbers. Frequent use should be made of apparatus such as the ball frame, which exhibits clearly grouping by tens. This will help to give significance to the number names " ten ", " twenty ", " thirty ", " fourteen ", " twenty-four", etc. ; and it will be an essential part of the teaching for the children to read and write numbers larger than ten. Before they complete the Infant School stage most children should have learnt to read and write numbers up to 100 and, in such a number as 14, to appreciate the significance of the 1 and the 4.

28. First ideas of magnitude, measurement, and money.—The children's growing competence in dealing with numbers should be accompanied by increasing exactness in their ideas of magnitude and measurement. The earliest ideas of quantity should be a matter of comparison rather than measurement, words such as "longer" and "heaviest" sufficing at first. Some of the materials given to the children to handle should, however, be so graded in size as to suggest increase by a regular unit. Opportunity should then be given to the children to experiment with improvised measures of all kinds—(strips, hand-breadths, paces for length, metal or cardboard discs for weight, cartons, bottles or toy pails for volume and so forth)—without any attempt being made at first to force standard units on them. In this way rudimentary ideas of measurement will take root and meaning will be given to the use of numbers in such expressions as "a four pound weight", "six inches", "five years old". Moreover, among the children's experiences involving operations or counting should be included some which also involve measures such as those which occur in simple shopping or in counting the groups of five minutes round the clock.

Before children pass out of the Infant School stage they should have had some acquaintance with coins, with measures most commonly used, such as pints and quarts of milk, and with such practical matters as telling the time and using the calendar. They should have become accustomed to the use of scales, weights, measuring-tape and foot-rule, and should have grown familiar with the idea that coins have different values according to their size and the material of which they are made, and that giving change is a common feature of shopping ;

for it will not be difficult for the average child to give change in pence from 6*d*. and 1*s*. 0*d*.

In short, the more realistic the school room procedure, the more likely children are to gain clear ideas of measures of quantity and of number relations generally.

III. MATHEMATICS AT THE JUNIOR SCHOOL STAGE

29. Continuation in the Junior School of work begun in the Infant School.—In the Infant School emphasis should fall not so much on the acquirement of a high degree of skill in computation as on bringing out and clarifying such notions of number and magnitude as are implicit in childish experience. The normal child on leaving the Infant School will probably have learnt rhythmic counting—e.g. in twos up to, say, forty,—and will have memorised the addition and subtraction tables up to a total of twelve. He will have been familiarised with multiplication and division, as performed with the aid of objects, though he will not have memorised the multiplication table as such. He will also have become acquainted with the commoner units of weight, length, and capacity, in use around him and he will have an intelligent idea of their use. The value of such training should be judged by the interest aroused and by the range of quantitative experience that has been explored, rather than by the systematic knowledge and skill obtained. It cannot be judged merely by the results of a formal test, especially of a written test. The teacher of the lowest Junior School class should be familiar with the course that each child has followed in the Infant School, so that she will be able to provide equally well for those who have done more or less than the average.

30. The range of work in the Junior School.—The importance of strictly limiting the amount of mechanical work required of each child, so that the balance of the syllabus may be maintained, has already been emphasised. In the Junior School, however, a certain emphasis must fall on the acquirement of skill in calculation, for the children are at the age when they most readily form simple mental habits, and if the right habits are not formed they are difficult to acquire afterwards. Accuracy should be secured in such " rules " as are taught, but no child should spend so much time in learning rules as to leave no time for simple problems or for the introductory practical and oral work that serves to give the rules meaning.

There are obvious practical advantages in assigning a minimum of knowledge and skill which every normal child will be expected to acquire before the end of the Junior School stage ; this might well be settled by local agreement for each group of re-organised schools. A suitable minimum, to be thoroughly and permanently known, will be found suggested in *Senior School Mathematics*. It will be noted that this does not include long multiplication and division of money, weights and measures, or any work with decimals, and further, that restricted range of number is suggested. For example, exercises in weights and measures may well be confined to three-unit quantities, and fractions to simple denominators that will not involve teaching the rules for H.C.F. and L.C.M. It is, of course, assumed that the brighter children will attempt more, and there will be a small minority who cannot attempt so much.

Many teachers have been deterred from simplifying their syllabus of Arithmetic, to the extent that is desirable, by the requirements of the Special Place Examination. It is important that the scope of this examination should not be too wide, especially when the papers are set to a complete age group. A suitable range is that suggested in Chapter II of *Senior School Mathematics*. Further, the questions set should not be too complex or too long. Papers consisting of a large number of short problems ranging from very easy to very difficult have been found to do the work of discrimination at least as well as those consisting of a few difficult ones. A paper in mental arithmetic may have high selective value. When a paper of mechanical exercises is set it should be long enough to test speed as well as accuracy. Moreover, due emphasis should be given to the more important rules taught at the beginning of the Junior School course. The long rules in weights and measures, taught usually in the year preceding the examination, are relatively unimportant.

31. The importance of providing alternative courses.—Throughout this chapter it has been emphasised that Arithmetic is taught in order to be applied, not merely in order that the child may pass tests in formal rules ; and that young children are only able to apply what they are taught, when it has been sufficiently related at the outset to their experience by means of practical work. The younger or duller the child, the wider the basis of experience that is needed for the grasp of each abstract conception. For the " C " child in the Junior School, for example, it may be necessary to base most of the oral and written exercises on real-life problems. The classroom shop for example, may provide most of the exercises in money and weighing, and full use will be made of such real-life experiences as arise naturally in the course of the school life, e.g. planning an excursion or laying out a garden. The " C " child will also profit from much brisk oral work designed to give facility in handling small numbers. Such exercises, with the more formal practical work, which will also have to be emphasised, take a great deal of time. His formal written work on the other hand may have to be limited by omitting all or nearly all the long rules, by using only small numbers or two-unit quantities, and the simplest

fractions. And it will have to be graded much less steeply than is customary, so that difficulties may be taken up one at a time and overcome before passing on. With such children in particular it is not only a waste of time but a source of great discouragement to teach formal rules that are not carried to the stage of working accurately and that will probably never be applied.

Even where brighter children are concerned interest and variety may be given to the work by the judicious use of catalogues and railway and other time-tables and of games, puzzles and problems that arouse their interest.

32. The tables and table-learning.—The practical work of the Infant School will be continued, and apparatus will be used to bring out the meaning of essential operations : e.g. that multiplication is an operation with groups and not with units,—(a fact which the child who builds up tables by moving objects one by one is apt to miss) ; how " 17 + 8 " and " 27 + 8 " follow at once from " 7 + 8 " ; how the different multiplication tables are related to one another, e.g. the tables of fours and eights ; how they are related to the number series, as shown for example by the patterns made on the number chart by the tables of nines and twelves. In short, the purpose of the practical work is not merely to discover the values of the items, (e.g. that " 6 × 7 " = 42), but also to bring out other relations. Unless the teacher is alert to its wider purpose, table building may be as mechanical as table repetition.

The four fundamental tables have to be memorised. Every child, if he is to avoid wasting time in subsequent work, must reach a high standard of accuracy, not far from 100 per cent., in the items. For example, by the end of the first year of the Junior School the addition-and-subtraction table up to a total of 20 should have become automatic. Points worth noting are that the addition table is at least as important as the multiplication table; that such a combination as " 31—27 " follows at once from " 11—7 "; that memorising a table means being able to recall each item as required, not merely in table order; that attention to pattern, e.g. that of the table of nines, greatly facilitates learning; that the traditional order and range of the tables learnt is not necessarily the best. There is much to be said, for example, for learning the table of twelves before the tables of sevens and elevens; also for memorising the tables of fourteen and sixteen when they are required in connection with weights.

Table learning should be supplemented by oral exercises designed to give general facility in calculation (e.g. exercises in rapid successive addition), in finding as many pairs of factors as possible for a given number, in recognising the prime numbers (e.g. between 60 and 70) etc.

33. The simple rules.—The weight of evidence suggests that accurate subtraction is best attained by the method of equal addition. Many teachers also favour approaching short division by the long division arrangement, thus showing the essential unity of the two methods. It is now generally accepted that the best method in long multiplication is to begin with the left-hand digit of the multiplier. In all the rules numbers involving one or more zero figures give much trouble and call for special attention.

34. The compound rules : money, weights and measures.—It should not be assumed that all children have been sufficiently familiarised in the Infant School even with the commoner coins and units. Some, for example, will need teaching how to tell the time or to use a pair of scales. All will need practical work to familiarise them with less common units and their relations. If the children are to have the varied individual experiences which will ensure a real understanding of weights and measures, it is obvious that there must be adequate equipment of the right type. At the Junior School stage there should be rulers exactly twelve inches long marked in fourths, eighths and tenths, without angle measurements, yard sticks, plywood cut to one foot square size and also to one inch square, weights of $\frac{1}{4}$ oz. to 1 lb., and separate measures of $\frac{1}{4}$, $\frac{1}{2}$, 1 and 2 pint capacity. Children should also know certain useful and familiar measures that will serve as standards where estimates are made. For example, a child may know his own height or the height of the classroom door, his own weight or how much he can easily lift, how long it takes him to walk a mile, or how far it is from home to school. His attention may be drawn to familiar measures in common use, e.g. that a cricket pitch is one chain, that three pennies weigh an ounce, and that the school milk bottle contains a third of a pint. The teacher who is familiar with the history of our weights and measures will be able to draw much interesting material from it.

The compound rules involve a new operation, unit-changing—changing one step up to a larger unit and one step down to a smaller. This process, though no more than an extension of the notation principle, is of fundamental importance, and needs careful treatment. It not only forms the basis of all the rules, but its intelligent application saves much time in solving problems. The meaning of unit-changing should be carefully demonstrated, by using objects and diagrams where possible, in relation to all the tables. And before learning, for example, the formal rule for reduction of money, oral practice should be given in solving small number exercises involving changing shillings to sixpences, sixpences to half-crowns, pounds to florins etc. The first rule work should consist of two-unit exercises arising out of oral work.

(a) *The money rules.*—Shopping exercises, which may be graded in difficulty so that a wide range of calculation is involved, are invaluable for providing an interesting approach to the money rules.

The pence-table need not be separately learnt, if the tables of twelves and its pattern on the number chart are well known. Counting backwards and forwards by steps of 3d., 1½d., 2s. 6d. etc. is a useful exercise.

In long multiplication and long division of money and other compound quantities the superiority of the " column " method is now established.

(b) *Weights and measures.*—Most of the applications to everyday life situations involve quantities of no more than two units, and the teaching of the rules should reflect this fact. Few problems involve quantities of more than three units. The " reduction " rules should not be taught until unit-changing is thoroughly grasped. Children who are taught them too soon and too thoroughly often handle the units met with in problems very unintelligently.

The factors and properties of certain numbers that occur often in relation to our English weights and measures are worthy of some special study, e.g. 112 and 1760. Further, certain tables lead naturally to the more important groups of fractions. The statement " one gallon = 8 pints " easily leads to its correlative " one pint = $\frac{1}{8}$ gallon." Similarly, the $\frac{1}{12}$ notation may be introduced in relation to shillings and pence or feet and inches.

35. Fractions. — Fractions should be introduced gradually through practical exercises. The work might begin with the halves, quarters, eighths family, and go on to the thirds, sixths, twelfths family. So long as the work is confined to such simple families, problems and operations involving fractions should be based on commonsense methods rather than on formal rules. The extension of notation to sixteenths, twenty-fourths, and of fifths, tenths, and hundredths as an introduction to decimals and percentages at a later stage will probably include as much as most normal children can thoroughly master by the age of 11. The relation of unit fractional parts to simple division should be understood, e.g. that $\frac{1}{4}$ of $23 = \frac{23}{4}$. Though the course may be extended for brighter children to include fractions with larger denominators that may be treated by the factor method of finding H.C.F. and L.C.M., it is more important at first to work a wide variety of exercises with a small range of fractions than to learn the formal rules of manipulation.

If the emphasis is placed on the intelligent use of fractions rather than on learning the rules, the importance of adequate practical work will be realised. Some standard apparatus will probably be needed. One useful type of individual apparatus can be made from stout strawboard or plywood by taking strips 12″ by 1″, marking one whole strip into 24 equal parts, cutting the others into 2, 3, 4, 6, 8, and 12 equal pieces respectively and labelling the pieces on one side, some in figures and some in words, e.g. "$\frac{1}{3}$" or "one third." By matching and super-imposing various pieces the child can discover for himself the equivalence of fractions and can easily state orally (though not at first in writing) that $1 = \frac{1}{3} + \frac{1}{4} + \frac{1}{6} + \frac{3}{12}$; that $\frac{1}{3}$ is greater than $\frac{1}{4}$ by $\frac{1}{12}$; that $\frac{1}{4}$ may be divided into 3 equal parts, each of which is $\frac{1}{12}$; that four times $\frac{1}{6}$ is $\frac{2}{3}$; that $\frac{1}{3} + \frac{1}{8} = \frac{11}{24}$; and so on. Measurement, especially measurement involving parts of an inch, is especially valuable. Enough of this should be included in the course for both boys and girls to form a basis for the appreciation of both fractional and decimal notation.

Decimals, if taught, will arise naturally as alternative notations for tenths and hundredths, and will be illustrated by ruler work. The treatment of hundredths, however, involves estimation on the ruler, and other apparatus may be preferred. Children should know the decimal equivalents of halves, quarters and fifths. The decimal notation can be illustrated through addition and subtraction but the formal rules for multiplication and division of decimals are best left to the Senior School.

36. The connexion of Mathematics with other subjects.—The other subjects of the curriculum, e.g. Nature Study, Geography, Needlecraft and Handwork, will provide occasions and material that can be used as a basis for Geometry, Mensuration and Graph-work, such as measurements of all kinds, and practice in estimating ; drawing simple shapes and patterns with the aid of ruler, set square, compass, squared paper, etc.; drawing rough diagrams and plans, not to scale ; reading and drawing simple maps and plans to scale ; compass-bearings and direction, involving the right angle and very simple fractions of it, but not the use of the protractor ; reading and constructing simple graphs, e.g. a temperature chart or weather record.

It is for the teacher of Mathematics to discover what material is available, and to see how far it can be made to serve his own purposes. For example, he may teach the correct use of such geometrical terms as *right angle, perpendicular, vertical,* etc. in describing it. He may use it to illustrate mensuration e.g. the finding of areas. It is important, however, that in treating area problems (e.g. the formula for the area of a rectangle), the material used should be such as brings out the notion of surface area, i.e. it is better to cut out pieces of paper for the rectangle and the units of area, than to draw rectangular outlines.

Some of the diagram work may be introductory to the graph. The lengths or areas of diagrams may represent quantities that are not necessarily spatial, e.g. the different speeds of ships, engines, etc. may be represented by pictures of different lengths. This diagrammatic work may be used to help children to grasp the relative size of large numbers.

37. The importance of tests.—It is difficult in Arithmetic to assess the value of teaching without some form of test. It is probable that standardised tests, enabling each teacher to compare the results that he gets in any part of the subject with the " norm " for children of given age, will become increasingly available in the future. Such tests, if judiciously used and with due regard to circumstances, may be very helpful in setting a standard or in maintaining it from year to year.

Tests are useful not only to determine whether proper standards, e.g. of accuracy or speed, are attained at each stage. If properly constructed, they may be used to diagnose the specific mental habits which each child has formed or failed to form.

IV. MATHEMATICS AT THE SENIOR SCHOOL STAGE

A. INTRODUCTORY

38. Alternative courses desirable.—The recent publication of the Board's pamphlet *Senior School Mathematics** makes it unnecessary to consider here the general problems relating to the teaching of Mathematics. Teachers are advised to make a preliminary study of that pamphlet before undertaking any thorough study

---

* Board of Education Educational Pamphlet No. 101, printed and published by H.M. Stationery Office, London, price 1s. 0d.

of this section of the Handbook, the main purpose of which is to deal more particularly with the preparation of schemes and with actual teaching methods.

The practice of dividing the Senior School into two, three or four streams has become common. In the selection of pupils for the various streams, arithmetical attainments will have carried considerable weight. For the sake of convenience, it will be assumed that the " A," " B " and " C " streams commonly found in the Senior School contain respectively, pupils of above average, average, and below average mathematical ability.

These wide differences in ability to which detailed reference is made in §39 and §40 of this Chapter, must be met by syllabuses which differ not only in content, but also in outlook and treatment. Each school therefore will normally provide at least two alternative courses in Mathematics.

The problems which arise in connexion with the teaching of " A " and " B " pupils are here dealt with together, but where topics and methods are more suited to the abilities of the " B " than of the " A " pupils, this is indicated. The suggestions regarding the teaching of " C " pupils are dealt with separately.

B. EARLY STAGES OF THE COURSE

39. The link between the Senior School and the Junior School.—The arithmetical attainments of pupils on entering a Senior School will vary considerably. Some of the pupils may not have covered the minimum syllabus indicated in §16 of *Senior School Mathematics*. The various tables and processes may be imperfectly known, roundabout and crude habits may have been learned and reasonable facility may not have been acquired. There will also be differences in the extent and variety of their practical experience.

Carefully designed tests should be applied to find out what each pupil knows, and can do, and where weaknesses lie. Individual records of the results will guide the teacher in prescribing the appropriate remedy. In multiplication, for example, a pupil who knows his tables may yet make continual mistakes in " carrying " : exercises should be designed to repair the real weakness, and more time than is necessary should not be spent on working long multiplication sums. Remedial exercises should not be applied indiscriminately to all members of a class. Reasonable facility in simple calculation and a fair knowledge of everyday weights and measures are all that is required at this stage. Methods should be the same as those taught at the Junior School stage, and where more than one school contributes pupils to a Senior School, uniformity of method should be agreed upon, if confusion and waste of time are to be avoided at the Senior School stage.

In revising and consolidating the foundation work of the Junior School it is essential that interest should be maintained. If a rule is imperfectly known, the skilful teacher will devise a fresh method of attack and will make sure that the pupil sees the need for any remedial exercise before he attempts it. Varied oral work, the introduction of a wide variety of real problems, team contests and the keeping of records by the pupils themselves are some of the ways of arousing and maintaining interest.

The work of consolidation should be spread over the first year, as the teacher finds it necessary.

40. Extension of the course in Pure Arithmetic.— Throughout the first year the pupils should spend a large part of the time in covering the remaining topics in " Pure Arithmetic " outlined in §47 of *Senior School Mathematics*, so that in the later years they may devote their attention in Arithmetic mainly to " Practical

Topics " as explained in Chapter IV, §§29—39, of that pamphlet. This will be possible with " B " pupils if the numbers involved are kept small and the problems are easy.

(a) *Multiplication and Division of money, lengths, times, weights and capacities by numbers greater than* 12. As these rules are relatively unimportant they need only be learnt by the brighter pupils.

(b) *Vulgar Fractions.*—The introduction of unusual vulgar fractions with large denominators, and the manipulation and simplification of long fractions are now not so common as formerly. Even for the " A " pupils the rule for finding the L.C.M. should not figure prominently. It may be avoided altogether for the " B " pupils, if the work is mainly confined to the units found on the foot-rule used in craft-work.

Fractions should be associated with money and the standard weights and measures, and with groups of objects as well as with abstract numbers.

(c) *Decimal Fractions.*—The decimal notation is employed in daily life in measuring with a rule marked in tenths, a clinical thermometer, a cyclometer or a surveyor's chain. As the need, however, of decimals of more than two or three places seldom occurs in everyday life, the introduction of long and complex decimal fractions is useless and wasteful.

If the pupils are familiar with the idea that a vulgar fraction is a way of expressing a division, the conversion of a vulgar fraction into a decimal is an easy step. The pupils should know the decimal equivalents of $\frac{1}{2}$, $\frac{1}{4}$, $\frac{3}{4}$, $\frac{1}{8}$, $\frac{3}{8}$, $\frac{5}{8}$, and $\frac{7}{8}$.

In multiplication and division the main objective is to teach the pupils where to place the decimal point in the answer. The easiest and safest rule in multiplication is to ignore the decimal points, to multiply as in ordinary multiplication, and then to insert the point in the answer after counting the total number of decimal places in the two numbers being multiplied. This brings the multiplication of decimals into line with ordinary multiplication. If each of the two numbers to be multiplied is small and has only one place of decimals, the pupils will place the point in the correct position in the answer in accordance with what they know about the size of the numbers ; but the rule can also be made intelligible by means of squared paper marked in inches and tenths of an inch.

The easiest and safest rule in division of decimals is to set down the sum in fractional form, with numerator and denominator, make the denominator a whole number, adjust the position of the point in the numerator and then proceed as in ordinary long division.

The " standard form " method of division is preferred by some teachers on the ground that a rough approximation to the answer is easily obtainable. The sum is first set down as in the above method, and the decimal point is adjusted so that the denominator has only one digit before the point.

The selection of the method to be used in multiplication and division must be left to the teacher ; provided the method adopted is made intelligible to the pupils, their proficiency in using it is then the final test of the teaching. Whatever method is chosen, it should be used throughout the school.

Some reference should be made in the teaching to the Metric System, but the extent to which the topic is developed will be largely determined by the use made of it in the Science course. There is no need to introduce the Metric System as applied to money or the decimalisation of English money and its converse process until the rules are required in the " Practical Topics " taken later in the course.

It is desirable to discuss what is meant by " degree of accuracy " in measurement, and, with " A " pupils at any rate, care should be taken to ensure that calculations based upon measurement are not carried to a number of significant figures clearly unjustified by the data. No elaborate estimate of the reliability of results is necessary. For example, in the calculation of the area of a rectangle from measurements which are correct to the nearest tenth of an inch it is easy to identify the figures in the multiplication, which arise wholly or in part from approximate figures in the data ; the conclusions can thence be drawn that it would be misleading to use the last figure of the answer, i.e. in this case, the hundredths of a square inch, and that some of the other figures are more or less doubtful. Similarly it can be shown that, if an approximate decimal form of the value of π is used (for example, in calculating the circumference of a circle from measurement) the number of figures which it is useful to retain in the value of π depends on the number of significant figures in the measure of the diameter.

(d) *Ratio, Percentage and Rate.*—One way of comparing two quantities of the same kind, e.g. two heights, is to use the vulgar fraction or ratio.

The method of percentage enables two or more fractions to be compared at a glance. For example, where classes are of different sizes, the ratios of absentees to the number on roll may be more readily compared by expressing each ratio as a percentage or decimal than in fractional or ratio form. Percentage should, therefore, be taught in close association with fractions and decimals. The method should be applied to class attendances, lengths, areas, weights and other measurable quantities. Its application to money transactions should be left until the pupils are studying the practical topic of " Savings " later in the course.

The essential difference between a rate and a ratio is not always clearly understood. The former is also a comparison between two quantities, but the quantities are of different kinds ; and whereas a ratio is an abstract fraction, a rate always involves a unit, e.g. feet per second, gallons per minute, pounds per annum.

> (e) *Proportion.*—The unitary method will have been used at the Junior School stage. Later, however, the method becomes cumbersome, often involves absurd statements, and tends to obscure the fact that proportion is a comparison of two ratios. It should, therefore, be superseded in the Senior School by the " fractional method."

The fundamental idea underlying proportion, viz. that of one quantity varying either directly or inversely with another, is best taught through a wide variety of real and, wherever possible, practical examples which should not be confined to Arithmetic. The subject should be linked up with " height problems " in Surveying and " area problems " in Map-reading, and with the relation between the dimensions and volumes of similar solids. Other illustrations may be drawn from Science, e.g. from experiments on the extension of a loaded spring, and on the variation in volume of a given mass of air under different pressures. The " A " pupils should, later in the course, learn to draw the graphs of related quantities, to read such graphs, to apply numerical and graphical tests for proportionality and to express a proportion by means of a formula. Further reference to this is made in §41 (b) below.

> (f) *Averages.*—There is no need to define the term " average " for the pupils. The underlying idea can be understood by them after working a

few examples in connexion with such familiar matters as attendances, temperatures, rainfall and ages, weights and heights of pupils in the class. The idea of " average reading " in connexion with linear and angular measurements is also important. The length of a classroom, for example, should be measured by several pupils and, after ignoring those readings which are obviously inaccurate, the average reading taken as being a more reliable estimate of the length than any of the individual readings. Frequent use should be made of the idea in outdoor Surveying.

(g) *Factors, Square root.*—It is often necessary in calculations arising in mensuration to determine the square root of a number. The process should be taught as the need arises. The notion of squares and square roots may be given at an early age : when pupils have learnt that " $7 \times 7 = 49$," it is easy to teach them the idea and notation of " $7^2 = 49$ " and " $\sqrt{49} = 7$." Practice should be given in finding the square roots of numbers which are readily resolvable into factors, and in making rough approximations to the square root of numbers by comparison with known squares and by checking through multiplication.

The pupils should also be made familiar with the use of a " table of squares " and a " curve of squares " for estimating both squares and square roots. It will be desirable, with " A " boys at all events, to teach the rule for the extraction of square roots. The rule is easy and may subsequently be illustrated by a diagram.

The notion of cube root and the recognition of the cube roots of the smaller numbers may be dealt with in a way similar to that adopted in the case of square root, but the rule for extraction of cube roots should not be taught. Pupils who have arrived at the stage when cube roots of more difficult numbers are required should be trained to use Tables of Logarithms.

41. Further new work in the First Year.—Some form of new work apart from that in Arithmetic should be attempted from the outset of the course if the pupils' expectations on entering the Senior School are to be realised. Concurrently with work aiming at consolidating the foundations and with the teaching of fresh rules in Pure Arithmetic should go exercises in Geometry and Mensuration, and in Graphic Representation of Statistics.

(a) *Geometry and Mensuration through practical activities : earlier work.*—The pupils will already have acquired a foundation of geometrical notions and a simple knowledge of shape. This preparatory knowledge is best extended through purposeful activities which give meaning to the work and which stimulate the pupils' interest and arouse in them a feeling of need for further knowledge and skill. Outdoor exercises in Surveying are eminently suitable for this purpose. Practical Drawing in connexion with Bookcraft, Woodwork and other forms of Craftwork also provides opportunities for giving the pupils a knowledge of Geometrical facts. By itself, however, Practical Work is not sufficient to develop definite geometrical ideas. The experiences need to be analysed and adequately discussed, and the new facts and principles made explicit. Supplementary concrete problems, bearing on the work in hand, are desirable, and may even be found necessary to assure mastery of the facts.

The following are some types of exercise in Surveying, which will be found suitable in the early stages of Geometry and Mensuration :

(1) Measuring distances in the playground and in the playing-field by means of a tape-measure ;

finding the length of a pupil's pace ; (2) estimating lengths of roads, fields, etc. ; verification of estimates; (3) drawing plans of classrooms and finding their areas ; (4) drawing a plan of the playing-field, using chain and cross-staff, and finding the area in square chains and acres ; (5) drawing a simple plan of a winding road using sighting compass and tape-measure ; (6) levelling of rising and undulating roads, using an improvised levelling-sight and levelling staff : plotting level sections.

The rules for the mensuration of solids may also be taught through Practical Drawing in connexion with Woodwork. The actual handling and measuring of objects by the pupils themselves should form the foundation of the instruction.

There is for girls no one practical subject which takes the place of Woodwork in giving interest and purpose to their course of Mensuration and Geometry. The girls' course will be generally less extensive than that of the boys and will be drawn from a greater variety of fields.

Further reference to the teaching of Geometry is made in the latter part of this section, and details regarding the approach to Practical Drawing appear in §97 and §98 of *Senior School Mathematics*, under the heading " Mechanical Drawing."

(b) *Graphic Representation of Statistics*.—The graphic representation of Statistics involves such simple ideas that it may profitably be taught to " B " as well as " A " pupils. The method should be introduced at an early stage both because of its intrinsic interest and because of the use to which graphs may be put in the teaching of Geography, Gardening, etc. The treatment suggested here is more exhaustive than is possible in the first year or with " B " pupils but is given somewhat fully for the sake of continuity.

The reading of pictorial and bar graphs of school attendances, rainfall, wages, etc., forms an easy approach to the subject, and it is an easy step to the more abstract form of graphic representation, namely, the smooth curve graph. A brief explanation is all that is needed to enable the pupils to supply information contained in bar graphs.

A smooth curve graph may similarly be introduced and the pupils asked to supply information contained in it. Elaborate explanations at this stage tend to cloud the issue and waste time. Statistical graphs relating to temperature readings, barometer readings, and ages and heights or ages and weights of pupils are appropriate for this purpose, but the Geography teacher will be ready to supply others.

The use of interpolation in finding probable values, where one of the observations is missing, can readily be shown by means of such graphs as age-and-weight and age-and-height graphs. Whether or no a comparison should be made at this stage or later between two such graphs as a barometric height graph and a graph relating to the area of circles and their radii, to bring out the validity of interpolation, will depend upon the mathematical ability of the pupil.

The idea of maximum and minimum values will readily follow from such questions as " What is the greatest length ? ", " What is the shortest length ? ", when applied to a graph representing the varying lengths of the shadow cast by a vertical stick at different times throughout the year.

The pupils' attention may be directed quite early to the idea of " rate of change." It is convenient to introduce this by examining actual changes in graphs of discontinuous quantities, in which the points do not lie on a smooth curve but are joined by straight lines in order to show the changes more clearly. Graphs relating to imports, exports, prices and wages are suitable for this purpose. " In which year or years were the exports greater than those of the preceding year ? In which less ? " " In which year was the increase or decrease greatest or least ? " are examples of questions which will lead the pupils to associate the greater or smaller changes with the corresponding greater or less steepness of the lines joining the points. The general idea of associating rate of change with steepness of a continuous graph will follow easily, if the earliest example chosen shows strongly contrasting slopes at different points and refers to practical matters thoroughly well understood. For example, if a curve of growth shows any marked irregularity of rate of growth, this will generally be associated with the steepness of the curve. The drawing of freehand graphs from dictation will help still further to clarify and enforce the idea. At a later stage it will be possible to extend the idea of " rate of change " to smooth-curve graphs in which the rate of change at any point is measured by the slope of the tangent to the curve at that point.

It is essential that the pupils should come to realise the advantages that graphic representation of statistics possesses over the tabular form. When statistical graphs have been taught, use should be made of them by teachers of other subjects, and the pupils themselves should be encouraged to use the method on all suitable occasions. There is need for a greater variety of graphs than is usually found in schools : the teacher should gradually collect a portfolio of interesting graphs. Practice in reading graphs is even more important than drawing them. The pupils should, therefore, be frequently asked to give a description of the " story " contained in the graph, whether it is one which they have constructed for themselves or one derived from some other source.

The drawing of graphic ready-reckoners is also appropriate at this stage, and should deal with such matters as numerical equivalents, rates of exchange, gas and electricity costs, simple interest, Centigrade and Fahrenheit readings and squares and cubes of numbers. With very bright pupils, the construction of graphic ready-reckoners in connexion with formulæ might profitably be taken, but the distinction between graphs of statistics and those graphs obtained from formulæ should come at the appropriate stage in the treatment of the formula.

C. LATER STAGES OF THE COURSE

42. Practice in the fundamental operations and problems illustrating them.—The groundwork of Pure Arithmetic will normally be covered by the end of the first year even by the " B " pupils, provided that only small numbers and simple problems are involved. During that period efforts will have been concentrated on consolidating the work of the Junior School stage, on extending the fundamental processes to fractions, decimals, etc., and on giving the pupils practice in solving problems dealing with familiar matters and designed to illustrate the use of those processes. No scheme for the " B " pupils can, however, be considered satisfactory if it reduces the needful amount and variety of practical experiences and of easy problems, or sacrifices reasonable facility in computation, in order to cover the whole of the groundwork in one year.

So necessary is this facility and accuracy in computation that during the remainder of the course the pupils should have regular practice in reviewing and mastering the Arithmetic of the first year. " B " pupils may need more than one period a week for practice of this kind. These lessons should be kept fresh and interesting. A typical period might devote, say, the first ten minutes to brisk oral problem work or to mechanical exercises designed to develop speed and accuracy. The practice should be varied either by keeping the exercises to one topic or, at other times, by introducing exercises from different topics. The remainder of the lesson should be devoted to written work. In selecting examples, the aim in view should not be forgotten. Elaborate, artificial and complex sums are unprofitable ; they test perseverance and patience rather than mastery and accuracy, and they often induce discouragement through failure. Interest will be added to the work, if pupils are encouraged to keep graphic records of their performances. In revision work of this kind there is no need to differentiate between the needs of boys and girls.

43. Applied Arithmetic. Selection of Practical Topics.—The new material for study in the later years will be grouped round such practical topics as seem likely to be of most value in the domestic, social and economic life of the pupils when they leave school.

Some of the topics will be of interest and of use to both boys and girls, but others to boys or to girls only. Many of the topics may fittingly be studied by the " B " as well as the " A " pupils, but the extent to which a topic is developed will depend upon the capabilities of the pupils. Topics will also be selected that are appropriate to the conditions and environment of the school. For example, where Poultry-keeping is one of the practical activities in a rural school, the mathematics of this subject could well form one of the topics. It will probably be neither possible nor desirable to treat a topic exhaustively in one year : the better plan is to deal with the topics concentrically.

The following are examples of the kind of " Money Transaction " topics which might be made the basis of exercises :

(1) The Family Income and Expenditure ; (2) Purchasing and Planning a House ; (3) Family Savings and Investments ; (4) A motor Cycle— buying, insuring ; running costs and records ; (5) The Money of the Local Authority ; (6) The Money of the Nation.

The method of treatment accorded each topic is just as important as the right selection of topics. If they are used mainly as a means of obtaining further practice in arithmetical operations, they will have little educational value in training the pupils in that type of thinking and quantitative judgment which the topics are largely designed to develop. The aim will be further obscured, if the material is taken ready-made from a text-book. It will, therefore, be important to maintain a proper balance between preparatory work with oral or dictated problems and written exercises.

The preparatory work should usually consist of a general survey of the topic or of the particular situation arising out of it, discussion of the method to be adopted, and the collection of any necessary information or data. Use should sometimes be made of catalogues, daily papers, year books or time-tables.

The treatment of the topic " Family Savings and Investments " might take the form of discussion of, and problems on :

(a) The Post Office Savings Bank. Information on how to deposit and withdraw money. Rate of interest and how calculated ; (b) Local Banks. Deposit and Current accounts, Interest and Commission ; (c) National Savings Certificates ; (d) Insurance for children, Endowments at specified ages, Old Age Pensions, Insurance against accidents, National Health and Unemployment Insurances; (*e*) Methods of Hire Purchase, Money-lenders and their charges; (*f*) Renting or buying a house, Mortgages, Building Societies; (*g*) Investments suitably treated for young pupils, e.g. a continuous study of the shares of a well-known firm.

The mathematics of Poultry-keeping could be treated under such headings as:

(*a*) Housing; (*b*) Foodstuffs; (*c*) Produce; (*d*) Accounts.

The treatment of the topic " Housing " might include:

(*a*) Study of commercial price lists of houses and equipment. Estimating amount and cost of materials for constructing and equipping a home-made poultry house. Comparison of catalogue and own-construction costs; (*b*) Measuring houses and runs, with simple calculations on areas and capacity, allowing 3 square feet floor space per bird, and 200 birds to the acre; (*c*) Drawing a plan and elevation of a poultry house. Plan of farm lay-out; (*d*) Calculations on capacity of houses and runs relating to intensive, semi-intensive and free range systems of poultry-keeping; (*e*) Comparison of results from different systems tried in the locality.

44. Geometry and Mensuration in connexion with outdoor activities.—The general aims of the teaching of Geometry are dealt with at length in *Senior School Mathematics*.

Outdoor exercises in Surveying and Practical Drawing in connexion with Bookcraft, Woodwork and Metalwork afford an excellent means of teaching and applying the principles of Geometry through practical activities.

Useful supplementary exercises can be drawn from concrete problems in Map-reading, " Buried Treasures," Navigation and Compass Bearings, Latitude and Longitude. Gardening and Housecraft can be used to illustrate the application of geometric principles.

Already in the first year the teacher will have used Surveying as one of the best means of teaching the principles of Geometry in an interesting and a systematic form. It is suitable for boys and girls, for urban as well as rural schools, and many of the very easy exercises are within the powers of the less able pupils.

Unity and coherence are added to such a course if the problems are grouped under practical topics. Chain-surveying, traverse surveying, the measurement of inaccessible heights, surveying by triangulation, levelling and contouring, and the measurement of inaccessible distances have in many schools proved suitable topics. Practically all the necessary instruments can be constructed in the Handicraft room, and some can be improvised from quite simple material.

Within each of the foregoing topics it is possible to devise many practical problems which can be arranged systematically and in order of difficulty. It is not advisable to treat one or more topics exhaustively in any one year of the course. They should be dealt with on the concentric plan, easy problems from each topic appearing in the first year and more difficult ones in each of the succeeding years.

The following is an illustration of the development of a practical topic, but no attempt is made to allocate the problems to particular years. The suggested treatment is somewhat exhaustive, and only in a school where Geometry is a special feature would all the problems be covered in the three years.

The Measurement of Heights

(i) Accessible objects including flagstaffs, buildings, and telegraph poles.

(1) Finding heights by means of : (*a*) a shadow stick ; (*b*) a geometric square ; (*c*) an Astrolabe ; (*d*) a 45° set square (various methods) ; a 60° set square ; (*e*) a plumb-bob clinometer ; (*f*) an optical spirit-level clinometer ; (*g*) a theodolite ; (*h*) a sextant.

(2) Finding heights by means of various forms of direct height-finders.

(ii) Inaccessible objects including chimneys, steeples, etc., where the base-line points towards the object but does not extend up to it.

Finding heights by means of (*a*) a clinometer ; (*b*) a theodolite ; (*c*) various forms of direct height-finders.

(iii.) Inaccessible objects : using any base line that does not point towards the object.

Finding heights by means of (*a*) angle-meter and clinometer ; (*b*) a theodolite.

Nearly all the problems included in the above list involve exercises in scale drawing, while some lend themselves to numerical and trigonometrical calculations. The latter should be reserved until the pupils have made some advance in the construction and use of algebraic formulæ.

Every problem should be designed either to introduce a new principle or to provide further practice in applying one already known. Before introducing a problem, the teacher should have clearly in mind the principle he intends to teach and should see that the new principle is made explicit before leaving the problem. For example, finding the height of a flagstaff in the playground might be used to teach the fact that similar triangles have the ratios of corresponding sides equal. The pupils should come to realise the nature of the problem by having their attention drawn to the shadow cast by the flagstaff. Experiments with three or four shadow sticks of different lengths should follow. They should be first stood vertically in the sun, so that the pupils may observe the varying lengths of the shadows. The sticks should next be arranged in a straight line so that the ends of their shadows coincide. By laying a long stick from the end of the shadow and touching the tops of the sticks the pupils will observe that a number of right-angled triangles are formed of the same shape.

Discussion on similar triangles should follow. By measuring the shadow sticks and their respective shadows, the ratio property of similar triangles can be verified by the pupils. Since the flagstaff and its shadow form the two sides of a right-angled triangle similar to those cast by the shadow sticks, the ratio of the lengths of the flagstaff and its shadow will equal the ratio previously found. The pupils will thus be able to calculate the height of the flagstaff. The new principle will then be expressed in words and committed to memory. Further practice in the application of the principle will then be provided.

45. Geometry and mensuration in connexion with indoor crafts.—In the construction and decoration of books and in the making of working drawings in connexion with Woodwork and Metalwork real problems arise, which may be used to teach many of the elementary principles of Geometry. Most, if not all, of the fundamental constructions, such as bisecting an angle, dividing a straight line into a number of equal parts will frequently occur. The properties of parallel lines, of plane figures, of symmetrical and similar figures, and of circles can well be taught through such work. The making of

Geometric designs and rhythmic patterns can also be used for the purpose.

In making hand-sketches and ruled drawings the pupils should obtain their own measurements, and should frequently be set to work calculations on the size of the objects and on the amount and cost of the material. Further detailed suggestions appear in §98 and §99 of *Senior School Mathematics* under the heading of " Mechanical Drawing."

Material for additional exercises in Mensuration are provided in rural areas by such things as stacks, potato clamps, and tree-trunks. Urban schools, especially those in industrial areas, should be furnished with many suitable objects such as metal washers and nuts, small pieces of piping, metal plates and ball-bearings which may be used to provide a wide range of purposeful practical exercises.

When the pupils have made some advance in Practical Drawing, they should be allowed to construct cardboard models of regular solids, and the " A " pupils might attempt more difficult exercises involving sections of regular solids towards the end of the course.

46. The use of algebraic methods and graphic representation in numerical calculations in Arithmetic, Geometry and Science.—(a) *The construction and use of formulæ.*—Algebraic methods are best introduced through the construction of formulæ in connexion with simple rules in Arithmetic and Mensuration. In this way meaning and purpose are at once given to the methods. They should not be introduced too early or abruptly, as the step of making a generalised verbal statement in Arithmetic is difficult for all but the more able pupils ; but once made this statement can readily be changed into the algebraic form. From time to time during the early stages of the Arithmetic courses opportunity will thus be taken in oral lessons to arrive at generalised statements and to translate them into algebraic form, until the pupils are thoroughly familiar with the procedure.

The formula should be regarded merely as a piece of shorthand, providing a handy way of writing a rule. It should be first expressed in equational form and the important words should then be replaced by their initial letters, thus :

Area of a rectangle equals length multiplied by breadth :

$$A = L \text{ multiplied by } B.$$
$$= LB.$$

As the course in Mathematics proceeds, the pupils should always be allowed to translate rules of this kind into the shorthand of simple formulæ. The multiplication, division and index notation will be introduced as the need arises.

Exercises in substitution should follow the construction of formulæ in order to develop speed and accuracy in their use, and from the results of formulæ involving two quantities the pupils will occasionally construct graphic ready reckoners. Practice will follow in reading and interpreting simple formulæ.

Next the pupils should be shown how it is possible by transposing a formula to obtain new formulæ. Thus, by memorising one rule in shorthand form, there is no need to memorise others that may be obtained from it. For example, the formula for the area of a triangle is $A = \frac{1}{2} bh$. The new formulæ to be derived from it are $b = \dfrac{2A}{h}$ and $h = \dfrac{2A}{b}$. If these formulæ are stated verbally, two new rules will thus have been derived from the original rule. The step of deriving new formulæ is a difficult one and may only be fully understood by the brighter pupils.

Most pupils delight in solving " missing number " problems and these can be used to introduce simple equations. They also afford practice in converting verbal statements into algebraic form and in transforming equations.

Factorisation or rearrangement of various simple types of formulæ—chiefly in connexion with numerical calculations in Mensuration, such as " $A = Ka \pm Kb$ "; " $A = Ka^2 - Kb^2$ "; and " $A = (a \pm b)^2$ "—can be readily appreciated as a time and labour-saving device of wide application. In each case the enquiry should arise out of a practical problem and be illustrated geometrically.

(b) *The formula and its graphic representation.*—In some Elementary Schools, those, for example, which send on an appreciable proportion of their pupils to Evening Technical Schools of certain types, or retain their pupils for a fourth year, it may be profitable to proceed further with the brighter pupils. There is no need to teach any algebraic processes except in so far as they are actually needed in the solution of applied problems. The introduction of any but the simplest exercises in addition, subtraction, brackets etc. should be avoided. The subsequent work should deal with the formula and its graphic representations.

The distinction between graphs of statistics and graphs obtained from formulæ should be made clear to the pupils and lead them to the idea of related quantities. In order to give the pupils a basis of comparison between different types of functionality, a direct proportion graph and an inverse proportion graph should be compared with a curve of squares and a curve of cubes. Only the two simple types of functionality namely, direct and inverse proportion, however, need be dealt with in detail at this stage, and it is essential that these should be taught through concrete problems. The connexion between a direct proportion formula and its corresponding graph should follow. This means that pupils should be able not only to draw a graph from its formula but translate a graph into its formula. It will then be possible for them to obtain working formulæ from experimental data obtained in the Science room. Inverse proportion graphs and formulæ should be treated and used in the same way.

The pupils will come to associate a straight line graph through the origin with direct proportion and with formulæ of the type $y = kx$ and a rectangular hyperbola with inverse proportion and with formulæ of the type $y = \dfrac{k}{x}$.

The difficulty of recognising an inverse proportion curve is a convincing reason for considering the relation of the inverse proportion formula to the direct proportion formula. In an experiment leading to the law of levers, instead of plotting W (weight) and D (distance) and obtaining a curve which cannot be recognised at a glance, the pupils will plot $\dfrac{1}{W}$ and D and obtain a straight line, and from it the formula connecting D and $\dfrac{1}{W}$ will be obtained.

Similarly, simple experiments can be introduced to shew the relation of the formula for the curve of squares or the curve of cubes to the direct proportion formula.

Another type of formula, e.g. the Simple Interest formula $A = IT + P$ (where "I" is the interest on the Principal for one year, "T" the time in years and "P" the Principal) may be introduced at this stage. Formulæ for calculating the cost, including the meter rent, of electricity and gas are familiar instances. The pupils should be able to draw the graph from its formula, and also to translate a graph into its formula. Where the study of simple machines forms part of the Mathematics course, practical use may be made of this latter method in obtaining formulæ from experimental data.

The solution of arithmetical puzzles and problems involving two unknowns forms an interesting introduction to the solution of simultaneous equations, leading on to the verification of given laws in connexion with simple machines.

Quadratic equations might be approached through the solution of arithmetical puzzles and problems. The subject may be further developed through a number of interesting experiments, such as tracing the path of an oiled ball-bearing projected obliquely up a slightly inclined blackboard or tracing the path of a jet of water starting horizontally from a small hole in the side of a vessel. The graphical test for a parabola should be explained to the pupils and then they will proceed to the discovery and verification of formulæ connecting vertical heights and horizontal displacements obtained from the above experiments.

Where conditions are particularly favourable, the construction and use of a slide rule can be taught. The subject may be approached through the study of the unique property of all Compound Interest graphs, which enables the " Abscissa " axis to be so graduated that numbers may be multiplied and divided, and roots and powers of numbers found from it. It is then an easy step to the construction of two such scales which can be used as a slide rule.

47. Logarithms.—Where logarithms are taught they should be introduced sufficiently early, say before the beginning of the third year, so that reasonable facility may be acquired before the end of the course.

Some teachers will probably decide to teach the mechanical use of logarithms. Others may take the view that the pupils ought to be convinced of the reasonableness of the methods, even if they are not completely understood. The first step then is to make the pupils realise that the figures in the table of logarithms are merely powers of 10. One way of doing this is to plot such powers of 10 as are easily calculable, and to shew that the figures in the table agree with those obtained from the resulting graph. For example, assuming that the pupils are familiar with the methods of multiplying and dividing numbers using the index notation, and that the meaning of an index has been extended to fractional values, then the logarithms of 2, 3 and 7 can be obtained from the statements :

$$2^{10} = 1024 = 10^3 \text{ approximately.}$$
$$3^4 = 81 = 8 \times 10 \quad ,,$$
$$7^4 = 2401 = 3 \times 8 \times 10^2 \text{ approx.}$$

From the logarithms of 2 and 3, those of the remaining integers up to 9 can be found. If the results are suitably plotted, from the resulting smooth curve, the logarithm of any number may be obtained correct to two decimal places and compared with that given in the table. The graph may be used to multiply and divide numbers, and to obtain any root or power, providing that in the case of numbers less than 1 or greater than 10, they are first expressed in " Standard Form." The use of the table should then follow without delay.

48. Mechanics.—Where conditions are suitable Mechanics can usefully be taught in the Senior School as the subject provides a good field for experiment, observation and the discovery, interpretation and verification of algebraic laws. Much of the work will be done in the Science room, but the readings obtained from experiments can best be dealt with by the Mathematics teacher.

Originally Mechanics was the science of mechanical contrivances such as the screw and the block and tackle, which men devised to enable them to handle weights too heavy for their unaided muscles. The study of such contrivances makes a good beginning in a Senior School. It is best to use real machines and to handle fairly heavy loads. Where this is not possible, the pupils should be acquainted with the working of the real machine, and the model used for experiments should resemble it closely in design and be strong enough to withstand fairly large forces. It may well be constructed by the pupil as an exercise in handicraft.

A qualitative study of " how it works " may be followed by plotting efforts and loads on a graph and perhaps by translating the graphs into formulæ. Where Algebra is carried far enough, it will be possible to study the connexions between time and distance for a ball rolling down a groove or for a wheel with its pivot on metal runners. The notions of speed at a point and average speed should be dealt with. Simple apparatus can be devised to illustrate the rule that doubling the speed of a car quadruples the stopping distance. The motion of projectiles and the law of the pendulum may be studied by graphical methods.

In rural schools Mechanics is equally valuable, but the subject belongs to rural Science more than to Mathematics. Farm and garden implements, from the spade to the mechanical harvester, afford endless examples of the Simple Machines, either singly or in combination, but the calculations that arise mostly consist of ratios either of lengths or numbers of cogs.

In some schools the notions of thrust and tension in beams and girders may be studied practically and the notion of couples, e.g. in the suspension of a farm gate.

D. BACKWARD PUPILS AND DULL PUPILS

49. The treatment of pupils who are backward but not dull.—Among the " C " pupils will be those whose backwardness has been caused not by any natural dullness of mind but by circumstances beyond their control, such as long absences from school, frequent migrations from one school to another, home conditions and differences of efficiency in the teaching given at the Junior School stage. In their case, the remedy lies in the use of a simplified revision course aiming at securing reasonable facility in simple calculations with small numbers and a fair knowledge of the weights and measures actually used in daily life. They should then be ready to undertake much of the easy work arranged for " B " pupils, but should not be expected to deal with large numbers or difficult problems.

Amongst the backward pupils will often be found those whose failure to learn Arithmetic arises from their disinclination to try. It is for such pupils that freshness of attack and a new appeal to their interests are particularly valuable in dealing with processes already familiar but imperfectly mastered.

50. The treatment of dull pupils.—(a) *Their limitations.*—Some pupils are definitely much below the average in arithmetical ability. As a rule the proportion of these dull pupils in any year group is appreciable and the difficulty of educating them is so great compared with the more normal pupils that the adoption of separate schemes and special methods of treatment is necessary. A full realisation of their many limitations is essential before the teacher is able to adopt the right measures.

Dull pupils will be distinguished from their fellows in the " A " and " B " classes by their lack of sustained attention and their inability to concentrate for any length of time. The lessons for the dull pupils must, therefore, be shorter than those arranged for the more normal pupils. A lesson should seldom exceed 30 minutes, except for practical work, and even then the period should be broken and may include say a few minutes mental practice or written work in addition to time for individual or group activities. The practical work suggested for Juniors in §23, §25 and §26 of the Board's pamphlet on *Senior School Mathematics* should be continued. Again, their interest is aroused only through purposeful experiences. Dull children understand processes by observing and using them in concrete situations but have difficulty in realising situations described in words. Furthermore they take longer to grasp a rule, need a longer time to memorise it and must have practice in revision at regular and short intervals in order to retain their knowledge and skill. In oral and written work they can only deal with small numbers.

(b) *Attainments on entry.*—A large proportion of the " C " class will have only reached the mental age of 12 by the time they have arrived at the statutory school-leaving age, while some may scarcely have reached 11. It is most unlikely, therefore, that dull pupils will have covered the suggested minimum syllabus outlined in §16 of *Senior School Mathematics*. The teacher's problem will be to find out, at the outset, the extent and limitations of the pupil's knowledge through diagnostic tests and close scrutiny of his work. Suitable individual records may be very helpful in meeting the varying needs. Particular defects of knowledge of number facts or " tables " should be met by specific remedies.

Revision work should never consist merely of a dull grind at mechanical exercises. The pupil's interest must be caught and held. A process that needs to be retaught may be approached through purposeful activities and games. Where one method of attack fails, the teacher should be ready with another. Nor should all the time be spent in revision. Fresh ground should be broken, for example, through practical exercises in Geometry, where lack of proficiency in the groundwork of Arithmetic is of little account.

(c) *The arithmetical needs of dull pupils when they leave school.*—The most important need of dull pupils is close familiarity with a wide variety of situations and experiences that they will normally meet in their home life. These will often involve only " mental " calculations. The knowledge of rules required in everyday life is not so extensive as is commonly imagined ; it is certainly much less than is covered by the ordinary school course. The need for working sums on paper seldom arises, and the range of rules is even more restricted. The minimum syllabus outlined in §16 of *Senior School Mathematics* includes more than is necessary and could only be covered by the dull pupils by encroaching on time that should be spent on other subjects. By the time the pupils leave school, however, confidence and proficiency should have been acquired in the limited range of calculations likely to be useful and some skill in the types of weighing, measuring and estimating needed in adult life.

(d) *General lines of treatment.*—Dull pupils learn best by " doing " and by dealing with real problems in situations which are familiar and interesting. It follows that the most effective way of teaching is to deal as realistically as possible with the pupils' everyday activities. Daily routine duties which involve calculations may be given to individual pupils, e.g. recording and calculating the cost of the school's supply of milk.

A growing practice is to arrange the scheme as a series of projects, such as the construction of a garden-frame or the planning of a holiday trip, due regard being paid to sequence. Interest is increased if the projects arise spontaneously and the pupils obtain their own data.

Similarly the work may be arranged under practical topics in connexion with the home and various school activities like gardening or poultry-keeping. These will be not unlike the practical topics that have already been suggested for normal pupils, but their interest will be more personal, the treatment simpler and the arithmetical processes involved much more elementary.

In addition to practical topics in Arithmetic, some of the very easy outdoor exercises in Surveying have been found suitable for dull boys. Many opportunities for measuring, sketching, drawing and calculating with small numbers will also arise in connexion with Wood-work.

In a girls' school, the general planning of a scheme based on Practical Topics might include :—

(1) Keeping the household accounts ; (2) The provision of meals ; (3) The provision of clothes ; (4) Soft furnishings and floor coverings for the home ; (5) Wall coverings for the home ; (6) Saving money.

Some of the above topics are equally suitable for boys, but in their case more emphasis might be placed on money topics or projects, e.g. keeping the accounts of the school camp, journey or sports.

The method of treatment is highly important ; no topic should be used merely as a means of obtaining further practice in arithmetical operations.

The following is given as an illustration of the development of one of the above topics :—

Soft furnishing and floor covering for the home :

(*a*) Planning of tray cloths, simple short curtains, cushion covers.

(*b*) Curtains with pelmets or frills. Cost of providing them in a four or six-roomed house. Curtains for modern windows and fittings for them.

(c) Floor coverings. Stair carpets.

(d) Bedding : mattress covers, sheets, pillow cases, quilts, etc.

The material for such topics cannot be drawn from any text-book. The situations will arise either in connexion with a housewifery course or with a project for fitting up a classroom or staff room as a sitting or bedroom. The whole purpose of such treatment is to train the children to extract for themselves the arithmetical data from the real situation. Essential facts, such as kinds of material, widths and prices, should be collected from reliable and if possible local sources. Technical questions will affect the difficulty of a problem, e.g. questions of cutting with warp, woof or on the cross, and with allowances for hems, joins or fullness. The teacher can to some extent grade her problems in difficulty and she can analyse them into easy stages for the pupils to tackle one by one. Some of the exercises under (a) in the example given above, for example, will be from one point of view harder than questions on stair carpets, as the latter involve length measures but not choice of width.

E. CONCLUSION

51. Selective Central Schools.—No reference has been made in this Handbook to the teaching of Mathematics in Selective Central schools. Much of what has been suggested for " A " pupils is applicable to the pupils of these schools ; and any special bias will be reflected in the choice and treatment of material. For pupils in Selective Central Schools as well as for pupils who remain in the non-selective Senior School beyond the age of 14 the topics suggested in the Board's pamphlet *Senior School Mathematics* will provide ample material for an extended course.

APPENDIX

THE LEAGUE OF NATIONS

I. Historical Background

To ensure the proper handling of this subject it is desirable, as indeed it is in the treatment of history in general, that the teacher should know a great deal more than he will ever have to teach. But it may be useful here to trace in the history of Europe those forces which have tended to strengthen the idea of international co-operation and to add a few notes on the more important articles of the Covenant and on the action that has been taken under them.

The establishment of the League of Nations was the direct result of the feeling which arose in every country during the Great War, especially in Great Britain and the United States, that, on the restoration of peace, some system or organisation must be set up to prevent the outbreak of a similar war in the future. The British Government appointed a Commission in 1917 to consider this problem, and on January 8, 1918, President Wilson declared publicly that at the peace :—

> " A general association of nations must be formed under specific covenants for the purpose of affording mutual guarantees of political independence and territorial integrity to great and small States alike."

In the early stages of the Peace Conference a " Covenant " was drawn up, largely based on proposals put forward by the British representatives, and was incorporated as a first chapter in all the Treaties of Peace. The object of the Scheme was, first, to establish a permanent Conference of the nations which should regulate matters of common interest and settle differences by a regular procedure of consultation, meditation, and arbitration ; and, secondly, in the last resort, to ensure joint action between the members of the League against any covenant-breaking State.

But these recent events do not really explain the League. The sense of unity and mutual obligation in the Western World and the idea of common organs for dealing with affairs of general interest are at least as old as the Roman Empire ; and Christianity gave new meaning and a wider scope to these conceptions. Hence the attempt during the Middle Ages to express the unity of Western Christendom in the persons of the Emperor as the representative of the Roman tradition of a common secular government and the Pope as the head of the religious community to which all belonged. But the Emperor was a head without a body ; his nominal Empire could not provide the peoples of Europe with a political organisation ; political unity had to be realised in narrower spheres before it could be expressed in the larger. The growth of national monarchies and national patriotism, with the increasing use of modern languages in place of Latin, while it weakened the traditional sense of European unity, was thus an essential stage in the history of European civilisation.

The development of nationalities tended to substitute war between nations for the conflicts of feudalism, and this tendency was accentuated when the ecclesiastical unity of Europe, already weakened by the struggles between the Papacy and the Empire and almost dissolved by the dissensions of the 15th Century, was shattered by the Reformation. But the nations of Europe, while struggling to organise themselves as independent units and to define their frontiers, were also always seeking to establish a settled European system. The conception towards which they worked was that of balance ; no nation was to be powerful enough to dominate Europe.

The ideas of a " system " or " concert " of Europe and of a " balance of power " were not clearly defined until the 18th and 19th Centuries, but they can be discerned as motives of policy as early as the days of Wolsey's diplomacy. And while statesmen were thus working out methods of common international action by diplomatic missions and conferences, the thinkers of Europe, from Grotius (1583–1645) onwards, were endeavouring to lay down the principles of an international law. These, therefore, are the main tendencies which have to be traced through the confused history of four centuries, viz. :—

   (i) the development of stable national units ;

   (ii) international diplomacy and agreements ;

   (iii) a system of international law.

Progress was slow. In the great treaties of Westphalia (1648), by which the Thirty Years' War was concluded, and of Utrecht (1713), at the end of the wars of Louis XIV, a division of the soil of Europe between governments was established and guaranteed. By this time the organisation and frontiers of the States of Western Europe had become so far defined as to make it possible for Great Britain, France, Holland, Spain and Austria to join in an alliance to maintain peace (1717 to 1720), but Central and Eastern Europe was weak and divided. The wars of the 18th Century, apart from their effects in America and India, were largely concerned with the emergence of Prussia as a new centre of national organisation in Germany and of Russia as a new force in the East. The idea of the balance of power had to be adjusted and extended to deal with these new factors ; and the partition of Poland (1772, 1793, 1795), together with the advance of Russia and Austria against the decaying Ottoman Empire showed how gravely the approximate balance hitherto secured in the West might be endangered by developments in the East.

Another new factor was introduced by the revolutionary and Napoleonic wars. Napoleon's renewed attempt to establish the dominion of a single Power was defeated, as the previous attempts of Charles V, Philip II and Louis XIV had been defeated, by the general revolt of European opinion against it ; but the struggles of this period led to a revival of national self-consciousness not only in Germany and in Italy, but also among the smaller nationalities of Europe. When, therefore, after the settlement of 1814–15 statesmen set themselves again to construct the " Concert of Europe," the European family of nations was still in a state of flux. Five wars had to be fought before Germany and Italy emerged as united nations ; four great ones before the Balkan nations secured their independence ; and it was not until after the Great War that the principle of nationality received something like full recognition in the new map of Europe.

Nevertheless, the " Concert of Europe " made some progress during this period. In its original form, that of the Holy Alliance (1815), it broke down because it developed the tendency to intervene in the internal affairs of other States and became indentified with a campaign against liberalism. More practicable was Castlereagh's idea of an alliance between the Great Powers, but from this also, after a series of conferences and congresses, the British Government felt obliged to withdraw, as it tended to become dominated by the policy of the Holy Alliance group. But the practice of summoning conferences to deal with disputes which threatened the general peace survived these failures, e.g., the coalition of England, France and Russia which determined the independence of Greece (1829) ; the Conference at London which settled the separation of Belgium and Holland (1839) ; the Congresses of Paris and Berlin and the London Conference which dealt with the problems of Eastern Europe in 1856, 1878 and

1913, and the Algeciras Conference (1906) which made the Moroccan settlement. These, however, were conferences specially summoned to meet emergencies or to conclude peace ; there was no established organisation which could automatically bring a conference into being. None the less the Concert of Europe even in this rudimentary form succeeded in realising some great reforms, such as the suppression of the slave trade ; it laid down the lines of a regular diplomatic and consular system for the conduct of ordinary international relations, and it developed for the joint administration of affairs of common interest such important organs as the Danube Commission (1865), the Postal Union (1874), and the Sanitary Union (especially the conventions of 1892 and 1897 dealing with cholera and plague). Here we touch a subject of the greatest importance : the influence of Science in facilitating communication between nations and compelling them to consult and act together to meet common problems. An important development took place in 1884-5 during the Berlin Congress, summoned to deal with African problems, when the States directly interested in the colonisation and partition of Africa combined in adopting agreed measures for the control of the liquor traffic, the slave trade, and the traffic in arms in certain portions of the continent—the so-called " conventional basin " of the Congo—thus recognising the common duty of civilised states in dealing with uncivilised peoples.

Meanwhile, the need for a more effective method of ensuring peace was impressed on men's minds ·by the growth of naval and military armaments. Suggestions for a mutual agreement for the reduction of armaments had been made by the Czar as early as 1815, and the idea continued to be discussed throughout the century. At the same time the work begun by Grotius had reached a point where the conception of a law of nations had become familiar to all the peoples of Europe. It was inevitable, in view of the character of European society, that this law should in the first instance be mainly concerned with the rules of war and that even these rules should be worked out and applied by national courts, e.g., the prize courts of the Napoleonic and American Civil Wars. None the less, by the end of the 19th Century the science of international law had grown greatly in authority and scope, and in many matters its principles seemed to have become definite enough to permit of the establishment of an international tribunal in whose decisions all nations could have confidence. The two ideas of "limitation of armaments" and "international arbitration" led to the Hague Conferences of 1897 and 1907.

These Conferences form an important landmark. Attended as they were by nations from every continent, they constituted a recognition of the fact that, not only Europe, but the civilised world as a whole, was bound together by a community of interests. The actual achievement of these Conferences was, however, small. A permanent Court of Arbitration was established at the Hague ; an alternative procedure for settling disputes by means of Courts of enquiry was worked out ; and treaties were drawn up laying down more definitely the rules of war. In the then existing condition of Europe nothing could be done for the limitation of armaments. In the language of the 18th Century, the balance of power in Europe was too unstable ; in the language of Mazzinian nationalism " the social idea could not be realised before the re-organisation of Europe was effected." The League of Nations is the attempt made by the European family of nations, as it has emerged from the Great War, to realise this balance or this social idea which for centuries different schools of thought have sought to express in different language, and statesmen, diplomatists, lawyers and idealists have worked towards in different ways.

This historical sketch has inevitably concerned itself mainly with European history, but during the last hundred years Europe has been profoundly affected by the political development of the New World and by the political resurgence of the Asiatic peoples. It would be impossible to deal at length with these factors, but before passing to a study of the League as it exists, reference must be made to what we in this country must regard as the most potent factor of all. Side by side with the growth in Europe of the principle of nationality another principle leading towards looser political organisation was being developed and tested elsewhere. At the end of the 18th Century American statesmen revived the idea of a federal union between sovereign states. The constitution of the United States was an attempt to work out on a grand scale the experiments in federalism made by Switzerland and the United Provinces of the Netherlands. Various forms of federal union had existed from early days in Europe, for instance in Germany and Northern Spain, but for the most part they had not been able to survive the centralising tendencies of European monarchies, and the history of the French Revolution showed that European Republics were no more friendly to the idea. German unity was later established on a federal basis and examples of the same idea are found in the constitutions of the great South American Republics, but the United States remains the best example of this type of political organisation. Under the stress of modern conditions, however, the distinction between these federal unions and what are sometimes called " unitary " states is in many ways tending to become less marked. The British Empire has found itself obliged to attempt an experiment in political organisation on an even grander scale, but on still looser lines. This experiment has developed into the voluntary co-operative union which we know as the British " Commonwealth of Nations."

The nature of that union has been described in the introductory statement prefixed to the Summary of Proceedings of the Imperial Conference of 1926 (Cmd. 2768), entitled "Status of Great Britain and the Dominions." This is by far the most novel and striking effort of political invention which has been attempted since the Reformation ; it is the peculiar contribution which our country has made to the solution of the problem of international co-operation ; and a careful study of it is essential to any proper understanding of that problem.

II. THE COVENANT

1. How the League works.—The League of Nations, in many of its aspects, developed out of the movement for co-operation between States which had grown with the growth of modern Europe, but comparison of the older machinery for international action with the modern methods of Geneva brings out contrasts as well as affinities. Two innovations in particular are changing and modifying the practice of diplomacy under the League Covenant. One is continuity, the other publicity. The fact that Conferences now take place at regular intervals, and not, as often heretofore, only under the shadow of impending crisis, and that a permanent organisation exists to carry out the decisions so taken, has entirely altered the atmosphere in which co-operation between States is fostered. It has also greatly increased the practical possibilities of producing results. The publicity given to the proceedings of the Council and Assembly profoundly influences decisions, by bringing public opinion to bear upon the points at issue. From another point of view, too, it is important, for it now becomes incumbent on every citizen of a State Member of the League to appreciate intelligently the work done at Geneva.

The value of public discussion depends largely on the educated good sense of the public. League Membership carries perhaps some peculiar responsibilities for the British nation, which must be considered by everyone of us who goes to Geneva, literally or figuratively. The League has now more than fifty Member States, and each government represented must explain to the others its own point of view and its own national position. League agreements are made by harmonising national interests, never by suppressing them. Strong national consciousness, strong national governments, are, therefore, necessities for strong international co-operation in the sense envisaged by the Covenant of the League. We in Britain have these essentials. As a people, however, we have a special difficulty of our own, namely, a lack of experience of many problems which pre-occupy continental nations. This part of our island heritage is apt to make us too unconscious of what other countries are feeling and doing. We may take the problem of general limitation and reduction of armaments, as a case in point. This question must naturally present itself differently to States with land frontiers and compact territories, and to those with long sea-boards and responsibilities overseas.

The League of Nations works under a written Constitution, the Covenant. This consists of twenty-six Articles embodying the principles on which the League acts, and setting up the main organs through which it acts, namely, the Council, the Assembly, the Permanent Secretariat, certain of its great standing Committees, and the Court of International Justice. Almost all the developments of its activity and its machinery which have been made since its establishment in 1920 derive from these. Thus some familiarity with the Covenant is an absolute essential to any study of the League. Whatever changes it may now seem desirable to make in the working of the League in the light of sixteen years' experience, much that has happened in the intervening years has made the statesmanship displayed in drawing up this document even more apparent than it was in 1920. Framing a constitution is a difficult task, even when the conditions to be met are more or less known. The League of Nations was launched in 1920, itself an experiment, on a world of which nothing could be predicted except that it would differ greatly from the world before the Great War. Too much definition of the League's functions might have wrecked the hopes of a League at all at the beginning.

The idea of an undefined Constitution, adapting itself to circumstances as they arise, does not present so much difficulty to us, who have seen our own Commonwealth of British Nations shape itself successfully under those very conditions, as it does to the logical mind of the French and other Latin races. All points of view had to be considered, however, while the final draft of the Covenant was being hammered out during the Paris Peace Conference. Fortunately much thought had been given to it even before the Armistice, in America and Britain especially. This bore fruit, and the Covenant as we have it, is, to quote President Wilson's words, "not a strait-jacket, but a vehicle of life."

2. The Covenant.—Only a detailed study of the Covenant in the light of the position at the close of the Great War will reveal the skill and care expended in its preparation. The aims of the League are stated in the Covenant in abstract form in the Preamble.* The first

---

*(THE PREAMBLE)
THE HIGH CONTRACTING PARTIES
In order to promote international co-operation and to achieve international peace and security
    by the acceptance of obligations not to resort to war,
    by the prescription of open, just and honourable relations between nations,
    by the firm establishment of the understandings of international law as the actual rule of conduct among Governments, and
    by the maintenance of justice and a scrupulous respect for all treaty obligations in the dealings of organised peoples with one another,
Agree to this Covenant of the League of Nations.

seven Articles,* concerned with the machinery through which the League acts, are precise and detailed.   But to

---

* Article 1 [Membership]

  * * * * * * * * *

Article 2 [Executive Machinery]
 The action of the League under this Covenant shall be effected through the instrumentality of an Assembly and of a Council, with a permanent Secretariat.

Article 3 [Assembly]
 The Assembly shall consist of Representatives of the Members of the League.
 The Assembly shall meet at stated intervals and from time to time as occasion may require at the Seat of the League or at such other place as may be decided upon.

  * * * * * * * * *

Article 4 [Council]
 The Council shall consist of Representatives of the Principal Allied and Associated Powers, together with Representatives of four other Members of the League.   These four Members of the League shall be selected by the Assembly from time to time in its discretion.

  * * * * * * * * *

 The Council shall meet from time to time as occasion may require, and at least once a year, at the Seat of the League, or at such other place as may be decided upon.

  * * * * * * * * *

 [The number of Members of the Council selected by the Assembly was increased to six instead of four, by virtue of a resolution adopted by the Third Assembly, Sept. 25, 1922 ; and to nine instead of six, by virtue of a resolution adopted by the Seventh Assembly, Sept. 8, 1926.]

  * * * * * * * * *

Article 5 [Voting and Procedure]
 Except where otherwise expressly provided in this Covenant or by the terms of the present Treaty, decisions at any meeting of the Assembly or of the Council shall require the agreement of all the Members of the League represented at the meeting.

  * * * * * * * * *

Article 6 [Secretariat]
 The permanent Secretariat shall be established at the Seat of the League.   The Secretariat shall comprise a Secretary-General and such secretaries and staff as may be required.

  * * * * * * * * *

Article 7 [Seat.   Qualifications for Officials.   Immunities]

  * * * * * * * * *

a British mind, accustomed to two-Chamber and Cabinet Government and to decisions reached by the votes of a majority, they present difficulties. The precise relations of the Council and the Assembly, the constitution of the Council and the reasons for the allocation of seats to certain Powers deserve further study. Similarly the implications of the article which provides that decisions shall require the agreement of all the members need careful consideration. The League of Nations is not a " Super-State ".

Article Eight,* however, which broaches the subject of reduction of armaments, suddenly breaks difficult ground and there is, so to speak, a change of pace in the very wording. The true relationship between the League and its Members is brought out very clearly in this Article. The League will impose nothing without the consent of the individual Governments. It provides

---

*Article 8 [Reduction of Armaments]

The Members of the League recognise that the maintenance of peace requires the reduction of national armaments to the lowest point consistent with national safety and the enforcement by common action of international obligations.

The Council, taking account of the geographical situation and circumstances of each State, shall formulate plans for such reduction for the consideration and action of the several Governments.

Such plans shall be subject to reconsideration and revision at least every ten years.

After these plans shall have been adopted by the several Governments, the limits of armaments therein fixed shall not be exceeded without the concurrence of the Council.

The Members of the League agree that the manufacture by private enterprise of munitions and implements of war is open to grave objections. The Council shall advise how the evil effects attendant upon such manufacture can be prevented, due regard being had to the necessities of those Members of the League which are not able to manufacture the munitions and implements of war necessary for their safety.

The Members of the League undertake to interchange full and frank information as to the scale of their armaments, their military, naval and air programmes and the condition of such of their industries as are adaptable to war-like purposes.

for them, however, through the action of the Council, the power of considering their own position as part of the whole.

3. Preservation of Peace.

—Article Ten,* which pledges League Members to protect each other against external attack, has perhaps caused more misgivings in some States, which have pledged themselves to be loyal League Members, than any other Article, for fear it should drag them into foreign wars against the interest and judgment of their people. It is best considered in connexion with the group of Articles† which succeed it which provide peaceful means of settling disputes before war breaks out. The sooner the use of these means becomes universal and habitual, the sooner will Article Ten which provides against cases of aggression become a dead letter.

4. Locarno Treaties.

—There is one school of thought which believes that the world-wide obligations of the Covenant would not in practice be honoured and that it is better to strengthen the Covenant by means of regional agreements between Powers specially interested in a certain area. We ourselves, under the Locarno Treaties of 1925, undertook a special obligation to lend immediate aid and assistance to France or Belgium if attacked by Germany and vice-versa.

The desirability of regional agreements is still warmly debated. On the one hand, the League's inability to solve satisfactorily the Sino-Japanese dispute of 1931 is used as an argument in favour of regional reinforcement of the Covenant; on the other hand, Germany's denunciation of Locarno in 1936, on the ground that it had been

---

*† See the " Extracts from the Covenant " given below on page 586.

T

invalidated by the Franco-Soviet Pact, shows that the whole question is more complicated than had been imagined.

5. The Collective System in operation.—The League has had to deal with a large number of political disputes, some trivial, others very serious. In general, it may be said that the collective system has worked well wherever the circumstances of a dispute have made its full application possible. An example of successful application is the settlement of the Greco-Bulgarian dispute in 1925. On October 19th, 1925, firing broke out between the sentries in a desolate region of the Greco-Bulgarian frontier. Greece assumed that the responsibility was Bulgaria's and invaded her territory in force. Bulgaria appealed to the League by telegram, the appeal reaching Geneva at 6 a.m. on October 23rd. The League Council met in Paris on October 26th and called on Greece and Bulgaria to withdraw their troops. The withdrawal was completed by October 30th. The League sent a Commission to the spot to investigate the origins of the quarrel. The Commission's report was presented to the Council in December. In accordance with its findings, Greece paid an indemnity to Bulgaria, and a Commission with a League chairman was set up on the frontier to prevent the recurrence of such incidents.

On many other occasions, the collective system has proved its value. In 1921, Albania was saved from invasion by Yugoslavia. In 1924 fighting on the frontier between Turkey and Iraq was stopped. In 1932 the League successfully obtained a " complete and final agreement " between Colombia and Peru over what threatened to be a dangerous dispute. As recently as 1934–5 the League scored two important successes. The plebiscite in the Saar, which was to settle the future of that area, threatened to give rise to a very grave dispute between France and Germany, as neither party trusted the other to stand aside and allow fair play. An international police force was constituted in pursuance of a resolution of the Council. Detachments of British, Italian, Dutch and Swedish troops, under a British Commander-in-Chief, were moved into the Saar territory, where they were placed at the disposal of the Governing Commission of the territory for the maintenance of order. The plebiscite passed off quietly. About the same time the King of Yugoslavia was assassinated in France and Hungary was accused of having sheltered the terrorists. A very similar situation in 1914 had led to the world war. This time the question was referred to the League. Responsibilities were duly assessed, offenders punished and precautions for the future taken.

On the other hand, experience to date has shown the great difficulty of getting the League States to act resolutely when they do not see their interests immediately affected, or when the offender is a large Power. In the case of Bolivia and Paraguay, fighting dragged on for years, without any resolute action being taken. When Japan invaded Manchuria in 1931 the League sent a Commission to the spot and proposed an equitable settlement, but did not attempt to enforce its recommendations, which thus remained on paper. When Italy invaded Abyssinia in 1935 fifty Members of the League found Italy guilty of violating the Covenant, and some economic sanctions were applied by 50 States, but the effect of the economic measures which the Members of the League were able to agree to apply collectively was not sufficiently rapid to prevent the conquest of Abyssinia, and it proved impossible to arrange for the drastic and effectual sanctions which alone might have saved Abyssinia.

6. Article 18* provides that all treaties entered into by Members of the League must be registered with the League. Treaties not so registered are invalid. Article 19,† which provides for consideration of possible change in the existing order is designed to supply the necessary elasticity without which the collective system would be dangerously rigid. It is a frequent criticism of the League that this Article has never become operative, and that States desiring change have resorted to force rather than to constitutional methods. But no State has yet taken the opportunity afforded by this Article to bring its case to Geneva, and in consequence the procedure to be followed in applying the Article has never been worked out. One of the problems of the future is how to apply the principle of this Article in order to bring about peaceful change in a given international situation.

7. Mandates.—Another outstanding Article is Twenty-two, that interesting experiment in practical idealism, on which the Mandate system is founded. The idea of a Mandate is not entirely new in its moral foundation in the sense of responsibility on the part of the administering government for the interests and welfare of the natives. British Colonial administration has been increasingly animated by the spirit of trusteeship for many years past. Attempts to formulate the idea are also found in some pre-war international Treaties.

---

*Article 18 [Registration and Publication of all Treaties]
    Every treaty or international engagement entered into hereafter by any Member of the League shall be forthwith registered with the Secretariat and shall as soon as possible be published by it. No such treaty or international engagement shall be binding until so registered.

†Article 19 [Review of Treaties]
    The Assembly may from time to time advise the reconsideration by Members of the League of treaties which have become inapplicable and the consideration of international conditions whose continuance might endanger the peace of the world.

The complete novelty in the Covenant plan is the system by which the State holding a Mandate gives an account of its stewardship to the League through yearly reports.

The history of the Mandates themselves, however, is naturally developing somewhat apart from that of the League, since the League supervises, without itself governing, the territories. The record is very variegated, as it must be since it describes the work of several civilised Powers, to one or other of whom is allotted the charge of peoples who differ as much in their stage of culture as do the Arabs and Jews of Palestine from the savages of New Guinea. No more interesting episodes than those connected with Mandates are to be read in the literature that is growing up round League work. One Mandate came to an end when Iraq received her independence and entered the League in 1932.

8. Human Welfare.—Article Twenty-three* follows

---

*Article 23 [Social Activities]

Subject to and in accordance with the provisions of international conventions existing or hereafter to be agreed upon, the Members of the League :

(*a*) will endeavour to secure and maintain fair and humane conditions of labour for men, women and children, both in their own countries and in all countries to which their commercial and industrial relations extend, and for that purpose will establish and maintain the necessary international organisations ;

(*b*) undertake to secure just treatment of the native inhabitants of territories under their control ;

(*c*) will entrust the League with the general supervision over the execution of agreements with regard to the traffic in women and children, and the traffic in opium and other dangerous drugs ;

(*d*) will entrust the League with the general supervision of the trade in arms and ammunition with the countries in which the control of this traffic is necessary in the common interest ;

(*e*) will make provision to secure and maintain freedom of communications and of transit and equitable treatment for the commerce of all Members of the League. In this connection, special necessities of the regions devastated during the war of 1914–1918 shall be borne in mind ;

(*f*) will endeavour to take steps in matters of international concern for the prevention and control of disease.

very naturally after Article Twenty-two. To many minds its constructive paragraphs for improving human health and happiness are the most interesting in the Covenant. Certainly the remarkable growth of activity that has sprung from them already seems to show that the times were ripe for them.

Thus the League has made determined efforts to cope with the drug problem. Several inquiries and conferences have been held and two important conventions adopted. One (1925) aims at restricting the manufacture of drugs and controlling and supervising the international trade. The second (1931) is a much more drastic instrument for limiting production. There are also special agreements affecting the Far Eastern countries.

Conventions of 1921 and 1933 aim at suppressing the traffic in women. Much subsequent work has been done in the same field, while a Child Welfare Committee has also attacked many problems. The League has also taken up problems relating to slavery and the slave trade. Temporary Committees on this subject were set up in 1924 and 1931 ; and an international convention was brought into force in 1926. In 1932 a Permanent Committee of Experts was constituted by the Assembly, on the initiative of the British Government, to advise the League on matters relating to slavery.

Any student of the League curious to understand the technique of its work on the social side should study the details of discussion of these questions. They present a lively picture of the process of harmonising various points of view that go to the make-up of sound international agreements. The zeal of experts, the discretion of governments, the cold criticism of the supervisors of League finance all play their necessary parts.

Article Twenty-three has been in a way the starting point from which the League has launched out to meet various kinds of emergency. The repatriation of great numbers of war prisoners from Central Europe, the relief and re-settlement of numbers of war refugees in the Levant, are examples of problems which private charity and even grants from single governments could not cope with alone. These episodes abound in picturesque stories.

The health work of the League has its own appeal to the imagination and is as varied as it is beneficient, ranging from general assistance in the organisation of health services in e.g. Bolivia, China and Greece to patient analysis and pooling of experience about malaria, tuberculosis, cancer, nutrition, infant welfare, etc., and the devising of methods of standardising potent biological remedies such as insulin, salvarsan and the various antitoxins. In these and in other ways the League has made valuable contributions to medical science, which knows no national boundaries.

Health and Welfare work is contributing more than its direct share to the process of binding League Members together by mutual interests, and producing a habit of mind in international relationships* which will in time go far in reducing the strain that arises in times of political crisis.

---

*Article 24 [International Bureaux]
There shall be placed under the direction of the League all international bureaux already established by general treaties of the parties to such treaties consent.

*   *   *   *   *   *   *   *   *

*Article 25 [Promotion of Red Cross]
*   *   *   *   *   *   *   *   *

9. European Reconstruction.—This is no attempt at a complete account of the League's work. The flexibility of its Constitution has enabled it to undertake some tasks which were quite unforeseen when its Covenant was framed. The most important of these are, perhaps, in the sphere of finance and economics. After the War Austria was on the verge of bankruptcy, and it seemed as if her whole administration must crash, and her people famish, and that a new threat of disorder in the heart of Europe might put the whole peace-settlement in the melting pot again. The Austrian Government appealed in despair to the League. From that appeal was evolved the idea of a loan, with its expenditure controlled by a League Commissioner, which has been applied since in Hungary and Greece and Bulgaria under different circumstances.

10. Protection of Minorities.—The economist finds so much to interest him in the details of this experiment that it seems absurd to dismiss it with a word. This is even truer of the League's Protection of Minorities, of which likewise no mention is made in the Covenant, which was framed before the series of Treaties that brought Poland, Czecho-Slovakia and the Baltic States into existence and gave new frontiers and new populations to the Old States of Central Europe. These Treaties confer upon every citizen in these countries the right to equal treatment in matters of religion, language and civic rights.

In accepting this responsibility the League put itself in a position where it may be forced to express an opinion on the domestic legislation of States, which in every other sphere it scrupulously avoids doing. The League procedure under which are examined the complaints of minorities in those countries which have accepted minority obligations is, nevertheless in harmony with the general tendency of modern thought to recognise the value in national life of the traditions and culture of racial minorities.

11. The Permanent Court.—In accordance with Article 14 of the Covenant, the League set up the first World Court of Justice at the Hague. By February 1936 the Court has handed down 23 judgments and 27 advisory opinions, many of them of great political importance.

12. The International Labour Organisation was set up in 1919 by Pt. XIII of the Treaty of Versailles on the ground that " the failure of any nation to adopt humane conditions of labour is an obstacle in the way of other nations which desire to improve the conditions in their own countries." The Organisation consists of a general conference of representatives of the members and an International Labour Office controlled by a Governing Body. The conference meets at least once a year and is composed of delegates representing governments, employers and workers. It can determine whether its proposals on any subject shall take the form either of a recommendation for submission to the member states with a view to effect being given to it by legislation or otherwise, or of an international convention for ratification, i.e. for incorporation in the law of any state which decides to ratify. The Governing Body consists of 16 representatives of governments, 8 of employers and 8 of workpeople. It controls the work of the International Labour Office and is responsible for passing the budget and for fixing the agenda of the conference. The International Labour Office prepares the agenda and performs the secretarial work, and also carries out the important function of collecting and distributing information on industrial subjects.

All the members of the League of Nations, with the United States of America, Japan, Brazil and Egypt in addition, are members of the Organisation. Up to July, 1936, 52 conventions and 47 recommendations had been adopted dealing with such questions as hours of work, the minimum age of admission to employment, the protection of women and young persons, social insurance, workmen's compensation, health, unemployment and the special problems of seamen, dockers, migrants, native labourers, etc.

EXTRACTS FROM THE COVENANT

Article 10 [Guarantees against Aggression]

The Members of the League undertake to respect and preserve as against external aggression the territorial integrity and existing political independence of all Members of the League. In case of any such aggression or in case of any threat or danger of such aggression the Council shall advise upon the means by which this obligation shall be fulfilled.

Article 11 [Action in Case of War or Danger of War]

Any war or threat of war, whether immediately affecting any of the Members of the League or not, is hereby declared a matter of concern to the whole League, and the League shall take any action that may be deemed wise and effectual to safeguard the peace of nations. In case any such emergency should arise the Secretary-General shall on the request of any Member of the League forthwith summon a meeting of the Council.

It is also declared to be the friendly right of each Member of the League to bring to the attention of the Assembly or of the Council any circumstance whatever affecting international relations which threatens to disturb international peace or the good understanding between nations upon which peace depends.

Article 12 [Disputes to be Submitted to Arbitration or Inquiry]

The Members of the League agree that, if there should arise between them any dispute likely to lead to a rupture, they will submit the matter either to arbitration or judicial settlement or to inquiry by the Council and they agree in no case to resort to war until three months after the award by the arbitrators or the judicial decision, or the report by the Council.

In any case under this Article, the award of the arbitrators or the judicial decision shall be made within a reasonable time, and the report of the Council shall be made within six months after the submission of the dispute.

Article 13 [Arbitration of Disputes]

The Members of the League agree that, whenever any dispute shall arise between them which they recognise to be suitable for submission to arbitration or judicial settlement, and which cannot be satisfactorily settled by diplomacy, they will submit the whole subject-matter to arbitration or judicial settlement.

Disputes as to the interpretation of a treaty, as to any question of international law, as to the existence of any fact which, if established, would constitute a breach of any international obligation, or as to the extent and nature of the reparation to be made for any such breach, are declared to be among those which are generally suitable for submission to arbitration or judicial settlement.

For the consideration of any such dispute, the court to which the case is referred shall be the Permanent Court of International Justice, established in accordance with Article 14, or any tribunal agreed on by the parties to the dispute or stipulated in any convention existing between them.

The Members of the League agree that they will carry out in full good faith any award or decision that may be rendered, and that they will not resort to war against any Member of the League that complies therewith. In the event of any failure to carry out such an award or decision, the Council shall propose what steps should be taken to give effect thereto.

Article 14 [Permanent Court of International Justice]

The Council shall formulate and submit to the Members of the League for adoption plans for the establishment of a Permanent Court of International Justice. The Court shall be competent to hear and determine any dispute of an international character which the parties thereto submit to it. The Court may also give an advisory opinion upon any dispute or question referred to it by the Council or by the Assembly.

Article 15 [Disputes not submitted to Arbitration]

If there should arise between Members of the League any dispute likely to lead to a rupture, which is not submitted to arbitration or judicial settlement in accordance with Article 13, the Members of the League agree that they will submit the matter to the Council. Any party to the dispute may effect such submission by giving notice of the existence of the dispute to the Secretary-General, who will make all necessary arrangements for a full investigation and consideration thereof.

For this purpose the parties to the dispute will communicate to the Secretary-General, as promptly as possible, statements of their case, with all the relevant facts and papers, and the Council may forthwith direct the publication thereof.

The Council shall endeavour to effect a settlement of the dispute and if such efforts are successful, a statement shall be made public giving such facts and explanations regarding the dispute and the terms of settlement thereof as the Council may deem appropriate.

If the dispute is not thus settled, the Council either unanimously or by a majority vote shall make and publish a report containing a statement of the facts of the dispute and the recommendations which are deemed just and proper in regard thereto.

Any Member of the League represented on the Council may make public a statement of the facts of the dispute and of its conclusions regarding the same.

If the report by the Council is unanimously agreed to by the members thereof other than the Representatives of one or more of the parties to the dispute, the Members of the League agree that they will not go to war with any party to the dispute which complies with the recommendations of the report.

If the Council fails to reach a report which is unanimously, agreed to by the members thereof, other than the Representatives of one or more of the parties to the dispute, the Members of the League reserve to themselves the right to take such action as they shall consider necessary for the maintenance of right and justice.

If the dispute between the parties is claimed by one of them, and is found by the Council, to arise out of a matter which by international law is solely within the domestic jurisdiction of that party, the Council shall so report, and shall make no recommendation as to its settlement.

The Council may in any case under this Article refer the dispute to the Assembly. The dispute shall be so referred at the request of either party to the dispute, provided that such request be made within fourteen days after the submission of the dispute to the Council.

In any case referred to the Assembly, all the provisions of this Article and of Article 12 relating to the action and powers of the Council shall apply to the action and powers of the Assembly, provided that a report made by the Assembly, if concurred in by the Representatives of those Members of the League represented on the Council and of a majority of the other Members of the League, exclusive in each case of the Representatives of the parties to the dispute, shall have the same force as a report by the Council concurred in by all the members thereof other than the Representatives of one or more of the parties to the dispute.

Article 16 [" Sanctions " of the League]

Should any Member of the League resort to war in disregard of its covenants under Article 12, 13, or 15, it shall *ipso facto* be deemed to have committed an act of war against all other Members of the League, which hereby undertake immediately to subject it to the severance of all trade or financial relations, the prohibition of all intercourse between their nationals and the nationals of the covenant-breaking State, and the prevention of all financial, commercial or personal intercourse between the nationals of the covenant-breaking State and the nationals of any other State, whether a Member of the League or not.

It shall be the duty of the Council in such case to recommend to the several Governments concerned what effective military, naval or air force the Members of the League shall severally contribute to the armed forces to be used to protect the covenants of the League.

The Members of the League agree, further, that they will mutually support one another in the financial and economic measures which are taken under this Article, in order to minimise the loss and inconvenience resulting from the above measures, and that they will mutually support one another in resisting any special measures aimed at one of their number by the covenant-breaking State, and that they will take the necessary steps to afford passage through their territory to the forces of any of the Members of the League which are co-operating to protect the covenants of the League.

Any Member of the League which has violated any covenant of the League may be declared to be no longer a Member of the League by a vote of the Council concurred in by the Representatives of all the other Members of the League represented thereon.

Article 17 [Disputes with Non-Members]

* * * * * * * * *

Article 22 [Mandatories, Control of Colonies and Territories]

To those colonies and territories which as a consequence of the late war have ceased to be under the sovereignty of the States which formerly governed them and which are inhabited by peoples not yet able to stand by themselves under the strenuous conditions of the modern world, there should be applied the principle that the well-being and development of such peoples form a sacred trust of civilisation and that securities for the performance of this trust should be embodied in this Covenant.

The best method of giving practical effect to this principle is that the tutelage of such peoples should be entrusted to advanced nations who by reason of their resources, their experience or their geographical position can best undertake this responsibility, and who are willing to accept it, and that this tutelage should be exercised by them as Mandatories on behalf of the League.

The character of the mandate must differ according to the stage of the development of the people, the geographical situation of the territory, its economic conditions and other similar circumstances.

Certain communities formerly belonging to the Turkish Empire have reached a stage of development where their existence as independent nations can be provisionally recognised subject to the rendering of administrative advice and assistance by a Mandatory until such time as they are able to stand alone. The wishes of these communities must be a principal consideration in the selection of the Mandatory.

Other peoples, especially those of Central Africa, are at such a stage that the Mandatory must be responsible for the administration of the territory under conditions which will guarantee freedom of conscience and religion, subject only to the maintenance of public order and morals, the prohibition of abuses such as the slave trade, the arms traffic and the liquor traffic, and the prevention of the establishment of fortifications or military and naval bases and of military training of the natives for other than police purposes and the defence of territory, and will also secure equal opportunities for the trade and commerce of other Members of the League.

There are territories, such as South-West Africa and certain of the South Pacific Islands, which, owing to the sparseness of their population, or their small size, or their remoteness from the centres of civilisation, or their geographical contiguity to the territory of the Mandatory, and other circumstances, can be best administered under the laws of the Mandatory as integral portions of its territory, subject to the safeguards above-mentioned in the interests of the indigenous population.

In every case of mandate, the Mandatory shall render to the Council an annual report in reference to the territory committed to its charge.

The degree of authority, control, or administration to be exercised by the Mandatory shall, if not previously agreed upon by the Members of the League, be explicitly defined in each case by the council.

A permanent Commission shall be constituted to receive and examine the annual reports of the Mandatories and to advise the Council on all matters relating to the observance of the mandates.

LIST OF BOOKS ON THE LEAGUE OF NATIONS AND ITS WORK FOR FURTHER STUDY

GENERAL

I. (1) Webster, C. K. and Herbert, S. *The League of Nations in Theory and Practice*. 1933. (Allen and Unwin). 10s. 0d.

(2) Jackson, J. and King-Hall, S. *The League Year Book*, annual since 1932. (Nicholson and Watson). 10s. 6d. each.

(3) Geneva Institute of International Relations. *Problems of Peace*, annual since 1927. (Allen and Unwin). 7s. 6d. each.

(4) Stawell, F. M. *The Growth of International Thought*. 1929. (Thornton Butterworth). 2s. 6d.

(5) York, E. *Leagues of Nations, Ancient, Mediaeval and Modern*. 1919. (Allen and Unwin). 8s. 6d.

(6) Jones, R. and Sherman, S. S. *The League of Nations from Idea to Reality*. 1929. (Pitman). 3s. 6d.

(7) Smith, N. C. and Garnett, J. C. Maxwell. *The Dawn of World Order*. 1932. (Oxford University Press). 3s. 6d.

(8) Rappard, W. E. *The Geneva Experiment*. 1931. (Oxford University Press). 5s. 0d.

(9) Gibberd, K. *The League of Nations, its Successes and Failures*. 1936. (Dent). 2s. 6d.

(10) Zimmern, Sir A. *The League of Nations and the Rule of Law*. 1936. (Macmillan). 12s. 6d.

(11) Stone, J. *International Guarantees of Minority Rights, Procedure of the Council of the League of Nations*. 1932. (Oxford University Press). 14s. 0d.

II. PUBLICATIONS OF THE SECRETARIAT OF THE LEAGUE, GENEVA :—

(12) *Essential Facts about the League of Nations*. 6th ed. 1936. (Allen and Unwin). 1s. 0d.

(13) *The League from Year to Year*. Annual 1926–1934. (Allen and Unwin). 1s. 0d. each.

(14) *Ten Years of World Co-operation.* 1930. (Allen and Unwin). 10s. 0d.

(15) *The Aims, Methods and Activity of the League of Nations.* 1936. (Allen and Unwin). 2s. 0d.

III. PUBLICATIONS OF THE LEAGUE OF NATIONS UNION, 15, GROSVENOR CRESCENT, LONDON, S.W.1 :—

(16) *The Covenant of the League of Nations.* 1935. 1d. and 3d.

(17) *The Covenant Explained,* by Frederick Whelen. 7th ed. 1935. 1s. 0d.

(18) *Organising Peace,* by Maxwell Garnett. 9th ed. 1934. 3d.

(19) *What the League has done,* by M. Fanshawe and C. A. Macartney. 9th ed. 1936. 1s. 0d.

(20) *Some Recent General Treaties.* Texts of treaties. 1934. 1s. 0d.

(21) *Maps.* League of Nations wall Map of the World. 40s. 0d. and 45s. 0d.
A new map of Europe. 3s. 0d. and 6s. 0d.

B. PARTICULAR ACTIVITIES

I. (22) Bentwich, N. *The Mandates System.* 1930. (Longmans, Green). 15s. 0d.

(23) White, F. *Mandates.* 1936. (Cape). 3s. 6d.

(24) Macartney, C. A. *National States and National Minorities.* 1934. (Oxford University Press). 18s. 0d.

(25) Alexander, F. *From Paris to Locarno and After.* 1928. (Dent). 5s. 0d.

(26) Bennett, J. W. Wheeler. *The Disarmament Deadlock.* 1934. (Routledge). 15s. 0d.

(27) de Madariaga, S. *Disarmament.* 1929. (Oxford University Press). 15s. 0d.

(28) Shotwell, J. T. *War as an Instrument of National Policy.* 1929. (Constable). 15s. 0d.

II. PUBLICATIONS OF THE INTERNATIONAL LABOUR OFFICE, GENEVA :—

(29) *The I.L.O. : The First Decade.* 1931. (Allen and Unwin). 12s. 6d.

III. PUBLICATIONS OF THE LEAGUE OF NATIONS UNION :—

(30) *Geneva* 1935, and annually by F. White. An account of the League Assembly. 1s. 0d.

(31) *Peace through Industry*, by Oliver Bell. 1934. 3d.

(32) *World Labour Problems*, an annual account of the International Labour Conference since 1927. 3d. each.

(33) *The League and Human Welfare.* 1934. 3d.

(34) *Minorities.* 1930. 4d.

(35) *World Disarmament* by M. Fanshawe. 1931. 1s. 6d.

(36) *What the League has Done.* (1920–1936). M. Fanshawe and C. A. Macartney. 1s. 0d.

C. Teaching Methods

I. (37) Board of Education. *The League of Nations and the Schools.* Educational Pamphlet No. 90. (H.M. Stationery Office). 1934. 6d.

(38) Parnell, N. S. *Education for Peace.* 1934. (National Union of Women Teachers). 6d.

(39) Evans, F. (ed.). *The Teaching of Geography in Relation to the World Community.* 1934. (Cambridge University Press). 1s. 0d.

II. Publications of the Secretariat of the League, Geneva :—

(40) *Bulletin of League of Nations Teaching.* Annually. (Allen and Unwin). 2s. 0d.

III. Publications of the League of Nations Union :—

(41) *Teachers and World Peace.* 4th ed. 1935. 6d.

(42) *The Schools of Great Britain and the Peace of the World.* 1927. 2d.

(43) *Education and the League of Nations.* 1929. 3d.

(44) *Geography Teaching in Relation to World Citizenship.* 1934. 4d.

(45) *Modern Language Teaching in Relation to World Citizenship.* 1935. 6d.

(46) *Report of the Guildhall Conference on Teaching World Citizenship.* 1935. 6d.

(47) *Report of National Conference on Junior Branches.* 1936. 9d.

---

*Prepared by the Education Committee of the League of Nations Union in co-operation with the Associations of Teachers and of Local Education Authorities.

INDEX.

This Index is not intended to be exhaustive. Reference should also be made to the *Summary of Contents* at the head of each Chapter.

The numbers of the pages on which a *Summary of Contents* is to be found are printed in the Index in heavier type.

In many cases where there are several references to a topic the principal reference is placed first.

A

B

C

LONDON
PRINTED AND PUBLISHED BY HIS MAJESTY'S STATIONERY OFFICE
To be purchased directly from H.M. STATIONERY OFFICE at the following addresses :
Adastral House, Kingsway, London, W.C.2 ;   120 George Street, Edinburgh 2 ;
26 York Street, Manchester 1 ;   1 St. Andrew's Crescent, Cardiff ;
80 Chichester Street, Belfast ;
or through any bookseller

1937

Price 2s. 0d. net

A Change from Textbooks

Textbooks of to-day, unlike those of the past, are often admirable, but there is still room for sources of information, not devised for school use, which will help the teacher to present his teaching in a lively form related to the environment and the period in which his pupils live.

¶ The physical environment, as illustrated in the geology of the surrounding area has, for instance, been treated in a popular series of Regional Surveys prepared by the Geological Survey. There are separate volumes on London and the Thames Valley, the Wealden District, Bristol and Gloucester District, South-West England, the Welsh borderland, Central England and North Wales. The price is 1s. 6d. each, and a full descriptive list of these handbooks will be supplied on request.

¶ Weather and climate form another aspect of physical environment dealt with in two books simple enough in style to facilitate an easy presentation of the subject by the teacher. These are a Short Course in Elementary Meteorology, price 2s. 6d. and The Weather Map, price 3s.

¶ The local history of districts containing ancient monuments under national care is illustrated by small guides sold at 2d. and 6d. While some are of value for local history, others, for example, the Corbridge Roman Station on the Roman Wall in Northumberland, Edinburgh Castle, Holyroodhouse Palace and Abbey, Richborough Castle in Kent (6d. each) can be utilised in illustrating general history. Each guide contains two or three photographs of the buildings.

¶ Of even greater service to an understanding and appreciation of the past are the three volumes of Regional Guides to Ancient Monuments, neat books bound in green cloth, with about 20 illustrations and a sketch map of the area dealt with in each. They each contain an historical survey of the area, and short descriptive notes on the principal historical remains. Apart from their use as teaching aids they are ideal books to take on a touring holiday. Volume I deals with North England, Volume II, England South of the Thames, Volume III, East Anglia and Central England; price 1s. each volume. A short list of all guides and other volumes relating to Ancient Monuments is also available free.

¶ The publications prepared by the Ministry of Agriculture include some which will profit the rural school with a school garden, for example, Allotments, price 1s., Collected Leaflets on Birds, price 1s. 6d., which contains in a handy loose-leaf cover some 20 illustrated leaflets describing the habits of common birds of agricultural importance. For the domestic science class, the Bulletin on the Domestic Preservation of Fruits and Vegetables is invaluable. For the geography class there is a Map of the World prepared by the Admiralty, printed in two colours, size $60'' \times 33''$ (5s.) which shows diagrammatically the position of British Empire shipping at a selected date in March, 1936, and thus brings out pictorially the concentration of British shipping along the principal trade routes of the world.

¶ Lastly there are the publications prepared by the Board of Education for the direct guidance of teachers. Some of them have been mentioned already in the text of this book. A full list will be supplied on application.

¶ Overleaf will be found the post free prices of the publications to which reference has been made above. Those listed represent only a few titles from the many which will interest the teacher either in his professional capacity, or as a citizen interested in this country's affairs. These and any other official publications can be obtained by using the order form included as a loose inset in this volume.

LIST OF BOOKS
mentioned in the two preceding pages

Obtainable from

HIS MAJESTY'S STATIONERY OFFICE

LONDON, W.C.2: Adastral House, Kingsway;
EDINBURGH 2: 120, George Street; MANCHESTER 1: 26, York Street;
CARDIFF: 1 St. Andrew's Crescent; BELFAST: 80, Chichester Street;
or through any bookseller.

Inspect the display of Government publications when you next visit one of these towns.

Government Publications as aids to teaching

Some of the publications issued by various Government Departments which are likely to be of interest to teachers are briefly described in three pages following the index to this volume.